Contents

Author's Acknowledgements

I have received a great deal of encouragement and advice in the preparation of this book. In particular, I am indebted to John Jones, Michael Jones, Chris Steer, Beverley Tarquini, Alun Watkins and Eric Wilmot. I would also like to thank the History Department at Lymm High School for their patience and support and sixth form students at Lymm for their interest and enthusiasm. Finally, I would like to thank my family and most of all my wife Linda, who typed the manuscript and provided constant encouragement.

FOR LINDA AND HANNAH LOUISE   JT

Editor's Preface

This book offers you the challenge of history. It encourages you to engage with the past in a creative and personal way; it also presents you with the many challenges which the past provides for present-day students. It demands a rigorous and scholarly approach. In return, we expect that you will increase your understanding, improve your skills, and develop a personal involvement in historical study.

The challenge is presented to you through the different components of each chapter:

Preview
Each chapter begins with a presentation which is designed to arouse your interest, and alert you to one or more of the major themes of the chapter.

Text
The text demands an active response from you. The book has been carefully written, designed and fully illustrated to develop your learning and understanding. Photographs, artwork, cartoons, statistical tables, maps, graphs are among the many visual images that reinforce the quality of the text.

Examining evidence
These sections present a wide variety of Historical sources, both primary and secondary. They encourage you to analyse the opinions of others, to assess the reliability of evidence, and to formulate and test your own personal views.

Focus
Focus sections zoom in on, and highlight, particular events, people and issues of the period. They are designed to enable you to see these more clearly and to find your way through the complexity of historical problems.

Talking Points
They are scattered widely throughout the book. By talking and listening, we can all learn about the major issues which translate the past into the present. In doing so, we question our own perceptions, test out our ideas and widen our range of interests.

Questions
Throughout the chapters. Questions encourage you to consider what you see and read. They invite your personal response and encourage you to share it verbally with your fellow students, and in writing with your teachers.

Review
Each chapter contains an exercise, often a formal essay or question, which enables you to revise the learning and understanding of the whole chapter. You will find supporting ideas and structures to help you to formulate your answer.

This book offers you many experiences of History. It opens up to you the thoughts and feelings of contemporaries; it classifies the distinctive nature of your period; it places people, events and issues in the context of the flow of History. Just as important, it invites and encourages you to formulate your own personal insights and opinions in a living and developing debate. The challenge of History is essential to the vitality and well-being of the modern world.

J.A.P. Jones

General Editor

Titles in the series

Dedication

Challenging History is dedicated, with affection, to the memory of Vince Crinnion. It was inspired by his humanity, and his vision, and by his belief that the study of history is an enjoyable, creative experience, through which we can challenge both our concept of the past and present, and our understanding of ourselves.

1 Germany under William II 1890-1914

PREVIEW

THIS PHOTOGRAPH OF WILLIAM, TAKEN IN 1880, SHOWS HIM IN FULL MILITARY REGALIA

1 What impression might a photograph like this create in the minds of the German people?

2 What qualities in a leader does this photograph attempt to portray?

3 Can we learn anything about a nation by looking at a photograph of its leader?

1 What criticisms of the Kaiser are made in this cartoon?

2 To what extent is the cartoon successful in deflating the image of the Kaiser shown in the photograph above?

3 Which of these sources is more valuable to the historian?

A FRENCH CARICATURE OF EMPEROR WILLIAM II 'Le Petit Journal Illustré'

The fall of Bismarck

The atmosphere at the Lehrter railway station in Berlin on 29 March 1890 was almost one of celebration. Soldiers from the light cavalry lined the platform on their magnificent horses. An army band played rousing tunes celebrating Germany's military prowess. A dazzling array of ambassadors, senior politicians and generals added to the spectacle. The local populace had turned out in force, waving their imperial flags and singing nationalist songs. The centre of attention was a balding, slightly stooped man of seventy five, Otto von Bismarck. Since 1862 he had dominated Prussian politics, and in the period since the unification of 1871 had been Germany's only chancellor. It was Bismarck's personality which had shaped the political complexion of the Second Reich. Now he was about to begin his retirement.

Although Kaiser William I (1871-88) had been proclaimed Emperor in 1871 with all the trappings of a traditional monarch, it had not been William but Bismarck who subsequently made most of the major decisions. He dominated German politics to such an extent that some historians have referred to a 'chancellor dictatorship'. Combining the posts of German Chancellor with Prussian Prime Minister, Bismarck assumed a degree of power far beyond the theoretical limits of the constitution. The charismatic Chancellor built up this power behind a smokescreen of monarchical tradition.

ON THE LEFT IS BISMARCK, WITH HIS DOCTOR, AT KISSINGEN, GERMANY IN JULY 1890

1.1 The German political system: theory and practice

Prussian Influence on the Constitution of the German Empire: 1871

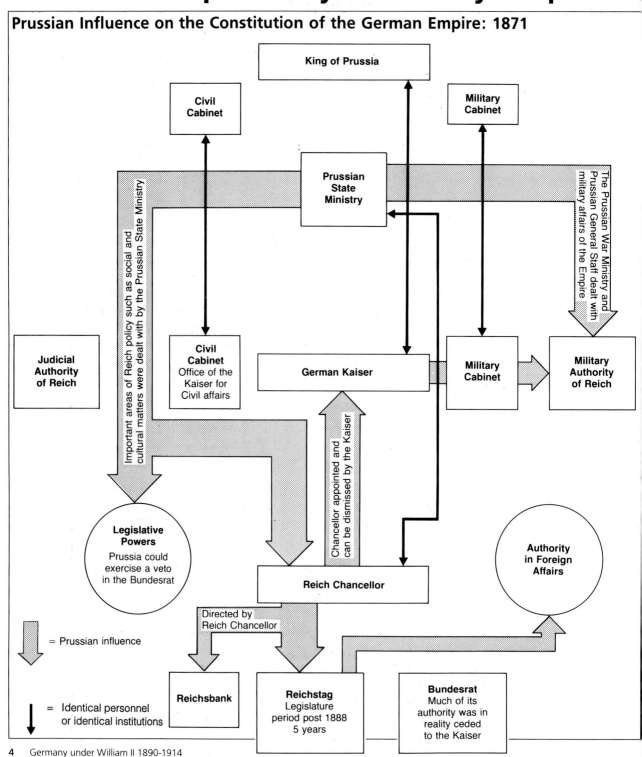

King of Prussia

Civil Cabinet

Military Cabinet

Prussian State Ministry

The Prussian War Ministry and Prussian General Staff dealt with military affairs of the Empire

Important areas of Reich policy such as social and cultural matters were dealt with by the Prussian State Ministry

Judicial Authority of Reich

Civil Cabinet
Office of the Kaiser for Civil affairs

German Kaiser

Military Cabinet

Military Authority of Reich

Chancellor appointed and can be dismissed by the Kaiser

Legislative Powers

Prussia could exercise a veto in the Bundesrat

Authority in Foreign Affairs

Reich Chancellor

Directed by Reich Chancellor

= Prussian influence

= Identical personnel or identical institutions

Reichsbank

Reichstag
Legislature period post 1888
5 years

Bundesrat
Much of its authority was in reality ceded to the Kaiser

William II
King of Prussia and German Kaiser

King of Prussia

- This was far and away the largest and most powerful state
- Prussia's conservative political tradition upheld monarchical privilege, obstructed reform and endorsed the rule of the old order
- The monarch had the power to appoint and dismiss all ministers and officials in the Prussian executive
- The constitution exercised few constraints on the autocratic rule of the monarch
- Prussian ministers were unable to exercise independence: they tended to be submissive and could lose their posts if they resisted
- The nature of this Prussian monarch tended to obstruct any attempt at political initiative

Did the king of Prussia exercise complete control?

German Kaiser

- The kaiser exercised personal command over the imperial army and navy, and controlled all appointments to the reich administration. William used his powers of patronage in both posts to appoint personal favourites and sycophants to key posts
- Critically, the kaiser could personally appoint and dismiss the chancellor
- The kaiser had the right to dissolve the Reichstag
- The kaiser had the last word in foreign policy and had the right to declare war and conclude peace
- William was 'supreme war lord' and the army in effect was his personal weapon

Did the kaiser exercise complete control?

Factors which tended to restrain the King and Emperor

- Certain individuals, such as Caprivi, did make some effort to exercise independence
- Germany's Federal nature meant that the other states could and did occasionally disagree with Prussian policy
- William himself led such a busy social life, and was so easily bored by paper work, that it was impossible for him to take all of the decisions
- After 1908, public demands for constitutional limitations on the Kaiser's authority reached new heights
- William was often bypassed by important officials
- William's personality meant that key individuals were able to influence him.

During the 90-day rule of William I's son Frederick I (1888-88), Bismarck remained at the helm. However, after Frederick's death from throat cancer his young son William II (1888-1918) became the new Hohenzollern family ruler. William was determined to reassert the authority of the monarchy at the expense of the elderly Chancellor. In 1890, after a series of disputes between Chancellor and Emperor, Bismarck resigned. The elaborate ceremony at the railway station served to disguise the bitterness that existed between the two men. After what Bismarck called 'a first-class funeral' the steam engine pulled out of the station and the old man retired to his estates. Provided with a converted hotel which would serve as a country house, and with an ample wine cellar of 13,000 bottles, Bismarck was now able to relax and watch others try to cope with the burdens of state.

SIR JOHN TENIEL'S FAMOUS *PUNCH* CARTOON OF 29.3.1890: 'DROPPING THE PILOT'.

The new Germany 1890-1900

The restless and exuberant new emperor who had ushered Bismarck from the political stage came to the throne at the age of 27. On the surface his country appeared remarkably well placed to enter the Twentieth Century with every confidence. Germany was internationally renowned for its rapid industrial growth and technological progress. Coal, agriculture, iron, steel, chemicals and textiles were all highly successful industries. The huge engineering combines of Bosch and Siemens typified the qualities of efficiency and innovation synonymous with German industry. Major breakthroughs such as the electric dynamo and the petrol engine were made in Germany.

Industrial strength was matched by cultural excellence. German citizens were able to enjoy top-class theatre, opera and classical music. Library provision was impressive, literacy rates were high, the leading national newspapers were forthright and independent, and Germany's ancient universities enjoyed an international reputation. The population was expanding rapidly - from about 41 million in 1871 to about 49 million in 1890 - while more than one third of the population was under 15 years of age.

Amid this atmosphere of youthful optimism then, few Germans regretted Bismarck's passing and in William II they seemed to have a leader whose personal energy and ambition tied in neatly with the qualities and aspirations of the German nation itself. Perhaps Germany would now have its Caesar. What was the nature of his government? William II often boasted that he had never bothered to read the German constitution. Even so, the document he neglected invested him with substantial powers. The constitution of the 'Kaiserreich' referred to the emperor as the 'all highest person' and the 'supreme war lord'. The emperor exerted absolute control over the government, the armed forces, the diplomatic network and the civil service. This was the framework for an autocratic, semi-absolutist state. The instruments of power were within the reach of the Kaiser and his advisers providing they had the ability to grasp them. An autocratic ruler could easily work outside the democratic niceties of the constitution. Was this William's intention?

Historian John Röhl has stated that 'gradually William II...created a government and an administrative apparatus of his own choosing' in which 'pliant tools of the imperial will' were appointed to 'all key offices'. Röhl claims that by 1897 William II had worn down resistance to his personal rule among the bureaucrats in the Wilhelmstrasse. The American historian Isabel Hull

'OUT OF THE SHADOW'

claims that the Emperor's ministers were 'like panes of glass...they were to shelter the Kaiser from hostile winds and at the same time allow his policies and his alone to shine through without distortion'.

It seems that the Kaiser's approach to ministerial appointments could sometimes be rather cavalier. Holstein, a key official in the 1890s, noted in a letter that the 'Kaiser has the habit of selecting his ministers like mistresses'. It could be argued that William had merely appointed a sychophantic clique which served only to feed his ego and separate him from political reality.

Of vital importance in the Kaiser's choice of personal appointments was the position of the chancellor, who could be appointed or dismissed by the emperor at his discretion. The chancellor was the emperor's key instrument in ensuring good relations with the parliament or Reichstag. This consisted of 400 deputies elected by direct, secret, male suffrage. When breaches occurred between the chancellor and the Reichstag the chancellor could take the measure of dissolving the Reichstag and calling fresh elections. On paper, despite the powers invested in the Emperor, the constitution rested formal sovereignty in the Federal Council or Bundesrat. The Bundesrat, which contained representatives from each of the German states, provided the federal element in the constitution. In practice this was dominated by Prussia, the largest state, which contained roughly three-fifths of Germany's area and population.

These parliamentary bodies revealed some of the divisions that existed within German society as a whole. Voting behaviour was strongly influenced by factors of class, race and religion. Increasingly the political parties became polarised between parties of the left and the right at the expense of the centre. While support for the Socialist party increased, there was also increasing representation for extreme nationalist and anti-semitic groups. German society came to have the largest socialist party in Europe but also the largest army. The fact that the Kaiser was notoriously close to leading military figures enhanced the feeling that the wishes of the population at large were not necessarily represented by the state. The German historian Hans-Ulrich Wehler says the central dilemma was that Germany's rapid economic and social development into a modern industrial society was not accompanied by similar progress in the political sphere. Rather Germany retained a political system which was outdated and anachronistic. The middle and working classes were increasingly influential and demanding but this trend was not reflected in political developments because of the hostility of the traditional ruling élites.

The verdict of some historians on the Kaiser's administration has been that the country was the most economically successful in Europe, but also one of the worst governed. The feeling is that the glamour of the court in Berlin has tended to distract attention from the chaos that the Kaiser, politicians, confidants and the military created in their struggle for power. While there is broad agreement among historians that the German government in the Wilhelmine era was ineffective, the question of who was actually in charge remains the subject of intense debate. We have already noted that in the period up to 1890 it was the chancellor who really ruled Germany. How much influence was exerted by the four men who occupied this post between 1890 and 1917?

PHILIP EULENBURG (1847-1921)

1.2 German chancellors (1890-1917): the Emperor's men?

L. Von Caprivi 1890-94 (1831-99)

Background/personality A middle-aged army general with substantial administrative experience.

Details of appointment It was hoped that a military figure would provide an impression of authority. William personally selected Caprivi from a list of generals because he was seen as an amenable man who would do what he was told. In fact, once in office he soon displayed a mind of his own.

Influence on policies Caprivi was an energetic administrator who adopted a conciliatory policy towards the Socialists and generally a policy of non-alignment, so that initially he received a good deal of support for his 'New Course' from the Reichstag. Much of this new legislation was Caprivi's personal policy.

Finance Bill Progressive income tax introduced.

Rural Administration Reform and modernisation.

Social welfare Restricted Sunday working and hours of labour for women and children.

Arbitration of industrial disputes Courts set up with workers' and employers' representatives to settle disputes. Anti-socialist laws from Bismarck's era lapsed.

Reform of Tariff Act of 1879 Germany was obliged to reduce her tariffs on cattle, timber, rye and wheat in order to gain overseas markets for German industrial exports in return.

Army Bill (1892) Increased peace-time army by 84,000. Reduced military service from 3 to 2 years. The Reichstag could debate the army grant every 5 instead of 7 years.

Dismissal Caprivi faced mounting opposition from powerful agrarian forces and when he also angered the Kaiser by refusing to draft a law against subversive elements his influence was coming to an end. He resigned at the end of 1894.

Prince von Hohenlohe-Schillingsfürst 1894-1900 (1819-1901)

Background/personality Bavarian aristocrat. Older when appointed than Bismarck was when he retired. Regarded as mildly liberal in political outlook and rather evasive in personality.

Details of appointment Personally appointed by William who wanted a mere figurehead whom he could control.

Influence on policies His age and indecision meant that he was unable to exert firm leadership during a period of transition. Liberals from the Caprivi era were dismissed and the initiative passed to key ministers such as Miquel and Koller. Their 'policy of concentration' led to reactionary anti-left measures such as the Subversion Bill (1894) and anti-union legislation (1899). These measures were opposed by the middle-class parties. Hohenlohe's main contribution was to restrain the Kaiser who talked wildly of subverting the constitution and removing the workers' vote.

Dismissal By 1900 he was tired of serving such an unpredictable master but his term of office had lasted long enough for the succession prospects of General Waldersee to have faded; when he resigned, the more moderate Bülow took over.

QUESTIONS

How much independence did each of the chancellors enjoy? Consider the following criteria:

(a) Their age

(b) Their relations with the emperor

(c) Their ability to instigate and implement policy

(d) Relations between the chancellor and powerful groups within German society

(e) Circumstances of dismissal

Assign each chancellor marks out of ten for each criterion.
1 = Factor making independence difficult
10 = Able to be completely independent

Baron von Bülow 1900-09 (1849-1929)

Background/personality An aristocratic landowner with extensive experience in the diplomatic service and foreign office. Relied heavily on personal charm and flattery. Sycophantic in his dealings with the Emperor. Known to his enemies as 'the eel'. Bülow favoured an adventurous foreign policy and concentrated his efforts in this area rather than domestic matters.

Details of appointment As early as 1895 William was writing critically of Hohenlohe and praising Bülow. Bülow's blatant flattery of the Kaiser made it certain that he would replace Hohenlohe.

Influence on Policies Beyond Bülow's personal flattery he did display a degree of independence as Chancellor. He helped to put a stop to the reactionary policies instigated under Hohenlohe. Instead he advocated a policy of rallying together Germany's disparate social groups in a Sammlungspolitik. The loyalty of the German people would be secured by the building of a prestigious fleet and the promotion of the Kaiser as a charismatic leader. In addition, Bülow restored tariffs to their pre-1892 level but resisted pressure from the Agrarian League to raise them much higher. Even so, in the 1903 election working-class resentment of higher tariffs enabled the Socialists to increase their votes by almost a million. Bülow also faced opposition from the Centre Party over tax reforms and colonial policy. In 1907 he dissolved the Reichstag and ran an election campaign on issues of defence and national security. After this election Bülow relied on a bloc of support from the Conservative and National Liberal Parties. In 1908 Bülow allowed William's notorious *Daily Telegraph* interview to go ahead.

Dismissal Bülow put the blame for this on the Emperor's personal government. Once William's depression over this incident lifted he was determined to see Bülow removed. In 1909 Bülow submitted his resignation after his Finance Bill had been rejected by the Reichstag. To his surprise this was immediately accepted and he left the government.

T. Bethmann-Hollweg 1909-17 (1856-1921)

Background/personality Bethmann had come up through the ranks of the Prussian administration, was made Prussian minister of the interior and in 1907 secretary of state in the Imperial Office of Internal Affairs.

Details of appointment Bethmann was not William's first choice and surprisingly, Bülow was able to put forward the claim of Bethmann as his successor. Once William accepted the idea he was typically enthusiastic: 'He is true as gold. A man of integrity, also very energetic, he will straighten out the Reichstag for me. Besides, it was with him in Hohenfinow that I shot my first roebuck'.

Influence on policies Historian Gordon Craig says that Bethmann was a 'careful and energetic administrator, an effective negotiator, and a man of courage and honour in time of crisis' but, like Caprivi, he lacked creative talent and his intellectual and political horizons were narrow. His ignorance of foreign affairs was - as Bülow had said - profound, and his knowledge of military problems minimal, and this robbed him of any confidence in two fields that were crucial to Germany's future. In other areas, too, he lacked verve and assurance. He was intelligent enough to see that the German political system was in need of reform but he was too conservative in his views, and too opposed in principle to the idea of parliamentary government, to favour any fundamental change in the existing system. During Bethmann's administration the Socialists became the largest single party in the Reichstag (1912), and in foreign policy he presided over the disastrous July Crisis of 1914.

Dismissal In 1917 Bethmann came under intense pressure from the Supreme Command led by Hindenburg and Ludendorff, and William was obliged to accept his resignation even though he was reluctant to do so.

The personal rule of William II

In the summer of 1900 the royal yacht *Hohenzollern* set sail from Germany to the North Sea. The imperial flag fluttering in the breeze showed that Emperor William II was on board, accompanied by his substantial personal entourage. Those who had been with the Reisekaiser (travelling Emperor) on earlier voyages knew that their master had a liking for physical jerks, practical jokes and elaborate or even bizarre fancy·dress parties. Nevertheless, the annual cruise was an opportunity for those entrusted with heavy burdens of state to relax and unwind. Accompanying William as usual was Philip Eulenburg, for many years his closest friend and confidant. It was Eulenburg's photograph which normally occupied pride of place on the Kaiser's desk in the imperial office in Berlin and in William's private hunting lodge at Rominten.

Yet on the night of 15 July, Eulenburg's easy familiarity was replaced by secrecy and alarm. He locked himself into his cabin and wrote a secret letter, the contents of which virtually amounted to treason. Addressed to the German chancellor von Bülow, the letter described in vivid detail how the

KAISER WILLIAM II AT POTSDAM, SURROUNDED BY MEMBERS OF HIS PERSONAL ENTOURAGE

Kaiser had thrown a terrifying fit of rage. Eulenburg said that 'H.M. is no longer in control of himself when he is seized by rage. I regard the situation as highly dangerous and am at a loss to know what to do'. He added that the Kaiser's personal physician was 'utterly perplexed' by his behaviour, and concluded with alarm that being on the yacht with the Emperor was like 'sitting on a powder keg'.

The contents of this recently-discovered letter have provided further evidence for historians who have tried to build up a full psychological profile of the last Kaiser. The impression has not been favourable. Born with a badly-withered left hand and plagued by a recurring ear infection, William's physical difficulties probably left their psychological mark. Some historians have claimed that his unloving mother instilled in him a sense of inferiority. It is possible that William suffered from a condition known as Attention Deficiency Disorder. This is said to be the result of minor brain damage at birth and makes the sufferer's behaviour unpredictable and irrational. William took great delight in turning the ornate rings on his good hand inward, enabling him to deliver with a vicelike grip an excruciating handshake to unsuspecting diplomats or dignitaries.

Probing further, some historians have concluded that William was a repressed homosexual who never came to terms with his own personality. On more than one occasion, members of William's inner circle were subject to damaging blackmail demands which implicated William himself. In 1896, for example, Philip Eulenburg was blackmailed by the owner of a Viennese bathhouse, and in 1908 members of the inner circle were involved in a protracted court case which received national attention. Contemporaries found William completely unpredictable. In 1888 Bismarck remarked that 'the Kaiser is like a balloon, if you don't keep fast hold of the string, you never know where he'll be off to'. Senior ministers went to ludicrous lengths to please him. On one occasion, Chancellor Bülow was wearing white trousers when William jokingly remarked that that would probably mean rain: Bülow promptly changed his trousers! More seriously, both contemporaries and historians have speculated about William's sanity. Whether all of this matters is now the subject of intense debate between two divided schools of historians.

English historians of the Second Reich - led by John Röhl - have maintained that there is still a great deal to learn about William, and that his personal neuroses must have had a direct impact on the decision-making process in pre-war Germany. They claim that William stamped his personality on the period 1890-1914, and that therefore their 'palace perspective' - concentrating on the Emperor and his court - is the correct one. They believe that the more light they can shed on William's personality the better our understanding will be of German society in this vital period.

However, a group of German historians led by Hans-Ulrich Wehler offers a totally different viewpoint. Wehler has described William as a 'shadow emperor' (*schattenkaiser*) without say or influence in pre-war Germany. Wehler says that William reigned but did not rule. His contention is that William simply lacked the ability to direct policy, command the army or influence the real decision-makers. Wehler believes that in 1890 the Kaiser launched a brief, unsuccessful bid to establish personal power but that after this date he abandoned this 'anachronistic game' and contented himself with making outspoken yet ultimately irrelevant speeches. Wehler argues that after the departure of Bismarck a power vacuum existed which William II was unable to fill. His thesis is that the glamour of the Berlin court and its trappings of power represent a powerful illusion which has beguiled historians fascinated by the Kaiser's personality. Beneath this veneer, he claims, the Emperor was increasingly out of touch and isolated. From this it therefore follows that the Kaiser's personality is also irrelevant, he exerted no real influence whether he was in a good mood or a bad mood. Wehler states that there is nothing more of interest to be discovered about the Kaiser. Historians like Röhl, who continue to search the archives for further information on the shadow emperor, are – according to Wehler – wasting their time in writing 'personalistic' accounts.

Wehler prefers a 'structural' approach. He contends that real influence was in the hands of powerful élite groups, members of which did not necessarily hold elected office but pulled strings behind the scenes. Such groups consisted of influential industrialists, agrarians, pressure groups and press barons. The objective of these rich landowners and businessmen was to prevent Germany's rapid industrialisation being accompanied by genuine democracy. In particular, they feared the growth of left-wing political parties and the participation of the working classes in the political system. For this reason they carried out a programme of social integration or *sammlungspolitik* by which they manipulated German society into accepting their continued domination. It worked in the following way. They used their influence to steer Germany towards a programme of colonial expansion for overseas markets (world policy or *weltpolitik*). This was sustained by the construction of a huge battle fleet and ultimately led to war and attempts at overseas conquest. The massive production of ships was intended to boost the economy, reduce unemployment and persuade the working class to remain loyal to the ruling élite rather than voting for the socialist parties. For their own self-preservation and personal profit, the élite favoured an increasingly ambitious armaments programme and aggressive foreign policy. They believed that success in this area would satisfy the population at large and preserve their position. The Kaiser, Wehler maintains, was merely a mouthpiece for this policy and, when it failed, a scapegoat.

In Röhl's words, Wehler is engaged in 'writing the history of the Kaiserreich without the Kaiser' or 'Wilhelmine Germany without William'. He argues that the reality is that William established an autocratic, semi-absolutist state in which his personal influence was paramount. Who is closer to the truth? Are there elements of the real answer in each of these verdicts? Consider the evidence that follows and see if you can reach a conclusion.

TALKING POINT
Should historians spend their time finding out more details about the private lives of important leaders, or should these details be regarded as irrelevant?

EXAMINING THE EVIDENCE

William II: personal ruler or shadow emperor?

Source A: 1888 - First impressions

Most people were impressed by the new ruler's vitality, his openness to new ideas, the diversity of his interests, and his personal charm. As his Court Marshal wrote later, William was 'a dazzling personality who fascinated everyone who appeared before him. He was well aware of his ability to do

this and developed this talent with much effort and refinement to an extraordinary perfection.'

G. Craig, Germany 1866-1945 (1981)

Source B: 1891 - Description of the Kaiser on a royal cruise

I would like to make one brief résumé, for your ear alone, of my impressions
of our trip. They are not exactly favourable in one respect: since last year,
H.M.'s autocratic tendencies have markedly increased. This … obtains in
matters great and small. And – quite between ourselves - it is not accompanied by any serious scrutiny or weighing of facts; he just talks himself into
an opinion.

Letter from Kiderlen-Wächter to Holstein, 1891. Quoted in G. Craig,
Germany 1866-1945 (1981)

Source C: 1896 - Criticism of the Emperor

The phrase current among all parties in the Reichstag, that the behaviour
of the Emperor can only be explained pathologically, is taking effect quietly
but devastatingly.

Holstein writing in November 1896

Source D: An historian's description of the changing role of the Emperor

A good deal has been written about William's 'Personal Rule' and there
can be little doubt that his strong desire to decide everything himself represented an important element in his character. Even more important was
the fact that, with the monarchy beset by manifold problems, a focal point
was needed. If the existing power structure was to be saved from the impact
of a changing industrial society, William II had to be turned into a people's
Kaiser whose charisma would help to reduce internal tensions and secure
Germany's position as an admired and respected world power.

V.R. Berghahn, Germany and the Approach of War in 1914 (1973)

Source E: Chancellor Bülow flatters his Emperor

I place my faith increasingly in the Emperor. He is so impressive! He is the
most impressive Hohenzollern who has ever lived. In a manner which I have
never seen before, he combines genius - the most genuine and original
genius - with the clearest good sense.

Letter to Philip Eulenburg from Bülow shortly after he
became Chancellor in 1900

Source F: Criticism of the Emperor

Look at Source F carefully. What would be the long-term effect, diplomatically, of such behaviour?

The main cause of alarm was William's lack of tact. Holstein wrote to
Eulenburg that 'the chief danger in life of William II is that he remains absolutely unconscious of the effect which his speeches and actions have upon
Princes, public men and the masses'. He astonished the British Ambassador
by the way he talked about the diminutive King of Italy whom he always
referred to as 'the Dwarf' while calling the Queen 'a peasant girl' and 'the
daughter of a cattle thief'. He was capable, when in the middle of a reception
for Prince Ferdinand of Bulgaria, of calling him 'the cleverest and most
unscrupulous ruler in Europe'. He later made fun of Ferdinand for being
'festooned with decorations like a Christmas tree.'

Michael Balfour, The Kaiser and his Times (1964)

Source G: William's view of himself
(i) Beware of the time when I shall give the orders.

Statement before he came to power

(ii) There is only one person who is master in this Empire and I am not going to tolerate any other.

From speech at Dusseldorf, 4 May 1891

(iii) I have often at night been kept from sleep for hours by the knowledge that in a speech delivered the previous day I had failed to observe the limitations on content and expression which I set myself in advance.

Sources i-iii are from M. Balfour, *The Kaiser and his Times* (1964)

(iv) You old asses.   Abuse regularly directed at the War Minister and the Chief of Military Cabinet

(v) All of you know nothing; I alone know something. I alone decide.

Statement to a group of Admirals

(vi) I will only send an ambassador to London who has My trust, obeys My will and carries out My orders.

William overruling advice from Bethmann-Hollweg and the Foreign Office in choosing Prince Lichnowsky to be his representative in London in 1912. Sources iv-vi are from *Kaiser Wilhelm II, New Interpretations* (edited by J.C.G. Röhl [1982])

Source H: The limitations of power
(i) He berated the Foreign Office for not showing despatches to him promptly, but he does not seem to have realised that sometimes, as in 1909, 1911 and 1914, important ones were not shown to him at all. A court official said to the Chief of the Military Secretariat 'It is extraordinary that in every department the Kaiser should have someone about who deceives him.'

(ii) Behind William's favourite pose of iron resolve, there was an acute lack of self-confidence, combined with an obstinate desire to have his own way... At critical moments, as in 1907, 1908 and 1918, this lack of confidence and staying power became a complete loss of nerve, accompanied by such physical symptoms as giddiness and shivering.

M. Balfour, *The Kaiser and his Times* (1964)

Source I: Contemporary views
(i) There is no stronger force in present-day Germany than the Kaiser.

Friedrich Naumann, 1900

(ii) All the most important political decisions of the past twelve years have been taken by him.   Maximillian Harden, 1902

(iii) When you mount to the peak of this highly organised people, you will find not only confusion but chaos.   Lord Haldane, 1912

Source J: The Kaiser's mental instability
(i) His face is completely distorted by rage...There can no longer be any question of self-control...I predict a breakdown of the nerves.

Extract from secret letter written by Eulenburg to Bülow during the Kaiser's North Sea cruises, 1903

(ii) There were periods when Wilhelm II became totally obsessed with one idea to such a degree that everything touching upon it even remotely, produced in him a violent rage...it was at this stage, surely, with his utterly relentless pursuit of one goal and angry determination to brook no opposition, that Kaiser Wilhelm's personality had the greatest impact on policy making. The pressure for an Army Bill in 1891-3, the demand for a crusade against 'subversion' in 1894-5, the obsession with naval expansion from 1895 onwards, his adoration of his grandfather in 1897, culminating in the 'lackeys and pygmies' speech...the thirst for revenge during the China expedition of 1900, the unbounded fury against Britain in December 1912 (quite possibly leading to a decision to go to war in eighteen months) are all good examples - and there are many others - of such moods affecting the direction of German policy.

J.G.C. Röhl, *Kaiser Wilhelm II, New Interpretations* (1982)

Source K: 1908 - The *Daily Telegraph* interview

(i) ...His majesty honoured me with a long conversation, and spoke with impulsive and unusual frankness. 'You English' he said, are mad, mad, mad as March hares. What has come over you that you are so completely given over to suspicions quite unworthy of a great nation? What more can I do than I have done?...I repeat', continued His Majesty, 'that I am a friend of England, but you make things difficult for me. My task is not of the easiest. The prevailing sentiment among large sections of the middle and lower classes of my own people is not friendly to England... I strive without ceasing to improve relations, and you retort that I am your arch-enemy. You make it hard for me. Why is it?

(ii) It was full of the Emperor's usual inept comments and was certain to offend the maximum number of people in the shortest possible time... The article was published in the *Daily Telegraph* on 28 October 1908. It aroused much criticism abroad, but this was completely dwarfed by the tremendous uproar in Germany... All the major parties, including the Conservatives, vehemently attacked the chancellor and his officials for their ineptitude in allowing the article to be published; nor did they spare the Emperor, who was severely censured for meddling once more in matters which were the proper concern of the government.

WILLIAM II SHOWN TAKING THE SALUTE. AT HIS SIDE ARE NUMEROUS GERMAN PRINCES

In fact William acted with constitutional propriety on this occasion. When Stuart-Wortley sent him the article, the Emperor passed it on to Bülow for approval. The latter was too preoccupied... Most likely he only glanced at it casually before passing it on... It can hardly be denied that Bülow's negligence was largely to blame for what happened. However, once the storm broke in the Reichstag... Bülow... joined in the attacks on William's 'personal government'... Shortly afterwards William promised in writing to respect the constitution and declared his complete confidence in the chancellor

William Carr, *A History of Germany* (1987)

The verdict of historians

Source L: J.C.G. Röhl - William as personal ruler

(i) A manically active, profoundly disturbed Emperor in charge of the mightiest military machine in the world; a clique of generals and courtiers who dress up as ballerinas and poodles to amuse him; a Chancellor who changes his trousers because he knows how dependent his control over the administration is upon the Kaiser's continuing support.

(ii) His very neuroses, once he became Kaiser, affected public policy.

(iii) William II's whole style of kingship was - for better or worse - his own invention, for his grandfather would not and his father could not be a 'Kaiser'. It may even be that the task he had set himself, of rallying the centrifugal nation behind his throne, was wildly over ambitious from the first, and that he failed as much because of its inherent impossibility as because of his personal weaknesses, however serious these were.

J.C.G. Röhl, *Kaiser Wilhelm II, New Interpretations* (1982)

Source M: H.U. Wehler – William as shadow emperor

(i) The Prussian-German power pyramid lacked an apex. Both in real terms and in terms of atmosphere, a power vacuum arose, which diverse personalities and forces tried to fill. Since neither they nor the parliament succeeded for any length of time in so-doing, there arose in Germany, behind the facade of a grandiose (personal) regime, a permanent crisis of state which led to a polycracy of rival power centres.

(ii) The last Hohenzollern Kaiser was incapable of ruling the Reich monocratically.

(iii) It was not Wilhelm II who impressed his stamp on Reich policy but the traditional oligarchies in conjunction with the anonymous forces of the authoritarian polycracy. Their power sufficed even without a semi-dictator.

H.U. Wehler, *The German Empire, 1871-1914*

Source N:

It was the Kaiser who was 'the ultimate authority in the Empire and who insisted on exercising that authority; it was he who dismissed Bismarck, for better or for worse; it was he who not only countenanced but encouraged the break-up of Germany's alliance system; it was he who was primarily

TALKING POINT
John Röhl uses the example of Bülow changing his trousers to please the Emperor. Do episodes like this suggest a strong emperor or a weak leader?

POLYCRACY – government by many people.
MONOCRACY – government by one ruler.
OLIGARCHY – government by a small group.

responsible for ruining Germany's relations with Britain by his ill-considered statements, by his reckless quest for colonies, and by his disastrous fleet programme; it was he, far more than Bismarck, who fostered the quality of grovelling servility in the German administration and who would only tolerate sychophants or mediocrities in his immediate entourage and in the highest positions of the German government including the German army.

N. Rich, Friedrich von Holstein, *Politics and Diplomacy in the Era of Bismarck and Wilhelm II* (Vol II 1965)

REVIEW

William II: personal ruler or shadow emperor?

Task

To build up a psychological profile of a ruler and his nation. You will need to look at Sources A-K in order to complete the exercise. In completing the list of headings you will need to indicate the source(s) and say briefly what it tells you, relevant to that heading. You will also need to consider its reliability. For example, you may not regard an outspoken comment by William himself as being completely accurate.

1 *Personal Profile.*

Use the following headings to analyse the sources

Physical description	Physical problems
Personal qualities	Personal problems
Personal faults	Evidence concerning William's sanity

2 *William's influence in decision-making*

Evidence from William himself suggesting strong rule
Evidence from William himself suggesting weak rule
Evidence from contemporaries suggesting strong rule
Evidence from contemporaries suggesting weak rule
Historians' verdicts

3 Assess the compatibility of your profile of William (1) with your picture of William at work (2).

4 What conclusions would you now draw? Was William a personal ruler or a shadow emperor?

5 You will need to return to this section after you have read Chapter Two. The notion under consideration will be: can a ruler influence a nation to such an extent that it comes to be a reflection of that ruler's personality (for example, William II=outspoken – Germany 1890-1914=outspoken)? When you have read Chapter Two, compile a list of characteristics which you feel describe the 'personality' of Germany. To what extent, if at all, do they mirror William's personality?

6 Essay: To what extent were the problems faced by Germany in the period 1890-1914 caused by the personal deficiencies of its ruler?

TALKING POINT

Historians who concentrate mainly on the personality and actions of the emperor are at fault because they are distracting attention from the collective responsibility of the German people for the outbreak of the First World War. Would you agree?

2 Germany and the Origins of The First World War 1890-1914

PREVIEW

The Kaiser's war?

'I am the sole master of German policy and my country must follow me wherever I go.'

'I am not the strong man - you must look elsewhere for him.'

Comments made by Kaiser William

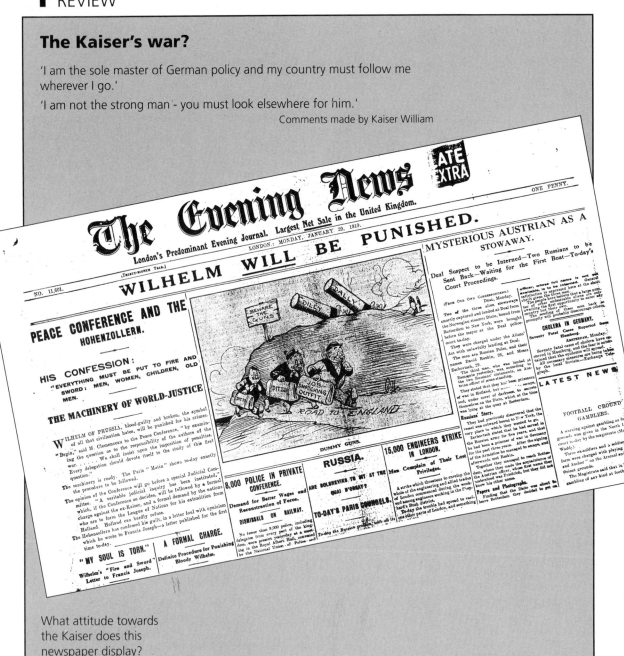

What attitude towards the Kaiser does this newspaper display?

Flight of the Kaiser

The 59-year-old man was roused in the middle of a cold and bleak night on 9 November 1918. He was told that the journey was about to begin and that there was no time to lose. Only one road out of the small German town of Spa remained open and that too might soon be closed. The journey to the frontier post with the Netherlands would have to be completed under cover of darkness. The convoy would consist of ten cars and, as an extra security measure, the royal motor car was stripped of all its insignia. Mutinous soldiers were known to be nearby. The small party arrived safely at the border at about 7.10 am.

Perhaps it was their elaborate cover which led to a delay, even though the Dutch authorities had already been warned to expect their important guest. At any rate, the royal party was detained in a bare waiting room for six hours before any decision was made. Eventually the royal train arrived at the railway siding and the party was accommodated on that. The man's fate was still undecided. The next day a Dutch nobleman, Count Betinck, offered to house the royal refugee in his castle at Amerongen. The Kaiser appeared to be safe. The abdication of William II, Emperor of Germany, was complete. However, the search for someone who could take the blame for the outbreak of a war that had lasted for more than four years had only just begun.

Seven months later the peacemakers at Versailles delivered this scathing verdict on the role played by the Kaiser in the outbreak of the war: 'The Allied and Associated Powers publicly arraign William II of Hohenzollern, former German Emperor, for a supreme offence against international morality and the sanctity of treaties'. Although William was never punished and lived out his exile in Holland until his death in June 1941, it is sometimes maintained even today that the First World War can justifiably be called the 'Kaiser's War'.

The objective in this chapter is to focus attention on a central issue. How much influence did William II actually exert on the conduct of German foreign policy between 1888 and 1914? Was the catastrophe of 1914-18 really the Kaiser's War?

EXAMINING THE EVIDENCE

How much influence did William II exert on German foreign policy between 1890 and 1914?

Source A: The decision not to renew the Reinsurance Treaty with Russia (1890-91)

(i) One can argue plausibly that the first foreign political action taken in... the Wilhelmine New Course was the most crucial of all those made between 1890 and the outbreak of the First World War and that it set in train the whole chain of calamity that led toward that catastrophe. If this is true, however, it has to be noted that, on this occasion, William II played an essentially passive role, the decisive force being exerted by the Foreign Ministry.

Gordon Craig, *The History of Germany* (1987)

CHANCELLOR CAPRIVI (1831-99)

CAPRIVI HAD ONLY JUST TAKEN OVER FROM BISMARK IN MARCH 1890 WHEN NEGOTIATIONS FOR RENEWAL OF THE TREATY BEGAN. HOLSTEIN, A SENIOR COUNCILLOR IN THE FOREIGN OFFICE PERSUADED CAPRIVI THAT RENEWAL WAS INADVISABLE. OTHER DIPLOMATS FROM THE BISMARCKIAN ERA BACKED UP THIS VIEW AND CLAIMED THAT GERMANY'S TIES TO AUSTRIA - HUNGARY AND ITALY WERE INCOMPATIBLE WITH THE RUSSIAN TREATY.

THE VISIT OF TSAR ALEXANDER III TO BERLIN. ALSO SHOWN ARE EMPEROR WILLIAM II, PRINCE BISMARCK, AND HIS SON HERBERT BISMARCK

What was the Reinsurance Treaty?

A secret agreement originally concluded with Russia by Bismarck in 1887. It stated that Russia would remain neutral if France attacked Germany, and Germany would remain neutral if Austria-Hungary attacked Russia.

William II had assured the Russians that the Treaty would be renewed, but backed down in the face of strong advice from the Foreign Office.

(ii) Then it isn't possible, much as I regret it.

> William II's comment after he had agreed to let the treaty lapse

Source B: The Krüger telegram (1895)

The German emperor was highly incensed by the Jameson Raid and insisted on immediate action. He talked wildly of declaring a protectorate over the Transvaal and sending troops to the Republic. His advisers persuaded him to settle for what they thought was a less harmful gesture of protest in the shape of a congratulatory telegram to Krüger, president of the Transvaal Republic…

The Krüger telegram was warmly applauded in Germany; Radical nationalists shared William's resentment of Britain and welcomed the ostentatious gesture of protest as a sign that Germany was now playing her rightful role in world politics. As a diplomatic manoeuvre the telegram was inept and unsuccessful..

> William Carr, *A History of Germany 1815-1985* (1987)

What was the Jameson Raid?

In 1894 Cecil Rhodes had been forced to curtail his attempt to gain control of a Boer railway in South Africa. The Jameson Raid was an attempt by an agent of Rhodes to invade the Transvaal. The raid was a total failure.

Source C: Naval expansion (1897)

(i) In my view, Germany will, in the coming century, rapidly drop from her position as a great power unless we begin to develop our maritime interests energetically, systematically and without delay.

> Tirpitz, 1895

(ii) In view of the changes in the balance of power in Asia and America, the Navy will, in the coming century, become increasingly important for our defence policy, indeed for our entire foreign policy.

> Tirpitz, February 1899

TIRPITZ BECAME THE NAVY SECRETARY IN 1897. BEFORE THE YEAR WAS OVER THE REICHSTAG HAD BEEN PRESENTED WITH A BILL WHICH PROVIDED FOR THE CONSTRUCTION OF SHIPS OF THE LINE WITHIN SEVEN YEARS.

In 1900 William proclaimed: 'Just as My Grandfather reorganised his Army, I shall unswervingly complete the task of reorganising My Navy so that it shall be in a position, internationally, to win for the German Reich that place which we have yet to achieve...'

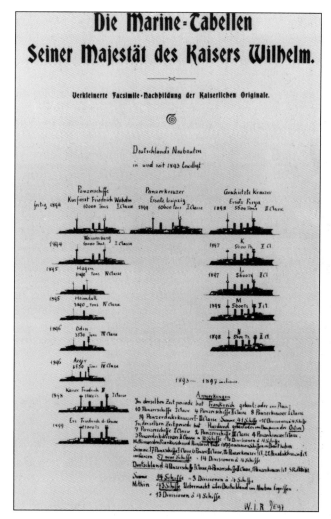

A NAVAL CHART, PERSONALLY DRAWN UP BY WILLIAM II

(iii) The slogans which William II proclaimed vociferously and which Bülow adopted without resistance, though in a somewhat smoother form, were world policy as a task, world power as the aim and naval construction as the instrument.

Fritz Fischer, 'World Policy, World Power and German War Aims'.
Essay in the *Origins of the First World War*, H.W. Koch (1972)

Source D: The First Moroccan Crisis (1905)

(i) Pressure was applied to France at her most vulnerable point, Morocco... In February 1905 France attempted to squeeze more concessions out of the Sultan. Whereupon Bülow and Hostein decided on an ostentatious gesture of protest; they asked the emperor to visit Tangier during his spring cruise in the Mediterranean. William was annoyed; he had no wish to quarrel with France in North Africa...Eventually he knuckled under and in March 1905 landed at Tangier; during his three-hour visit he was received by the Sultan's uncle and assured the latter, in tones reminiscent of the Krüger telegram, that Germany considered Morocco an independent state and expected her to resist French pressure.

William Carr, *A History of Germany 1815-1985* (1987)

(ii) Recent research has shown that the Kaiser's visit to Tangier was not the direct result of economic pressure group activities. The decision to intervene was based rather on considerations resulting from the changes which had taken place in the European balance of power since 1904. Holstein...apparently hoped to use the Moroccan crisis as a pretext for either a preventative war against France or, at least, the destruction of the as yet untested Entente Cordiale

V.R. Berghahn, *Germany and the Approach of War in 1914* (1973)

Source E: The Second Moroccan Crisis (1911)

(i) By seizing a (territorial) pawn, the Imperial Government will be placed in a position to give the Moroccan affair a turn which would cause the earlier setbacks (of 1905) to pass into oblivion... to obtain tangible advantages for Germany... (from the) liquidation of the Moroccan question would be important also for the future development of political conditions at home.

Alfred von Kiderlen-Wächter, State Secretary in the German Foreign Office. Extract from memorandum to the Kaiser, 3 May 1911

What was the outcome of the First Moroccan Crisis? Bülow insisted that an international conference on Morocco would have to be held. His hints that Germany would resort to war led to the resignation of the French foreign minister. When the conference was held in January 1906 Germany's isolation over Morocco became clear.

Why was there a Second Moroccan Crisis? Kiderlen Wächter, the Secretary of State for Foreign Affairs claimed that by sending troops to Morocco in April 1911 France was in breach of the 1906 agreement. Kiderlen insisted on sending the gunboat *Panther* to the Moroccan port of Agadir.

WILLIAM II INSTRUCTING A GROUP OF GENERALS DURING MILITARY MANOEUVRES BEFORE THE OUTBREAK OF WAR. HOW MUCH NOTICE DID THEY TAKE?

(ii) Keen to gain a success and...growing impatient.

Kaiser William's comment to Heinrich Class, leader of the
Pan German League, on the Chancellor's attitude towards Morocco

(iii) Had I ... allowed the war stage to be reached, we should now be somewhere in France, while the major part of our fleet should lie at the bottom of the North Sea and Hamburg and Bremen would be blockaded or under bombardment. The German people might well have asked me why? Why all this - for the fictitious sovereignty of the Sultan of Morocco?

Bethman-Hollweg's defence of his settlement of the Second Moroccan Crisis, in
a confidential letter to Carl von Weizsächer, Premier of
Württemberg (16 November 1911)

Source F: The Potsdam war council (December 1912)

(i) If Russia were to support the Serbs... If Austria were to invade Serbia, war would be inevitable for us... The fleet, of course, would have to face the war against Britain.

The Kaiser (8 December 1912)

(ii) In my opinion war is inevitable, and the sooner the better...the popularity of a war against Russia as outlined by the Kaiser, should be better prepared.

General von Moltke, Chief of the General Staff (8 December 1912)

(iii) Postponement of the great struggle by one-and-a-half years.

Admiral von Tirpitz (8 December 1912)

(iv) 'Pretty much nil.'

George Alexander von Muller, Chief of the Naval Cabinet. Verdict
on significance of Potsdam meeting

(v) He has 'accustomed' himself 'to the idea of... war.'

William's description of the Chancellor's frame of mind, to
Admiral Muller. (Note: Bethmann-Hollweg was not present at the meeting.)

Source G: The Kaiser's personal timetable

In his book *Germany 1866-1945*, Gordon Craig contends that William II's personal timetable was dominated by his love of military matters:

'He wore military dress whenever possible, if not that of his own regiments, then of foreign ones with which he had an honorary attachment. He saw to it that wherever he went he was surrounded by a cloud of uniforms; he preferred military companions, manners and advice to any other.

'This last ominous circumstance is illustrated by the ordering of the Emperor's working week. To be sure, he never worked for very long even when at home, but there is no doubt that a disproportionate amount of the time he spent on official business was devoted to military matters. He rarely met any of his Prussian ministers in person, except the War Minister, who had a weekly audience. The Reich Chancellor, except on extraordinary occasions, saw the Emperor on Saturday afternoon, although this was not invariable. In contrast, the Chief of the General Staff and the Chief of the Admiralty (later replaced by the Chief of the Marine Cabinet) each had one regular audience a week, while the Chief of the Military Cabinet met the sovereign every Tuesday, Thursday and Saturday morning'.

From G. Craig, *Germany 1866-1945* (1981)

What was the Potsdam war council Meeting? By 1912 Germany's aggressive foreign policy had taken its toll. Relations with Russia and France were poor. Internally 1912 also marked the emergence of the Social Democrats as the single largest party in the Reichstag. At Potsdam Moltke advised the Kaiser to launch an immediate 'preventative' war against France and Russia. Tirpitz wanted the war to be postponed for 18 months which would allow additional time to widen the Kiel Canal so that Germany's battleships would have easy access to the North Sea.

2.1 An analysis of the decision-making process in Wilhelmine Germany (1890-1912)

Powerful groups or individuals within German society	The Reinsurance Treaty	The Kruger telegram	Naval expansion	First Moroccan Crisis	Second Moroccan Crisis	Potsdam Coun…
Kaiser						
Chancellor						
Secretary of state for Foreign Affairs						
Chief of the General Staff						
Navy Secretary						
Powerful officials in the Foreign Office, for example Holstein						
Minister of War						
Chief of the Naval Cabinet						

EXERCISE

1 First copy out the table opposite. Then place the symbol which you feel is most appropriate next to each group or individual. For example, if you consider that the Chancellor initiated the Naval Programme, you will place an in column C, row 2

2 The search for a pattern: the role of power blocs
Now that you have filled in the grid consider whether any consistent pattern emerges
(i) Which figures or groups appear consistently? Why?
(ii) Which figures or groups appear erratically? Why?

3 The extent of the Kaiser's personal rule
a The Kaiser instigated and implemented all key decisions.
b The Kaiser instigated and implemented some decisions.
c The Kaiser was easily influenced by others.
d The Kaiser allowed others to make important decisions for him.
e The Kaiser reluctantly submitted to the advice of others even when his personal opinion was rather different.
f The Kaiser's influence diminished as time went on.
g The Kaiser's influence increased as time went on.
h Wilhelmine Germany was drifting along without any clear leadership from one individual in foreign policy.
i Decisions were not being freely made by any individuals at any time. Rather, Germany's leaders found their options limited by economics and political constraints. Room for manoeuvre in foreign policy was sorely limited.

Consider statements **a-i** very carefully. Working in small groups discuss which of them:

(a) You would instantly dismiss
(b) You feel contain an element of truth
(c) You feel accurately reflect the situation in the Kaiser's Germany.

What conclusions would you now draw about the decision-making process in Wilhelmine Germany?

Key
○ Took the initiative on this occasion

● Was asked for advice by the Kaiser

☐ Clearly exerted influence upon the Kaiser

■ Does not appear to have been immediately consulted by the Kaiser

★ Played a key role in reaching the final decision

? Role of this individual/ group uncertain on this occasion

FOCUS

2.2 The alliance system and the arms race up to 1914

It is essential to realise that while we have focused in this chapter on the role of the Kaiser in the origins of the First World War, other factors were also vital. What else contributed to the undermining of relations between Germany and Russia? Contemporaries and historians have pointed to the damaging effects of the alliance system and the accompanying arms race. Many Germans felt that France and Russia, joined by Great Britain, were deliberately pursuing a policy which was designed to 'encircle' Germany. On the other hand these powers, alarmed by Germany's naval expansion, colonial ambitions and outspoken diplomacy, felt that their alliance was an essential response to a malign attempt at disturbing the balance of power. Now decide whether you think Germany was entitled to believe that its security had deliberately been placed in jeopardy.

1882 Triple Alliance (Germany, Austria and Italy)

Following the German-Austrian treaty which had been signed in 1879, Italy had joined the German-Austrian alliance in 1882 and this was known as the Triple Alliance. This was renewed in 1907 and 1912.

1893 Franco-Russian Alliance

In 1890 Germany allowed the Reinsurance Treaty with Russia to lapse. In 1891, partly as a consequence of this, came the Franco-Russian Entente, in which the signatories agreed to consult each other in the event of threat of aggression to one of the powers. In 1892 came the Franco-Russian Military Convention and then the Alliance of 1893.

1902 Anglo-Japanese Alliance

In the autumn of 1901 Anglo-German alliance negotiations collapsed. Earlier Franco-German negotiations broke down. However, in 1902 Britain strengthened its position in the Far East by signing a defensive alliance with Japan.

1904 Entente-Cordiale (Great Britain and France)

This was a less formal agreement than a full-scale alliance. This entente, reached between England and France, was intended to settle past colonial differences between them, especially over Egypt and Morocco. In the same year Britain's relations with Russia were badly strained in the Dogger Bank Incident, the sinking of a British trawler by the Russian Fleet. Germany attempted to take advantage of this situation but her negotiations with Russia broke down.

1907 Anglo-Russian Entente

In the same year that the Triple Alliance was renewed for six years, Britain and Russia moved much closer together. The entente settled a number of imperial disputes, especially over Persia, Tibet and Afghanistan. Collectively, France, Britain and Russia now comprised the Triple Entente. Europe was now effectively divided into two major alliance systems and this remained the case up to 1914. How powerful were these alliances?

1 Naval strength of major European Powers in 1914

	France	Great Britain	Russia	Austria-Hungary	Germany	Italy
Dreadnoughts	14	24	4	3	13	1
Pre-Dreadnoughts	9	38	7	12	30	17
Battle Cruisers	0	10	1	0	6	0
Cruisers	19	47	8	3	14	5
Light Cruisers	6	61	5	4	35	6
Destroyers	81	228	106	18	152	33
Submarines	67	76	36	14	30	20

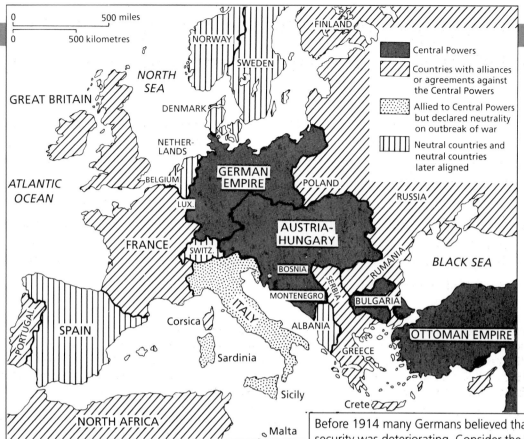

Before 1914 many Germans believed that their security was deteriorating. Consider the following:
(a) What justification was there for this view?
(b) Which alliance system appeared to be most powerful?
(c) What mistakes in German foreign policy do you feel are reflected here?

2 Total population of the Powers, 1890-1913

	1890	1900	1910	1913
France	38.3	38.9	39.5	39.7
Great Britain	37.4	41.1	44.9	45.6
Russia	116.8	135.6	159.3	175.1
Austria-Hungary	42.6	46.7	50.8	52.1
Germany	49.2	56.0	64.5	66.9
Italy	30.0	32.2	34.4	35.1

3 Military and naval personnel of the Powers, 1890-1914

	1890	1900	1910	1914
France	542,000	715,000	769,000	910,000
Great Britain	420,000	624,000	571,000	532,000
Russia	677,000	1,162,000	1,285,000	1,352,000
Austria-Hungary	284,000	255,000	322,000	345,000
Germany	504,000	524,000	694,000	891,000
Italy	284,000	255,000	322,000	345,000

2.3 Flashpoint! The Balkans and the origins of the First World War

Despite the apparent security provided by the alliance system, the actions of the great powers tended to be a reflection of their anxieties and hyper-defensive tendencies. Indeed, the extra commitments implicit in the logic of the system only served to heighten the notion, shared by many of the powers, that the actions of their rivals were inevitably malign. Nowhere was the anxiety more acutely felt than in the Austro-Hungarian Empire. Having witnessed the rapid disintegration of the Ottoman Empire amid rising demands for Slavic independence, the Austrians themselves felt increasingly threatened. In particular Austria regarded Serbia as the focal point of Slav nationalism, a problem which would one day have to be dealt with successfully if Austria were not to face total oblivion. In turn, Germany's rulers recognised that as Austria's closest ally their fate was inextricably linked with that of the Austro-Hungarian empire. On the other hand Russia's apparent sponsorship of Slav nationalism - the so called Pan-Slav policy - seemed bound to draw her into conflict with the Austrians. Why were the Balkans Europe's most volatile region?

The Austro-Hungarian Empire
Sought to preserve its empire by repressing the nationalist aspirations of her subject peoples

Russia
Encouraged through a policy of Pan-Slavism, the nationalist aspirations of these groups

The nationalities of the Habsburg monarchy in 1910

Cisleithanian Austria	%
Germans	35.6
Czechs (incl.Slovaks)	23.0
Poles	17.8
Ruthenians	12.6
Serbo-Croats	2.6
Romanians	1.0

Lands of the Hungarian crown including Croatia-Slavonia	%
Magyars	48.1
Germans	9.8
Slovaks	9.4
Romanians	14.1
Ruthenians	2.3
Croats	8.8
Serbs	5.3

Bosnia-Herzegovina	
Croats	21
Serbs	42
Mohammedans	34

1897 Emperor Francis Joseph makes state visit to Russia. This marked the start of an Austro-Russian entente over the Balkans. In effect this removed the Balkan issue as a source of disagreement for the next decade.

1903 The antagonistic racial policy pursued by the Hungarians aroused considerable ill-will among the Croats and Serbs who lived within the Dual Monarchy. By now Serbia had emerged as a critical force in the Balkans. The upsurge in Serbian patriotism was marked by the murder of King Alexander Obrenovich of Serbia in 1903. This dynasty, which had been fairly friendly towards Austria, was now replaced by the Karageorgevich family, which had traditionally been attached to Russia. After this date Russian influence prevailed in Belgrade and Serbian patriotic clubs were set up in Bosnia and Hungary. The first major test of the Austro-Russian entente came in 1903, when open rebellion erupted among the South Slavs in Macedonia which was strategically the key province of the Ottoman Empire in Europe. In the Mürzsteg agreement signed by the two powers in October, it was agreed to reaffirm the 1897 agreement and supervise reforms in the province.

1904 -1907 This period has been described as the golden age of the Austro-Russian Entente. While Austria was busy coping with domestic issues, Russia was preoccupied with the Far East arena, ultimately facing military defeat at the hands of the Japanese and domestic upheaval. However, by 1907 Europe's division into two power blocs, the Triple Alliance and the Triple Entente, was quite apparent. As Austria became more desperate to maintain her grip on the empire, and Russia switched her focus away from the Far East and towards Europe, the Balkans became an increasingly tense area. In particular, Austria was determined to take action to defend her interests in the Balkans.

1908-1909 The decision to annex Bosnia-Herzegovina in the autumn of 1908 was taken by the Austrian foreign minister Aehrenthal. Given the nature of the alliance system, Chancellor Bülow had no choice but to recommend German backing: `our position would indeed be dangerous if Austria lost confidence in us and turned away... in the present world constellation we must be careful to retain in Austria a "true partner"'. Russia and Serbia protested

in vain and Germany backed Austria completely. In March 1909 Germany suggested that Russia formally acknowledge the annexation. When Russia hesitated Germany underlined the suggestion in terms strong enough to constitute an ultimatum. Germany knew that Russia was in no position to go to war over Bosnia and Russia's recognition of the annexation was soon forthcoming.

The significance of these events was two-fold. Germany was now fully committed to Austria's policy in the Balkans. Russia had been humiliated but was now closer to Britain and France than ever before. In effect an Austrian war with Serbia would involve Russia, Germany and France.

1912 Balkan League formed, comprising Serbia, Greece, Bulgaria and Montenegro. In the First Balkan War these states attacked Turkey and drove her out of all her European territories. Austria's sense of crisis was acute but decisive action against Serbia was not forthcoming. Germany's advice was to await the break up of the Balkan League before Austria attacked Serbia.

1913 Disputes within the Balkan League led to war between Bulgaria and the rest. Bulgaria was quickly defeated. Although Serbia responded to an Austrian ultimatum demanding the withdrawal of Serb troops from Albania, the fact remained that the Balkan states were growing in strength.

1914 By the time Franz Ferdinand was assassinated by Bosnian terrorists during a visit to Sarajevo, the capital of Bosnia, it was clear that the balance of power in the Balkans had moved steadily in favour of Russia. The response to the murder, as we will now see, was tinged with desperation on the part of Austria and Germany.

`The Balkans were in a highly disturbed state in the first decade of the twentieth century. As the Turkish Empire declined, the independent Balkan states were becoming increasingly restive.'

From William Car A *History of Germany,* (1987)

`For some years there had been indications that both the Ottoman and Austro-Hungarian empires faced a deadly threat from the resurgent nationalism of the Balkan peoples.'

From L.F.C. Turner *Origins of the First World War,* (1970)

The July Crisis

Sunday 18 June 1914

The month of June was coming to a glorious conclusion. All over Europe people were basking under a prolonged heatwave which showed no sign of coming to an end. Prospects for the summer were superb. Although the season had only just begun, seaside towns were already crowded with visitors, many eager to display the latest daring fashions in below-the-knee swimwear. In the leafy suburb of Wimbledon the groundsmen spent all of Sunday watering the courts in preparation for the lawn tennis championships which were due to resume the next day. Meanwhile, butlers and manservants across the continent put the finishing touches to their employers' traditional routine of

THE LADIES FINAL AT WIMBLEDON IN JULY 1914

THE ARREST OF GAVRILLO PRINCIP AFTER HIS ASSASSINATION OF ARCHDUKE FRANZ FERDINAND

1 Why do you think Franz Ferdinand made his state visit to Bosnia when it must have been clear to him that such a visit might be dangerous?

2 Why do you suppose Franz Ferdinand was a special target for Slav terrorists?

hunting expeditions, holidays, spas and cures which characterised the summer months. In Germany, Kaiser William II had left behind weighty matters of state, donned his sailing outfit and spent the day under the blazing sun racing his yacht *Meteor* at Kiel.

Meanwhile, several hundred miles to the south, Archduke Franz Ferdinand - heir to the throne of Austria-Hungary - was spending his wedding anniversary with his wife, Countess Sophie, on a state visit to Sarajevo. They received a very warm welcome and the glorious weather enabled them to drive through the crowded streets in an open-topped car. However, Sarajevo was the capital of the former Turkish province of Bosnia, a state inhabited by Slavs but occupied since 1908 by the Austro-Hungarian Empire. A south Slav terrorist organisation consisting of ultra-nationalist officers and student intellectuals (calling itself the 'Black Hand' gang) regarded the Austrian prince as the figurehead of an occupying empire which stood in the way of Slav independence. At the centre of this radical group, and beyond the direct control of the Serbian government, was Gavrillo Princip who had decided to lead an assassination attempt against the Austrian prince.

The bungling nature of these amateur assassins meant that two attempts on the Heir Apparent's life were necessary. After a hand grenade had missed its intended target but injured 20 onlookers, officials decided that the visit should be cut short and the route home changed. In retrospect, one of the most startling aspects of that fateful day in Sarajevo is that the authorities were unable to guarantee Franz Ferdinand's safety after the first assassination attempt had failed. Crucially, the driver of the first vehicle in the four-car entourage did not follow the fresh instructions and made a right turn back along the original route. It was only when the second car, containing the royal couple had followed suit that officials shouted out instructions to stop and turn back. As the driver of Franz Ferdinand's car tried in vain to find reverse gear, Princip stepped out of the crowd and onto the running board. With his victim helpless and within a few feet, Princip almost lost his nerve. The sight of Countess Sophie made him hesitate but then nationalism overcame chivalry and at point-blank range he fired several shots. A few minutes later the couple were dead.

William II was still aboard his yacht when Admiral Muller, the Chief of the Naval Secretariat, pulled alongside in a launch and shouted that he had a telegram to pass across. William, never a man renowned for his patience, demanded that the news should simply be shouted across immediately. Observers were struck by the calm, almost off-hand manner in which the Kaiser reacted. William requested advice on whether it would now be good form to call off the yachting race. Yet the time for graver decisions was almost at hand.

Franz Ferdinand's blood splattered blue tunic and his car with its famous running board have now become museum exhibits. The spot from where Princip fired his shots in Sarajevo is a popular tourist attraction. However, the central questions about the political consequences of his murder remain controversial. Why did an isolated act of terrorism in an area of which few Europeans had even heard lead to a prolonged and widespread political crisis throughout July? Why did this culminate in the wholesale declarations of war which scarred the first days of August and led to the most horrendous conflict in European history? It is unlikely that any period in the history of mankind has been subject to more intensive historical research than that between 28 June and 4 August 1914. There is no shortage of primary evidence and with one or two important exceptions, diaries, diplomatic exchanges and private memoirs, varying in their accuracy, abound. What does it all reveal? Who was making the key decisions in German foreign policy during the July Crisis? The role played in the crisis by the Chancellor, Theobald von Bethmann-Hollweg, has aroused intense debate. The traditional view saw the Chancellor as a peace-loving, liberal statesman who reminded some people of Abraham Lincoln. Supporters of this viewpoint praise Bethmann-Hollweg for his valiant efforts to keep the radical militarists at bay and prevent them from indoctrinating the Kaiser with their warlike talk. This viewpoint has been sustained by extracts (the accuracy of which are now very much under review) from the diary of Kurt Reizler, Bethmann-Hollweg's personal assistant and confidant. These extracts portray the chancellor as a helpless victim of circumstances beyond his control, trying at all costs to avoid war but being dragged to the brink by inflexible military strategies, belligerent generals and a headstrong Emperor.

Fritz Fischer's formidable study *Griff Nach der Weltmacht* (Grasping at World Power), published in 1961, presents a radically different picture of Bethmann-Hollweg. Fischer places the Chancellor much closer to military extremists like General Ludendorff. He claims that Bethmann-Hollweg had far-reaching war aims which followed closely the ideas put forward by leading German industrialists and by the radical lobbying of the Pan German League. These ideas, Fischer argues, were there for all to see in an influential memorandum of 9 September 1914 in which Bethmann-Hollweg stated that the aim of the war must be: 'The security of the German Empire in the West and in the East for the foreseeable future. To this end, France must be so weakened that she cannot rise again as a Great Power, Russia must be pushed as far as possible from the German frontier, and her rule over non-Russian subject peoples must be broken'. Fischer is convinced that these ideas must have been formulated before the war had begun. Moreover, he provides damaging evidence of close personal links between the Chancellor and Walther Rathenau, director of the powerful German electrical combine: the A.E.G. Fischer shows that Rathenau was a regular guest at the Chancellor's magnificent country estate in Hohenfinow. Other like-minded industrialists and merchant bankers were also made welcome there. Perhaps as they sat by the open fire and chatted into the small hours, their expansionist ideas came to exert a powerful influence over the Chancellor. You should now consider which view of Bethmann-Hollweg is most accurately reflected in his conduct during the build-up to war.

There is no doubt that long before the July Crisis the Chancellor found himself full of doubts and apprehension. In 1913 he remarked to a friend that 'the more distant future is quite dark'. Overlooking the park of his estate near Berlin, the gloomy Chancellor told his son that there was no point in planting new trees for 'in a few years the Russians would be here anyway'. Bethmann-Hollweg confessed that the pressures of high office had taken their toll and made him weary. In particular, the Chancellor complained that 'the men who should lighten my burden professionally, His Majesty and the Conservatives, make things as difficult as they can'. Germany's international

TALKING POINT

From the moment Franz Ferdinand was assassinated, the alliance system and the Balkan situation made war inevitable. Do you agree?

TALKING POINT

The German government objected strongly to Fischer's book and stopped him lecturing on the subject. Why do you think they reacted so strongly?

isolation cannot have relieved the Chancellor's growing sense of pessimism. As a gloomy military memorandum of May 1914 put it: 'At the moment Italy is still on the side of the Triple Alliance and Emperor Franz Joseph's personality still holds the hotch-potch Danubian monarchy together...But for how long? Will these things perhaps not change in favour (of the Entente Powers) quite soon?'

This growing sense of urgency tinged with gloom and pessimism was heightened by the events in Sarajevo on 28 June 1914. When Kaiser William II received an official report on the assassination from the German ambassador in Vienna, his reaction was less restrained than it had been when he had first heard the news on his yacht. The vitriolic comments which the Kaiser scribbled in pencil in the margins of the memorandum have become history in themselves. 'Now or never' exclaimed the Kaiser, 'The Serbs will have to be straightened out and soon'. William II had set the tone for the regime's reaction and had personally added a dreadful momentum to events.

The crucial issue was whether action of whatever type against Serbia could be carried out without Russian intervention. The critical contribution of the military at this stage was to urge the Kaiser to meet this risk head-on and launch a preventative war against Russia. They argued that with Russia still a few years away from being at full military capacity, a much greater chance of victory was to be had in 1914 than a few years later. They undoubtedly succeeded in getting their views across but for the time being at least, it was the more sophisticated counsel of the Chancellor which prevailed.

In his book *Germany and the Approach of War in 1914,* Volker Berghahn estimates that within Germany no more than 12 people were consulted over the main decisions. Moreover, the crucial steps in the July Crisis were made by individuals within the Court, the German Foreign Office and the General Staff. The leading industrialists, despite their power and influence, do not appear to have been consulted at this stage.

Meanwhile, the Austrian monarchy had not reacted to the assassination with as much zeal as its German counterpart. In marked contrast to their official anguish and despair, the private actions of the Austrian royal family suggested that Franz Ferdinand would not be sorely missed. The fallen prince was buried with such an astonishing lack of pomp and ceremony that it was referred to as a 'third-class funeral'. Rather than seeking out immediate revenge, Emperor Franz Joseph made it clear that he would prefer to hear the results of an inquiry into the assassination before approving any action against the Serbs. Only Conrad, the chief of the General Staff, proposed immediate action. Meanwhile Berchtold, the Austro-Hungarian foreign minister, was concerned that Germany 'would leave us in the lurch' and this prompted Franz Joseph to write a personal letter to William II asking for clarification of the German position at the highest level.

Count Berchtold's personal envoy was sent to deliver the letter in person and after lunch with the Kaiser in the Royal Palace, emphatic clarification was forthcoming:

'I gave the autograph letter and the enclosed memoir into the hands of His Majesty. In my presence the Kaiser read both with the greatest attention. The first thing he assured me was, that he had expected some serious step

TALKING POINT

It seems that William's famous comment 'Now or never' was an instinctive, off-the-cuff remark rather than a considered statement. Is it therefore best to disregard this type of comment in the final analysis?

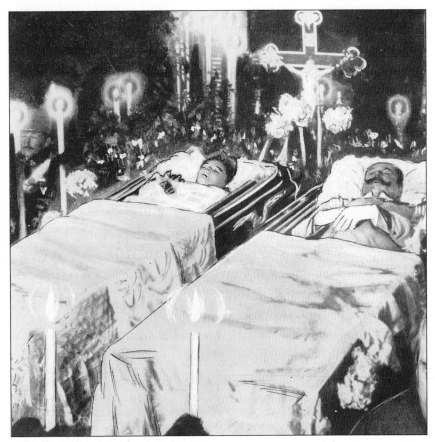
FRANZ FERDINAND LYING IN STATE

on our part towards Serbia, but that at the same time he must confess that the detailed statement of His Majesty made him regard a serious European complication possible and that he could give no definite answer before having taken council with the Imperial Chancellor.

After lunch, when I again called attention to the seriousness of the situation, the Kaiser authorised me to inform our gracious Majesty that we might in this case, as in all others, rely upon Germany's full support. He must, as he said before, first hear what the Imperial Chancellor has to say, but he did not doubt in the least that Herr von Bethmann Hollweg would agree with him. Especially as far as our action against Serbia was concerned.'

This offer of support to Austria from the Kaiser was so wholehearted that it has become known as the 'blank cheque'. It represented a key step in unlocking the complex mechanisms of treaty obligations which would ultimately unleash a world war. The Kaiser, without obtaining prior approval from the Chancellor but assuming it would be given later, had personally issued full, unconditional support to the Austrians and had underlined this 'blank cheque' with the advice that the Dual Monarchy should not hesitate to take action against the Serbs. The Kaiser's bellicose mood was not diminished by the holiday atmosphere. Indeed as William prepared to set sail for Norway on the evening of 6 July he told the industrialist, Krupp, 'This time, I shall not chicken out'. Krupp regarded this more as a pathetic show of bravado than genuine aggression but nevertheless, the Kaiser's nervous energy was having a profound effect on those around him.

Bethmann-Hollweg quickly realised that the sort of 'action' against Serbia which the Kaiser envisaged could easily trigger the whole process of alliance commitments and lead to a major war. It is to Bethmann-Hollweg's credit that he was quickly able to come up with an alternative plan which had sufficient credibility to persuade the Kaiser to take his holiday as planned and leave things to the Chancellor. The military men were pressuring him but Bethmann-Hollweg had at least obtained some breathing space.

William II explained the plan to officials with some enthusiasm: 'the Austrian Government will demand the most far-reaching satisfaction from Serbia and will, as soon as this is not given, move its troops into Serbia'. Russian intervention was regarded as highly unlikely 'because the Tsar will not lend his support to royal assassins and because Russia is at the present moment, militarily and financially totally unprepared for war'. What could go wrong?

Ingenuity had been provided by the Chancellor. Two further ingredients, secrecy and speed, were necessary to ensure complete success. There was a greater degree of ostentation than usual therefore when the Kaiser set off on his annual cruise while the military men also went their separate ways on vacation. They could hardly have gone to greater lengths to assure the watching world that nothing was amiss.

Now it was up to the Austrians to draw up a definitive ultimatum to Serbia. Fatally, it took until 19 July for the Austro-Hungarian ministerial council to approve a suitably-worded ultimatum. Surely now it could be passed on and the initiative regained? It was not to be. Chance intervened when the Austrians realised that between 20 and 23 July, Raymond Poincaré, the French President, would be on a state visit to St Petersburg. If the ultimatum were presented to Serbia during this period then there was every possibility that the response would come not just from the Serbs alone but as a coordinated move from Serbia, her protector Russia and Russia's ally France. The ultimatum would have to be shelved until Poincaré left Russia. Yet even before Poincaré arrived in St Petersburg the Russians had cracked the cipher used by the Austro-Hungarian Foreign Ministry and had a clear idea that the Austrians were planning some sort of decisive action against Serbia. Nevertheless, when the ultimatum was finally delivered to Serbia on 23 July, its harsh terms and 48-hour time limit for a reply sent shock waves through the foreign offices of Europe. The British foreign secretary, Sir Edward Grey, described the ultimatum as 'the most formidable document I had ever seen addressed by one State to another that was independent'. The hard-pressed Serbs skilfully produced a reply which while conciliatory in tone did not meet all of the demands. The Serbian reply was delivered to the Austrian representative moments before the 6 pm deadline on 25 July. Its contents were scarcely considered. Following prior instructions the Austrian official immediately announced his dissatisfaction and returned to Vienna on the 6.30 pm train. Austria announced that it had broken off relations with Serbia but the real intentions behind the smokescreen of the ultimatum had been laid bare.

Meanwhile, in Germany, Bethmann-Hollweg remained at the helm,

1 What were the strengths, and

2 What were the weaknesses of Bethmann-Hollweg's plan?

lamenting the lethargy of the Austrian response and realising the risks inherent in his plan. He began to sink into his familiar melancholy. According to Reizler, Bethmann-Hollweg said on 7 July: 'An action against Serbia can lead to world war'. A week later he admitted that he was taking 'a leap into the dark' but this constituted his 'gravest duty'. By now Bethmann-Hollweg seemed to think that there was no way out: 'Secret intelligence gives a shattering picture...the military might of Russia is growing fast'. By 25 July it was becoming painfully apparent that Russia and Britain were not prepared to stand by and observe the defeat of Serbia. Universal diplomatic condemnation of the ultimatum and the way it had been handled by the Austrians ensured that Bethmann-Hollweg's elaborate plan had failed. Over his shoulder the harassed chancellor could sense Moltke and the other leading military figures gathering against him. By 26 July they had all returned to Berlin. Their time had come.

The struggle between the General Staff and the civilian politicians lasted for three days. One account tells us that Moltke 'uses all his influence that the singularly favourable situation be exploited for military action'. The prospect of a swift military victory resolving Germany's complex foreign and domestic problems was an intoxicating one, and the optimism of the General Staff ensured that the military now gained the ascendancy over the civilians. The Chancellor exclaimed that he now saw the 'force of fate, stronger than the power of humans, hanging over Europe and our people' On the same day Bethmann-Hollweg informed the Kaiser of his new priorities: 'in all events Russia must ruthlessly be put in the wrong'.

The events of the last few days of July and the first few days of August now took on an alarming European dimension. On 28 July Austria-Hungary declared war on Serbia and shelled Belgrade, although general mobilisation against Russia had not yet occurred. When the French took the precaution of recalling soldiers from Morocco the Germans warned that further steps would force Germany to proclaim the 'state of imminent danger of war' which directly preceded mobilisation. In Russia, two alternative decrees - one for partial mobilisation and one for general mobilisation - had already

been signed by the Tsar. Germany's firm warning to Russia now followed, but backfired since the Russian foreign minister, the war minister and the chief of staff unanimously agreed to respond with general mobilisation. The Tsar only hesitated because of the intervention of William II. Evidence that the Kaiser was now beginning to have second thoughts is provided by his personal telegram to his cousin the Tsar which ended: 'I am exerting my utmost influence to induce the Austrians to deal straightly to arrive to a satisfactory understanding with you. I confidently hope you will help me in my efforts to smooth over difficulties that may still arise. Your very sincere and devoted friend and cousin Willy'.

Events were now moving with such pace and complexity that it becomes difficult and perhaps unfair at this stage to attach personal responsibility for war guilt to any one individual. It may be that for their conduct in the last days of July and the first days of August, Europe's decision-makers should be burdened with a collective responsibility because they had allowed the control of events to slip from their grasp and assume an inexorable momentum. When analysing the leaders involved in the July Crisis, the Italian historian Luigi Albertini was alarmed by 'the disproportion between their

GERMAN ARTILLERY PASSING THROUGH BRUSSELS (26 AUGUST 1914)

intellectual and moral endowments and the gravity of the problems which faced them, between their acts and the results thereof'. More specifically, many individuals who tried to deal with Berlin at this stage in the crisis were struck by a sense of chaos and helplessness. The experience of the Austrians in the last days of peace illustrates the point and suggests that at the eleventh hour the Kaiser and the Chancellor were having serious misgivings.

On 27 July Grey - the British foreign secretary - sent an urgent message to Bethmann-Hollweg asking Germany to persuade the Austrian government to accept Serbia's reply to the ultimatum. In return, Grey was urging the Russians to act with restraint. The telegram was passed to the Kaiser who replied that the Serbian response had indeed removed grounds for war but nevertheless recommended that Austria should occupy Belgrade and stay there to provide some guarantee that the Serbs would fulfil their promises. However, while the civilian Berchtold was weighing up the Kaiser's 'halt in Belgrade' proposal, General Conrad was being reminded by Moltke (the chief of the German general staff) that any further delay in Austrian action against the Serbs would have disastrous consequences. It is no wonder that such conflicting advice had Berchtold in despair, to the extent that he is said to have exclaimed: 'Who actually rules in Berlin, Bethmann or Moltke?' Austria's subsequent announcement that it was too late to delay operations against Serbia suggests that the advice of the German military was now carrying more weight. On 30 July Austria-Hungary ordered general mobilisation for the next day. Russia immediately followed suit. At noon on 31 July news of Russian general mobilisation became known in Berlin.

The news moved the civilian and military factions in Germany together. Bethmann-Hollweg was satisfied that the press would be able to bring together the German people in a wave of anti-Russian patriotism. The generals knew that their demands for full German mobilisation could no longer

How would you have answered Berchtold's question?

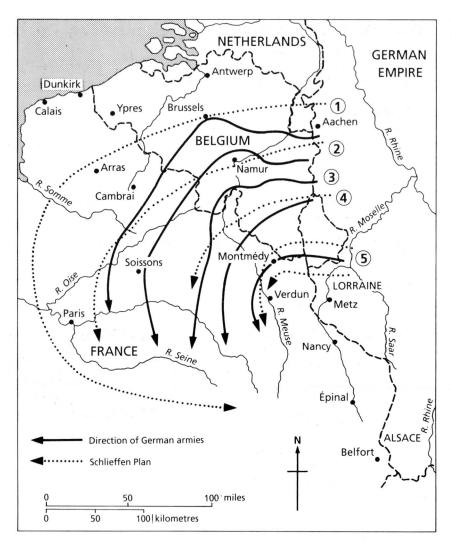

NETHERLANDS

GERMAN
EMPIRE

Dunkirk

Calais

Ypres

Brussels

Antwerp

Aachen

BELGIUM

Namur

Arras

Cambrai

R. Somme

R. Oise

Soissons

Montmédy

Verdun

Metz

LORRAINE

Paris

FRANCE

R. Seine

Nancy

Épinal

Belfort

ALSACE

R. Rhine

R. Moselle

R. Meuse

R. Saar

R. Rhine

Direction of German armies

Schlieffen Plan

0   50   100 miles

0   50   100 kilometres

N

be resisted. Allegations in the German press that Russian patrols had tres-
passed on to German soil on 2 August ensured that left-wing opposition to
the war was brushed aside amid alarmist talk of the imminent invasion by
the 'Russian barbarians'. On 1 August Germany declared war on Russia and
mobilised her troops. The harsh logic of the alliance system meant that on
3 August Germany also declared war on France.

Germany's military strategy, based on a plan drawn up in 1892 by General
Schlieffen, made it unlikely that Britain would remain neutral. In the expectation that it would be several weeks before the Russian mobilisation would
take full effect, Germany's soldiers would outflank the French army by
marching through southern Belgium. This was in direct violation of the
Treaty of London, Britain's guarantee to Belgium made in 1839. Britain
declared war on Germany on 4 August. The chain was complete, but was
the Kaiser chiefly to blame or does more responsibility rest with his
Chancellor, Bethmann-Hollweg?

The role of Bethmann-Hollweg in the July Crisis

1 Sympathetic viewpoint
The Chancellor was a peace-loving liberal statesman. He fought a constant battle to restrain the expansionists. He did his best to avoid war.

2 Neutral viewpoint
The Chancellor lost control of events during the July Crisis. He tried to bring about a limited punishment of Serbia but did not desire a more general European war.

3 Critical viewpoint
The Chancellor was an aggressive expansionist whose aim coincided with the industrialists, the army generals and the Kaiser.

Which viewpoint of the Chancellor do you feel is closest to the truth? Consider the following factors before you make your decision.

Influence
How much influence did each exert on the other?

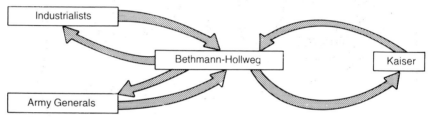

Actions
What did Bethmann-Hollweg do to:
(a) make a limited war more likely?
(b) make a general European war more likely?
(c) avoid war?
Could he have acted differently?

Intentions
What did Bethmann-Hollweg want to do?
(a) What do his private comments reveal?
(b) Did he have a set of definite war aims?

Other questions
(a) Were there any key groups that Bethmann-Hollweg chose not to consult?
(b) What were Bethmann-Hollweg's relations with the Austrians?
(c) Were there any other leading individuals whom you feel bear greater moral responsibility for what happened?

Task
(i) Write out the three statements concerning the Chancellor's role in the July Crisis.
(ii) Consider in turn each of the factors listed.
(iii) Now write a paragraph supporting each of the viewpoints 1, 2, 3.
(iv) Finally, offer your own analysis of the July Crisis.

EXAMINING THE EVIDENCE

The outbreak of war: what was the popular mood in 1914?

Source A

Russian soldiers preparing to leave to leave for the front. What is your impression of their feelings at the outbreak of war?

Source B

British recruits at Southwark Town Hall, in the recruitment campaign of 1915. Contrast this photograph with the Russian one.

1 Which of the sources A–F contain evidence to suggest that the popular mood in 1914 supported the outbreak of war?

2 What evidence is contained in these sources to suggest the existence of doubt and dissent?

3 What difficulties does an assessment of the popular mood present for the historian?

4 What conclusions would you reach on the basis of the evidence presented here?

Source C: The mood in Russia. An extract from a novel

What had happened? Only a month or three weeks ago no thinking Russian citizen had doubted the fact that the ruler of Russia was a despicable individual, unworthy of serious mention; no one would have dreamed of quoting him except as a joke. Yet in a matter of days everything had changed... throughout her long journey Vanya had observed the effects of war - the loading of troop-trains, the farewells. Especially at small stations, the Russian leave-taking was an almost joyous affair, with the reservists dancing away to balalaika music and raising the dust on the trampled earth of the trackside...'

Alexander Solzhenitsyn, *August 1914* (1972)

Source D: The mood in Germany. The findings of an historian

Using sources from the city of Hamburg, he found that the *Hamburgische Correspondent*, a respectable middle-class paper, reported that the news of the mobilisation had been received 'in silent earnestness'. Ulrich moreover found the diary of a member of the socialist Youth League which contains the following passage: 'Excitement among the population which expressed itself in a panicky run on savings banks and grocery shops. Most people were downcast, as if they were to be beheaded on the following day'. And finally there is the response of an older Social Democrat in Hamburg who wrote on the day the Reichstag voted the war credits: 'In front of the trade union offices in Besenbinderhof many comrades assembled day after day. We watched the commotion rather dumfounded. Many asked themselves: "Am I mad or is it the others?"'

Volker Berghahn citing Volker Ulrich in *History Sixth Magazine* (May 1988)

Source E: The mood in Austria. The viewpoint of the British ambassador in Vienna

The British ambassador noted that the Austrian reaction to the news of a breach with Serbia was to 'burst into a frenzy of delight, vast crowds parading the streets and singing patriotic songs till the small hours of the morning.' An Austrian socialist added, 'The party is defenceless...Demonstrations in support of the war are taking place in the streets...Our whole organisation and our press are at risk. We run the risk of destroying thirty years' work without any political result.'

Quoted in James Joll, *The Origins of the First World War* (1984)

REVIEW

Debate this motion using the details and evidence contained in the chapter you have just read.

Motion

The Kaiser was responsible for the outbreak of the First World War.

Source F: The mood in Britain. The findings of James Joll, an historian

Reports on the mood of the English varied: 'There is strained solemnity on every face,' Beatrice Webb noted in London on 5 August. But others felt enthusiasm themselves and observed it in others. 'I may possibly live to think differently; but at the present moment, assuming that this war has to come, I feel nothing but gratitude to the gods for sending it in my time. Whatever war itself may be like, preparing to fight in time of war is the greatest game and the finest work in the world,' one radical reformer wrote shortly after volunteering for the army... Bertrand Russell remembered that 'I discovered to my amazement that average men and women were delighted at the prospect of war.'

James Joll, *The Origins of the First World War* (1984)

3 France and the Origins of the First World War 1890-1914

PREVIEW

THE PROCLAMATION OF WILLIAM I AS GERMAN EMPEROR, AT THE PALACE OF VERSAILLES (18 JANUARY 1871)

1 Why do you think Versailles was selected as the venue for the proclamation of William I?

2 Analyse the painting carefully. Can it provide us with any information about the embryonic German society?

3 How would such a painting be perceived by a French observer?

SIGNING THE TREATY AT VERSAILLES (28 JUNE 1919)

1 Why do you think Versailles was selected as the venue for the signing of the peace treaty?

2 Contrast the position of the Germans in 1919 with that in 1871. What words would you use to describe them in victory and in defeat?

3 How would this scene be perceived by a German observer?

Flashback! The Battle of Sedan, 1-2 September 1870

The battle had resumed at 4 am and daybreak, when it came, was obscured by the bonfires of war. The chill September mist was darkened by the smoke from soldiers' bivouac fires, the acrid aftermath of shell bursts and the crumbling remnants of blazing villages. Yet even amid the carnage of battle, the sun came out and a golden, autumn day was in prospect. As the mist lifted, King William I of Prussia was able to take advantage of a superb vantage point to witness his moment of triumph. In a forest clearing above Sedan the Prussian King was joined by his leading generals, Moltke and Roon, his political strategist Otto von Bismarck, and a glittering array of German princes. Using powerful field glasses, this exalted group were able to see the French soldiers, conspicuous in their red uniforms, wilting in the face of modern German artillery. Meanwhile, the French emperor, unable amid impending disaster to view the day's developments with his counterpart's easy detachment, found himself in the midst of battle. Once it was clear that defeat was inevitable, Emperor Napoleon III rode across the battlefield in a mood of grim abandon, ready to give his life for his country but finding death in battle strangely elusive. Finally, appalled by the carnage visited upon his countrymen, Napoleon personally ordered the hoisting of a white flag.

On 2 September the two sovereigns came face-to-face and Napoleon's capitulation was formally accepted. Finally, on 3 September the French troops watched through driving rain as their emperor, followed by his extensive wagon train, rode off into captivity.

The Prussian victory had been comprehensively sealed and the moment of German unification was almost at hand. The choice of venue for the formal proclamation of William I as German Emperor (Kaiser) was rich in irony. On 18 January 1871, William was proclaimed Emperor in a glittering ceremony at the Palace of Versailles, for so long the symbol of France's power and glory. On 10 May the two countries concluded the Peace Treaty of Frankfurt am Main. France ceded Alsace (except Belfort) and German Lorraine, including the fortresses of Metz and Strasburg. In addition, France

THE SURRENDER OF NAPOLEON III AFTER THE BATTLE OF SEDAN, 1870

was obliged to pay a war debt of fr.5,000 million, starting with fr.1,000 million in 1871. The final indignity was that France was also subject to military occupation.

The combination of crushing military defeat and humiliating peace treaty served to scar the collective memory of the French nation. Its statesmen, generals, writers and ordinary people gave eager support to the mounting desire for *revanche* or revenge. The French writer Charles Maurras described the idea of *revanche* as the 'Queen of France'. Most people came to regard the peace of Frankfurt as marking a brief truce, rather than a permanent solution to the to the problem of Franco-German relations. In particular, the future status of Alsace-Lorraine, an area rich in coal and iron reserves, became the focus of mutual ill feeling.

The assumption that France, as a defeated power, had been permanently humbled was soon dispelled. France made an economic recovery which in the words of the historian Maurice Baumont: 'astonished her friends and dismayed her enemies, conscious as they all were of the effort involved in her impatience to pay an exorbitant war debt. On 5 September 1873 the last few million francs were handed over. For Germany, France was henceforth a danger.' How long would it be before the opportunity for revenge presented itself?

Fast forward: the Peace of Versailles (January-June 1919)

7 May 1919

The moment of retribution was at hand. Representatives of 27 nations had crowded into the dining room of the Trianon Palace Hotel, at Versailles, to see the terms of the peace treaty being handed to the German delegation. The irony of the setting was apparent to both victor and vanquished. At the stroke of three the German politicians, pale and tense, were ushered in to hear their fate. Clemenceau, the French prime minister was the first to rise.

FROM A FRENCH MAGAZINE OF 1893. WHILE THE FRENCH DEPUTIES ARGUE, THE FIGURE OF THE REPUBLIC POINTS TO THE DANGER REPRESENTED BY THE SOLDIERS OF GERMANY AND AUSTRIA-HUNGARY. WHAT DOES THIS TELL YOU ABOUT FRANCO-GERMAN RELATIONS?

His mood was terse and cold, his sense of satisfaction at the turn of events was ill-concealed. He addressed the German delegation as follows; 'This is neither the time nor the place for superfluous words. You see before you the accredited representatives of the Allied and Associated Powers, both small and great, which have waged without respite for more than four years the pitiless war that was imposed on them. The time has come for a heavy reckoning of events. You have asked for peace. We are ready to grant it to you. I must of necessity add, that this second Peace of Versailles which is now to be the subject of our discussions, has been too dearly bought by the peoples represented here, for us not to be unanimously resolved to use all the means in our power to obtain every lawful satisfaction that is due to us. There will,' Clemenceau stressed, 'be no verbal discussion, and observations must be submitted in writing. The plenipotentiaries of Germany will be given fifteen days in which to submit their written observations on the entire treaty.' The peace terms, with drastic implications for Germany, were handed over in a large, white, folio volume. The recipient - the head of the German delegation, Count Brockdorff-Rantzau - accepted the folder with a bow and began his reply.

To the astonishment of the onlookers he delivered his reply sitting down. The discourtesy was intentional. 'We are under no illusions' he stated, 'as to the extent of our defeat and the degree of our powerlessness. We know that the strength of German arms is broken. We know the intensity of the hatred which meets us, and we have heard the victor's passionate demand that as the vanquished, we shall be made to pay, and as the guilty, we shall be punished.' It was now, with a note of defiance, that Brockdorff-Rantzau raised his objections. 'We are required to admit that we alone are to blame for the war: such an admission on my lips would be a lie.' The German politician told the Allies that he was 'far from seeking to absolve Germany from all responsibility for this World War, and for its having been waged as it has.' However, 'we emphatically deny that Germany, whose people were convinced that they were waging a war of defence, should be burdened with sole responsibility.'

In this chapter we will examine the nature of French foreign policy between 1890 and 1914. To what extent did French desire for revenge contribute to the outbreak of the First World War? How much truth was there in Brockdorff-Rantzau's claim that Germany alone was not to blame? Was France entitled in 1919 to lay blame entirely at the hands of the Germans, or should she have shared some of the responsibility?

TALKING POINT

Should Brockdorff-Rantzau have conducted himself differently?

The period of recovery, 1890-1904

The French leaders and people were reluctant to assume the demeanour of a defeated country. Indeed, in the inter-war period (1871-1914) France displayed many of the characteristics of a country which had regained its national self-confidence. In his study of the *Rise and Fall of the Great Powers*, Paul Kennedy points out that 'France was immensely rich in terms of mobile capital, which could be (and systematically was) applied to serve the interests of the country's diplomacy and strategy. The most impressive sign of this had been the very rapid paying off of the German indemnity of 1871, which, in Bismarck's erroneous calculation, was supposed to cripple France's strength for many years to come.'

The economic historian T. Kemp summarises French economic progress as follows: 'This period saw a great development in banking and financial institutions participating in industrial investment and in foreign lending. The iron and steel industry was established on modern lines and great new plants were built, especially on the Lorraine orefield. On the coalfields of northern France the familiar ugly landscape of an industrial society took place. Important strides were made in engineering and the newer industries. France had its notable entrepreneurs and innovators who won a leading place in the late nineteenth and early twentieth century in steel, engineering, motor cars and aircraft. Firms like Schneider, Peugeot, Michelin and Renault were in the vanguard.'

This economic well-being enabled France to develop links with other great powers to the extent that economic co-operation developed into full-blown military alliances. The most important example of this trend concerned Franco-Russian relations. During the 1880s loans from France to Russia steadily increased and the first formal contract between French banks and the Russian government was signed in November 1888. By the early years of the 1890s, Russia was borrowing up to two million francs annually from French financial institutions.

The cultural barriers which divided tsarist autocracy from the French republic also began to break down in the 1880s. Translations of the works of Tolstoy and Dostoyevsky became tremendously popular. The French press stressed the positive qualities of Russian order and military strength.

In July 1891 a French military delegation visited Kronstadt and French loans to Russia were stepped up. Meanwhile, the Tsar conferred Russia's highest decoration on the French President. The process was assisted further by German failure to renew the Reinsurance Treaty in the wake of Bismarck's resignation in 1890. In August 1891 the two nations exchanged letters in which they agreed to act together 'on all questions likely to upset the general peace'. This Franco-Russian *entente* was extended a year later with the secret military convention of August 1892.

The full commitment of an Alliance was now virtually inevitable. James Joll highlights the logic behind such an agreement. 'A rapprochement between France and Russia, in spite of the differences of political system between the Third Republic and the tsarist autocracy had been a logical consequence of the new balance of power established in 1870. As Karl Marx had put it at the time of the Franco-Prussian War, "If Alsace and Lorraine are taken, then France will later make war on Germany in conjunction with Russia". The annexation by Germany of the two French provinces meant that there could be in the long run no reconciliation between France and Germany; and although at some moments the French government and public temporarily forgot about the lost provinces, the hope of recovering them was always likely to ensure that in a European war France would join the side opposed to Germany.'

In January 1893 the Franco-Russian Alliance was agreed and in December 1893 the Franco-Russian military convention came into force. Although the terms of these agreements were kept secret their existence was widely known. It was also apparent that the Dual Alliance of France and Russia would, in the event of war, be pushed into confrontation with the Triple Alliance of Germany, Austria-Hungary and Italy. Britain's position remained unclear, and it is arguably the central achievement of French diplomacy that by 1904

Why would a potential alliance between France and Russia be regarded with alarm in Germany?

Do these developments change your perception of Germany's decision not to renew the Reinsurance Treaty?

THE FIRST LANDING AT FASHODA.
LORD EDWARD CECIL INTRODUCES
CAPTAIN KEPPEL TO MAJOR
MARCHAND

the position had changed to the extent that France and Britain had become much closer whereas Germany's isolation had been heightened.

Paul Kennedy's description of Anglo-French relations highlights the fact that the early signs were distinctly unpromising; 'from 1884, the two countries were locked into an escalating naval race, which on the British side was associated with the possible loss of their Mediterranean line of communications and (occasionally) with fears of a French cross-Channel invasion. Even more persistent and threatening were the frequent Anglo-French colonial clashes. Britain and France had quarrelled over the Congo in 1884-1885 and over West Africa throughout the entire 1880s and 1890s. In 1893 they seemed to be on the brink of war over Siam. The greatest crisis of all came in 1898, when the sixteen-year rivalry over control of the Nile Valley climaxed in the confrontation between Kitchener's army and Marchand's small expedition at Fashoda. Although the French backed down on that occasion, they were energetic and bold imperialists. Between 1871 and 1900, France had added 3.5 million square miles to its existing colonial territories, and it possessed indisputably the largest overseas empire after Britain's.'

Before any agreement between Britain and France could be concluded it was essential to lay to rest the colonial differences which had divided the countries in the 1890s. This process was carried along by the French foreign minister Théophile Delcassé. He recognised that Britain might be prepared to make concessions over Morocco in return for French concessions over Egypt. The leverage France needed came through her membership of the Caisse de la Dette, the international commission responsible for overlooking Egypt's financial affairs. Britain needed the approval of this commission to carry out a reform of the Egyptian financial system, an essential step in the consolidation of Britain's position which she had been seeking since her occupation of Egypt in 1882. It was therefore in the mutual interests of France and Britain to make an agreement and this came about in 1904.

The Entente Cordiale of 1904 settled Anglo-French colonial disputes in North Africa and agreed to leave Siam as an independent buffer state between French Indo-China and British possessions in Burma. However, the real significance of the agreement was that it laid the groundwork for further co-operation in the future.

The German view was that the Entente was superficial and would crumble as soon as it was put to the test. The opportunity Germany was looking for presented itself shortly after war had broken out in the Far East between Japan and Russia in 1904. As part of the Russian fleet made its way from the Baltic to the Far East, shots were fired at some British fishing boats on the Dogger Bank in the North Sea. Russia was quick to apologise for the sinking of these vessels, claiming that they had been mistaken for Japanese submarines. Germany, however, was eager to take advantage of the situation. Amid a brief but powerful upsurge of anti-Russian sentiment in Britain, the German government proposed to the Russians a continental league against Britain. German intentions were made clear with the suggestion that France might also wish to join the league. However, Delcassé steered a skilful course through the crisis, urging mediation between Britain and Russia and advising Russia to pay the compensation which the British were demanding. The Dogger Bank incident was short-lived, but it had further discredited Germany and offered evidence that the agreements between France, Britain and Russia were based on fairly firm foundations.

Focus

3.1 Crises in Morocco (1905 and 1911)

Chronology

1880 The Madrid Convention. Established international guarantees of Morocco's status.

1900-03 During the period of personal rule by Abdul Aziz, popular uprisings by the Berber tribes meant that by 1903 he retained control over only a fraction of his former lands and even the Moroccan capital, Fez, came under attack.

1900 Secret Franco-Italian agreement to support each other's interests in Morocco and Tunisia, respectively.

1904 Franco-Spanish treaty on Morocco.

1905 Germany's attempt to interfere with France's status in Morocco was marked by Kaiser William II's visit to Tangier in March. He made it clear that Germany regarded Morocco as an independent state, and encouraged the Sultan to resist French pressure.

Key Treaties/Alliances

1882 *Triple Alliance* between Germany, Austria - Hungary and Italy. Renewed in 1887, 1891, 1902 and 1912.

1893 *Dual Entente* formed between France and Russia, offering mutual assistance in event of war with Germany.

1904 *Entente Cordiale* signed between Britain and France, settled colonial disputes and promised future friendship.

1907 *Triple Entente* between Great Britain, France and Russia, established after agreement between Britain and Russia over spheres of influence in Asia.

1905

TWO'S COMPANY (PUNCH) ▶

▼ WILLIAM'S ENTOURAGE RIDING THROUGH TANGIER IN 1905

Germany's mounting isolation after the Kaiser's visit

'If there is a war between France and Germany, it will be very difficult for us to keep out of it. The Entente and still more the constant and emphatic demonstrations of affection…have created in France a belief that we shall support them in war. If this expectation is disappointed, the French will never forgive us. There would also I think be a general feeling that we had behaved badly and left France in the lurch.'

Sir Edward Grey, British Foreign Secretary, February 1906

Consequences of the 1905 crisis: shifting allegiances

Using the material shown here draw arrows between the countries to indicate either a growth in antagonism or support during the period 1904-06. Alongside the arrow indicate the reason for your choice (Eg, German antagonism towards France causing the resignation of Delcassé).

GREAT BRITAIN

FRANCE   RUSSIA

GERMANY

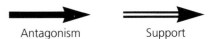

Antagonism   Support

1911

Chronology

1905 Germany did not receive international support for her stance, but insisted that France agree to an international conference. Amid German threats of aggression the French foreign minister, Delcassé, was forced to resign.

1906 At the Algeciras Conference the crisis was settled peacefully but Germany emerged more isolated than before. During the talks Great Britain and France held military discussions.

1909 France and Germany signed an agreement recognising French political status in return for open economic competition.

1911 Germany renewed pressure on France in Morocco by sending the gunboat *Panther* to Agadir. Lloyd-George publicly warned Germany in the Mansion House speech that Britain would not stand by over Morocco. Crisis talks settled the dispute as Germany recognised the French protectorate in Morocco and France offered Germany land and money

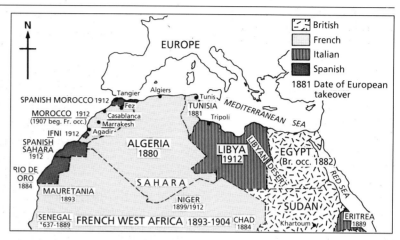

The British reaction: Lloyd-George's 'Mansion House' speech

'If a situation were to be forced upon us, in which peace could only be preserved by the surrender of the great and beneficient position Britain has won by centuries of heroism and achievement, by allowing Britain to be treated, where her interests were vitally affected, as if she were of no account in the Cabinet of Nations, then I say emphatically that peace at that price would be a humiliation intolerable for a great country like ours to endure.'

21 July 1911

The Verdict of a German military leader

'I am beginning to get sick and tired of this unhappy Moroccan affair... If we again slip away from this affair with our tail between our legs and if we cannot bring ourselves to put forward a determined claim which we are prepared to force through with the sword, I shall despair of the future of the German Empire.'

Extract from letter written by Molke to his wife 19 August 1911

Consequences of the 1911 crisis: shifting allegiances

Repeat the exercise shown opposite, only for the period 1909-11 (Eg, Mutual antagonism between Germany and Britain).

GREAT BRITAIN

FRANCE   RUSSIA

GERMANY

Antagonism   Support

3.2 The rise and fall of great powers: Franco-German economic rivalry

The antagonism which existed between Germany and France was not purely political. In the latter part of the Nineteenth Century both countries had developed into modern industrial economies. Clearly the relative strength of the economy had massive implications for a nation's ability to conduct diplomacy, win friends, alienate enemies and, ultimately, to wage war. What then, were the relative strengths of these two nations in economic terms?

France

Population

(a) National population in millions
1851 – 35.8   1881 – 37.4   1890 – 38.3   1913 – 39.7
(b) Population of Paris in thousands
1850 – 1,053   1900 – 2,714

Agriculture

(a) Output of grain crops: annual averages in million quintals
1885-94 – 160.1   1905-14 – 171.9
(b) Output of wheat: thousands of metric tons
1913 – 8,690

1 Study the figures carefully and then prepare a detailed comparison.

2 Present your comparison in the form of a chart, placing the figures side by side.

3 Devise a scale which (a) determines the relative importance of each statistic (b) indicates the stronger nation in each case.

4 Once you have assessed the individual points, decide which was the strongest economy overall.

Industry

(a) Output of coal and lignite: annual average for quinquennia in million metric tons
1890-94 – 26   1895-99 – 31   1900-04 – 33
1905-09 – 36   1910-14 – 40
(b) Pig iron: annual production in million metric tons
1880 – 1.7   1910 – 4.0
(c) Output of steel in million metric tons
1890 – 0.7   1900 – 1.6   1910 – 3.4
(d) Motor vehicles (commercial and private) produced in thousands
1910 – 38
(e) Railway mileage open in kilometres
1880 – 23,089   1900 – 38,109   1913 – 40,770
(f) Merchant ships registered by country in thousand tons
1880 – 920   1910 – 1,452
(g) Value of external trade in millions of francs
1870 – 5,669   1900 – 8,807

Germany

Population

(a) National population in millions

1851 – 33.4	1881 – 45.2
1891 – 49.0	1901 – 56.4
1913 – 66.0	

(b) Population of Berlin in thousands

1850 – 419	1900 – 1,889

Agriculture

(a) Output of grain crops: annual averages in million quintals

1885-94 – 304.6
1905-14 – 457.9

(b) Output of wheat: thousands of metric tons

1913 – 5,094

GERMAN INDUSTRIAL DEVELOPMENT: THE FIRST 4-WHEELED DAIMLER CAR (1886)

Industry

(a) Output of coal and lignite: annual average for quinquennia in million metric tons
1890-94 – 94   1895-99 – 120   1900-04 – 157   1905 –09 – 201   1910-14 – 247

(b) Pig iron: annual production in million metric tons
1880 – 2.7   1910 – 14.8

(c) Output of steel in million metric tons
1890 – 2.2   1900 – 6.6   1910 – 13.7

(d) Motor vehicles (commercial and private) produced in thousands
1910 – 10

(e) Railway mileage open, in kilometres
1880 – 33,838   1900 – 51,678   1913 – 63,378

(f) Merchant ships registered by country in thousand tons
1880 –1,104   1910 – 2,890

(g) Value of external trade in millions of marks
1870 – 5,741   1900 – 10,380

Domestic problems: a case study

In addition to concern over foreign policy, the Third Republic was plagued by a series of domestic crises. None of these scandals has attracted more attention than the trial, conviction and subsequent rehabilitation of the French army captain, Alfred Dreyfus.

Examining the evidence
The Dreyfus Affair
Source A: The arrest of Dreyfus, 15 October 1894

It was at the end of September 1894 that the French Intelligence Service, discreetly called at that time the 'Statistical Section' and run by Colonel Sandherr, was shown a missive informing the German military attaché, Lieutenant-Colonel Maximilian von Schwartzkoppen. stationed in Paris from 1892 to 1897, of the despatch of confidential French military documents. This unsigned letter, soon known as the '*bordereau*' (memorandum), implied a long-standing relationship. The information sheets to which it referred have never been found, and it is difficult to judge the importance of the information which they are supposed to have contained. The precise origin of the *bordereau* is still discussed today; it was very probably the work of Major Esterhazy, as Dreyfus's supporters thought at the time and as Esterhazy himself admitted later.

> Jean-Marie Mayeur and Madeleine Rebérioux, *The Third Republic from its Origins to the Great War, 1871-1914* (1987)

Look at Source A carefully. What is the significance of Major Esterhazy in this affair?

Source B: The *bordereau*

Without news indicating that you wish to see me, nevertheless, Sir, I send you some interesting information:
1. A note on the hydraulic buffer of the 120 and the way in which this gun behaves;
2. A note on the covering troops (some modifications will be made under the new plan);
3. A note on a modification to the artillery formations;
4. A note about Madagascar;
5. The preliminary Firing Manual of the Field Artillery (14 March 1894).

The last document is extremely difficult to come by and I can only have it at my disposal for a very few days. The War Office has sent a limited number to the Corps, and the Corps are responsible for them. Each officer holding one must return it after manoeuvres. If therefore you wish to take from it what interests you then keep it for me, I will fetch it. Unless you would like me to have it copied in extenso and only send you the copy.
  I am just off to manoeuvres.

> Keith Randell, *France: The Third Republic 1870-1914* (1986)

Why was the information contained in the *bordereau* so important?

Source C: The evidence against Dreyfus

Three conclusions were rapidly reached from a study of the contents of the *bordereau*. The writer was probably an expert in artillery because of the nature of documents 1, 3, and 5. He must be a member of the War Office to have access to such a range of documents, and was probably one of the officers recently appointed to the War Office because such people spent a few months in each section and therefore would have come across all the documents listed in the *bordereau*. Each member of the War Office was checked in turn to see whether or not he fitted. When the name of Captain Alfred Dreyfus was considered it immediately seemed obvious to Major Henry and his colleagues that here was their man. Dreyfus was an artillery officer, he was in the process of spending an amount of time in each section of the War Office, and he seemed the type of person who was likely to come under suspicion for some malpractice or another. He was generally unpopular being both arrogant and overkeen. He was not 'one of the lads'. His zeal in studying the detail of documents he was shown had already caused some questions to be asked. But most of all he was suspect in Major Henry's anti-semitic mind because he was a Jew. In fact, he was the first Jew ever to be posted to the War Office… It was decided that Dreyfus was the culprit. When some handwriting experts were prepared to say that the *bordereau* had been penned by Dreyfus the case seemed solid to Major Henry.

Keith Randell, *France: The Third Republic 1870-1914* (1986)

Analyse the role of Major Henry in the Dreyfus Affair.

Read Extract C very carefully. What was the nature of the allegations against Dreyfus? What other factor made him liable to conviction?

THE CLOSING SCENE OF THE TRIAL OF DREYFUS AT RENNES: READING THE VERDICT

Source D: The conviction of Dreyfus, 22 December 1894

The trial of Captain Dreyfus by the senior Paris court martial opened on 19 December and took place behind closed doors. There was still no firm proof to support the circumstantial evidence. They were still based solely on the writing in the memorandum. Alfred Dreyfus had denied everything right from the start...

It was necessary for Major Henry, speaking semi-officially in the name of Colonel Sandherr, to throw into the scales all the weight of the Intelligence Service, and for the Minister of War to send to the president of the court, under totally illegal conditions, a 'secret file' which neither the accused nor his defender, maître Demange, had ever set eyes upon; it consisted of a few documents cobbled together by Henry and Sandherr. At least two of these documents had been forged by the Intelligence Service; the abuse of power was thus added to the abuse of the rule of law.

On 22 December the court martial unanimously pronounced Dreyfus guilty and sentenced him to deportation for life to a fortress prison. On 5 January 1895 he had to submit to the painful ceremony of cashiering. On 21 February he embarked for Devil's Island.

Jean-Marie Mayeur and Madeleine Rebérioux, *The Third Republic from its Origins to the Great War, 1871-1914* (1987)

What role was played in the trial by the 'secret file'?

Cashiering - to be formally stripped of all military rank and status

THE DEGRADING OF DREYFUS

Source E: Doubts emerge

There the matter might have rested had it not been for two factors: the Dreyfus family was convinced of Alfred's innocence and was determined to prove it, and there was appointed to the leadership of the Statistical Section in 1895 a man, Major Picquart, who was scrupulously honest. Between them, although working totally independently, they were able to establish the probability that a great mistake had been made.

The Dreyfus family, because they were not able to gain access to the secret files at the War Office, were forced to pin their hopes of obtaining a retrial on the grounds of some procedural irregularity... Picquart's position was even more difficult... His apprehension turned to real concern when it became clear that the German Embassy was still receiving secret documents, and to near panic in 1896 when the Embassy's waste-paper baskets yielded a letter, presumably thrown away because the writer was not happy with the wording, addressed to a Major Esterhazy in terms which seemed to indicate that he was a spy. Picquart's conscience was troubled almost beyond endurance when Esterhazy's handwriting was shown to be identical with that of the *bordereau*.

Keith Randell, *France: The Third Republic 1870-1914* (1986)

What was the significance of Picquart's discovery?

Source F: The *faux Henry*

Major Henry, whose determination to protect the honour of the army was extreme, decided that incontestable evidence of Dreyfus' spying activity must be provided. Because he had no doubt that the ends justified the means, he proceeded to forge what was necessary. Pretending that it had come to him in pieces from the German Embassy's waste-paper baskets, he wrote a letter from the Italian military attaché to his German opposite number. It read:

'I have read that a deputy is going to interpellate [ask questions in parliament] about Dreyfus. If new explanations are needed at Rome, I shall say I have never had relations with this Jew. You understand. If you are asked, say the same thing, for no one must ever know what happened with him.'

This forgery, known as the *faux Henry*, was shown to the jubilant army leaders who were now able to say with even greater confidence that there was no possibility that the decision of the court martial had been wrong. At the same time, Henry, who realised that Picquart could not be relied on to remain silent for ever, set about a complicated process of discrediting him in the eyes of his superiors. This involved forging more evidence, and working closely with Esterhazy who was prepared to tell whatever lies he was instructed to as long as he remained safe himself.

Keith Randell, *France: The Third Republic 1870-1914* (1986)

Explain the importance of the faux Henry.

Source G: The intervention of Zola

On 13 January 1898...two days after the acquittal of Esterhazy...*L'Aurore* published in an edition of 300,000 copies a 'Letter to the President of the Republic' signed by Emile Zola and topped by Georges Clemenceau with the withering title, 'J'accuse'. The intervention of Clemenceau, a redoubtable controversialist, and above all that of Zola, resulted in the Affair having extraordinary repercussions.

Jean-Marie Mayeur and Madeleine Rebérioux, *The Third Republic from its Origins to the Great War, 1871-1914* (1987)

Source H: 'J' accuse', 13 January 1898

I accuse Lieutenant Colonel du Pary de Clam of having been the diabolical worker of the judicial error, I would like to believe unconsciously, and of having afterwards defended his baneful work for three years by the most absurd and culpable machinations.

I accuse General Mercier of having been an acomplice, at least by reasons of weakness of spirit, in one of the greatest iniquities of the century.

I accuse General Billot of having had in his hands certain proofs of the innocence of Dreyfus and of having suppressed them, of having incurred the guilt of this crime of betraying humanity and justice for a political end and to save the compromised General Staff...

I accuse the three handwriting experts, Messrs. Belhomme, Varinard, and Couard, of having made lying and fraudulent reports, unless a medical examination finds them stricken by diseased views and judgement.

I accuse the offices of the War of having led an abominable press campaign, especially in *L'Eclaire* and in *L'Echo de Paris*, to mislead opinion and conceal their blame.

I accuse, finally, the first Court-Martial of having broken the law by condemning the accused on secret evidence, and I accuse the second Court-Martial of having hidden this illegality, on orders, and of committing in turn the juridicial crime of knowingly acquitting a guilty man...

Zola quoted in Keith Randell, *France: The Third Republic 1870-1914* (1987)

> Summarise in your own words the points made by Zola in his 'J'accuse' letter

Source I: The significance of the Affair

By the time of the Fashoda crisis, however, the army had, as a result of the Dreyfus affair and the division between those who accepted the army's claim to be above criticism and those who saw the army's treatment of Dreyfus and its handling of the case as a shocking infringement of the rights of man, become the object of political dispute rather than of political consensus.

James Joll, *The Origins of the First World War* (1985)

Source J: France divided

Politically conscious France had been divided into two camps, Dreyfusards and the anti-Dreyfusards, for there were very few people of any education or social standing who were able to remain neutral. Often according to previous prejudice or general disposition, each person felt obliged to be either for Dreyfus or against him. Those who were anti-Semites, fervent nationalists, in favour of a militarily strong France, believers in discipline and authority, hostile to a parliamentary democracy or supporters of the Catholic Church tended to be against Dreyfus. Those who were active Republicans, socialists, pacifists, or anti-clericals tended to be in favour of him... In the summer of 1898 the army's case crumbled further. The *faux Henry* was re-examined and was found to be a forgery. Henry, in making it, had stuck together pieces of paper that appeared to be identical but which were actually clearly different... He confirmed his guilt by taking his razor and cutting his throat.

Keith Randell, *France: The Third Republic 1870-1914* (1987)

> To what extent do you think domestic crises affected France's international relations? Give reasons for your answer.

Source K: Clearing Dreyfus's name

How was it possible for Dreyfus to be cleared?

According to Sources J and K, what was the significance of the trial for France generally?

It was only on 3 June 1899 that the Court set aside the judgement of 1894 and ordered that Dreyfus should appear before a new court martial in Rennes. This time the revisionists were full of confidence, but again they were wrong. After a month's deliberations the court martial found Dreyfus guilty a second time, but only, to tell the truth, by a majority; and they also surprisingly qualified the verdict with a number of mitigating circumstances. It looked like the collapse of the revisionists' struggle. But no: on 19 September 1899 Loubet, the President of the Republic, signed the pardon of Alfred Dreyfus, who accepted it without renouncing action to secure the public recognition of innocence. On 2 June 1900 the Senate voted an amnesty. Nevertheless, it was not until 12 July 1900 that the Supreme Court of Appeal set aside definitively the Rennes verdict and thus cleared Captain Dreyfus of any accusation. He was to die in 1935.

Jean-Marie Mayeur and Madeleine Rebérioux, *The Third Republic from its Origins to the Great War, 1871-1914* (1987)

1 We have seen very clearly that the evidence against Dreyfus was extremely limited.

(a) Why then, did it take so long for him to be given justice?

(b) Why did some Frenchmen think Dreyfus should stay in prison even after it was evident that he was innocent?

2 What divisions in French society do you feel are revealed by the events of the Dreyfus affair?

3 What do you consider to be the significance of the affair in relation to:

(a) The role of the army in French society?

(b) The development of nationalist feeling in France?

(c) Anti-semitism in French society?

Source L

THE LAW GIVES THE ARMY A KICK IN THE FACE: REVISION OF CHARGE AGAINST DREYFUS, NOVEMBER 1898

The importance of Alsace-Lorraine to Franco-German relations

We have already seen that the most bitterly-resented aspect of the peace of Frankfurt was the annexation of Alsace-Lorraine by Germany. It is not entirely coincidental that this disputed area was once again the centre of dispute on the eve of war in 1913. Ironically, the president at this time was himself from Lorraine. Why was this area the source of so much antagonism?

FOCUS

3.3 Alsace-Lorraine: symbol of Franco-German antagonism

These provinces, rich in coal and iron reserves, were annexed by Germany in 1871 and became the subject of endless dispute

▲ FRENCH CARTOON SHOWING THE GRAVESTONE OF A SOLDIER KILLED IN 1870

FRENCH CARTOON DEPICTS CHILD GAZING ▶ TOWARDS THE LOST PROVINCES OF ALSACE-LORRAINE

The view of an Alsace-Lorraine deputy, Edouard Teutsch

'Germany has exceeded her rights as a civilised nation in compelling defeated France to sacrifice a million and a half of her children… We protest against the abuse of strength of which our country is the victim… It was with a knife at her throat that France, bleeding and exhausted, signed us away. Give us our self-determination. Give us justice.'

18 February 1874

Poincaré: The view of an historian

Because in a war with Germany in 1870 France had lost the two provinces of Alsace-Lorraine, it was suggested that for virtually the next half century she had prepared for a war of *revanche* against Germany to regain the lost territories. Because from 1912 France's new leader, Raymond Poincaré, who was a Lorrainer into the bargain, was determined to apply resolute policies and to strengthen the links with France's allies, particularly with Russia, it was suggested that he plotted a war of *revanche* against Germany… The criticism levelled against France struck out at the Franco-Russian alliance for having caused the war. Poincaré was charged with having encouraged Russia to begin the conflict. The idea of Poincaré la-guerre gained currency.

J. Keiger, *France and the Origins of the First World War* (1983)

Poincaré: The verdict of an historian

Too much has been made of his Lorraine origins, supposedly synonymous with *revanche*. Without question the defeat of 1870 had a profound effect on him… It inculcated in him a profound mistrust of Germany, an ardent patriotism and a deep feeling of national pride. But this was tempered by his experience of the chaos and destruction of war. If anything, it made him wish to guard against further defeat and further war by ensuring that France would always be prepared militarily and diplomatically.

J. Keiger, *France and the Origins of the First World War* (1983)

Raymond Poincaré: personification of révanchism?

1860 Born in Bar-le-Duc in Lorraine

1870 The defeat of 1870 had a profound and lasting impact on Poincaré, then a 10-year-old obliged to leave his home and to live under German occupation

1887 Elected a deputy in Meuse, a seat he retained until 1903

1893-94 Education Minister

1894-95 Finance Minister

1906 Senator and Finance Minister

1912 After a six-year absence he became Prime Minister

1913-20 Served as President on the eve of, and during, the First World War

The Zabern Incident: an historian's description

A young German officer of this small town in Alsace (Zabern) insulted the civilian inhabitants and encouraged his men to beat them up; and when the citizens of Zabern protested and insulted the officers in their turn, the commander of the regiment finally arrested twenty-seven of them and locked them up in the cells of the barracks. The matter was raised in the (German) Reichstag, but although a majority carried a vote of censure on the Chancellor for his handling of the matter, nothing much came of this, and the commander of the regiment in Zabern was acquitted by a court-martial of a charge of illegal arrest, though some of the officers concerned were transferred elsewhere… The War Minister, the Crown Prince and senior members of the officer corps expressed their contempt for parliament and politicians and made it quite clear that they would never allow the army to be subject to them.

James Joll, *The Origins of the First World War* (1984)

---

1 Why was Alsace-Lorraine the cause of so much ill-feeling between Germany and France?

2 What role did Alsace-Lorraine play in the origins of the First World War?

The Zabern incident

Although the Zabern incident damaged relations between the inhabitants of Alsace-Lorraine and the occupying German army, its real significance was in what it revealed about German society. Although criticism of the army was made openly in the Reichstag, revealing limited progress towards a more democratic society, the fact remained that the chancellor could ignore a parliamentary vote of censure and the army seemed indifferent to the criticisms made of it. In addition, the Kaiser appeared contemptuous of the criticisms made of his soldiers. The incident paled into insignificance when it was set against the crisis of July 1914.

July 1914: Crisis or confusion?

In the sultry summer of 1914 the story which gripped the attention of the whole nation was one which contained all the classic ingredients of a typical French murder mystery. Passion, intrigue, corruption, adultery and revenge all played a part, set against the background of high politics. In the spring of 1914 Gaston Calmette, editor of *Le Figaro*, had become preoccupied with his newspaper's intensive investigation into the private life of a cabinet minister: Joseph Caillaux, the finance minister. *Le Figaro* obtained and published love letters which his second wife had sent to him when he was still married to the first Madame Caillaux. On 16 March 1914, unhindered by other staff, the new Madame Caillaux walked briskly into Calmette's office. The journalist's final act was to look up and recognise the woman who had so regularly featured on the front pages of his newspaper. At close range she fired six shots into the body of the newspaper editor. He died instantly.

Four months later, as the trial of Madame Caillaux moved to a dramatic conclusion, the story continued to dominate the French press. On 29 July, for example, the renowned newspaper *Le Temps* - with its reputation for thorough coverage of international issues - devoted more space to the surprise acquittal of Madame Caillaux than to any other story.

The trial's significance in the context of foreign affairs was twofold. First, it constituted a major, unsettling scandal which rocked the government, especially when rumours began to circulate that Calmette had obtained detailed transcripts of Caillaux's secret negotiations with Germany during the Moroccan crisis. Secondly, and more importantly, the protracted scandal and its heavy press coverage served to distract public attention completely away from the European diplomatic crisis; something to which it was already almost oblivious. Elsewhere in Europe the 'July crisis' concerned the intense diplomatic activity sparked off by the assassination of Archduke Franz Ferdinand on 28 June; in France, the same term would probably have been interpreted as a reference to the Calmette murder. However, it would not be long before the graver implications of the political crisis would command the attention of all the French people. When did their politicians realise that a major crisis was developing? How did they react? What were the consequences of their actions?

Initially, the murder of Franz Ferdinand did not cause undue alarm in French political circles. After all, the mechanisms for peace had prevailed in a series of crises since 1890. Why should this one be any different? The

TALKING POINT

Read through this section on the July Crisis. When, in your opinion, did the French politicians realise that a major crisis had developed?

low-key funeral of Franz Ferdinand seemed to offer confirmation that the incident would only briefly disturb the tranquillity which had marked the first six months of 1914. As the politician Jules Cambon commented, 'I am far from believing that at this moment there is anything in the air which could be a threat to us, on the contrary.'

The false sense of security was compounded by the relative inexperience of some of Poincaré's key ministers. Although Viviani, the new prime minister, combined the premiership with the office of secretary of state for foreign affairs, he had no previous experience of foreign policy. His new under-secretary of state for foreign affairs, Abel Ferry, was similarly inexperienced.

Amid this background of relative naïvety, the seasoned campaigner Poincaré was able to reassert himself after the temporary demise of his influence under the premiership of Doumergue. News of Franz Ferdinand's assassination reached the President on the afternoon of Sunday 28 June while he was attending the races at the Longchamp course. Although the news caused some distress and the Austrian Ambassador was obliged to leave the race meeting, there was no sense of crisis. Poincaré saw no reason to cancel his long list of summer engagements and his major political concern continued to be the Caillaux scandal. French diplomatic documents for the first two weeks in July reveal no significant change in issues and priorities to those under discussion before 28 June. Crucially, it appears that the French diplomats remained unaware that a formidable ultimatum, drawn up by the Austrians with the forceful backing of Germany, would shortly be delivered to Serbia. As the Central Powers finalised their plan of action the French decision-makers were moving into a period of startling isolation.

THE ARRIVAL OF PRESIDENT POINCARÉ IN RUSSIA, JULY 1914. SHOWN WITH NICHOLAS II ON BOARD THE YACHT *STANDARD*

This period in limbo began when the presidential train pulled out of the Gare du Nord at 11.30 pm on Wednesday 15 July. On board were Poincaré and Viviani, France's two senior politicians. Following their arrival at Dunkirk they set sail aboard the battleship *France* in the early hours of Thursday morning. Their trip, a state cruise to Russia and Scandinavia, had been planned several months earlier and was scheduled to last until 31 July. In retrospect, their decision to set to sea at such a crucial point (and when the transmission and reception of radio messages were totally unreliable) appears startling. The problems raised by these logistical difficulties were made worse by the inexperience of those left behind at the Quai d'Orsay. The result was, as the historian John Keiger puts it, that 'on the eve of the war, French leaders were literally and metaphorically at sea'.

During their four days at sea, Poincaré took the opportunity to discuss with Viviani a number of important foreign policy issues. The briefing sessions were not a great success. Poincaré was alarmed by Viviani's 'frightening' ignorance of foreign affairs. The question of Austria and Serbia does not seem to have been on the agenda and Poincaré's advice to Viviani regarding Germany was that he had 'never had any serious difficulties with Germany because I have always used great firmness with her'. It is clear that Poincaré was in urgent need of a briefing himself: the man to provide it was waiting to meet him in Russia.

Since 14 July the Russian foreign minister, Sazonov, had been receiving transcripts of decoded Austrian telegrams. They revealed that the Austrian ultimatum to Serbia was drawn up but that its delivery would be deliberately withheld until Poincaré and Viviani left Russia for Sweden on 23 July. The thoroughness of the Central Powers' planning was such that they had even taken account of the differences in time zones to make certain that Poincaré and the Russian foreign minister would not be able to discuss the ultimatum. However, the skill of the Russian cryptographers meant that Sazonov would at least be able to provide Poincaré with a general picture of Austria's intentions.

Early in the afternoon of Monday 20 July the French battleship pulled into the port of Kronstadt where Tsar Nicholas II was waiting to greet Poincaré. In the early evening, before a magnificent banquet at the Winter Palace, diplomatic discussions were held between the two heads of state, and secondly between Viviani and Sazonov. Clearly these talks are of major interest to historians but unfortunately the minutes of these and subsequent discussions have disappeared. Although information is therefore scanty, several key points can be discerned. First, Poincaré's first-hand view of the widespread strikes and social upheaval in St Petersburg in the summer of 1914 offered evidence that Russia was not ready for war. Second, in a conversation with the Austrian Ambassador, Count Szapary, it was made clear to Poincaré that Austria was ready to take stern action against Serbia. Third, a telegram sent from Paris told Poincaré that Germany had made it clear that she would support Austria's demands against Serbia and would not act as a mediator. Finally, in discussions with Poincaré and Viviani, Sazonov seemed far more worried than at the start of the visit. The extent of this growing sense of alarm and heightened realism was conveyed by Sazonov's expressed concern at the difficulty Russia would face in mobilising the peasants whilst they were busy harvesting.

On Wednesday 22 July, unbeknown to the Russians and French, the text of the Austrian ultimatum was reported to the German foreign minister, von Jagow. Meanwhile, Sazonov conveyed to the Austria foreign minister a polite but firm message, warning of the possible dangers which could result from Austria making excessive demands of Serbia. It is clear that Sazonov - and therefore his French counterpart - were still under the impression that firm warnings from the great powers would make the Austrians act with due caution.

It should be added at this point that the Austrians and the Germans had misconceptions of their own. This extract from a letter written by the German secretary of state for foreign affairs, von Jagow, to the ambassador in London, Lichnowsky, reveals some of the Central Powers' flaws in reasoning:

'We must attempt to localise the conflict between Austria and Serbia. Whether this is possible will depend in the first place on Russia and in the second place on the moderating influence of the other members of the Entente. The more boldness Austria displays, the more strongly we support her, the more likely is Russia to keep quiet. There is certain to be some blustering in St Petersburg, but at bottom Russia is not now ready to strike. Nor will France and England be anxious for war at the present time.'

On 23 July the *France* set sail from Kronstadt bound for Sweden. When the battleship was safely out to sea, the Austrians delivered their ultimatum to Serbia. It was not until the next day that Poincaré, despite problems with reception, received a series of faint radio messages informing him that in the diplomatic gamble the stakes had once again been raised.

By the time Poincaré reached Stockholm on 25 July he was seriously considering whether to abandon the visit and return at once to France. His growing sense of urgency was highlighted by the decision that he and Viviani would henceforth take over control of foreign affairs from Paris. Even so, it seems clear that Poincaré was essentially reacting to, rather than controlling, the course of events. Indeed, on the following day, as he sailed towards Copenhagen, the French President admitted that he felt powerless. News passed on by the King of Sweden, that the Austrian ultimatum had expired without resolution, did nothing to ease Poincaré's pessimistic frame of mind. While he continued to agonise over whether to abandon his cruise, the German Kaiser interrupted his own trip to the fiords and returned to Kiel on 26 July.

The decision to go back, typically, came neither from the President nor the Prime Minister. On 27 July, with the ship bound for Denmark, telegrams were received from the government in Paris requesting a prompt return home. The visit was - at last - abandoned and the battleship turned around and headed for Dunkirk.

Viviani's rapid initiation into the dangers and complexities of foreign affairs at a time of crisis soon overwhelmed him. Physical and mental exhaustion rendered him incapable of offering any sort of leadership. Poincaré observed that his prime minister was 'nervous, agitated and never ceases pronouncing imprudent words or sentences which show a complete ignorance of foreign affairs'. By the time they arrived at Dunkirk on the morning of Wednesday 29 July it was obvious that the fate of the Republic was in the hands of its president, not its prime minister. As Poincaré stepped back on French soil he was filled with a profound sense of personal mission. At last he was ready to take control of events. Yet perhaps it was already too late.

Belatedly, Poincaré was brought up to date with a series of detailed messages concerning critical developments in Russia which he ought to have received on his cruise. Poincaré's frustration at the apparent inability of the Eiffel Tower transmitter to send clear messages to the *France* became anger at the news that Germany's transmission service at Metz had deliberately jammed the French frequencies.

Meanwhile (as Poincaré had feared), the acting foreign minister, Jean-Baptiste Bienvenu-Martin, had conveyed an impression of indecision and weakness during the President's absence. Consequently, the German and Austrian ambassadors in Paris reported back that France would not provide enthusiastic support to the Russians. Yet it is vital to appreciate that this was not the impression which had been created in Russia itself. At a critical moment the French decision-makers were unable to convey a clear and unified stance to either friend or foe. To a considerable extent this was due to the unpredictable behaviour of the Franch ambassador in St Petersburg, Maurice Paléologue.

Ever since his appointment, the flamboyant ambassador had cultivated, falsely, the impression that he was a close confidante of Poincaré. He therefore implied to the Russians that when he spoke it was with the full backing of the President of the Republic. This was certainly the view taken by the foreign minister Sazonov. As the historian James Joll puts it, Paléologue, 'a man wholly committed to the Russian alliance, felt free to strengthen the resolve of Sazonov, whose changes of mood contributed to the complexity of the situation, by assuring him of France's readiness to fulfil her obligations as an ally'.

Sazonov was told the contents of the Austrian ultimatum on the morning of 24 July. He immediately resolved to request partial mobilisation from the Tsar and his ministers. A meeting of the Council of Ministers was already planned for 3 pm that afternoon. In the interim, Sazonov sought the backing of the British and French ambassadors. Whereas Sir George Buchanan remained non-committal, Paléologue made it clear that as far as he was concerned France would honour all her alliance obligations to Russia. Paléologue's influence on events was extended by his failure to keep the foreign ministry in Paris fully informed of this discussion and the military preparations which Russia now began making.

On the night of 25/26 July, with the Tsar's approval, Russian troops moved into the 'pre-mobilisation' period against Austria, whereby reservists were moved into frontier positions to strengthen the troops already stationed there. The failure of the Russians to distinguish between the Austrian and German frontiers led to German alarm, and protests from Bethmann-Hollweg. Despite the fact that Poincaré was not being fully informed of these developments, the French had already begun to take precautionary measures themselves. Leave was cancelled, soldiers hastily recalled, and units based in Morocco ordered to return. In addition - perhaps out of concern that Russia seemed exclusively concerned with Austria and not Germany - General Joffre, the French chief of staff, and Adolphe Messimy, the war minister, conveyed a message to the Russian high command that should war break out, they hoped that the Russians would immediately take the offensive in East Prussia. Yet even as late as 29 July German Intelligence suggested that France was 'setting all levers in motion at St Petersburg to exercise a moderating influence there'.

Meanwhile, dramatic events elsewhere seemed to offer confirmation that these military preparations would indeed be necessary. On 28 July Austria declared war on Serbia. The next day the Tsar signed two mobilisation orders, one for partial, one for general mobilisation, should circumstances demand it. That evening the German ambassador showed Sazonov a telegram he had received from Chancellor Bethmann-Hollweg: 'Kindly impress on M. Sazonov very seriously that further progress of Russian mobilisation measures would compel us to mobilise and that European war could scarcely be prevented'. This seemed only to harden the resolve of the Russian foreign minister, the war minister and the chief of staff, all of whom agreed to immediate general mobilisation. Only the Tsar's personal telegram from his cousin 'Willy' (Kaiser William II) had prevented this measure from being taken immediately. All of these alarming developments had taken place by the 29th, the day Poincaré arrived back in France.

At 5 pm that afternoon Viviani's depression mounted when the German ambassador called to say that if France continued her military preparations Germany would order *Kriegsgefahrzustand* - the 'danger of war' period which came one step before general mobilisation. Meanwhile Paléologue, Sazonov and the Russian ambassador in France, Isvolsky, were all working to cement Franco-Russian co-operation. It was still not clear to Viviani that Paléologue had expressed unequivocal support for the Russians. However, when Isvolsky passed on a message of thanks from Sazonov to the French government 'for the declaration, which the French Ambassador made to me in his government's name, that we may count completely on the allied support of France' the truth finally emerged. A distressed Viviani was so alarmed by this that he personally went to the Elysée Palace and had Poincaré awakened to tell him the latest development. Yet it was now too late for France to exercise restraint. Within 24 hours, on the night of 30/31 July, red mobilisation notices began to appear in public places throughout St Petersburg. Paléologue, anxious that his government might now express vehement opposition to Russian mobilisation, deliberately delayed sending his telegram to the Quai d'Orsay. Critically, the telegram did not arrive in Paris until 8.30 pm on the evening of 31 July. Yet the Germans had been aware of Russian mobilisation as early as the morning of 31 July. While France was still coming to terms with the significance of Russian mobilisation, the Germans had already proclaimed the 'danger of war' and, when Russia continued to take military measures, Germany declared war on Russia at 6 pm on 1 August. That evening France, no longer in control of events, proclaimed general mobilisation.

It is vital to appreciate that throughout these developments, France had been unable to obtain from Britain a clear expression of full military support. Fortunately, while Cambon was asking 'whether the word "honour" should not be struck out of the English vocabulary,' Britain finally decided to act. On the evening of 2 August the Cabinet decided that any violation of Belgian neutrality would compel Britain to intervene. At the same time German troops had already crossed into Luxemburg and were demanding free passage through Belgium. The next day, Germany declared war on France. On the morning of 4 August, German troops - ignoring the British guarantee - crossed into Belgium. After their ultimatum was ignored, Britain declared war on Germany at 11 am.

James Joll summarises what happened next. 'In the succession of declarations of war from 1 to 4 August, the Austrians were almost overlooked: the final breach with Russia only occurred on 6 August… France and Britain declared war on Austria-Hungary on 12 August, rather reluctantly and with expressions of personal esteem and regret from both Grey and the Austrian ambassador. The terms and timing of the actual declarations of war had been largely determined by the efforts of all the governments concerned to present themselves in the best light so as to justify their actions to their citizens; and for the moment they had little difficulty in doing so. Almost everywhere war was accepted not only with resignation but in many cases with enthusiasm. Very few people foresaw what the nature, duration and consequences were likely to be. What was the extent of France's contribution to these events?

TALKING POINT

In certain respects the French leaders seem to have acted incompetently and to have lost control of events. Does incompetence equal shared responsibility for the outbreak of war? To what extent were French leaders to blame?

REVIEW

To what extent was France responsible for the outbreak of the First World War?

1 Look at the following statements.

(a) France was motivated throughout this period by a fervent desire for revenge.
(b) Her economic and colonial expansion contributed to the intense national rivalry between France and Germany.
(c) France carefully exploited the Alliance system ensuring that Germany became increasingly isolated and, eventually, encircled.
(d) During the July Crisis the negligence and ineptitude of the French leaders contributed by default to the outbreak of the war.
(e) France and her allies were as much to blame for the mobilisation and declarations of war as her rivals.

Go through the chapter and make notes under the headings (a) - (e)

2 In what ways would you say that France was not to blame?

3 Write an essay under the title shown above, balancing your points for and against French responsibility.

4 Russia in Turmoil 1894-1917

PREVIEW

The death of an autocrat

In April 1918 the Russian royal family were moved for the third time in a year. Tsar Nicholas II, the Tsarina Alexandra and their four daughters were taken from Siberia to the remote town of Ekaterinburg in the Ural mountains. With a small number of servants they were taken to a large town house referred to by their communist captors as a 'House of Special Purpose'. It was heavily guarded and barricaded. Escape seemed impossible. Later the prisoners were joined by the heir to the throne, the Tsarevich Alexei. The Tsar's son suffered from haemophilia: an incurable and painful disease in which the blood clots slowly and bleeding is very difficult to control. He had been too ill to travel to Ekaterinburg with his family but now the Romanovs were back together. Perhaps they would be rescued? At

THE CORONATION OF NICHOLAS II AT THE ASSUMPTION CATHEDRAL, 1896

THE GRAND DUCHESSES OLGA AND TIIANA WITH MEMBERS OF THE IMPERIAL COURT, WORKING IN THE
GROUNDS OF THE PALACE OF TSARKOE SELO DURING THEIR IMPRISONMENT (1918)

TALKING POINT
Why does the
assassination of a ruler
make so much impact on
a people, even though
most would probably
never have met their
leader?

the start of July, Royalist White Russians who wanted to restore the Tsar to the
throne were poised to storm Ekaterinburg. The guard around the house was
stepped up. As the heat of summer became stifling, the captors took the
ominous step of whitewashing all the windows. Whatever happened inside
the house was clearly intended to be kept secret.

What follows is therefore speculation. Some historians maintain that on the
night of 16 July the imperial family were crowded into a cellar, shot and
bayonetted. They believe that the royal corpses were soaked in acid and then
burnt. Others have claimed that only the Tsar and his son were killed and that
the females were taken away. In 1989 a Russian investigator claimed to have
discovered the remains of the Tsar. The rest of the affair remains shrouded in
mystery. The Romanov family had ruled Russia from 1613 to 1917. Why did
they lose the throne in 1917? How was it possible for the absolute ruler of the
largest land empire in the world to end his life as a helpless murder victim?

An absolute ruler: Tsar Nicholas II 1894-1917

When Nicholas became Tsar in 1894 his personal authority seemed completely secure. With the Imperial crown came the imposing titles of Tsar of all the Russias, Grand Duke of Poland and Grand Duke of Finland. Appointed by God, the holder of these titles was the absolute ruler of an empire covering roughly one-sixth of the earth's total land surface. This empire stretched from the Baltic to the Black Sea and from Poland to the Pacific. Such was its extent that the capital, St Petersburg, was actually closer to New York than to Vladivostock. It was the home of many different racial groups including Latvians, Poles, Ukrainians and Mongols. Of a population in 1917 of 163 million, ethnic Russians constituted only 40 per cent.

RUSSIA AND THE WORLD IN 1914

The royal family enjoyed massive personal wealth and owned estates which were larger than several European countries. Their huge empire was held together by the largest standing army in Europe, which was one million strong. While the prestige of the Russian empire rested on the strength of the army, its political security was in the firm hands of an extensive secret police network which was usually brutally effective. As these features suggest, the Tsar was at the helm of a highly authoritarian, heavily centralised police state which did not appear to respond to pressure from any social class. Political parties were banned. Radical critics of the regime generally found themselves in prison or in exile. The press was heavily censored and public meetings were carefully controlled. Yet loyalty to the Tsar or 'Father' was intense, typified by the peasants' widespread practice of displaying an icon of him on the walls of their huts.

Absolute power rested in the hands of one man. The tone of Nicholas II's personal rule was set by his unequivocal response in 1895 to a request from the provincial *zemstvo* (local council) of Tver for an extension of representative institutions: 'I am informed that recently in some zemstvo assemblies, voices have made themselves heard from people carried away by senseless dreams about participation by members of the zemstvo in the affairs of internal government: let all know that I, devoting all my strength to the welfare of the people, will uphold the principle of autocracy as firmly and as unflinchingly as my late unforgettable father.'

The Emperor had made it clear from the outset that his word was literally law. Any earlier legislation could simply be overruled by an oral instruction from him. There were no legal or constitutional restraints on the choice of ministers, the exercise of political power or the formulation of national policy. The extent of the Tsar's authority was heightened by the corresponding weakness of Russia's limited political institutions. The Council of Ministers

NICHOLAS II AND HIS FAMILY, TAKEN AROUND 1905. THEIR NEW SON, ALEXEI, HAD INHERITED HAEMOPHILIA

held no collective talks and each minister was responsible to the Tsar alone. The governors of the Russian provinces exercised considerable authority but they remained the personal appointments of the Tsar and could be instantly dismissed. The historian Hans Rogger makes the telling observation that 'at the accession of Nicholas II, Turkey, Montenegro and Russia were the only European countries without a parliament'.

The problems of the tsarist regime

On 1 March 1881 Tsar Alexander II carried out a routine inspection of the royal guard in St Petersburg. The formalities over, the elaborate procession set off on the return journey to the Winter Palace. As the horses' hooves clattered on the cobbled streets a bomb was thrown with deadly accuracy at the royal carriage. It exploded under the back axle, destroying the carriage and injuring the horses. Miraculously, the Tsar stepped out of the wreck unscathed. His personal guards, who had been breached with alarming ease, must have heaved a collective sigh of relief. Then, from out of the rapidly

AN ENGRAVING SHOWING THE ASSASSINATION OF ALEXANDER II IN 1881

THE WOUNDED TSAR TAKEN BACK TO THE WINTER PALACE BY COLONEL DVORKETSKY

EMPEROR ALEXANDER III
(1845-94)

gathering crowd, a second assassin stepped forward. From only a few feet away a second bomb was dropped at the Tsar's feet. With some difficulty Alexander's horribly mutilated body was taken back to the palace. Despite massive injuries to the legs, stomach and face, the Tsar was still conscious when he was carried up the marble stairs of the palace. Yet the loss of blood was massive and the royal surgeons watched helplessly as his life drifted away. Before Alexander lost consciousness a pale, 13-year-old boy in a sailor suit was ushered into the room to see his stricken grandfather. It was an experience that the future Nicholas II would never forget.

The impact of the assassination on the Tsar's successor, Alexander III, was equally traumatic. Shocked by his father's death, Alexander resolved to restore the autocracy to its traditional, feared position. He cast aside the reforms of his father and came increasingly to rely on the reactionary ideas of Constantin Pobedonostsev. No analysis of the reign of Nicholas II can afford to neglect the pervasive influence of this key minister. As Procurator of the Holy Synod (the government minister responsible for the church), Pobedonostsev combined religious orthodoxy, virulent anti-semitism and absolute autocracy. He dismissed reformers as 'half-wits and perverted apes' and maintained that 'the whole secret of Russia's order and prosperity is in the top, in the person of the supreme authority'. Police repression reached new heights and the Jewish community suffered in a succession of violent pogroms. Most lasting of all was the destruction of every trace of democracy and constitutionalism. Government policy was set out in a notorious memorandum: to prevent the children of 'coachmen, servants, cooks, washerwomen, small shopkeepers and other similar persons' questioning the 'natural and inevitable inequality in social and economic relationships'. While Russia's economy progressed, her political development had been stopped in its tracks. To make matters worse, Pobedonostsev found time to engage in some private tuition: his pupil was an impressionable young man named Nicholas. When the time comes to assess the downfall of Nicholas II the damaging legacy of Pobedonostsev must not be forgotten.

The premature death of Alexander III at the age of 49 meant that the

POBEDONOSTSEV - Konstantin Petrovich (1827-1907).
1860-65 Prof. of Constitutional Law, Moscow University
Tutor to Alexander III and Nicholas II
1872 Became member of Council of the Empire
1880 Appointed Procurator of Holy Synod. Advocated oppression of non-Russian nationalities

KONSTANTIN POBEDONOSTEV, PROCURATOR GENERAL OF THE RUSSIAN SYNOD (1827-1907)

RELIGIOUS PROCESSION IN KURSK GUBERNIYA (1883). OBSERVE THE DREADFUL POVERTY, THE PRESENCE OF SECURITY POLICE, AND THE BARREN COUNTRYSIDE

reins of power were passed to his son Nicholas II when he was only 26 years old. He came to the throne ill equipped to wield power and with a personality more suited to the role of a purely ceremonial figure-head. Little had been done to prepare him for the job into which he was now thrust and which was ultimately to overwhelm him. The omens were not good. In 1895 a glittering coronation ceremony was marred when hundreds of onlookers on Khodyanka field were trampled to death.

Nevertheless, at first it appeared that the heritage passed on to Nicholas was a healthy one. The empire was at peace and Europe was enjoying a welcome period of tranquillity. The domestic situation was stable and Alexander III had presided over a period of intense industrial expansion, typified by the ambitious project to build a trans-Siberian railway. St Petersburg and Moscow were now major industrial centres. Foreign investment poured into

WOMEN PULLING RAFTS ALONG THE VOLGA. DREADFUL WORKING CONDITIONS SUCH AS THIS WERE COMMONPLACE

Russia, promoting massive growth in railways, iron, steel, cotton, silk, chemicals and banking. Spectacular progress was made in the mines of the Ukraine and the oilfields of the Baku, while cotton production was boosted by the widespread introduction of new machinery.

Most historians are agreed, however, that beneath the veneer of autocratic rule and industrial growth, the tsarist regime entered the Twentieth Century heading towards a major crisis. Russian society was in need of substantial social, economic and political reform if this impending crisis were to be averted. The new ruler, though, was a man who regarded even minor reform as dangerous and for whom the autocracy was sacrosanct. What was the nature of Russia's problem and why was reform so limited?

It is essential to recognise that the industrial growth which the Tsars eagerly promoted carried with it major social problems. In general, the Russian people had endured the difficulties of an industrial revolution without experiencing any of its benefits. The capital, St Petersburg, had seen rapid industrial growth but the conditions which accompanied this were horrendous. Its huge textile factories were poorly lit, ill ventilated and contained fast-moving machinery without protective guards. The average working day

A PEASANT FAMILY IN THEIR HOME

in the 1890s was between 12 and 14 hours. Discipline was harsh, rules inflexible, foremen brutal and fines severe. Larger firms offered their workers company accommodation in dismal barracks. The alternative was to search for housing in the grim backstreets of the capital. Such housing was notoriously expensive, overcrowded and insanitary. Within a mile of the Winter Palace families lived in indescribable filth and squalor.

The glaring contrast between the glittering opulence of the ruling aristocracy and the awful conditions endured by the working class could have sounded an alarm for the Tsar, but its warning clamour was completely ignored. Strike action, while still limited in the 1890s, reached a peak for that decade in 1899, with 97,000 participants. Perhaps this figure reflects the fact that more and more factory workers were developing a sense of political awareness and class consciousness. For the time being, the ban on trade unions and the strength of the police state meant that working-class dissatisfaction was largely ignored. However, the sense of injustice which increasingly prevailed in the cities would not always fall upon deaf ears; eventually, these areas would prove to be a hotbed of radical political activity.

In the countryside the situation was generally even worse. Approximately 80 per cent of Russia's population comprised peasant farmers, subsisting in conditions which were exceptionally harsh. Less than one third of the peasantry could read and write. Average life expectancy in the countryside was under 40. Farming equipment was primitive and investment virtually non-existent. Generally, individual peasants did not own private land. Instead the commune (*obshchina*) owned land, organised the collection of taxes and allotted strips of land to each household. The power of the commune was underlined by the fact that peasants could not leave the village without the consent of the village elders. Discipline was imposed through locally-appointed officials known as Land Captains, and corporal punishment was commonly used until 1904. Moreover, serious breaches of communal law could be punished by exile to Siberia. Communal farming did little to protect its members from famine. In 1891 severe drought and crop failure led to a major famine which combined with outbreaks of cholera and typhus to produce a death toll of 400,000. The alarming extent of peasant deprivation is reflected in the fact that in 1890 about 64 per cent of peasants called up for military service were declared unfit on health grounds. In the famine year of 1891 the figure reached a staggering 78 per cent. Nevertheless, the historian Hans Rogger estimates that between 15 and 25 per cent of peasant households were relatively prosperous. He argues that generally it was the shortage of land rather than the shortage of food which caused most irritation. Between 1877 and 1897 the rural population grew by 25 per cent and this growth rate was repeated in the following 20 years. Yet the amount of land in peasant hands, and the size of individual peasant allotments, completely failed to keep pace with this. Later the peasants' demand for land would assume an urgency which would prove impossible to resist, but for the time being they retained their faith in the tsar. Meanwhile their hunger for food and land was ignored.

It is clear, then, that at the turn of the century there was considerable scope for future dissatisfaction with the tsarist regime in both the cities and the countryside. Yet the relative passivity of the population and the repressive apparatus of the state created an atmosphere of complacency and political stagnation. This complacency was temporarily disturbed by the events of 1904-5 when tsarism was shaken to its foundations by what appears, in retrospect, to have provided a dress rehearsal for the revolutions of 1917. Although the revolution of 1905, sparked-off by the dramatic events of Bloody Sunday, appears to have a convenient starting point it is important to note that long before this date, discontent was already growing. In May 1896 the textile mills around St Petersburg were hit by a wave of strikes, notable for the militant action of many female factory workers. In Rostov-on-Don massive street demonstrations in 1902 were quelled by troops. Between 1901 and 1907 arson in the countryside became commonplace as rioting peasants set fire to the manor houses of the aristocracy. An economic depression hard on the heels of the 1890s boom led to renewed strike action and demonstrations. In 1904 the minister of the interior, Plehve, was assassinated by a Social Revolutionary.

TALKING POINT

Would you say that the main features of the tsarist regime represent a strong autocratic regime or a weak one?

1 Which aspects of Russian Society would you say were most in need of reform at the turn of the century?

2 Were there any positive aspects to Russian society at this time?

The regime's problems were exacerbated by a disastrous war with Japan which took place between 1904 and 1905. The war was fought over the control of Korea and Manchuria, and its outbreak was initially greeted with some enthusiasm. However, this turned to concern after major setbacks at Port Arthur and Mukden early in 1905. At the end of May, the Russian Baltic fleet was annihilated by the Japanese in the straits of Tshushima. In August 1905 the Russians were obliged to sign a humiliating peace treaty which gave Japan control over Korea and southern Manchuria. A campaign which it was hoped would boost the government's waning popularity had ended in ignominious defeat. It is in this context of mounting problems at home and abroad that the events of 1905 are best understood.

Can you see any connection between Russia's domestic problems and her defeat by the Japanese in 1905?

The revolution of 1905

The procession set off for the Winter Palace early on the morning of 22 January 1905. The boots of the marchers crunched the hard-packed snow and a biting wind blew fresh flurries into their faces. Despite the freezing conditions, approximately 200,000 people, forming five separate processions, had turned out to present their petition to the Tsar. At the head of the huge procession was a priest, Father Gapon. The peaceful intent of the marchers was underlined by the icons of the Tsar which many of them proudly held aloft. Their demands now appear fairly modest: 'We ask but little: to reduce the working day to eight hours, to provide a minimum wage of a rouble a day, and to abolish overtime'. Added to these requests for social

LEFT: FRENCH CARTOON SHOWS THE TSAR FACING THE SWORD OF DAMOCLES. LOOK CAREFULLY AT THE GRAVESTONES

RIGHT: THE TSAR, HAUNTED BY THE REVOLUTIONARY EVENTS OF 1905

change was a more ambitious call for constitutional reform. However, long before they reached their destination, those at the front of the lengthy procession came to a jarring halt. Armed guards and mounted cossacks had been deployed in a massive but unnecessary show of force. They ordered the demonstrators to turn back but the sheer size of the group made this impossible. As the crowd surged forward the edgy soldiers opened fire and the cossack horsemen charged the crowd. Crimson patches stained the snow as unarmed men, women and children were cut down in an unrestrained massacre which left hundreds dead and wounded.

Those who survived must have wondered why the Tsar had not come out to receive their petition. In fact, alarmed by warnings of a mass demonstration, he had taken his family to the elegant town of Tsarkoe Selo some 15 miles away. The consequences of his soldiers' actions however, were inescapable. Amid a wave of revulsion, St Petersburg was paralysed by a general strike. On 4 February the tsar's uncle, the governor-general of Moscow, was assassinated. Traditional loyalties were being strained to the limit. Clearly the regime was facing a major crisis. The extent of the crisis remains the subject of debate. Some historians have used the term 'revolution' in relation to it. How appropriate is this term?

Your brief is to produce a satirical criticism of the regime in 1905.
You need to produce the following:
(a) A name for the Tsar.
(b) A cartoon, with a caption, depicting the regime in 1905.
(c) A brief article about the regime's conduct.

IMPERIAL TROOPS FIRE AT DEMONSTRATING WORKERS
OUTSIDE THE WINTER PALACE (JANUARY 1905)

4.1 Was there a revolution in 1905?

Naval Mutiny
May Kronstadt. This was not directly connected with the incidents in the Black Sea.

Workers' Soviets
April The lst workers' council was set up in the Urals.
May The textile workers in Ivanovo followed suit. Soon there were 60 such workers' councils, despite their illegality.

National uprisings
Non-Russian groups within the empire rose up in Poland, Finland and Georgia.

St Petersburg
22 January Bloody Sunday.
January General Strike throughout the city.
October St Petersburg Soviet of Workers Deputies set up.
16 December Leaders of the Soviet were arrested.

Naval Mutinies
June Mutiny at Odessa on board the battleship *Potemkin*. The crew eventually sailed her to Romania.

FINLAND
KRONSTADT
BALTIC SEA
ST. PETERSBURG
IVANOVO-VOZNESENSK
MOSCOW
POLAND
ODESSA CAUCASUS
SEBASTOPOL
BLACK SEA
TURKEY
CASPIAN SEA
IRAN
URAL MOUNTAINS

February Assassination of the Govenor-General of Moscow, Grand Duke Sergei, the Tsar's uncle.
October Moscow badly affected by the national general strike.
December A poorly equipped uprising was crushed by the Semenovsky regiment from St. Petersburg. More than 500 lives were lost.

'The historian cannot do without the word "revolution", shapeless and slippery smooth though it is, after much use and abuse

J. M. Roberts *The French Revolution* (1978)

Strike!

October The Union of Railway Workers began a strike in Moscow demanding better wages, hours, civil liberties and a democratically elected constituent assembly. The railways across the country were quickly paralysed.

The example of the railwaymen was followed by doctors, lawyers, teachers, printers, postal workers, industrial workers, students, telegraphers, professors, actors and even dancers of the imperial ballet.

In most cities barracades were erected and there were major clashes between police and strikers. The St. Petersburg Soviet called off the general strike at the end of October as many strikers were starving.

Repression

The government was unsparing in its use of force to suppress the uprisings. Throughout the countryside hangings and beatings of peasants were common. The government used gangs of strike-breakers – known as the Black Hundreds – to attack workers, especially in the oil industry in the Caucasus.

Peasant unrest

The peasants' harvest was ruined by drought. Illegal pasturing and wood felling on gentry land, burning and looting of manor houses throughout the countryside. At first these outbreaks were sporadic and dispersed, but later, a National Peasants' Union was formed

MANCHURIA

KOREA

QUESTIONS

The pictures show some of the classic features of a revolution.

(a) Which features were present in 1905?

(b) Which features were absent?

(c) You now need to decide whether it is accurate to use the term 'revolution' to describe the events of 1905. Justify your answer.

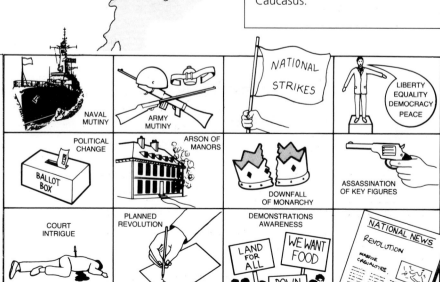

The Tsar's ministers

Despite the autocratic nature of the tsarist regime, Nicholas II depended heavily on the work of key ministers. Two figures dominate his reign, one serving before the revolution of 1905, the other being asked to pick up the pieces afterwards. To what extent were they able to implement major reforms within the framework of autocracy?

Sergei Witte (1849-1915)

Witte is regarded by many historians as a bold, imaginative statesman and possibly the ablest man to serve the last two Tsars. Following an early career in the railway industry, Witte served as minister of communications during the 1880s. He became minister of finance in 1892, with particular responsibility for commerce, industry and labour relations. The Ministry was the most important agency dealing with Russia's economic system.

Witte was able to build on the progress made by his two predecessors,

THIS PAINTING DEPICTS A PEACEFUL DEMONSTRATION BEING DISPERSED BY COSSACKS (JANUARY 1905)

Bunge (1881-86) and Vyshnegradskii (1887-92). Bunge had expanded a railway-building programme, helped several industries with a programme of tariff protection, set up a factory inspectorate and established the Peasant Land Bank which helped peasants to buy additional land from the nobles. Vyshnegradskii had imposed high tax burdens on the peasantry which helped to balance the national budget but left them ill-prepared to cope with the famine of 1891. Despite these problems, Vyshnegradskii had laid the foundations of a national railway network, stabilised the rouble and produced a significant surplus in exports.

Witte's contribution was to continue with the expansionist economic policies favoured by his predecessors and instil a new sense of energy and urgency. In short, Witte created a climate for industrial development and ensured that more government resources than ever before went into investment and new technology. His ministry coincided with the greatest industrial boom in Russia's history, although this was hindered by a major slump in 1899. Witte lost his post in 1903. His major achievements are set out here:

Foreign Capital: Witte encouraged foreign investment and loans in Russian industry to a massive degree. Between 1893 and 1896, foreigners invested in Russian businesses 40 million roubles more than the Russians themselves (144.9 compared to 103.7 million roubles). Even a traditional industry like cotton relied on foreign investment for 20 per cent of its finance. Foreign financing speeded the growth of Russian mining, industry, railways, credit and commerce.

Trade: Witte brought about a threefold improvement in the nation's trade balance. Higher taxes were imposed but Witte claimed that there was also a higher level of consumer consumption. Industry was safeguarded by a series of protectionist tariffs.

Finance: In 1897 the rouble was elevated to the Gold Standard which made it freely convertible with foreign currencies, although this in turn meant that wheat was freely exported making famine more likely.

Peter Arkadyevich Stolypin (1862-1911)

Stolypin's rise to ministerial status needs to be set against the national disturbances of 1905 and the limited constitutional concessions reluctantly granted by the Tsar in that year. During the revolution of 1905 Stolypin was serving as the Governor of Saratov province. The energetic and effective manner in which he crushed the rural disturbances there earned him favourable attention from the Tsar. Perhaps this able administrator could perform a similar repressive function on a national scale.

In July 1905 Stolypin was appointed minister of the interior and later in the same year replaced Goremykin as Prime Minister. Although Stolypin was not completely hostile towards the idea of the Duma, he disliked the political complexion of the first one and dissolved it in 1906. His intention was to produce a second, more pliant Duma, but the dissolution provoked widespread dissent. A major protest from the Duma deputies, sporadic peasant uprisings, political assassinations and mutinies at Sveaborg and Kronstadt meant that once again the country faced a major crisis. Stolypin's own residence was bombed, injuring two of his children.

In August 1906 Stolypin established the field court-martials, consisting of senior military officers who met in secret to deal with serious anti-government crimes. All cases had to be concluded within two days and were conducted without a defence counsel. Death sentences could not be commuted and were always carried out within 24 hours.

Historian Chris Read estimates that literally thousands were killed, not just over a short time but year after year. Such was the notoriety of the system that the gallow's noose became known as the 'Stolypin neck tie'. Thousands more were banished to distant provinces. It is important to note that in retaliation more than a thousand government agents were killed in the same period. Rogger notes that in February 1907 Stolypin proposed the end of the field court-martials but this was personally rejected by the Tsar. When the second Duma was called in March 1907 it was vehemently critical of the government's repressive measures.

PETER STOLYPIN (1862-1911)

Some historians feel that Stolypin was losing his influence with the tsar by 1909, and he was assassinated by a Social Revolutionary in 1911. Nevertheless, his brief administration gave rise to a series of major reforms, some of which continued to flourish after his death.

The land reforms: These were the most fundamental of Stolypin's reforms. His objective was to ensure that the regime could recapture the inherent loyalty of the 'sturdy peasant'. Stolypin wanted to distract the peasants' gaze from the estates of the nobility and focus their attention on the communal land. To achieve this, the main cause of peasant discontent - 'communal land tenure' - would have to be removed. Instead, each peasant would become the owner of scattered strips which would be consolidated into small farmsteads. By 1915, almost half of peasant households held land individually. Credit was made available through Peasant Land Bank loans to help the peasants buy land from the nobility. In a major programme of 'internal colonisation' peasants were encouraged to move to western Siberia where more farming land was available.

Health services: These were extended in the provinces by the zemstvos and in 1912 a system of health insurance for workers was established.

Education: In 1908 the government announced its aim of providing compulsory universal education within ten years. By 1914 the government had provided 50,000 extra primary schools. Secondary and higher education were also extended by Stolypin.

1 What were the main problems which Stolypin was trying to solve?

2 Which of Stolypin's reforms do you consider to be the most important?

3 Did Stolypin's repressive tactics outweigh the value of his reforms?

An experiment in constitutional government (1906-1914)

Alongside the economic and social reforms of Witte and Stolypin, the period 1906-14 also witnessed Russia's first attempt at some form of democratic government. These developments came as a concession after the upheaval of 1905, but those who believed that the Tsar and his advisers had been converted to western ideas of democracy were soon to be disappointed. Historian David Floyd gives this assessment of the Duma period: 'It was true that the Duma never became a parliament in the western European sense. It was never able to exercise effective control over the actions of the government or the Tsar. But it would be a mistake to dismiss Russia's "parliamentary experiment" as worthless. It was impossible for a country so large and so backward as Russia to become a parliamentary democracy in a matter of six years, after centuries of autocratic rule. It was surprising, however, how much progress was made in that short period and how much business was done by the four Dumas. The simple fact of the existence of the Duma was important in itself'.

Analyse the conduct of the first four Dumas and decide whether you agree with Floyd's assessment.

The First Duma: April 1906 - July 1906

The regime made its promise of political reform in the October Manifesto of 1905 and in February 1906 a new manifesto set out details of the representative system. The upper house was to be known as the Council of State, with half the members to be nominated and half to be elected by the zemstvos and higher orders of society. The lower house, the Duma, was to consist of around 500 deputies elected by universal suffrage from all classes of Russian society, with direct voting in the five largest cities and an electoral college elsewhere.

However, on 23 April the Tsar proclaimed the Fundamental Laws which defined the precise powers of the Duma. These laws proclaimed that 'Supreme Autocratic power belongs to the Emperor of All Russia' and that 'no law can come into existence without His approval'. When the Duma met for the first time in the Tauride Palace in St Petersburg on 27 April, it was clear that its powers were strictly limited. It could neither pass laws independently of the government, nor appoint ministers, nor exercise control over parts of the budget concerning the military; and it was liable to be dissolved at the Tsar's will. Despite these limitations, the radical complexion of the First Duma, with a majority of Constitutional Democrats but also some Mensheviks and (despite a party boycott) Social Revolutionaries, meant that it was frequently critical of government policies. A clash between

THE ARRIVAL OF THE IMPERIAL FAMILY AT THE WINTER PALACE FOR THE OPENING OF THE DUMA (MAY 1906)

the Duma and the government over land reform led to the dissolution of the first Duma in July 1906, a move which coincided with the appointment of Stolypin as premier. Russia's first major experiment in constitutional politics had lasted for ten weeks.

The Second Duma: February 1907-June 1907

Stolypin's hopes for a more pliable Duma were quickly dashed. The lifting of the socialists' boycott increased left-wing representation while the extreme right-wing, anti-semitic Union of the Russian People also gained ground. This shift to the extremes of left and right took place largely at the expense of the Kadets, and meant that the second Duma was much more divided than the first. Again, the Duma tried to assert itself but floundered in the face of government hostility. On 6 March 1907 Stolypin presented an inimical Duma with his proposals for land and tax reform, workers' insurance, compulsory primary education and an improved police system. His objective was to reach a middle ground with the Duma at the expense of the extremists. However, land reform was once again a stumbling block. The Duma advocated the confiscation of land but Stolypin found this proposal, with or without compensation, completely unacceptable. The government's unease about the Duma was reflected in a concerted campaign to discredit it which culminated in the summer of 1907. On 1 June Stolypin called for the removal of parliamentary immunity for all Social Democratic deputies on the grounds that some of them had conspired to subvert the armed forces and incite a revolution. A committee was set up to look into these allegations but before it had concluded its work, the order of dissolution was issued on 3 June 1907.

The Third Duma: 1907-12

Dissatisfied with the attitude of the first two Dumas, Stolypin now took the step of altering the electoral procedures in order to produce a Duma acceptable to the government. Stolypin breached the Fundamental Laws by restricting the franchise in favour of the rich urban classes and the landed gentry at the expense of the workers and peasants. Therefore when the Third Duma was convened in November it was very different in its political make-up to its predecessors. The Octobrists, who happily accepted the limitations of the Fundamental Laws, were now the largest party in the Duma. The extreme right became more powerful while representation for the Social Democrats and Trudoviki collapsed. Stolypin had finally got what he wanted. The Third Duma was generally a compliant, conservative organ acting as a rubber stamp for government legislation. Even so, this Duma was also suspended at times, but the fact that the deputies reconvened without protest meant that it was the first Duma to survive the allotted five-year span. The experiment in constitutional politics had been stopped in its tracks and this served to widen the gulf between government and the masses.

The Fourth Duma: 1912-17

The Fourth Duma was elected on a restricted franchise and was dominated by men of property and wealth who returned a parliament even more conservative than its predecessor. However, the period between 1912 and 1914 saw a marked deterioration in relations between the Tsar and the classes within Russian society which had previously been so loyal to him. In par-

Kadets
The Kadets took their name from their full title, Constitutional Democrats, also known as `Party of the People's Freedom'. Under the Tsar they consisted of propertied Liberals. They advocated political reform and later comprised the First Provisional Government when the Tsar was overthrown.

Populist Socialists
Also known as the Trudoviki (Labour Group). Numerically small, they attracted intellectuals, conservative peasants and leaders of co-operative societies. They reflected populist ideas but often followed the line taken by the Kadets.

Bolsheviks
Originally Lenin and other leading Bolsheviks had been members of the Russian Social Democratic Labour Party. At a party congress held in 1903 the party split into two factions, of which Bolsheviki signified `members of the majority'. This group supported proletarian insurrection.

Socialist Revolutionary Party
The SRs, founded in 1901, were the major rivals to the Social Democratic parties. They brought together radicals from earlier organisations, such as Land and Liberty and The People's Will. They relied heavily on support from the peasants.

Mensheviks

After the split of 1903, the Mensheviki ('members of the minority') encompassed a range of socialists who maintained that society would naturally evolve towards socialism. The Mensheviks attracted a more 'elitist', educated following than their Bolshevik rivals.

Left Socialist Revolutionaries

Many peasants who left the SRs joined this party instead. They advocated confiscation, without compensation, of the great landed estates.

Maximalists

Having branched out from the Socialist Revolutionary Party in the revolution of 1905, they demanded the application of a full (maximum) socialist programme.

ticular this élite group became increasingly concerned about the bizarre relationship between Nicholas and Alexandra and their 'friend' Gregory Rasputin (1871-1916). Rasputin was a member of an extreme religious sect from Siberia. His influence in St Petersburg high society was made possible by his apparently miraculous powers to cure the bleeding of the heir to the throne, the Tsarevich Alexis. Rasputin's well-founded reputation as an uncouth, womanising drunkard alarmed the conservative members of the Duma, but rumours of an affair between the monk and the Empress caused scandal and outrage. Nicholas's apparent reliance on this 'holy-man' was an important factor in a distinct cooling-off in relations between the Duma and the Tsar. While loyalist groups within the Duma were expressing increased concern about Rasputin, the opposition members were reaching the conclusion that membership of the Duma was really a pointless exercise. The Fourth Duma then was marked by stagnation and dissatisfaction, temporarily relieved when it voted for war credits in August 1914.

The eve of war: 1912-14

Clearly the Dumas did not satisfy critics of the regime who had anticipated more genuine democratic reforms. With the death of Stolypin the problems which had afflicted Russia in 1905 began to return. In 1912, striking gold miners in Siberia were brutally attacked, resulting in 200 fatalities. The regime's heavy-handed response served to underline the fact that nothing had really changed. The structural problems which Russia faced at the turn of the century were still present but the Tsar's most imaginative ministers had left the scene. Despite these problems, the well-orchestrated celebrations held in 1913 to commemorate 300 years of Romanov rule were greeted with genuine enthusiasm. The reservoir of goodwill which the Tsar had always enjoyed was still not exhausted. Indeed in August 1914 it appeared that he was as popular as ever. Russia's declaration of war against Germany prompted a wave of patriotism. Yet less than three years later Nicholas was forced to abdicate and Romanov rule came to an end. Why did this happen?

Assess each of the four Dumas according to the following criteria:

(a) The range of political opinion represented in each one.
(b) Its ability to influence the Tsar.
(c) Its degree of independence.
(d) Its overall contribution to Russia's political development.

RASPUTIN, SURROUNDED BY FEMALE ADMIRERS

EXAMINING THE EVIDENCE

Why did the Tsar abdicate in February 1917?

Source A

Celebrations for the Romanov tri-centenary in Moscow (1913). Tsarevitch Alexis is being carried by a cossack

1 The photograph shows that by 1913 the public had forgiven the regime for Bloody Sunday. Explain whether you agree with this statement.

2 Explain the significance of Source B in Russia's political development.

3 To what extent do Sources A, B and C suggest that by 1914 Russia had overcome its problems?

Source B: Growth of population in St Petersburg 1881-1917

1881	928,000
1890	1,033,600
1897	1,264,700
1900	1,439,600
1910	1,905,000
1914	2,217,500
1917	2,300,000

Source C: August 1914 - a wave of patriotism

THE GERMAN AMBASSADOR IN ST PETERSBURG HAS DELIVERED A NOTE CONTAINING A DECLARATION OF WAR
Resolute mood in Petersburg and Moscow... Ban on sale of spiritous liquours in both capitals.

GOD STRIKE THE AGGRESSOR!
A crowd of a hundred thousand kneeling in front of the Winter Palace with national flags dipped in salute...Arise, great nation of Russia!

Newspaper extracts quoted in Alexander Solzhenitsyn, *August 1914* (1972)

Source D: A note of caution

That the patriotic intoxication might be neither deep nor lasting, least of all among the masses who would bear the brunt of the burdens of war, was apparent to fearful conservatives even before hostilities began. In February 1914, P.N. Durnovo, now a member of the Council of State, pleaded with the emperor for an accommodation with Germany in order to avoid war. He predicted social revolution, the disintegration of the army, and hopeless anarchy in the likely event of military setbacks.'

Hans Rogger, *Russia in the Age of Modernisation and Revolution 1881-1917* (1983)

Source E

RUSSIAN SOLDIERS IN THE FACE OF A GERMAN GAS ATTACK

Source F

CASUALTY FIGURES FOR THE RUSSIAN ARMY, 1914 -18

Standing armies & trained reserves	Total mobilised	Killed in action or died of wounds	Total military casualties
5,971,000	12,000,000	1,700,000	9,150,000

1 Explain the significance of Sources E and F in the light of the comments made by Durnovo in Source E.

2 Look again at Sources E and F. Explain how these sources could be interpreted by

(a) A supporter of the regime
(b) An enemy of the regime.

Source G: October 1916 - a warning sign

The brilliant success of the offensive of General Brusilov in the spring of the present year and the current solution to the problem of supplying the troops proved convincingly that the task undertaken by the Government and the community has been fulfilled more than successfully. The question of the organisation of the army supply may be held to have been satisfactorily settled...But, on the other hand, the disintegration of the rear, that is of the whole country, which is now steadily increasing has today reached such monstrous and extreme form that it has begun to be a menace to the success

NICHOLAS II AND HIS PERSONAL RETINUE AT THE TSAR'S HEADQUARTERS IN MOGILEV

obtained at the front, and in the very near future promises to throw the country into chaotic, spontaneous and catastrophic anarchy.

...all these things have led to an unfair distribution of foodstuffs and articles of prime necessity, an immense and rapid increase in the cost of

RUSSIAN SOLDIERS KNEEL BEFORE THE TSAR AND A HOLY ICON DURING WORLD WAR 1

What light does the Petrograd police report (Source G) shed on the problems being faced by the regime in the Autumn of 1916?

Read Source H very carefully.

1 In 1905 the troops fired upon the crowds, What reasons does this extract provide to explain why they behaved differently in 1917?

2 What additional reasons can you suggest to explain the troops' mutiny in 1917?

3 What appears, at face value, to have been the attitude of the generals towards the mutiny?

4 Can you discern any ulterior motive behind General Alekseev's telegram?

living, and to inadequacy in sources of supply and means of existence. These factors show that the neglect of the rear is the prime cause of the disorganisation of the huge machine of the state...a terrible crisis is already on the way...

There is little doubt that rumours that Russia is on the eve of a revolution are exaggerated as compared to the actual conditions, but nevertheless the situation is serious enough to deserve immediate attention.

Petrograd police report for October 1916

Source H: February 1917 - mutiny in Petrograd

General Khabalov around midday on the 27th reported to his Majesty that one company of the Pavlovsky Regiment's reserve battalion had declared on February 26 that it would not fire on people... On February 27 training detachments of the Volynsky Regiment refused to proceed against the rebels, and its commander shot himself. Then this detachment together with a company of the same regiment proceeded to the quarters of the reserve battalions, and men from these units began to join them...

On February 28 at 1 am His Majesty received a telegram from General Khabalov stating that he could not restore order in the capital. The majority of the units have betrayed their duty and many have passed over to the side of the rebels. The troops which have remained faithful to their duty, after fighting the whole day, have suffered many casualties.

We have just received a telegram from the Minister of War stating that the rebels have seized the most important buildings in all parts of the city. Due to fatigue and propaganda the troops have laid down their arms, passed to the side of the rebels or become neutral...

Extracts from a telegram of 28 February 1917 from General Alekseev, Chief of Staff of the Supreme Commander to all the commanders in chief

A DEMONSTRATION IN FRONT OF THE WINTER PALACE IN PETROGRAD, 1917

Source I: The Tsar is asked to abdicate

On 2 March two members of the Duma, A.I. Guchkov and V.V. Shulgin, met the Tsar on the royal train at Pskov. The account which follows was given by Shulgin in the 1960s.

'I said "Petersburg is a mad-house." Guchkov went on to say that under the present circumstances the only way out of the situation might be to abdicate the throne. At that moment, General Ruzskii came in. He sat down between Count Fredericks and myself. Leaning towards me, he whispered in my ear: "The decision has already been made: yesterday was a difficult day."

There was a storm. The Tsar spoke simply and precisely. Only his accent, which was a little strange, betrayed his emotion. "I have taken the decision to abdicate the throne. Until 3 o'clock this afternoon, I thought that I would abdicate in favour of my son, Alexis. Since then I have changed my decision in favour of my brother Mikhail."'

Shulgin speaking in the 1960s

Read Source I very carefully.

I What appears to have been the intention of Guchkov and Shulgin?

2 Which other groups aside from the Duma politicians appear to have influenced the Tsar in making his decision to abdicate?

THE ABDICATION OF THE TSAR (MARCH 1917)

Source J: Nicholas II abdicates

We have judged it right to abdicate the Throne of the Russian State and to lay down the Supreme Power. Not wishing to be parted from Our beloved Son, We hand over Our succession to Our Brother, the Grand Duke Mikhail Alexandrovich and bless Him on his accession to the Throne of the Russian State...May the Lord God help Russia!

Tsar Nicholas II, Pskov, 3.00 pm, 2 March, 1917

The verdict of historians

Source K

About 80,000 metal and textile workers went on strike on 23 February. It also happened to be International Women's Day. It had not been organised by any political party, it was the spontaneous expression of increasing exasperation at the privations and shortages, exacerbated by war. There were 160,000 troops garrisoned in the capital, Petrograd. The regime did not appear to be in danger. The strike gradually spread throughout the city, bringing vast numbers of people onto the streets. On 26 February the troops fired on the demonstrators and drew blood but by the following day the mood of the army was different. The Volhynian regiment went over to the people and set out to convince others to do the same. Other regiments followed. The Cossacks, formerly the most reliable of the imperial guards, changed sides and this doomed the dynasty. The revolution had almost been bloodless; only 587 civilians, 655 soldiers and 73 policemen sealed its victory with their blood.

Martin McCauley, *The Soviet Union Since 1917* (1981)

Source L

The government vigorously suppressed strikes in late 1916. Its nerve seemed unbreakable: a revolt in central Asia by Moslems unwilling to be conscripted was brutally quelled. But the regime's power was in fact weakening. Workers remained the vanguard of the opposition. In February 1917…demonstrations filled the capital's thoroughfares. The Petrograd garrison mutinied. The emperor's appeal to front-line headquarters for armed intervention was made too late and indecisively; in any event, the disenchantment with the monarch had by then spread even to the high command. No civilian or military group wanted autocracy preserved.

Robert Service, *The Russian Revolution 1900-1927* (1986)

Source M

Meanwhile the tsar, still refusing political concessions, attempted to return from army headquarters at Mogilev to his family at Tsarskoe Selo outside the capital. He was prevented from doing so by the presence of revolutionary troops, and the royal train was diverted to Pskov. There, with surprising ease once the real situation in the capital was brought home to him, he abdicated for himself and for his sick son Alexei on 2 March.

Beryl Williams, *The Russian Revolution 1917-1921* (1987)

Source N

Despite the disaffection of the military, however, it was neither the high command nor the Duma politicians, still less the revolutionary parties, which finally brought about the downfall of 'Bloody Nicholas'. It was caused by the upsurge of the politically radicalised masses.

Alan Wood, *The Origins of the Russian Revolution 1861-1917* (1987)

Source O

Many historians consider the February Revolution to be the archetype of a spontaneous revolution and indeed this is how it appears. In Petrograd strikers took to the streets. Soldiers mutinied in sympathy with the crowd. But the regime had already survived far worse. Only by looking beyond the streets and considering the activities of the elite can we really understand why the monarchy fell. In 1905, in the face of the revolutionary threat, the elite had, when it mattered, fallen into line behind the autocracy. This is the crucial difference. In 1917 most of the elite abandoned the monarch.

Chris Read, *The Decline of Tsarism*, Warwick History Video (1987)

Source P

RUSSIA IN TURMOIL 1914-1917

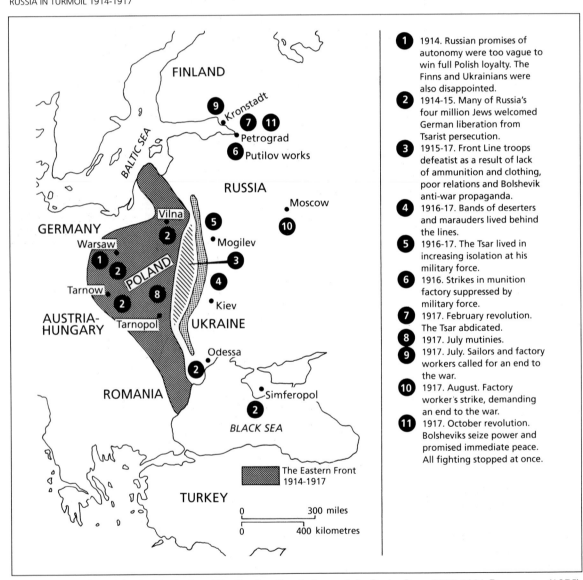

1. 1914. Russian promises of autonomy were too vague to win full Polish loyalty. The Finns and Ukrainians were also disappointed.
2. 1914-15. Many of Russia's four million Jews welcomed German liberation from Tsarist persecution.
3. 1915-17. Front Line troops defeatist as a result of lack of ammunition and clothing, poor relations and Bolshevik anti-war propaganda.
4. 1916-17. Bands of deserters and marauders lived behind the lines.
5. 1916-17. The Tsar lived in increasing isolation at his military force.
6. 1916. Strikes in munition factory suppressed by military force.
7. 1917. February revolution. The Tsar abdicated.
8. 1917. July mutinies.
9. 1917. July. Sailors and factory workers called for an end to the war.
10. 1917. August. Factory worker's strike, demanding an end to the war.
11. 1917. October revolution. Bolsheviks seize power and promised immediate peace. All fighting stopped at once.

Adapted from Martin McCauley, *The Russian Revolution and the Soviet State 1917-1921 Documents* (1975)

Source Q

THE FALL OF THE MONARCHY 1917

Russian territory under German military control in February 1917

* Principal strikes and the mutiny in Petrograd (Sources H, K, L)

⟶ Troops sent against the strikers, but disarmed at Tsarskoye Selo and Luga

+++++ Railways which were largely controlled by railway workers hostile to Tsardom

→ — Route of the Tsar's train. He was prevented from reaching Petrograd on 1 March and abdicated 2 March. (Sources I, J, M)

⟹ Lenin's train route from exile in Switzerland, reaching Petrograd 3 April.

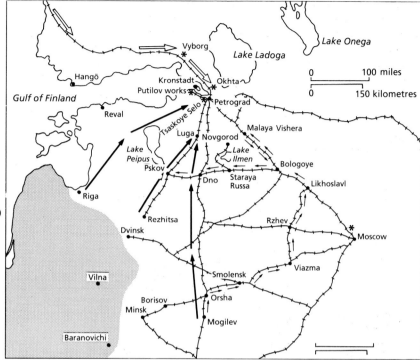

Adapted from Martin McCauley, *The Russian Revolution and the Soviet State 1917-1921 Documents* (1975)

I Look carefully at Sources A to I. Decide how much influence each factor exerted on the Tsar's position. The influence may be favourable (+) or damaging (–).

For each piece of evidence shade in the appropriate ring of the sector to show how much influence it would have had on the Tsar and put a + or –. Eg. Source A - celebrating the Romanovs' anniversary - might be a moderate and positive influence on the Tsar's position so shade in ring 3 of sector A as shown.

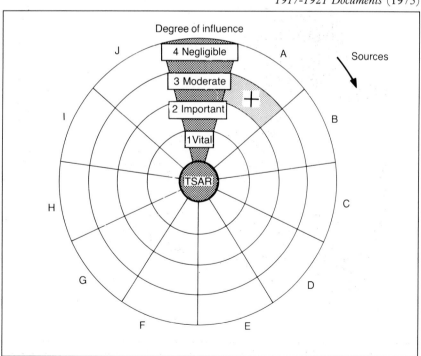

REVIEW

Analysis of causation

Here is a list of factors covered in this chapter which may have helped bring about the Russian Revolution in February 1917.

Factors

1 The damaging legacy of Alexander III and Pobedonostsev.
2 Limitations of Russia's constitutional reform and the weakness of Russia's political institutions.
3 Personal failings of Nicholas II.
4 Dreadful conditions in the towns and factories.
5 Harsh conditions in the countryside and lack of meaningful land reform.
6 Establishment of politically aware, radicalised masses.
7 Bloody Sunday and defeat by Japan.
8 Acute shortages of food in the towns.
9 Widespread strike action in February 1917.
10 Mutiny of soldiers and sailors in February 1917.
11 The limitations of Witte's policies.
12 Repressive aspects of Stolypin's policies.
13 Massive casualties and military reverses in the First World War.
14 The illness of the Tsar's son and the rumours of a relationship between Rasputin and the Tsarina.
15 Dissatisfaction of the Duma and the ruling élite with the Tsar.
16 Disaffection among the General Staff.

Questions

1 Consider the notion that it was solely the defeat in the war which caused the revolution in February 1917. Select factors from the list which support this idea. Construct an argument based entirely on supporting this notion.

2 Which aspects of this mono-causal explanation do you consider to be unsatisfactory? Is it possible to explain a major historical event by looking at a single cause?

3 Consider the short-term causes of the Revolution which exerted influence in February 1917. Select factors from the list which would support the idea that the regime's downfall was based mainly on events in the final few weeks of its existence. How closely were these events connected to the war itself?

4 Look at the long-term structural problems in the autocratic system which Nicholas inherited and did little to change. To what extent were these problems really the underlying causes of the Russian Revolution? Did the war simply accelerate the regime's inevitable downfall?

5 Now consider this recent examination question. 'It was defeat in the war which was the real cause of the Russian Revolution.' Discuss this statement.

2(a) Decide from the sources which separate groups of people were influencing the Tsar.
(b) Look at your finished diagram and decide who had the most influence on the Tsar's position.

3 Read Sources K to O. These are the points of view of five historians. Decide who each historian feels was chiefly responsible for the abdication of Tsar Nicholas. Summarise the viewpoint of each one. Finally, which historian's viewpoint do you find the most convincing and why?

5 The Struggle for Peace 1918-20

PREVIEW

TALKING POINT

Is it possible after war on such a scale to search for peace rather than victory?

FIRST WORLD WAR MEMORIAL

THE WALKING WOUNDED. A CAPTURED GERMAN SOLDIER IN THE FIRST WORLD WAR

The casualty figures of the major powers

	Standing armies and trained reserves	Total mobilised	Killed or died of wounds	Total military casualties
Austria-Hungary	3,000,000	7,800,000	1,200,000	7,020,000
British Empire	975,000	8,904,000	908,000	3,190,235
France	4,017,000	8,410,000	1,363,000	6,160,800
Germany	4,500,000	11,000,000	1,774,000	7,142,558
Italy	1,251,000	5,615,000	460,000	2,197,000
Russia	5,971,000	12,000,000	1,700,000	9,150,000
Turkey	210,000	2,850,000	325,000	975,000

The forgotten peace: the Peace of Brest-Litovsk

While the Peace of Versailles, which marked the end of the conflict in the west, has continued to be the subject of much historical debate, the Peace of Brest-Litovsk which formed the basis of the settlement in the east has received much less attention. Nevertheless, the treaty had massive implications not only in terms of its domestic impact on Russia and Germany but also with regard to the final outcome of the First World War. Indeed, the allegedly brutal manner in which the Russians were treated by Germany was often brought up to defend the Versailles peace against German accusations of unfairness.

In 1914 Lenin had forecast that the massive strain imposed by the 'capitalist' war would eventually bring down the tsarist regime. In the aftermath of the first revolution in March 1917 Lenin was able to see at first hand Kerensky's failure to turn the war around during the summer of that year. Finally, Lenin was well aware of the importance of his promise to withdraw Russia from the war in enabling the Bolsheviks to triumph over Kerensky in November 1917.

Peace with Germany at any price was therefore necessary for practical as well as ideological reasons. In any case, the Bolsheviks would have been unable to consolidate the domestic revolution and continue the war in the east. Lastly, Lenin hoped that the general feeling of war weariness among the demoralised troops at the front would lead to desertion on a vast scale among German as well as Russian troops. In his biography, Adam Ulam writes that to some extent 'the Bolsheviks had been taken in by their own propaganda: they would take over power, issue a worldwide appeal for peace, Russian soldiers would begin fraternization with those in the opposing trenches. Soon the German armies would dissolve into a mass of soviets, kick out their officers and conclude a people's peace: very simple.'

However, two things quickly became apparent to Lenin: first, Russia's western allies were not even prepared to recognise the Bolshevik Government let alone join in negotiations for a general European peace. Secondly, the separate peace which Russia would therefore have to conduct with Germany and Austria-Hungary would be negotiated with the old military and political establishment, not the representatives of the soldiers in the trenches.

So it was that Leon Trotsky, the revolutionary People's Commissar for War came face to face with the aristocratic German officer corps. The setting was the small provincial town of Brest-Litovsk close to the Russian border

Why did the issue of whether or not to continue with the war assume so much importance in Russia?

Why were the Allies so hostile to the Bolshevik regime and its negotiations with Germany?

RUSSIAN SOLDIERS ATTEMPT TO COPE WITH FREEZING CONDITIONS ON THE EASTERN FRONT

with Germany. At stake was all the territory gained by Russia in the previous 300 years. Trotsky was initially optimistic that he would be able to resist Germany's territorial demands, but the German historian Fritz Fischer indicates the severity of the problems he faced in the following extract from *Germany's Aims in the First World War:*

'Lenin's victory over Kerensky on November 6 and 7, 1917 could not but seem to the German government to be the crown of their military and political campaign against Russia since the autumn of 1914. At last the Russian colossus had collapsed under the pincer movement of military pressure and the social revolution fostered by Germany through the Bolsheviks... The new rulers in Petersburg were in a dilemma: on the one hand, they had come to power under the slogan of peace, and they therefore needed an immediate end to hostilities...On the other hand, they could not accept peace at any price, for fear of strengthening the right-wing Social Revolutionaries and the Mensheviks...

'The German government saw the Bolsheviks' dilemma and decided to exploit it ruthlessly, in order not only to secure the comprehensive solution in the east for which it had so long been working, but also by concluding a separate peace with Russia, to decide the issue in the west and thus achieve the whole of their war aims.'

Trotsky had proved himself to be a brilliant revolutionary, a supremely gifted writer and orator. At Brest-Litovsk his inexperience in diplomacy and foreign affairs was to be put to the test.

Assess the strengths and weaknesses of

(a) Russia
(b) Germany

approaching the negotiations at Brest-Litovsk.

TROTSKY AND THE RUSSIAN DELEGATION RECEIVED AT BREST-LITOVSK BY GERMAN OFFICERS (JANUARY 1918)

5.1 Brest-Litovsk: the forgotten peace.
The anatomy of a peace conference

1 Russia's aims at Brest-Litovsk

(i) 'The Russian Revolution will not bow its head before German imperialism...The Bolsheviks will sign only an honourable peace.'

Remark made by Trotsky to Russian soldiers on his way to Brest-Litovsk (November 1917)

(ii) 'We no longer desire to participate in this purely imperialist war... In the expectation of the near moment when the oppressed working classes of all nations will, as happened in Russia, take power in their own hands, we take our army and nation out of war...the war is to be discontinued; peace is not to be signed, and the army is to be demobilised.'

Trotsky (28 January 1918)

(iii) 'The position of Comrade Trotsky represents no policy at all...In October we talked about the sacred revolutionary war, because we were promised that one word "peace" would bring about a revolution in the West. But that has not come to pass.'

Stalin's view of Trotsky's 'Neither Peace Nor War' formula (February 1918)

(iv) 'If the Germans should demand the overturn of the Bolshevik Government, then, of course, we should have to fight. All other demands can and should be granted. We have heard the statement made that the Germans are going to take Livonia and Estonia. We can very well sacrifice these for the sake of the Revolution. If they demand the removal of our troops from Finland, well and good. Let them take revolutionary Finland. Even if we give up Finland, Livonia and Estonia we shall retain the Revolution. I recommend that we sign the peace terms offered to us by the Germans.'

Lenin proposes acceptance of the German terms (February 1918)

2 Russia's view of German war aims

'The principles of a general democratic peace without annexations are accepted by the nations of the Central Powers...Germany and its allies have no plans whatsoever of territorial aggrandizement.'

Statement by Russian peace delegation, headed by Joffe and Trotsky as reported in the Petrograd press (January 1918)

3 Germany's aims at Brest-Litovsk

(i) 'As regards Russia, we have to solve the extraordinarily difficult task of establishing a good economic and political relationship with the new Russia, in order to keep our rear militarily completely free, while at the same time detaching huge areas from the present Russia and building up these districts into effective bulwarks on our frontier.'

Kuhlmann to Hindenburg

(ii) 'There is only one thing for them to choose now - under what sauce are they to be devoured.'

Private comment by Kuhlmann to Count Czernin, the Austrian Foreign Minister, at Brest-Litovsk.

(iii) 'A peace which only assured the territorial status quo would mean that we had lost the war. Such a peace in the east has never been considered. In the west things are not yet clear.'

General Ludendorff (January 1918)

(iv) 'The Russian delegation talks to us as if it stood victorious in our countries and could dictate conditions to us. I would like to point out that the facts are just the reverse: that the victorious German army stands in your territory.'

General Hoffman to the Russian delegation at Brest-Litovsk

Territory lost by Russia

Western boundary of the Ukrainian Republic (Treaty of 9 February 1918)

Furthest extent of the Central Powers' occupation of Russia and the Ukraine by May 1918

| 0 | | 250 miles |
| 0 | | 500 km |

FINLAND

Stockholm

Hanko

St. Petersburg

ESTONIA

RUSSIA

Moscow

Riga

LATVIA

Orel

Voronezh

Tannenberg

Kursk

Brest Litovsk

GERMANY

Warsaw

Kiev

Lublin

Kholm

R. Dnieper

Lemberg

R. Don

Gorlice

UKRAINE

BUKOVINA

AUSTRIA-HUNGARY

Vittorio
Veneto

Caporetto

ROMANIA

SERBIA

BULGARIA

ALBANIA

Salonika

TURKEY

Dardanelles

Smyrna

Dodecanese

Cyprus

Damascus

Crete

Jerusalem

Gaza

QUESTIONS

1 What divisions are apparent in the Russian stance over peace negotiations?

2 Look at Section 2. What light does this shed on Russian perceptions of German war aims? Was this perception shared by Lenin?

3 Which extract in Section 3 tells us most, in your opinion, about the true nature of Germany's intentions?

4 What perception did the German delegates seem to have of Russia's position? How do you explain this?

5 Look at the above map. What conclusions would you draw from it?

Brest-Litovsk: the verdict of historians

Source A: A German historian

Judgements on the 'forgotten peace' range between condemnation of it as a peace of force, as foreign critics saw it at the time, and the ebullient praise given to it by Wilhelm II as one of the 'greatest successes of world history'...After 1919 the Allies often retorted to German criticisms of the Treaty of Versailles by pointing to the ruthless severity of the Peace of Brest-Litovsk...It is also often pointed out that the Brest-Litovsk Treaty did not take away a single square yard of ethnically Russian territory, so that they cannot be held up as examples of German annexationism.

Fritz Fischer, *Germany's Aims in the First World War* (1967)

Source B: An American historian

On 1 March the Soviet delegates again reached Brest-Litovsk...to sign the most humiliating peace in Russia's modern history...On March 3 the treaty was signed. Russia had lost the Ukraine, Finland, her Polish and Baltic territories. In the Caucasus she had to make territorial concessions to Turkey. The treaty placed the German sphere of occupation close to Petrograd, which on its other side was precariously close to Finland, where the Finnish Bolsheviks were being ejected by the nationalists with German help. Three centuries of Russian territorial expansion were undone.

Adam B. Ulam, *Lenin and the Bolsheviks* (1966)

TALKING POINT
Brest-Litovsk: a true reflection of the military situation or an unjust 'carve-up'. Which view would you support?

Collapse in the West: the peace of 1918-19

The First World War finally came to an end on 11 November 1918 when the Germans formally surrendered to the Allies. The armistice was signed at 5 am in a railway carriage in a forest clearing at Compiégne. The peace took effect at 11 am when the guns finally fell silent on the Western front. However, Britain and France had channelled all their energies into winning the war and had given little prior thought to planning the peace. The sudden collapse of the German war effort took everyone by surprise, and so it was agreed that the details of the peace settlement would be drawn up at a conference to be held in the New Year.

Germany would be obliged to send representatives to receive and agree to the terms, but they would not be invited to take part in the meetings or discussions. Nevertheless, it is vital to appreciate that at this stage Germany fully expected the peace settlement to be based on the principle of 'Peace without victory' announced by US President Wilson; a principle which had been at the centre of the preliminary talks leading to German surrender.

The Great War had cost the lives of more than 8 million men while over 21 million others were wounded. Russia lost 1.75 million men and the Germans almost 2 million. 250,000 French buildings were destroyed and 8,000 square miles of agricultural land were laid waste. It was estimated that the war had cost Britain almost £9 billion.

The horrendous casualty figures and the enormous physical damage had two major political consequences. First and perhaps not surprisingly they

MILITARY LEADERS OUTSIDE THE RAILWAY CARRIAGE WHERE THE ARMISTICE WAS DECLARED

1 Why were the Germans anxious to see an armistice based on US peace proposals?

2 What would have been the attitude of the Allies towards separate negotiations between Germany and the US?

SIGNING THE ARMISTICE

combined to create among the victors an overwhelming desire for revenge against Germany. Secondly, it would soon become apparent that the so-called victors were physically and economically exhausted. The European powers were completely drained and in retrospect it was plain to see that the power-base had shifted towards the emerging powers of the USA and Japan.

Those who desired revenge were particularly keen to see Kaiser William II brought to justice, and the slogan 'Hang the Kaiser' seemed to dominate the popular press in the build-up to the conference. However, two days before the armistice was signed, the Kaiser abdicated and slipped across the border to the Netherlands where he was to live out his political exile in the comfort of an imposing castle. Meanwhile, General Ludendorff, second only to Hindenburg in the German military establishment, had donned false whiskers and spectacles and made his escape to a safe haven in Sweden. Ludendorff could not accept that Germany had lost the war and placed the blame on the socialists in the Reichstag. Before his hasty departure he commented: 'I have asked His Majesty to bring those circles into the government to whom we mainly owe it that we are in this position. We will therefore now see these gentlemen assume ministerial posts. They are now to make the peace which must now be made. They shall now eat the soup they have brewed for us.'

Many of the factors that were to dominate the peace settlement were already falling into place. The trauma of defeat had led the old political establishment to abdicate responsibility, leaving the representatives of German's embryonic democracy to face the stigma of accepting defeat and punishment. The desire for revenge felt by the people of France and Britain was only heightened by the Kaiser's exile. Pressure for severe anti-German measures from the press represented a relatively new but highly significant ingredient. In these circumstances it was clear that the Americans - who had occupied the high moral ground as the only disinterested party - would play a key role in the making of the peace.

What changes in Germany's government were brought about by the collapse of the war effort?

Russia's dramatic withdrawal from the war in the east served to heighten the importance of the US entry in April 1917. Having played such an important part in swinging the balance of the war towards the Allies, America now sought to play an equally important role in the peacemaking process. On 4 December 1918 the US cruiser *George Washington* set sail from New York harbour for the port of Brest in France. On board was Woodrow Wilson, 62 years old, leader of the Democratic Party and, since 1912, President of the United States of America. In the following extract J.A. Thompson highlights the importance of his mission.

'Woodrow Wilson was the first American President to leave the Western Hemisphere during his period of office, and, as befitted him, the circumstances in which he did so were neither casual nor frivolous. He went to Europe in late 1918 to take part in the peace conference following a war that the United States had played a crucial part in bringing to a decisive end. His aim was to secure a peace that accorded with the proposals he had set out in his Fourteen Points address of January 1918 and in other speeches - a peace that would be based upon justice and thus secure consent, that would embody liberal principles (the self-determination of peoples as far as practicable, the prohibition of discriminatory trade barriers) and that would be maintained by a new international organisation in which the United States,

1 What factors were contributing to the development of isolationist feeling in the US at this time?

2 What impact did the US casualty figures have on American public opinion?

3 Can you explain why Wilson might have failed to appreciate the changes in public opinion at this time?

4 What was the significance of these developments for Wilson's standing at the peace conference?

AMERICAN TROOPS ARRIVE AT LE HAVRE, 1918. HEAVY CASUALTIES WERE SOON TO FOLLOW, CHANGING THE MOOD OF THE AMERICAN PUBLIC

breaking its tradition of isolation, would take part - a league of nations that would provide a general guarantee of "political independence and territorial integrity to great and small states alike."'

As the *George Washington* sailed out of Hoboken harbour in New York it was passed by a shipload of American troops returning home from the battlefields of the Great War. It was rather ironic that the President who wanted to step up American intervention in Europe was heading in one direction while the dead and the wounded were being brought back home in the other.

The psychological impact on the American public of seeing the wounded and the dead brought back home was immense. Even though the USA had not joined in the war until April 1917, almost three years after the fighting in Europe had started, 115,000 American troops were killed before the war was brought to a close by the German surrender of November 1918. It seems fair to say that at this stage, Wilson's preoccupation with Europe may have led him to underestimate the increasing desire for isolationism in America. However, the high casualty figures were enough to convince most Americans that the USA should never again become involved in a European conflict.

To make matters worse, Wilson had caused a political storm when he made clear that his diplomatic team in Paris would not include any members of the Senate and would contain only one member of the Republican Party. Wilson had ignored the convention of consultation with the Senate and had made powerful enemies who were eager for revenge when he returned to Washington in July 1919.

The *George Washington* arrived in Brest on 13 December 1918. The French President, Raymond Poincaré sent his own train to bring Wilson from the port to Paris and he arrived in the capital to a hero's welcome. The

French people made their gratitude to America clear but it was also apparent that they expected the American President to support them in their desire for revenge. Indeed the choice of Paris as a venue for the peace conference seemed solely designed to heighten anti-German sympathies. Wilson's steadfast refusal to commit himself to the French point of view highlighted the fact that there was a substantial difference between the French, with their desire for revenge, and the Americans who stood for a more abstract 'Peace without victory'.

The polarity of these positions meant that the stance adopted by Britain would be absolutely vital. The importance of public opinion in influencing the politicians was heightened by the fact that a general election was being fought out in December 1918. It was difficult for any politician to resist climbing onto the popular bandwagon of 'Hang the Kaiser' and 'Make Germany Pay' which was being whipped up by the popular press in the build-up to the election at home and the peace conference in Paris. Look carefully at the evidence that follows, not only to establish what differences existed in the aims of the 'Big Three' but also to assess the various factors involved in leading the politicians to arrive at these policies.

Examining the Evidence

Versailles - the aims of the peacemakers

Source A: Great Britain - Lloyd-George

(i) There will be vigorous attempts made in certain quarters to...induce and cajole the Government to here and there depart from the strict principles of right, in order to satisfy some base and some sordid, and if I may say squalid, principles of either revenge or avarice. We must relentlessly set our faces against that.

Lloyd-George speaking to liberals at a pre-election meeting, 12 November 1918

(ii) Our first task must be to conclude a just and lasting peace, and so to establish the foundations of a new Europe.

Extract from Lloyd-George's election manifesto, 22 November 1918

(iii) We propose to demand the whole cost of the war from Germany.

Lloyd-George, 11 December 1918

(iv) We are a government and people seeking no selfish and predatory aims of any kind, pursuing with one mind and one unchanging purpose: to obtain justice for others. We desire neither to destroy Germany nor diminish her boundaries: we seek neither to exalt ourselves nor to enlarge our Empire.

Lloyd-George, 5 January 1919

(v) He was especially interested in the question of reparations, and said that if I would help him out in this direction, he would be extremely grateful. By 'helping him out' he meant: to give a plausible reason to his people for having fooled them about the question of war costs, reparations and what not. He admitted that he knew Germany could not pay anything like the indemnity which the British and French demanded.

Colonel House (Senior US delegate) note of a conversation with Lloyd-George in Paris.

LLOYD-GEORGE, David (1863-1945)

British Liberal statesman.

1890-1945 Member of Parliament

1915-16 Minister of Munitions

1916 Secretary for War

1916-22 Prime Minister. Dynamic and efficient wartime leader

1919 Attended Paris Peace Conference

Source B: The USA - Woodrow Wilson

(i) It must be a peace without victory...Victory would mean peace forced upon the loser, a victor's terms imposed upon the vanquished. It would be accepted in humiliation, under duress, as an intolerable sacrifice, and would leave a sting, a resentment, a bitter memory upon which terms of peace would rest, not permanently, but only as upon quicksand. Such a peace was the 'only...sort of peace that the peoples of America could join in guaranteeing.'

Woodrow Wilson, Address to the Senate, 22 January 1917

(ii) A Summary of Woodrow Wilson's Fourteen Points

1 Open covenants of peace, openly arrived at, after which there shall be no private international understandings of any kind.

2 Absolute freedom of navigation upon the seas...alike in peace and in war.

3 The removal, so far as possible, of all economic barriers.

4 Adequate guarantees given and taken that national armaments will be reduced to the lowest point consistent with domestic safety.

5 A free, open-minded and impartial adjustment of all colonial claims, based upon a strict observance of the principle that the interests of the population concerned must have equal weight with the equitable claims of the government whose title is to be determined.

6 The evacuation of all Russian territory and...a settlement of all questions affecting Russia.

7 Belgium...must be evacuated and restored.

8 All French territory should be freed and the invaded portions restored, and the wrong done to France by Prussia in 1871 in the matter of Alsace-Lorraine...should be righted.

9 A readjustment of the frontiers of Italy should be effected along clearly recognizable lines of nationality.

10 The peoples of Austria-Hungary...should be accorded the freest opportunity of autonomous development.

11 Romania, Serbia and Montenegro should be evacuated; occupied territories restored; Serbia accorded free and secure access to the sea;...and international guarantees of the political and economic independence and territorial integrity of the several Balkan States should be entered into.

12 The Turkish portions of the present Ottoman empire should be assured a secure sovereignty, but the other nationalities which are now under Turkish rule should be assured...an absolutely unmolested opportunity of autonomous development, and the Dardanelles should be permanently opened as a free passage to the ships and commerce of all nations under international guarantees.

13 An independent Polish State should be erected which should include the territories inhabited by indisputably Polish populations, which should be assured a free and secure access to the sea.

14 A general association of nations must be formed under specific covenants for the purposes of affording mutual guarantees of political independence and territorial integrity to great and small states alike.

From Ruth Henig, *Versailles and After (1919-1933)* (1984)

(iii) We have used great words, all or us; we have used the great words 'right' and 'justice', and now we are to prove whether or not we understand these words and how they are to be applied to the particular settlements which must conclude this war.

Woodrow Wilson, Buckingham Palace, 27 December 1918

Source C: France - Poincaré and Clemenceau

(i) Mr President. A few months ago you cabled to me that the USA would send to invaded France ever increasing forces able to submerge the enemy under an overwhelming flow of new divisions, and in fact, flowing more that a year a continuous tide of youth and energy has poured onto the shores of France. Eager though they were to meet the enemy they were yet unaware when they arrived of his monstrous crimes. To obtain a proper view of the German conduct of war, they had to witness the systematically burnt down cities, the flooded mines and the crumbling factories. You will have the opportunity, Mr. President, to inspect with your own eyes the extent of that disaster.

The French government will also furnish you with authentic documents in which the German general staff develops its plan of plunder and industrial annihilation. Should it remain unpunished...the most splendid victories would be useless.'

Speech of welcome, President Poincaré to Wilson, Paris, 14 December 1918

CLEMENCEAU, Georges (1841-1929)

French radical statesman.

1871 Entered National Assembly

1876 Elected Deputy

1876-93 Leader of the extreme Left

1893 Lost seat in chamber - returned after supporting Dreyfus

1902-20 Senator

1906 Minister of the Interior

1906-09 Prime Minister

1917-20 Appointed Prime Minister again and Minister of War

1919 Presided at Paris Peace Conference

1920 Lost presidential election

1 Did Lloyd-George maintain a consistent position before and during the conference?

2 What evidence is there that Lloyd-George gave a rather misleading impression during the election campaign?

3 Read Poincaré's speech of welcome very carefully.

(a) What phrases would you pick out to highlight the damage done by the Germans?

(b) What would you say was Poincaré's main objective in making this speech?

4 Based on the evidence of his intentions, write a draft speech of reply which could have been given by Wilson.

The Versailles settlement: a bitter peace

The preliminary peace conference was opened at the French Foreign Ministry in the Quai d'Orsay on 18 January 1919 and concluded when the peace terms were presented to the German delegation on 7 May. Although 32 states were officially represented, the whole conference only came together six times. Ultimately the talks were dominated by the 'big four': President Wilson of the USA, Prime Minister Lloyd-George of Great Britain, Premier Clemenceau of France and Prime Minister Orlando of Italy. Much of the historical verdict on the manner in which the negotiations were carried out has been critical. The historian Sally Marks describes how the big four 'proceeded in slipshod fashion without agenda, minutes, or any record of decisions until the secretary of the British delegation, the supremely efficient Colonel Sir Maurice Hankey, insinuated himself into their midst and rescued them from disaster. Even then, the agenda darted from topic to topic, and the big four were startlingly erratic in either accepting, ignoring or rejecting expert reports.'

The range of problems facing the main protagonists was immense but the range of agreement was narrow. Relations between Wilson, Lloyd-George and Clemenceau began coolly and got worse. Clemenceau, nicknamed 'the Tiger' and with a fearsome appearance that matched his reputation, soon made it clear that he was not impressed by Wilson's idealism: 'God gave us the Ten Commandments and we broke them, Wilson gave us the Fourteen Points. We shall see'. On another occasion Clemenceau asked: 'How can I talk to a fellow who thinks himself the first man for two thousand years who has known anything about peace on earth?' Wilson soon began to feel the strain of dealing with Clemenceau and fell ill on 3 April. Clemenceau was scarcely able to conceal his delight, telling Lloyd-George, 'He is worse today', before doubling up with laughter. Clemenceau showed that his ill-feeling was not confined to Wilson when, after a heated debate, he threatened to assault Lloyd-George. An assassination attempt on Clemenceau that left the 78-year-old premier with a grazed lung added to the morbid atmosphere that seems to have characterised the conference.

It is when this personal animosity is set against the background of the range of technical problems which were faced that the shortcomings of the conference can be most easily understood. The historian A. Lentin in his book *Guilt at Versailles* highlights the practical problems encountered by Wilson in seeking to implement the worthy ideal of national self-determination. 'He was ignorant, when he promised Italy the South Tyrol, that its population was Austrian. When he approved the boundaries of Czechoslovakia, he had no idea that they contained three million Germans. When he assented to the incorporation of Transylvania within Roumania, he was unaware of sanctioning an act of annexation.'

Ultimately the complexities of the problem were pushed aside in order to produce a finished treaty. After four months of argument the treaty was hurriedly brought together at the end of April. When it was rushed to the printers at the beginning of May nobody had read the document - with its 440 clauses and more than 200 pages - in full or obtained a clear idea of its overall stance. The treaty was presented to the Germans, essentially in the form of an ultimatum, at a tense ceremony on 7 May 1919. It was made clear to Germany that refusal to sign the treaty would mean that they would once

PUNCH CARTOON SHOWS
GERMAN HUMILIATION AT
VERSAILLES

GHOSTS AT VERSAILLES.

again be at war. It was hard for the Germans to see any common ground
between the 14 points and the severity of the new treaty. In a terse speech
the head of the German delegation, Brockdorff-Rantzau, set the tone of bitterness and resentment which was to characterise the German response. 'We
are under no illusions as to the extent of our defeat and the degree of our
powerlessness.'

A SCENE FROM THE VERSAILLES CONFERENCE, 1919

What would be your
major criticisms of the
way the peacemakers
went about their
business?

Germany's outspoken resentment at the manner in which the terms had been dictated to them only served to harden the position on both sides, and the only amendments made to the treaty were minor ones. On 28 June 1919 the conference finally came to an end when the Germans signed the treaty in the Hall of Mirrors in the glittering Palace of Versailles. The very room that had been the scene of German's unification and triumphant victory over France in 1871 now symbolised national humiliation. The fate of Germany had been decided and when the terms were made public they dismayed the German nation.

EXAMINING THE EVIDENCE

Versailles: the verdict

The terms of the Versailles Peace Treaty

Among the 440 Articles of the Treaty were:

Article 42: Germany is not to maintain or construct any fortifications either on the left bank of the Rhine or on the right bank to the west of a line drawn 50 kilometres to the east.

Article 45: As compensation for the destruction of the coal mines in the north of France, and as part payment towards the total reparations due, Germany gives to France the coal mines of the Saar. At the end of 15 years, its inhabitants shall be asked under which government they wish to be placed.

Article 80: Germany acknowledges and will respect strictly the independence of Austria...she agrees that this independence will be inalienable.

Article 102: The Principal Allied and Associated Powers undertake to establish the town of Danzig...as a Free City. It will be placed under the protection of the League of Nations.

Article 119: Germany renounces in favour of the Principal Allied and Associated Powers all her rights and titles over her overseas possessions.

Article 160: By a date not later than 31 March 1920, the German army must not consist of more than seven divisions of infantry and three of cavalry (ie, not more than 100,000 men).

Article 231: The Allied governments affirm, and Germany accepts, the responsibility of Germany and her allies for causing all the loss and damage to which the Allied governments and their peoples have been subjected as a result of the war.

Article 232: The Allied governments recognise that the resources of Germany are not adequate to make complete reparation for all such loss and damage...But they require, and Germany undertakes, that she will make compensation for all the damage done to the civilian population of the Allied powers and to their property during the war.

Article 428: As a guarantee that the treaty shall be carried out, the German territory to the west of the Rhine will be occupied by...Allied troops for 15 years.

The German reaction to the Versailles settlement.

The German Delegation has just been handed details of the peace terms. The key points are shown opposite.

(a) Write a brief assessment from the German standpoint indicating which terms are most severe and which are easier to accept.

(b) Now set out your arguments for revision of the treaty before it is signed.

You could emphasise the impact the terms might have on Europe as a whole, as well as Germany.

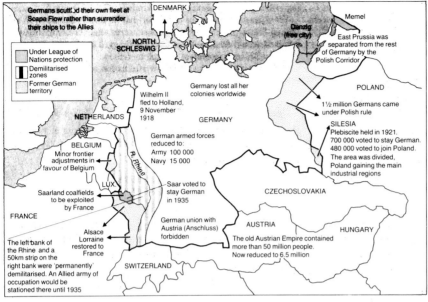

Germans scuttled their own fleet at Scapa Flow rather than surrender their ships to the Allies

Under League of Nations protection

Demilitarised zones

Former German territory

DENMARK

NORTH SCHLESWIG

Memel

Danzig (free city)

East Prussia was separated from the rest of Germany by the Polish Corridor

Wilhelm II fled to Holland, 9 November 1918

Germany lost all her colonies worldwide

POLAND

1½ million Germans came under Polish rule

NETHERLANDS

GERMANY

German armed forces reduced to:
Army 100 000
Navy 15 000

SILESIA
Plebiscite held in 1921.
700 000 voted to stay German.
480 000 voted to join Poland.
The area was divided, Poland gaining the main industrial regions

BELGIUM
Minor frontier adjustments in favour of Belgium

R. Rhine

LUX

Saarland coalfields to be exploited by France

Saar voted to stay German in 1935

CZECHOSLOVAKIA

FRANCE

Alsace Lorraine restored to France

German union with Austria (Anschluss) forbidden

AUSTRIA

HUNGARY

The old Austrian Empire contained more than 50 million people. Now reduced to 6.5 million

The left bank of the Rhine and a 50km strip on the right bank were 'permanently' demilitarised. An Allied army of occupation would be stationed there until 1935

SWITZERLAND

THE MAIN TERMS OF THE TREATY OF VERSAILLES

I Which of the terms seem to have been designed to

(a) Punish Germany
(b) Improve French security
(c) Reward the victors.

2 Which clauses do you think Germany found most offensive and why?

3 Does your analysis suggest that Wilson restrained Clemenceau or not?

4 What was more important to the national delegations: self-interest, or the achievement of a satisfactory European peace settlement?

The contemporary response

Source A

There follow several extracts from *The Economic Consequences of the Peace*, a famous contemporary criticism written by a brilliant young economist who resigned from the British delegation at Paris with the words that he was walking away from the scene of a nightmare.

(i) 'The future life of Europe was not their concern: its means of livelihood was not their anxiety. Their preoccupations, good and bad alike related to frontiers and nationalities, to the balance of power, to imperial aggrandisements, to the future enfeeblement of a strong and dangerous enemy, to revenge, and to the shifting by the victors of their unbearable financial burdens on to the shoulders of the defeated.'

(ii) 'Europe, if she is to survive her troubles, will need so much magnanimity from America, that she must herself practise it. It is useless for the Allies, hot from stripping Germany and one another, to turn for help to the United States to put the states of Europe, including Germany on to their feet again.'

KEYNES, JOHN MAYNARD (1883-1946)
British economist. Worked at Treasury during WW1. Chief representative at negotiations prior to Treaty of Versailles. Criticised reparations plans in *The Economic Consequences of the Peace*, 1919. Resigned from British delegation at Versailles.

(iii) 'Most estimates of a great indemnity from Germany depend on the assumption that she is in the position to conduct in the future a vastly greater-trade than she has ever had in the past.'

John Maynard Keynes, *The Economic Consequences of the Peace* (1919)

Source B

If there is one country that the Germans are determined to get even with it is France. The Germans will try by every means to...isolate France...[to] render the pledges of the United States null and void is the dominating idea of the individual German...and one hears talk about a next war, first with Poland, later with France. Never was it more necessary for the Allies to watch Germany closely.   *The Times*, 2 July 1919

Source C

Not stern merely, but actually punitive...There is not a single person among the younger people here who is not unhappy and disappointed at the terms. The only people who approve are the old fire-eaters...If I were the Germans, I shouldn't sign it for a moment.'

Harold Nicolson, *Diary*, 1919

Source D

We are all so disgusted with the peace that we have ceased to discuss it.

Beatrice Webb, 1919

THE RECKONING
PAN-GERMAN 'MONSTROUS, I CALL IT. WHY, IT'S FULLY A QUARTER OF WHAT *WE* SHOULD HAVE MADE *THEM* PAY, IF WE'D WON.'

The verdict of historians

Source A

The fundamental significance of Versailles...was emotional rather than rational. Allied statesmen, urged on by the pressure of public opinion, had made peace in a spirit of revenge. The cries of 'Hang the Kaiser' and 'squeezing the German lemon until the pips squeak' were indicative of the desire not merely for a guarantee of future security, but for the national humiliation of Germany...The Germans saw every difficulty in subsequent years as a further indignity that they alone must suffer as a result of the hated Treaty of Versailles.

Anthony Wood, *Europe 1815-1960* (1986)

Source B

It was a wise precept of Machiavelli that the victor should either conciliate his enemy or destroy him. The Treaty of Versailles did neither. It did not pacify Germany, still less permanently weaken her, appearances notwithstanding, but left her scourged, humiliated and resentful. It was neither a Wilson peace nor a Clemenceau peace, but a witches' brew concocted of the least palatable ingredients of each which, though highly distasteful to Germany, were by no means fatal.

A. Lentin, *Guilt at Versailles* (1984)

Source C

Severe as the Treaty of Versailles seemed to many Germans, it should be remembered that Germany might easily have fared much worse. If Clemenceau had had his way, instead of being restrained by Britain and America, the Rhineland would have become an independent state, the Saarland would have been annexed to France and Danzig would have become an integral part of Poland...However, the Germans as a nation were not inclined to count their blessings in 1919...Most of all they resented the

Prepare three leading articles that could have appeared in the press immediately after the peace terms had been signed:

(a) From the French standpoint
(b) From the American standpoint
(c) From the British viewpoint.

Each piece of writing (about 10-15 lines) should assess the success of the peace.

moral stigma of sole war-guilt which they did not feel...Finally, the fact that the treaty was not negotiated but dictated to Germany and signed in humiliating circumstances made it certain that the German people would accept no responsibility for its fulfilment. To the discerning it was clear from the beginning that the Versailles settlement would last only as long as the victorious powers were in a position to enforce it on a bitterly resentful people.

William Carr, *A History of Germany 1815-1945* (1985)

1 Summarise the criticisms of the peace conference made by Keynes: what do they have in common?

2 Have the criticisms made by Keynes been repeated and endorsed by historians or rejected?

3 To what extent would you now say that Germany's punishment was psychological rather than physical?

4 Was Germany's hostile reaction to the Treaty justified
(a) at the time?
(b) in retrospect?

Review

Debate:

The motion is that the Versailles Treaty was harsh and short-sighted.

Two students should speak in favour of the motion. They:
(a) Could outline factual support and detailed points to illustrate ways in which the treaty may have been unduly harsh;
(b) Could criticise the treaty in a more general sense, for example by pointing to its underlying principles and the catastrophic consequences which followed it.

Two students should speak against the motion. They:
(a) Could argue against the motion on a factual basis;
(b) Could criticise the motion in a more general sense. Was the treaty really as harsh as the Germans made it out to be. Couldn't it have been a lot harsher? What about the peace of Brest-Litovsk when Germany imposed a harsh settlement on Russia?

Woodrow Wilson: America fails to join the League

Four months of bitter negotiations with Clemenceau had taken their toll on Wilson and on 29 June, with the ink scarcely dry on the Treaty of Versailles, he set sail for home. A band played the Star Spangled Banner as the *George Washington* pulled out of Brest harbour, but Wilson was weary and in no mood for celebration. To many observers he had been unable to restrain the French president in his overwhelming desire for revenge. Wilson's personal correspondence from this time seems to reveal a man who was close to the end of his tether. He complained to his personal physician of sleeplessness, headaches and indigestion. The feeling of euphoria which had accompanied his arrival in France must have seemed a distant memory to

Article 10 of the Covenant of the League of Nations

'The members of the League undertake to respect and preserve as against external aggression the territorial integrity and existing political independence of all Members of the League. In case of any such aggression or in case of any threat or danger of such aggression the Council shall advise upon the means by which this obligation shall be fulfilled.'

TALKING POINT

Why do you think Wilson regarded Article 10 as the cornerstone of the League? Should he have agreed to its removal in order to secure American membership of the League?

him as he contemplated the struggle which he knew awaited him back in the USA.

When Wilson finally arrived at the Union Station in Washington DC on 8 July he was welcomed by a crowd of 100,000 well-wishers. He knew that when he presented the treaty and the Covenant to the Senate for signature the reception would be less warm.

America could only join the League of Nations if the Senate gave its approval but Wilson's failure to consult the Senate before he went to Paris had not been forgotten or forgiven. Within the Senate a group known as the Irreconcilables had been formed under the leadership of Senator Borah. These politicians would not consider American membership under any circumstances. A second, more moderate group of senators led by Henry Cabot Lodge wanted Wilson to remove Article 10 of the Covenant before they would sign.

On 10 July Wilson was ready to present the Treaty of Versailles to the Senate. As he walked into the Senate Chamber with the treaty under his arm, Senator Lodge, who was walking by his side, inquired, 'Mr. President, can I carry the treaty for you?' Wilson is reputed to have smiled and said 'Not on your life', making everyone around him laugh. Yet the time for humour was almost over. Wilson refused to compromise over the content of the Covenant and at the end of August he decided to tour America in a bid to gain public support in place of the political support which he was being denied.

The schedule which the ageing President now faced was awesome. In 22 days it was proposed to cover 8,000 miles and deliver 37 hour-long speeches. Jolting train journeys, searing temperatures, and the fact that even in large arenas Wilson's voice received no amplification, combined to make the whole venture seem ill-advised. As you read the evidence that follows it may be an opportune moment for you to consider the role of the individual in history. Would a younger, fitter man have succeeded where Wilson failed? Were Wilson's persistent refusal to compromise and his subsequent ill-health to blame for America's failure to join the League, or were there wider factors?

EXAMINING THE EVIDENCE

Woodrow Wilson: stubborn old man or heroic crusader?

Source A

In Pueblo, on September 25, no longer master of his emotions, Woodrow Wilson bursts into tears when he addresses the crowd. His headaches rob him of sleep. When he sleeps, saliva drops from the corner of his mouth. Fever assails his body. Catastrophe is at hand.

At four o'clock in the morning, on September 26, Grayson knocks at Tumulty's compartment. 'The President is seriously ill. I greatly fear that the trip may end fatally if he attempts to go on.'

When Tumulty arrives at the President's drawing-room, he finds him fully dressed and seated in his chair. Speech no longer flows freely. His tongue stumbles. His lips refuse to articulate. His face is ghostly pale, one side of it seems to have fallen, like a ruined house. Tears stream down the President's cheek...

The sick man pleads with his doctor and his secretary. 'Don't you see that if you cancel this trip, Senator Lodge and his friends will say that I am a quitter, and that the western trip was a failure, and the Treaty will be lost!...'

Wilson is unable to persuade Tumulty. His left arm and leg no longer function.

The train slides into a siding near Wichita, Kansas...Mrs Wilson, now thoroughly alarmed, takes command of the situation...A sign from her ends the sad crusade...the train turns homeward. Blinds down, it heads swiftly to Washington.'

G.S. Viereck, *The Strangest Friendship in History* (1933)

Source B

PRESIDENT WILSON ON HIS SPEAKING TOUR IN ST PAUL, WITH HIS PRIVATE SECRETARY, TUMULTY (SEPTEMBER 1919)

Source C

The President pushed himself beyond endurance. After the Pueblo speech and a sleepless night on the train he collapsed. He told Tumulty...'I seem to have gone to pieces. The doctor is right. I am not in condition to go on. I have never been in a condition like this, and I just feel as if I am going to pieces'. He choked, wept as he turned to look away out of the window. The train sped back to Washington, where in a few days he suffered the massive stroke from which he never recovered.

R.H. Ferrell, *Woodrow Wilson and World War 1 1917-1921* (1985)

TALKING POINT

The role of the individual in history:

People do not control events, they react to them. Discuss this statement.

Source D

It did not kill him, to his misfortune; but it incapacitated him for government, and turned his native obstinacy and assurance to granite... Compromise of some kind was essential to save the treaty, but from his sickbed Wilson refused it implacably; his will hurled the Democrats into unsuccessful battle against the Republicans and when the Lodge amendments were passed, he forced his supporters to vote against the entire document. Borah and his irreconcilables voted against it too, and thus it was Wilson himself, in collaboration, as it were, with his bitterest enemies, who made America take the first steps back down the isolationist path.

Hugh Brogan, *The History of the U.S.A.* (1985)

Source E

In 1919 the United States was strong enough to have made the world safe for democracy. It possessed one of the richest portions of the globe, the world's largest economy, had created the largest army, and was building the largest navy.

R.H. Ferrell, *Woodrow Wilson and World War 1 1917-1921* (1985)

TALKING POINT

Where did Wilson go wrong? Is it possible to choose a specific moment when Wilson lost his chance to obtain American membership of the League? If so, was it his fault that things went wrong?

The peace settlement in Eastern Europe

The leading statesmen had hurried away from Paris as soon as the Peace of Versailles was signed, leaving completion of the remaining treaties to their diplomats and officials. A huge amount of work remained and was carried out piecemeal until its completion in August 1920. The future of Austria, Hungary, Bulgaria and Turkey constituted the bulk of the work which remained. Rather than writing out four entirely new treaties it was decided that much of the material and ideas from the Versailles Treaty could be re-applied. Each of the subsequent treaties incorporated the League Covenant. Disarmament clauses, reparations, customs restrictions and economic clauses very similar to those at Versailles were employed on a smaller scale. Finally, written into all four treaties was an acknowledgement of the transformation of Serbia into the new kingdom of the Serbs, Croats and Slovenes which was eventually to become known as Yugoslavia.

Focus

5.2 The peace settlement in Eastern Europe

Legend:
- Austria-Hungary until 1918
- Plebiscite Areas
- Former territory of Imperial Russia

```
0                    100 miles
0                    150 kilometres
```

Austria

Treaty of St. Germain: September 1919

Austria was severed from Hungary and reduced to a tiny rump state, land-locked and with nearly one third of its population concentrated in Vienna and the rest scattered in fairly unproductive, German-speaking Alpine lands. Much of Austria's wealthiest territory went to create the Czech portions of Czechoslovakia.

The rest was distributed as follows: *Galicia* went to Poland; *Istrian Peninsula, Trentino, South Tyrol* to Italy; *Bukovina* to Romania; *Bosnia-Herzegovina, Dalmation Coast* to Yugoslavia. Austria's grand capital remained but the economy to support it had been destroyed.

Hungary

Treaty of Trianon: June 1920

Reduced to a rump state. Territorial losses even more severe than Austria:

Slovakia and Ruthenia went to Czechoslovakia; *Croatia - Slavonia and part of the Banat* - to Romania. Hungary also surrendered its last remaining outlet to the sea, *Fiume*, although this became the subject of a dispute between Italy and the other powers.

Map labels: Berlin, Poznan, Weimar, Breslau, GERMANY, SAXONY, Prague, Munich, BAVARIA, Vienna, AUSTRIA, CZECHOSL[OVAKIA], Graz, HUNGA[RY], Trento, Trieste, YUGOSLAVIA, CROATIA, Sarajevo, ITALY, ADRIATIC SEA, BOSNIA, MONTENEG[RO]

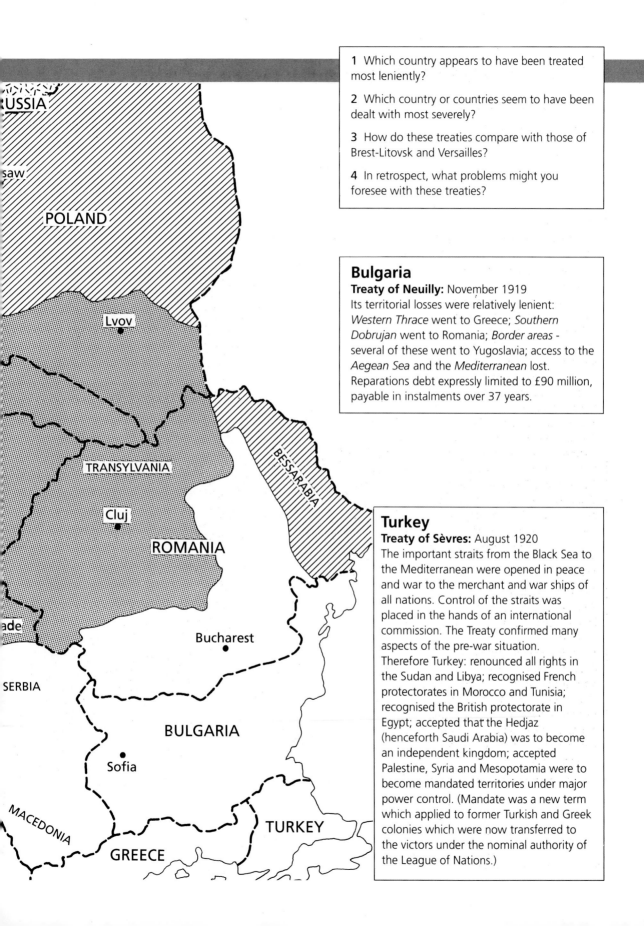

1 Which country appears to have been treated most leniently?

2 Which country or countries seem to have been dealt with most severely?

3 How do these treaties compare with those of Brest-Litovsk and Versailles?

4 In retrospect, what problems might you foresee with these treaties?

Bulgaria
Treaty of Neuilly: November 1919
Its territorial losses were relatively lenient: *Western Thrace* went to Greece; *Southern Dobrujan* went to Romania; *Border areas* - several of these went to Yugoslavia; access to the *Aegean Sea* and the *Mediterranean* lost. Reparations debt expressly limited to £90 million, payable in instalments over 37 years.

Turkey
Treaty of Sèvres: August 1920
The important straits from the Black Sea to the Mediterranean were opened in peace and war to the merchant and war ships of all nations. Control of the straits was placed in the hands of an international commission. The Treaty confirmed many aspects of the pre-war situation.
Therefore Turkey: renounced all rights in the Sudan and Libya; recognised French protectorates in Morocco and Tunisia; recognised the British protectorate in Egypt; accepted that the Hedjaz (henceforth Saudi Arabia) was to become an independent kingdom; accepted Palestine, Syria and Mesopotamia were to become mandated territories under major power control. (Mandate was a new term which applied to former Turkish and Greek colonies which were now transferred to the victors under the nominal authority of the League of Nations.)

6 Instability in Europe 1919-39

PREVIEW

'There weren't over-many of us there in the third German trench. I'd lost my Lewis-gunner somewhere or other, and I was on my own for ten minutes or a quarter of an hour and then I picked up another Lewis-gunner. We all knew that, once you occupy a trench, you have to set up a post to consolidate it and defend it in case the Jerry attacks again. Well, we were looking round for a place to plant our gun over the Jerries' side of the trench and, walking round it, I found a Jerry who was wounded sitting on the ground. As we walked up to him very carefully, with bayonet at the ready to stab him if he started being naughty, he looked up and he said "Water, Tommy, water"

He was badly wounded. What could you do but give him water? So, I slung my rifle and told the other chap to keep watch, and I took my bottle and gave him a drop of water. And then, when he'd drunk it, in a very strange manner - he hadn't got a steel helmet, they had little round hats - he took his little blue hat off and he handed it to me and, in good English, he said, "Lucky souvenir, you, Tommy". And he died. Just died, there and then. I was glad I'd given him water. I stuck the hat in my pocket and forgot all about it.'

Corporal Bob Thompson, Lewis-gunner, 13 (S) Batallion, The Rifle Brigade

SOLDIERS ON THE WESTERN FRONT TRYING TO COPE AMID DREADFUL CONDITIONS

CELEBRATIONS ON ARMISTICE DAY

An uneasy peace (1920-29)

The widespread revulsion at the suffering of 1914-18, combined with a general feeling of war-weariness, served to create an atmosphere which embraced new notions of openness, discussion and morality at the expense of secrecy and power-politics. As C.P. Scott said in the *Manchester Guardian* in February 1919, 'the organised opinion of the world is a tremendous weapon. It may well prove also to be a growing one.' Balfour, referring to the creation of the League of Nations enthused that, 'all has been done that could be done to make war in the future difficult and peace easy'. The new optimism was carried forward and in 1924 the Bishop of Manchester asserted 'the steadily growing sense that Machiavellian statescraft is bankrupt'.

However, the historian A. Lentin in his book *Guilt at Versailles* argues that this sense of optimism was in itself dangerous:

'The mirage of the League of Nations as an entity somehow different from the erring states which composed it, the myth of the actual efficacy of peaceful aspirations, was to prove among the most infectious and tenacious of the illusions born of the Peace Conference.'

In *The Illusion of Peace*, Sally Marks makes the important point that:

'The advent of peace was highly relative. The major powers were no longer in bloody collision, but civil war raged in Russia, Ireland, China, Turkey, and briefly in the Ruhr. Foreign troops remained in Russia; the Baltic area was a battleground; and Poland invaded Russia while Hungary marched briefly on Poland, Romania and Slovakia. There was fighting on the Finnish frontier and in Fiume; in Silesia Germans and Poles waged an undeclared war; most Balkan borders were aflame; and in Anatolia the Turks fought the Greeks, backed by the British. Yet the world was officially at peace.'

As the map shows, the period of 'peace' between 1919 and 1939 was punctuated by war, civil unrest, famine and dispute.

Alsace Lorraine

Ruhr

Rhineland

1939 Invasion or annexation with dates

Refugees

1920-23 War with dates

Civil war with dates 1917-20

Resolution of dispute by League

Nazi invasion

Severe famine

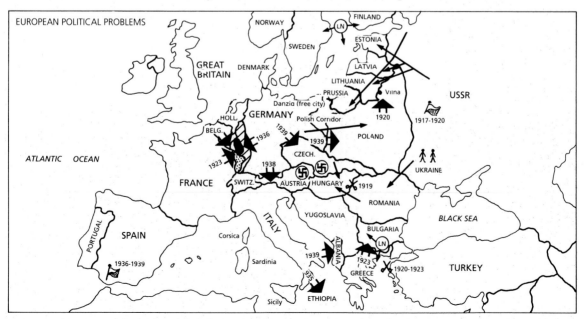

EUROPEAN POLITICAL PROBLEMS

6.1 The League of Nations - could it keep the peace?

When the war ended in November 1918 at least it was possible for most people to assume that nothing on this scale would ever happen again. However, 20 years later Europe found itself on the brink of all-out war once again. What was wrong with the structures established by the politicians of 1918 to ensure that Europe would embark on a new period of peace, stability and democracy? Why did Europe face a Second World War only 21 years after the First had come to an end? In 1919, many people believed that in the future peace would be preserved by the League of Nations. What was the nature of this organisation?

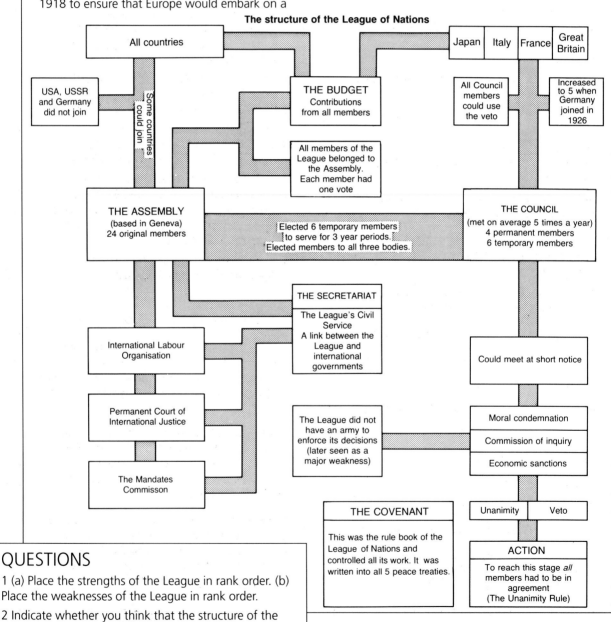

The structure of the League of Nations

All countries

Japan | Italy | France | Great Britain

USA, USSR and Germany did not join

Some countries could join

THE BUDGET
Contributions from all members

All Council members could use the veto

Increased to 5 when Germany joined in 1926

All members of the League belonged to the Assembly. Each member had one vote

THE ASSEMBLY
(based in Geneva)
24 original members

Elected 6 temporary members to serve for 3 year periods. Elected members to all three bodies.

THE COUNCIL
(met on average 5 times a year)
4 permanent members
6 temporary members

THE SECRETARIAT

The League's Civil Service
A link between the League and international governments

International Labour Organisation

Could meet at short notice

Permanent Court of International Justice

The League did not have an army to enforce its decisions (later seen as a major weakness)

Moral condemnation

Commission of inquiry

Economic sanctions

The Mandates Commisson

THE COVENANT

This was the rule book of the League of Nations and controlled all its work. It was written into all 5 peace treaties.

Unanimity | Veto

ACTION

To reach this stage *all* members had to be in agreement
(The Unanimity Rule)

QUESTIONS

1 (a) Place the strengths of the League in rank order. (b) Place the weaknesses of the League in rank order.

2 Indicate whether you think that the structure of the League was potentially adequate to keep the peace.

Strengths

- The League had a clearly-defined organisation and Covenant.
- 24 nations, including Britain and France, had joined the League.
- There was a genuine mood of co-operation amongst the Members.
- The League had the potential to impose damaging economic sanctions on aggressive nations.
- The League would defend the interests of all Member nations, not just the large ones.
- The aims of the League enjoyed widespread support.
- The League was a revolutionary step forward in international relations, away from the old alliance system.
- The League undertook a wide range of humanitarian and economic activities.

The changing membership of the League

There were 24 original Members. Important additions and departures included:

Country	Date of Entry	Withdrawal
Austria	December 1920	*December 1939
Ethiopia	September 1923	
Germany	September 1926	October 1933
Ireland	September 1923	
Italy	Original Member	December 1937
Japan	Original Member	March 1933
Spain	Original Member	May 1939
USSR	September 1934	*December 1939

*Declared to be no longer a Member of the League, by Council Resolution, 14 December 1939.

Weaknesses

- The United States refused to join the League.
- Britain and France were not as powerful as they had once been.
- The League had no armed forces of its own.
- The membership was predominantly European and the shift in power towards countries like Japan and the USA had not been recognised.
- The most enthusiastic members were the smaller European countries, which could do little themselves to guarantee peace, but relied on peace for their own survival.
- Certain countries - such as Germany - were hostile towards the whole peace settlement.
- As historian Hugh Brogan puts it, the League 'depended on the goodwill of the nations to work, though it was the absence of goodwill that made it necessary', *Longman History of the USA* (1985).
- Britain's government tried to make the obligations of the League less binding.

Early successes of the League

1920 The Health Organisation of the League organised medical assistance and the distribution of vaccines to combat the epidemics of typhus, cholera and dysentery which swept Europe.

1921 A dispute arose between Sweden and Finland over the Aaland Islands in the Baltic. The League ruled in favour of Finland and the Swedes accepted settlement in the face of international opinion.

1925 In October, Greek troops entered Bulgaria backed up by their airforce. Many Bulgarians were killed. The League halted the Greek invasion and ruled that Greece should pay an indemnity to Bulgaria.

Early problems for the League

The power of the League of Nations to resolve these disputes was not always apparent. In the absence of the US - whose Senate finally rejected the Versailles Treaty in March 1920 - it was essential that the remaining powers were in agreement on major issues. This was by no means the case. Indeed Ruth Henig points out that the 'repudiation by the United States of the entire peace settlement increased the reluctance of successive British governments in the 1920s to underwrite in any tangible way the European territorial settlement'. In the dispute between Turkey and Greece of 1920-23, Britain and France took opposite sides. While France endorsed Poland's aims in Russia and Silesia, Britain pointedly did not. In addition, the distractions caused by major problems in Ireland and the Empire made it impossible for Britain to concentrate on upholding the interests of the League before national concerns. While France fretted about Germany, Britain sought to redevelop trade links with her former enemy. Sally Marks points out that the powers had assumed that the treaties would be honoured although this was emphatically not the case:

'The Dutch refused to relinquish the Kaiser, and Germany did not surrender alleged war criminals. Nor did she disarm on schedule or meet reparations quotas. Austria could not and did not pay reparations. Poland did not accept her frontiers; Italian troops did not evacuate Fiume; and Turkey did not accept the Treaty of Sèvres. Nothing much happened. The will to enforce the treaties was lacking or at best divided.'

Despite, or perhaps because of, these problems, the 1920s were marked by a series of conferences and treaties. As we will see, it was not always the intention at these conferences to uphold the peace settlement.

TALKING POINT

America's refusal to join the League was the critical weakness of the League itself. Do you agree?

The Washington Conference (1921)

American sponsorship of this conference marked the brief return of the United States to the international scene. Held between November 1921 and February 1922, the conference was mainly concerned with the discussion of naval disarmament and the issue of the Pacific and the Far East.

America, having embarked on a period of isolationism and burdened with the maintenance of two ocean-going navies was eager to see limits imposed on the world's major fleets. In addition, the US was increasingly concerned with Japan's rising strength in this area. On 6 February 1922 the major powers signed a Five-power Treaty which was broadly in line with American requirements. Naval tonnage for capital ships was limited to 525,000 for Britain and America, 300,000 for Japan and 175,000 for France and Italy. However, despite this agreement, the Washington Conference highlighted the growing international isolation of France which had reluctantly accepted the humiliating fact that in future her navy would be on a par with Italy's.

The Washington Conference was also concerned with key issues in the Far East. America and Canada were eager to see Britain distance herself from her pre-war alliance with Japan. In addition, it was intended to relieve China of some of the more pressing demands forced upon her by Japan in 1915. The Nine-power Pact of 6 February 1922 affirmed, though with no commitment to defend, the territorial integrity of China and endorsed the notion of the 'Open Door' through which all nations could trade with China on an equal basis.

Overall, it had been America's ambition at the conference to achieve in the Pacific and the Far East a new system of co-operative relations in keeping with the Western system under the League. It was hoped that the treaty would mark an end to naval arms races and expansionism but this rested on the unfounded assumption that all nations would indefinitely abide by its terms, regardless of their changing status or ambitions.

The Rapallo Treaty (April 1922)

The details of the Rapallo Treaty between Germany and Russia were made known while the great European powers were still in conference in Genoa. The Genoa Conference had marked the limited re-admission of Russia into the international community. Russia had been completely isolated by the revolutions of 1917 and the subsequent reluctance of the powers to recognise Lenin's government. The failure of the allies to invite Russia to the Versailles Conference and Lenin's repudiation of tsarist war debts damaged relations even further. At Genoa, while France insisted that Russia should still honour her war debts, Lloyd-George made every effort to court Russian favour. Alarmed by this trend, Germany went ahead with her growing commitment to Russia (there had been a secret Russo-German military collaboration in 1921) sending delegates away from Genoa to nearby Rapallo to negotiate with the Russians. On 16 April the terms were made known: the German and Soviet governments reintroduced diplomatic relations and pledged their future co-operation. Germany fully recognised the Soviet government and both powers denounced reparations. In addition, the Rapallo Treaty provided for close economic co-operation. In the future, military co-operation would become just as important.

As Marks explains: 'On the Russian plains, far from the prying eyes of military control commissions, Germany could and did build factories, produce the airplanes, poison gases, and tanks forbidden by the Versailles Treaty, test them, and train military personnel, both German and Russian, in their use. While this mutually beneficial arrangement had its ups and downs, it flourished throughout the twenties and to a lesser degree until the advent of Hitler.'

In the short term, the announcement of the Rapallo Treaty increased the difficulties which the Genoa Conference was running into and the negotiations eventually broke down over the insistence by France that Russia should honour its pre-war debts.

The Geneva Protocol (October 1924)

By 1923 it had become clear that the League of Nations was substantially weaker than individual members such as Britain, France and Japan. Two attempts were made, in 1923 and 1924, to bolster the strength of the League and make real progress on security and disarmament. The first of these initiatives was the Draft Treaty of Mutual Assistance presented to the League Assembly in September 1923. The terms would have obliged all members to come to the assistance of a victim of aggression, with the League Council

determining individual responsibilities. Although the majority of European states including France approved the draft treaty, it was rejected out of hand by Britain with the backing of many of the Empire states in July 1924.

The second initiative was the Geneva Protocol for the Pacific Settlement of International Disputes, which was presented in 1924. This provided for compulsory arbitration in all disputes and stated that the aggressor would be defined as the nation unwilling to submit its case to arbitration. Once again, the decisive note in rejecting this attempt to strengthen the powers of the League was sounded by Britain and her Dominions. In March 1925 Britain formally rejected the Geneva Protocol. The Dominions in particular had made it clear that they did not wish to jeopardise trading links by the application of economic sanctions on behalf of the League.

The Locarno Conference (1925)

The Locarno Conference marked a critical turning point in the post-war fortunes of Germany. Two years earlier, Gustav Stresemann had called off passive resistance to the French occupation of the Ruhr. This gesture seemed to many observers to symbolise Germany's new willingness for international co-operation. Stresemann had persuaded many of his opponents that Germany had finally given up her hostility towards the peace of Versailles. He reaped the benefits of this apparent change of heart at Locarno in October 1925. The leading statesmen came together for this vital conference in the picturesque Swiss town on Lake Maggiore, ready to readmit Germany to the international community on equal terms. Yet like most other German politicians, including Hitler, Stresemann wanted to restore German power and free his country from the shackles of Versailles. Indeed Sally Marks has gone so far as to say that 'no man in the Weimar Republic did more to destroy the Versailles Treaty' than Stresemann.

At the time, the Locarno Pact seemed to herald a new era of co-operation and goodwill. The key terms included:

1 The Rhineland Pact. Germany, France and Belgium agreed to respect their mutual frontiers, recognising them as permanent, including the demilitarised zone of the Rhineland. Britain and Italy acted as guarantors to the agreement.
2 It was agreed that French troops would complete their withdrawal from the Ruhr.
3 A Treaty of Arbitration between France and Germany provided for settlement of all disputes through the League of Nations.
4 Plans were made for German admission to the League of Nations which were carried out in 1926.

When news of the agreement was announced church bells rang out, fireworks exploded and celebrations carried on late into the night. France seemed to have been offered some guarantee of border security and Germany had shown more goodwill than ever before. Britain was pleased to have made only a limited guarantee to France without undertaking wider obligations, for example in Eastern Europe.

However, in reality Germany was already in breach of the disarmament clauses of the Versailles settlement through her secret military co-operation with Russia. Sally Marks says that 'the real spirit at Locarno behind the facade of public fellowship was one of bitter confrontation between a fearful France and a bitter Germany'. It would not be too long before the true nature of international relations in Europe would once again become the subject of political concern.

The Kellogg-Briand Pact (August 1928)

The International Treaty for the Renunciation of War as an Instrument of National Policy was signed at the Quai d'Orsay in Paris on 27 August 1928. Fifteen nations signed this renunciation of war, with a subsequent endorsement by 31 additional countries. Confined to two paragraphs, the declaration stated that the signatories would in future seek to resolve disputes only by peaceful means. In practice, countries were still left free to exercise self-defence and fulfil their treaty obligations. The sense of optimism engendered by this show of goodwill was heightened when the US Secretary of State, Frank Kellogg, came to Paris to place his signature next to that of his French counterpart, Aristide Briand. This was taken as a sign that the US was poised to return to a central position in world affairs, but this was a mistaken notion.

America was to remain aloof from European affairs, and the Wall Street Crash of October 1929 heightened her sense of domestic preoccupation. In the same month, Stresemann, who had risen from his sickbed to sign the Kellogg-Briand Pact, died and Germany too entered a period of intense domestic crisis. The Pact had genuinely represented a moment of international goodwill and stability. However, the Great Depression which began in 1929 was to have much more far-reaching consequences. The economic crisis precipitated a shift from democratic, liberal regimes to authoritarian and even totalitarian government in many European countries. What was the nature of these changes and why did they take place?

In addition, the economic crisis and the authoritarian governments which it helped to produce heralded a period in which international co-operation gave way to acts of aggression and expansionism. It was in the critical period between 1931 and 1939 that the League of Nations and its mechanisms for international security would really be put to the rest. Would it survive?

1 What justification was there for optimism in international relations in the period from 1919 to 1929?

(a) What developments had taken place which boded well for peace?

(b) What developments had taken place which seemed to threaten future peace?

(c) What conclusions would you now draw?

TALKING POINT

The 1920s: a period of peace and calm, or a period of dispute and tension. Which is nearer the truth?

FOCUS

6.2 The collapse of democracy: changes in European government (1919-41)

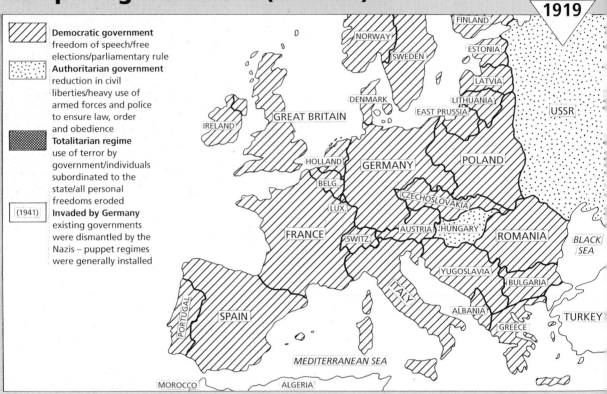

Legend:

- **Democratic government** — freedom of speech/free elections/parliamentary rule
- **Authoritarian government** — reduction in civil liberties/heavy use of armed forces and police to ensure law, order and obedience
- **Totalitarian regime** — use of terror by government/individuals subordinated to the state/all personal freedoms eroded
- (1941) **Invaded by Germany** — existing governments were dismantled by the Nazis – puppet regimes were generally installed

1919

Country/State	Details of changes in regime	Date of change
Albania	Ahmet Zog self-proclaimed King Zog	1928
Austria	Moved to Right under Dolfuss	1932
Belgium	Democracy dismantled by Nazis	1939
Bulgaria	King Boris set up personal rule	1934
Czechoslovakia	Democracy dismantled by Nazis	1939
Denmark	Democracy dismantled by Nazis	1940
Estonia	Päts established authoritarian rule	1934
Finland	Democracy remained intact	-
France	Democracy dismantled by Nazis	1940
Germany	Hitler's fascist regime	1933
Great Britain	Democracy remained intact	-
Greece	Metaxas established authoritarian rule	1936
Holland	Democracy dismantled by Nazis	1940

Country/State	Details of changes in regime	Date of change
Hungary	Short-lived Communist regime: Bela Kun overthrown Horthy took control	1919 1920
Ireland	Democracy remained intact	-
Italy	Mussolini's fascist regime	1922
Latvia	Ulmanis established authoritarian rule	1934
Lithuania	Smetona set up authoritarian rule	1926
Luxemburg	Democracy dismantled	1940
Norway	Democracy dismantled by Nazis	1940
Poland	Pilsudski established control of Poland	1926
Portugal	Firm rule established by Salazar	-
Romania	King Carol ruled without parliament	1938
Spain	After Civil War, General Franco in control	1939
Sweden	Democracy remained intact	-
Switzerland	Democracy remained intact	-
USSR	Lenin and Communism 1917 - then Stalin	1917
Yugoslavia	King Alexander set up personal rule	1929

Examining the Evidence

The collapse of the League of Nations: failure or scapegoat?

In examining the reasons for the failure of the League of Nations we will need to assume a broad perspective. As Richard Overy explains in *The Road to War:*

'There was a much larger cast of actors in the drama of international relations than the traditionalist's three-hander: Britain, France and Germany. The shaping of policy looks very different when viewed from the perspective of Washington, Moscow, Rome or Tokyo rather than exclusively from London, Paris or Berlin. Each government, in a world still made up of nation states, felt the immediate pressures of national or domestic preoccupations.'

Richard Overy, *The Road to War* (1989)

Japanese expansionism (1931-37)

Source A: The Japanese invasion of Manchuria (1931)

On November 14 (1930) Prime Minister Yuko Hamaguchi was shot at Tokyo Station. Drastic surgery saved his life, but the assassination attempt was followed by a succession of plots hatched by the army and patriotic societies...Democracy in Japan was now facing a severe test...It was soon evident that Tokyo had lost control of the headstrong generals of the Kwantung Army as incidents escalated that summer along the Manchurian railway line their troops were guarding. Three years earlier, in pursuit of their goal of turning Manchuria into a satellite state of Japan's, they had dynamited the train of the venerable Marshall Chang Tso-lin, disposing of the Chinese warlord who appeared to be transferring allegiance to the Nationalist cause. The final stage of their takeover plan went into operation on September 18, 1931, when another explosion on the tracks outside Mukden provided the excuse the Kwantung Army needed to send its troops marching out across Manchuria in pursuit of 'Chinese bandits'. As the conquest of Manchuria got under way it was applauded by the rightists, the 'Strike North' faction of the army, and influential patriotic groups led by the Cherry Blossom Society.   John Costello, *The Pacific War* (1981)

Source B: The US response to Japanese aggression

Recognising that unless Japan honoured her obligations under the Nine Power Pact the whole Washington Treaty system would collapse, Secretary of State Henry Stimson urged that America should take the lead on threatening sanctions: 'If we lie down and let them treat them (the treaty system) like scraps of paper, nothing will happen and the future of the peace movement will receive a blow that it will not recover from for a very long time.' President Herbert Hoover, although an old China hand himself, and equally determined to 'uphold the moral foundations of international life,' feared that sanctions would lead to war.

John Costello, *The Pacific War* (1981)

US PRESIDENT HERBERT HOOVER

Source C

AFTER THE JAPANESE INVASION OF MANCHUKUO, JAPANESE SOLDIERS BEAR THE CREMATED REMAINS OF SOLDIERS KILLED THERE

Source D: The response of the League of Nations

The League responded by sending a Commission of inquiry led by Lord Lytton to investigate the situation in Manchuria. The Japanese made little attempt to hide the consolidation of their control of what was now a mainland satellite state even while the League Commission under Lord Lytton was in Manchuria on its fact-finding investigation...The Lytton Commission's report in January 1933 was far from the total condemnation that Washington expected. However, the League's refusal to recognise Manchukuo was enough to precipitate Japan's withdrawal as her Kwantung Army marched southwest toward Peking into Jehol Province, and the militarists in Tokyo believed they had now shed themselves of all restraint.

America's consistent refusal to invoke nothing [sic] more than words in support of the League and the treaty system her own diplomats had engineered had shown just how toothless and helpless the international community was when it came to upholding and enforcing the fragile framework on which peace rested. A dangerous precedent had been set.

John Costello, *The Pacific War* (1981)

TALKING POINT

The League's first major mistake was the fatal one. If Japan had been punished in 1931, later acts of aggression could have been stopped. Do you agree?

Source E: Japanese aggression - the international perspective

'The Manchurian Incident caused a profound reappraisal of Japan's position within the international system. Until 1931, she had been regarded as a loyal but junior member of the concert of nations. From 1931 onwards two distinct interpretations of Japan's international status began to develop. For some Westerners, the issue was clear-cut: Japan had used force in Manchuria, so she became a pariah-state, the first government to defy the League of Nations: the only plausible Western response was ostracism or some form of punishment. The strongest advocates of a hard line were the Far East specialists in the State Department, although their policy proposals often fell on deaf ears in Washington. There were many more supporters for a soft line: the military and naval adventurism was, they whispered, only temporary. If Japan could be seen to 'benefit' from the international system, then the Militarist cause would wither...Britain and the United States had huge investments in both China and Japan; 300,000 jobs in the United States depended on the Japanese silk trade...The Western governments did not want to invite retaliation by precipitate action over Manchuria...The ethical issues were also confused...A letter to the British Foreign Secretary, Sir John Simon from an old friend, the Master of Peterhouse, Cambridge, accurately reflected private rather than public British attitudes: 'This I know sounds all wrong, perhaps immoral, when she (Japan) is flouting the League of Nations, but (1) she has had great provocation, (2) she *must* ere long expand somewhere - for goodness sake let (or rather encourage) her to do so there instead of Australia and (3) her presence fully established in Manchuria means a real block against Bolshevik aggression.'

Richard Overy, The Road to War (1989)

The Italian invasion of Abyssinia (1935): the application of sanctions against Italy

Source F

'Instead of recognising the just rights of Italy, the League of Nations dares to speak of sanctions. Until there is proof to the contrary, I refuse to believe that the free people of Great Britain want to spill blood and push Europe on the road to catastrophe in order to defend an African country, universally stamped as unworthy of taking its place among civilised peoples.

Benito Mussolini, 2 October 1935

Source G

Mussolini judged correctly that neither Britain nor France wanted to go to war (or blockade, or close the Suez Canal) to stop an Italian conquest, even though for many in Geneva this was a test case of the League's capacity to enforce its system of collective security. Cautiously, the League imposed limited economic and financial sanctions. These sanctions were meant to wear down Italy's fighting capacity over the two years it was estimated the war would run. But sanctions were limited, slow to work, and only partially supported...In the short run, stockpiling...allowed Italy to absorb these irritations without damage to the African campaign. Mussolini played on British and French fears in his threat of European war should sanctions be extended to oil. A. Sbacchi, *Ethiopia under Mussolini* (1985)

Source H: President Roosevelt's response to the Italian invasion

When Italy attacked Abyssinia in 1935, Roosevelt, against the advice of his diplomatic representatives and in advance of the League of Nations, promptly declared a state of war to exist between Italy and Abyssinia and imposed an arms embargo which he knew full well would affect Italy more than land-locked Abyssinia...and even though he dare not align the United States openly with the League of Nations in applying sanctions, he and Cordell Hull urged businessmen not to trade with the belligerents. When Italian purchases of raw materials rose sharply Hull threatened to publish the names of exporters...It was not president or secretary of state who let the League of Nations down but Britain and France by their surrender to Mussolini's demands.

William Carr, From Poland to Pearl Harbor (1985)

Source I

THE ITALIAN INVASION OF ABYSSINIA (1935). BLACKSHIRTS DISEMBARK AT MASSAWA, ITALIAN ERITREA

Source J

Source K

ITALIAN AMMUNITION COLUMN ON THE MOVE IN ABYSSINIA, 1935

German revision of the Versailles Treaty

Source L

What a use could be made of the Treaty of Versailles! ...How each one of the points of the Treaty could be branded in the hearts and minds of the German people until sixty million men and women find their souls aflame with a feeling of rage and shame; and a torrent of fire bursts forth as from a furnace, and a will of steel is forged from it, with the common cry...We will have arms again.

Adolf Hitler, *Mein Kampf* (1925)

Source M

ENFORCING THE TREATY OF VERSAILLES. GERMAN TANKS AND ARMOURED CARS TRANSFORMED INTO PLOUGHS AND AGRICULTURAL MACHINERY

Source N: The French response to German reoccupation of the Rhineland (March 1936)

The day after the occupation, a clear violation of the terms of Versailles, French military leaders came together to determine their response.

Present: General Gamelin (Chief of the French army), Admiral Durand-Viel (Navy), General Pugo (Airforce).

Admiral Durand-Viel: 'The government has asked the military, "Are you prepared to drive the Germans out of the zone?"'

General Gamelin: 'By the fact of our entry into the zone, war would be unleashed. Such action would thus require general mobilisation...We can only enter the Rhineland zone...at the same time as the guarantor powers of Locarno (England and Italy). British and Italian contingents must be with us.'

Admiral Durand-Viel: 'At the moment England could give us nothing but moral support.'

French diplomatic records, 8 March 1936

Source O: Poland and the free city of Danzig (1939)

The League of Nations commissioner...Carl Burckhardt, whose task it was to maintain the integrity of the free City was far from committed to its independent survival. Lord Halifax, the British Foreign Secretary from February 1938, thought the status of Danzig and the Corridor 'a most foolish provision of the Treaty of Versailles'. Moreover the city whose independence was to provoke a general European war was, by 1938, a Nazi city. The Nazi Party had taken control of the Danzig parliament in May 1933...Despite League objections the Nazi Party by 1936 had established virtual one-party rule and had imported the repressive apparatus of the parent model...

Without firm allies, Poland's chances of persuading other powers to help her safeguard a Nazified Danzig against a predatory Germany seemed remote. Hitler had not chosen his moment idly. Poland was isolated and shunned, Danzig a Nazi outpost abandoned by the League. Two things transformed the situation: the Polish decision that they would fight rather than abandon the Free City, and the British decision to side with Poland if it came to a fight.

Richard Overy, The Road to War (1989)

Source P: Hitler's plans to invade Poland (May 1939)

...Germany was outside the circle of the Great Powers. A balance of power had been established without Germany's participation. It is not Danzig that is at stake. For us it is a matter of expanding our living space in the East and making food supplies secure and also solving the problem of the Baltic States...The problem 'Poland' cannot be dissociated from the showdown with the West...There is therefore no question of sparing Poland and we are left with the decision: To attack Poland at the first suitable opportunity. We cannot expect a repetition of Czechia. There will be war. Our task is to isolate Poland. Success in isolating her will be decisive.

Extracts from Hitler's comments to senior Army commanders,
23 May 1939. Quoted in Noakes and Pridham, Nazism 1919-1945,
A Documentary Reader, Volume 3 (1988)

Source Q

GERMAN TROOPS COVERED BY A TANK, MOVE INTO DANZIG

Source R

HITLER IN CONVERSATION WITH GENERAL VON BLOMBERG, AND GENERAL VON FRITSCH

Conclusion

Source S: Responding to the dictators

Hitler...stood outside the normal Western pattern of discussion, debate and compromise: such a creature was beyond the understanding of most of the statesmen who faced him. They had built an international system based on reason, or at the very least on the principles of political horse-trading. Hitler in Germany, and those who followed the 'war path' in Japan and Italy, were not traders but hunters, belonging in a sense to an earlier stage of human history. In the context of the 1930s they were radical, violent states seeking a new order at home and abroad. A strategy to confront these forces was difficult to formulate. There was no easy answer to the challenge.

Richard Overy, *The Road to War* (1989)

REVIEW

The League of Nations

Essay

'An unmitigated failure.' How far is this a fair estimate of the League of Nations?

Prepare notes under the following headings:

(a) The nature of the League: its strengths and weaknesses
(b) The early successes of the League
(c) The Japanese invasion of Manchuria (1931)
(d) The Italian invasion of Abyssinia (1935)
(e) German reoccupation of the Rhineland (1936)
(f) Further acts of German aggression (1938-39)

> For c-f you should include subsections on
> i) The nature of aggression
> ii) The response of the League
> iii) Impact of League's action
> iv) Consequences of these events
> v) Whether the League was to blame
> vi) Other factors

(g) Factors outside the League's control

(h) Did individual members of the League make matters worse by their own actions (eg, British Naval Pact with Germany, 1935)?

(i) Could any international organisation based on reason and goodwill have prevented leaders like Mussolini and Hitler committing acts of aggression?

(j) Conclusions: for and against the essay title.

The Russo-German Non-Aggression Pact

Although the League of Nations had not been able to resist acts of aggression in the 1930s, there was still a possibility in August 1939 that Hitler might have been restrained. However, the prospects of international, concerted action against Hitler were dealt a massive blow with the announcement of the Nazi-Soviet Non-Aggression pact of August 1939. Why did Stalin sign such an agreement with Hitler?

Role-playing exercise

A critical turning point in the road to the Second World War came with the announcement in August 1939 that Germany had concluded a non-aggression pact with the Soviet Union. This seemed to clear the way for Hitler's move against Poland which, in turn precipitated a much wider conflict. Why did Stalin - the arch Communist - sign an agreement with his ideological opposite, Adolf Hitler? Could the agreement have been avoided if France and Britain had acted differently? Did Stalin seek an agreement with the Western democracies before turning to Hitler?

Imagine it is the beginning of August 1939. The following section will reproduce some of the complexities surrounding top-level negotiations between the great powers in this critical year. Your perspective for this exercise will be the Soviet one. In particular, consider the dossier of information from the viewpoint of a senior official in the Soviet foreign ministry. A variety of dates will be made available, but some details will be based on speculation rather than hard facts. Part of the information is based on coded messages between the powers, which your cryptographers have attempted to unlock. Such information was often deliberately 'planted' in the knowledge that the code would be easily broken; the content of the message was therefore intentionally misleading. For this reason you will need to weigh up the validity of this information very carefully. To make matters worse, the actions and intentions of your leader, Stalin, are at best unpredictable. The essence of this exercise is for you to interpret the information that is available at the time, weigh up the options available and recommend a choice accordingly. You need to be fully briefed before you can complete this exercise. Read over the background information very carefully

Key incidents, 1938-39

1938

Feb 4   Von Ribbentrop appointed as German foreign minister.

March 12   German army marches into Austria.

March 28   Hitler encourages German minority in Czechoslovakia to agitate for the break-up of the state.

April 24   Germans in Sudetenland demand complete autonomy.

April 29   Britain reluctantly supports France in diplomatic action in defence of the Czech government.

May 9   Russia promises to help Czechoslovakia in the event of a German invasion if Poland and Romania will allow the passage of Russian troops. This is refused by both nations.

May 21   Czechoslovakia moves to partial mobilisation in response to German troop movements on her border.

May 22   Britain warns Germany of dangers of military action but tells France that she does not favour military action herself.

Aug 12   Germany begins to mobilise.

Sept 11   Poland and Romania again refuse to allow the passage of Russian troops to help Czechoslovakia.

Sept 15   In their first meeting, at Berchtesgaden, Hitler tells Chamberlain of his determination to annex the Sudetenland on the grounds of self-determination.

Sept 18   Britain and France agree to persuade the Czechs to hand over territory to Germany in areas where over half the population is German. The Czechs at first reject this proposal but then agree to it.

Sept 22   In the second meeting between Hitler and Chamberlain, at Bad Godesberg, Hitler demands immediate occupation of the Sudetenland and names the date of the invasion as 28 September.

Sept 29   Hitler suspends the invasion pending the Munich Conference at which Chamberlain, Daladier, Mussolini and Hitler agree to the transfer of the Sudetenland to Germany, while guaranteeing the remaining Czech frontiers. The Russians are not invited to take part in the conference.

October   Japanese Cabinet begins discussion over a military alliance with Hitler.

December   Western press full of speculation that Hitler intends to attack the Ukraine.

1939

March 11   In a major speech to the Soviet Congress Stalin says that 'The Soviet Union is not going to pull the warmongers' chestnuts out of the fire!' This is interpreted as a warning to the Western powers not to try to provoke a German-Soviet conflict. Hitler may have read the same speech as a green light for his planned invasion of the remainder of Czechoslovakia.

March 15   German troops occupy rump Czechoslovakia. This secured Germany's rear in the event of war in the west.

March 28   Hitler denounces Germany's 1934 non-aggression pact with Poland.

March 31   Britain and France announce their guarantees of Poland's territorial integrity. Hitler responds furiously to what he regards as an act of obstruction.

April 18   Litvinov, Commissar for Foreign Affairs, proposes a tripartite military alliance between Russia, France and Britain. The offer is not taken up by the Western allies. At the same time similar discussions were taking place between Soviet officials and German secretary of state von Weizsacker.

May 3   Litvinov is dismissed by Stalin and replaced by Molotov, Stalin's longest-standing associate. The fact that Litvinov is jewish is regarded in some circles as significant.

July   The British press contains detailed reports of talks between top officials at the Department of Overseas Trade with Helmut Wohltata, Head of Goering's four-year plan.

Aug 12 Anglo-French mission arrives in Moscow to begin talks.

Aug 18 Germany signs a commercial agreement with the USSR.

Aug 22 Ribbentrop, the German foreign minister, arrives in Moscow.

Background information on individual countries

France   Military reports suggest that France is making ready to fight a siege type war along her frontiers with Germany. While France is willing to discuss a military agreement with the Soviet Union, it is not clear how serious her commitment is.

Germany   Overtures received from Germany in the summer seem to suggest that in return for a free hand in Poland, Hitler might be prepared to make significant concessions to Russia in eastern Poland, Bessarabia, the Baltic States and Finland. At the same time it has to be borne in mind that an agreement with Hitler might easily be violated in the near future.

Great Britain   Great Britain's true intentions are uncertain. Chamberlain seems to desire better relations with the Soviet Union. He is the first British premier to attend a function at the Soviet embassy since the revolution of 1917. At the same time there is some evidence to suggest that Britain is anxious to conclude an agreement with Germany. Talks in the summer indicated a desire for economic co-operation and the corollary of this might be British concessions to Germany over Poland.

Italy   Although Italy signed a pact with Germany in May 1939 and has so far stood by her ally, there is some evidence that Mussolini has reservations about the extent of Hitler's territorial ambitions and the likely consequences. Intelligence reports suggest that in discussions between Italian foreign minister Count Ciano and Ribbentrop in August 1939, the German foreign minister made it known that Hitler's ambitions extended beyond Poland.

USSR   We are in the position whereby negotiations are taking place with the so-called democratic countries of France and Great Britain and Fascist Germany. Whatever the outcome, it has to be said that while the country has made tremendous progress economically, industrially and militarily, the time is not ripe for a major war. Following the removal of certain generals and admirals in 1937, the new leadership is loyal but inexperienced and untested. Zhdanov, the party boss in Leningrad has rightly drawn attention to the lamentable state of that city's defences. Our entire transport system would be subject to great strain by any major invasion. It is imperative, therefore, that in these negotiations of 1939 the best possible option is secured.

Secret Intelligence material

This material needs to be read with great care - it may not be entirely reliable!

1 Source: Richard Sorge - secret agent for Stalin.
Contact: German ambassador in Japan.
Intelligence: The Japanese Cabinet has been debating German proposals for an alliance. There is general support for a narrow alliance which might be directed chiefly against the Soviet Union.

2 Source: Ozaki Hosumi - previously reliable agent.
Contact: Hosumi is an adviser to the Japanese Court and has contacts at the highest level.
Intelligence: The Japanese navy minister and the foreign minister have expressed opposition to a broader military alliance with Hitler.

3 Source: NKVD agent. Name withheld.
Contact: British Foreign Office, communications department.
Intelligence: Reports suggest that Chamberlain had used Mussolini to encourage Hitler to attack the Ukraine. (NB. There is some doubt over this source, and a suspicion that it has been deliberately 'planted' by Italian agents to move us away from Britain.)

4 Source: NKVD agent. Name withheld.
Contact: British Foreign Office.
Intelligence: Reports of Anglo-Soviet discussions are being passed to the German embassy in London. However, they have been deliberately slanted to

highlight areas of agreement. We have let the Germans know, for instance, that Britain refused to guarantee the status of Finland and the Baltic States. One interpretation of this could be that the British are deliberately leaving the way open for a German attack in this area.

5 Source: Military Intelligence.
Contact: Intelligence network in Germany.
Intelligence: It is now clear that following German absorption of Czechoslovakia, Hitler plans to take military action against Poland. He said as much in public speeches. Military Intelligence suggests that for such an operation to succeed it would need to begin in September before the autumn rains and the deterioration in the weather.

Other factors to consider

1 At the end of April 1939 routine press attacks on the Soviet Union, made in Nazi newspapers, suddenly came to an end.

2 In May, Stalin recalled the Soviet ambassador to Berlin. He has now been sent to a labour camp.

3 Although Ribbentrop is firmly anti-British, Hitler's attitude towards the British is ambivalent. However, his feelings about Communism are inherently hostile and he has major ideological doubts concerning an agreement with the Soviet Union.

4 The negotiations with the Anglo-French mission have not proceeded entirely satisfactorily. The British diplomatic entourage which arrived in August - on a slow steamship - seems to be alarmingly second-string. While the foreign minister, Lord Halifax, remained at home, the British sent a junior Foreign Office official, William Strang. Accompanying him were a group of second-rank officers without any real authority. Indeed, when Soviet Marshal Voroshilov asked the British and French what role they would want Russia to play in a war with Germany, their vague reaction seemed to indicate that this was not an issue to which they had given serious thought.

5 Commercial negotiations with German officials in August have led to the suggestion that Foreign Minister Ribbentrop would be prepared to fly to Russia at short notice to discuss military arrangements. It should, however, be underlined once again that Hitler has not shown himself to be the most reliable signatory of alliance agreements.

Summary of task: Preparation of top secret military report (20 August, 1939)
Your report must contain the following points.

1 A clear, but brief summary of the general diplomatic situation in August 1939.

2 The options available to the Soviet Union.
(a) An alliance with France and Britain
(b) An alliance with Germany

In both cases you need to set out detailed points for and against these options. Indicate what the nature of such alliances would be and state clearly the advantages to be gained, and the likely repercussions of each option. Summarise the information you have used to set out these options.

(c) Indicate clearly, and in detail, which option you think should be chosen and why.

Essay

Why did the Soviet Union make an alliance with Germany in 1939 rather than with France and Great Britain?

The Nazi-Soviet Pact: the outcome

Extracts from the secret agreement (23 August, 1939)

The Government of the German Reich and The Government of the Union of the Soviet Socialist Republics

directed by the wish to strengthen the cause of peace between Germany and the USSR and proceeding upon the basic provisions of the Treaty of Neutrality concluded between Germany and the USSR in April 1926, have reached the following agreement:

Article 1 The two contracting parties undertake to refrain from any act of violence, any aggressive action, or any attack against one another, whether individually or jointly with other powers.

Article 2 In case any of the contracting parties should become the object of warlike acts on the part of a third power, the other contracting power will not support that third power in any form.

Article 3 The Governments of the two contracting parties will in future remain in contact with each other through continuous consultation in order to inform each other concerning questions affecting their mutual interests.

Article 4 Neither of the two contracting parties will participate in any grouping of powers which is indirectly aimed against the other party...

Secret Additional Protocol
On the occasion of the signature of the Non-Aggression Treaty between the German Reich and the Union of the Soviet Socialist Republics, the undersigned plenipotentiaries of the two parties discussed in strictly confidential conversations the question of the delimitation of their respective spheres of interest in Eastern Europe. These conversations led to the following results:

1. In the event of a territorial and political transformation in the territories belonging to the Baltic States (Finland, Estonia, Latvia, Lithuania), the northern frontier of Lithuania shall represent the frontier of the spheres of interest both of Germany and the USSR. In this connection the interest of Lithuania in the Vilna territory is recognised by both parties...

Noakes and Pridham *Nazism 1919-1945*, vol III (1988)

RIBBENTROP AND MOLOTOV SIGNING THE NAZI-SOVIET PACT (22 AUGUST 1930)

DAVID LOW'S SATIRE ON THE NAZI-SOVIET PACT
FROM *THE EVENING STANDARD* (AUGUST, 1939)

7 Mussolini's Italy 1922-43

PREVIEW

'Fascism had aspirations to be "totalitarian"; Mussolini virtually invented the term. But… it is clear that Mussolini's grip on Italian society was not as firm, his influence so pervasive, as that of a Hitler or a Stalin.'
Adrian Lyttelton

A HUGE FASCIST RALLY. WHAT IMPRESSION DOES SUCH A PHOTOGRAPH CREATE?

The death of a dictator

In his prime he had presented himself as the strong man: a political leader whose main concern was to sustain his own power and exert his will over the whole of the Italian people; a man who had personally founded the Fascist movement and who had tried to turn Italy into a totalitarian state. Yet on 26 April 1945, as he attempted to flee the country he once ruled, Benito Mussolini was arrested as he tried to cross the state border into Austria. Although he had committed many crimes during his political career, there was now no question of him being brought to trial. With American soldiers only a few hours away, and the end of the Second World War in sight, the Communist partisans who had detained him were determined to exact a more instant form of justice. Two days after he had been taken prisoner, the 61-year-old former dictator and his mistress - Clara Petacci - were shot dead. Then the bodies were piled into a truck and driven to the Piazzale Loreto in Milan, where, in death, they were subject to a final indignity. Ropes were tied around the corpses' ankles and the bodies were strung up for display in the square. The man who had devoted his life to controlling the Italian people had met a terrible fate at their hands. What had been the extent of his control during his years in power?

Historians are agreed that Mussolini played a key role in the formulation of Fascist ideology and its subsequent implementation. However, the notion that Mussolini established a truly totalitarian state has now been called into question. Indeed, historians have pointed out the disparity between Mussolini's propaganda and rhetoric on the one hand, and the regime's actual performance on the other. They argue that the smack of firm government was conspicuously lacking from Mussolini's regime. Its real motifs, it is claimed, were indecision and confusion. Rather than genuinely seeking to establish a state in which the people became an instrument to serve the will of the leader, it is argued that Mussolini actually intended to weaken the powers of the state, since his only concern was to extend his own period in office. Finally, it is claimed that it was Hitler's Germany rather than Mussolini's Italy which witnessed the imposition of a genuinely totalitarian state. Hitler, it is said, achieved a degree of control and indoctrination far in excess of anything that happened in Italy. In this chapter we shall examine this issue, but first we must examine the circumstances which led to Mussolini's rise to power. Perhaps there too we will discover a difference between Mussolini's rhetoric and his performance.

THE CORPSES OF MUSSOLINI AND HIS MISTRESS

TALKING POINT

From Mussolini in Italy in 1945 to Ceausescu in Romania in 1989, dictators have often met a violent death with little or no attempt at a formal trial. Should formal methods of justice always be applied no matter what the circumstances?

FOCUS

7.1 Why did Fascism develop in Italy after the First World War?

The political development of Benito Mussolini

MUSSOLINI IN HIS SOLDIER'S UNIFORM OF THE FIRST WORLD WAR

1883-1912

Born in the Romagna, the son of a blacksmith and a schoolmistress. He embarked upon a stormy career in journalism and politics. His early career was characterised by an outspoken commitment to the radical Left. A fervent critic of nationalism he condemned Italy's conquest of Tripoli in 1912. He became a member of the PSI (Partito Socialista Italiano) and joined the local Socialist paper at Forli, *Lotta di Classe*. He then became editor of the official Socialist daily *Avanti!* in 1912, at the age of 29.

1914-17

Mussolini went through a major change in political outlook after the war broke out and his advocacy of Italian intervention meant that he lost his editorship of *Avanti!* and was expelled from the PSI. He set up his own newspaper, the *Popolo d'Italia* (a mouthpiece for the interventionists), but this was interrupted by his loyal but undistinguished military service, curtailed when he was wounded in 1917.

1919

Mussolini founded his own political movement, the Fasci di Combattimento, in Milan in March. The radical party programme did not instantly capture the public imagination. In the 1919 elections they did not win a single seat and the Socialists mockingly buried an effigy of Fascism. The newspaper, rather than the fasci, kept Mussolini in the political spotlight. In December 1919 the movement had only 870 members.

1920-21

The turning point came towards the end of 1920 with the establishment of paramilitary armed squads or 'squadrismo'. These squads took violent action against both striking urban workers and rural Socialist labour leagues. Meanwhile, in another temporary change of stance, Mussolini began preparing Fascism for a parliamentary campaign. In the summer of 1921 he took the risk of publicly endorsing a Pact of Pacification with the Socialists. This showed Mussolini's flexibility and his desire to create an aura of respectability. However, the move was soon abandoned and the emphasis returned to the Squadrismo movement. In October 1921 Mussolini formed the Fascist Party and by the end of the year the party had more than 200,000 members and 35 parliamentary deputies.

1922

By 1922 the government was relying increasingly on the Fascists to combat left-wing unrest. In particular, the Fascists played a key role in combatting the Socialists' general strike of 31 July. By the autumn, Mussolini was exerting growing pressure on the ruling élite to acknowledge his role by formally handing him a substantial degree of political authority, even though his electoral backing was not spectacular. In early October Mussolini was insisting on significant Cabinet representation and in the middle of the month was insisting on becoming prime minister. Mussolini's preparations for power reached a pitch at a mass rally of 40,000 Fascists in Naples on 24 October. It was now that the preparations were finalised for the March on Rome.

The context for the growth of Fascism in Italy
1900-12

In the years after 1900, Italy appeared to be moving through the formative stages towards a liberal, parliamentary democracy. There was an elected parliament with genuine influence alongside a monarch, the reticent Victor Emmanuel III (1900-46) who used the royal prerogative sparingly. Under the premiership of Giolitti, Italy experienced meaningful social reforms and some degree of economic prosperity. Of course, there was still a great deal of authority in the hands of the dynasty and the army but Italy appeared to be progressing democratically.

1915-18

Although Italy was involved in a war with Libya in 1911, Italy did not join in the European war until 1915. In May Italy entered the First World War on the Allied side and declared war on Germany and Austria. Rather than uniting the nation this brought about a split between those who supported the war - the interventionists - and those who opposed it (the neutralists). One historian has described this as a 'violent laceration of the political fabric, a bitterness of feeling, more characteristic of a civil than a national war'. A de Grand says the war marked a rupture in the course of Italian political development. The Italian army suffered a major defeat at the hands of the Austrians in the

Battle of Caporetto in 1917 but a year later the Austrians were defeated at Vittorio Veneto. In November 1918 Austria agreed to Allied peace terms. Italy had defeated her historic rival and had emerged with her monarchy and liberal institutions intact.

1919-20

The Italians made extensive territorial claims at Versailles only to be denied them by President Wilson. Arch nationalist D'Annunzio denounced the government and its 'mutilated victory' and agreed to lead a military coup on the disputed island of Fiume. His 'heroic' occupation and subsequent removal in the 'Christmas of Blood' of 1920 made the government appear both weak and unpatriotic. Meanwhile the introduction of proportional representation in the electoral system produced a series of weak and divided coalition

governments. In addition, a series of strikes disrupted the engineering, metal and steel industries. The government relied on the Fascist squads as the main bulwark against Socialist action.

1921-22

In 1921 Mussolini had founded the Fascist Party but despite some electoral success his influence was at its greatest outside parliament. In July 1922 the Socialists called a nationwide strike as an 'anti-Fascist' demonstration. Once again the government's dependency on the Fascists to control the Socialists and maintain services was evident. By the autumn of 1922 the key question in Italian politics was on what terms Mussolini and his followers would join the government.

CARTOON HIGHLIGHTING CONNECTION BETWEEN WAR AND THE GROWTH OF FASCISM

EXAMINING THE EVIDENCE

The March on Rome

Source A: the role of Balbo

'We are going, either with or without you, make up your mind.'

> Balbo's (leader of the Squadrismo) reputed comment to Mussolini, 16 October, 1922, quoted in S.J. Lee, *The European Dictatorships 1918-45* (1987)

Source B

'Today we enjoy the benefits of surprise. No one yet believes seriously in our insurrectionary intentions. In other words, in six months our difficulties will be ten times as great.'

> Balbo, 16 October 1922, quoted in A. Lyttleton, *The Seizure of Power* (1987)

Source C

Balbo later suggested that it was himself and Bianchi who advocated the March on Rome and that Mussolini was so cautious that it was considered necessary to tell him that the Fascists would march on Rome whether Mussolini agreed or not. This was not Mussolini's own version, and there is no doubt that, whether his apparent hesitation was contrived or not, it did enable him to maintain contacts with all his opponents, none of whom was certain until the last moment whether he might even then choose collaboration with them instead of leading a purely Fascist revolution.

> C. Hibbert, *Benito Mussolini* (1962)

Source D: The role of Mussolini

'Giolitti believes he can offer us two portfolios, but we want six or nothing. So we must put the masses in action to make an extra parliamentary crisis and come to power.'

> Mussolini, 16 October 1922, quoted in A. Lyttleton, *The Seizure of Power* (1987)

Source E

'What we have in view is the introduction into the liberal State, which has fulfilled its functions...of all the forces of the new generation which has emerged from the war and the victory...Either the Government will be given to us or we shall seize it by marching on Rome!'

> Mussolini, 24 October 1922, quoted in C. Hibbert, *Benito Mussolini* (1962)

Source F: The plan

The plan for the March on Rome had been drawn up in a secret meeting on 24 October in a Naples Hotel. The plan called for the occupation of public buildings throughout north and central Italy as the first stage in the seizure of power; in the second stage three columns would concentrate on the roads leading to Rome, at S. Marinella, Monterotondo and Tivoli, and converge on the capital. If the Government resisted the Ministries were to be occupied by force.

> A. Lyttleton, *The Seizure of Power* (1987)

SOME KEY FIGURES IN THE MARCH ON ROME. FROM LEFT TO RIGHT, GENERAL BALBO, GENERAL DE BONO, MUSSOLINI, DE VECCHI AND BIANCHI

Source G

The uncertainty is greatest among the police and prefectoral authorities. The Government has prescribed resistance including in case of necessity the use of arms. In other words the Government does not see the insurrectionary character of this whole movement, since in such a case it cannot be a question of a mere matter for the police, but for a real movement which should be treated as such, and therefore arrest of the leaders, military government etc...At Rome they don't understand a thing, and what is worse they give uncertain and contradictory information. At Milan, for example, they are in doubt even as to whether the telegraph and telephone offices should be guarded and they telephone from Rome that protection should be confined to the offices dependent on the Ministry of the Interior.

Letter from Camillo Corradini to Giolitti, 27 October 1922, quoted in A. Lyttleton, The Seizure of Power (1987)

Source H: The role of the King

KING VICTOR EMANUEL III. COULD HE HAVE PREVENTED MUSSOLINI'S RISE TO POWER?

By mid-October Mussolini could insist on becoming Prime Minister himself, unless the politicians used force against the massed Fascists. The Facta government, still formally in office, was obviously reluctant to do so. But early on 28 October, after much hesitation, it finally asked the King to sign a decree establishing martial law ('Stato d'assedio'). The King, after initially agreeing, refused. Why? No one can be sure, but his military advisers seem to have told him that the army might not be willing to fire on Fascists. Marshall Diaz is reported to have said, in a splendid phrase, 'Your Majesty, the army will do its duty; however, it would be well not to put it to the test.'

The King may also have worried about his cousin, the Duke of Aosta, who was near the Fascist headquarters in Perugia and might have been hoping for the crown.

M.Clark, *Modern Italy 1871-1982* (1984)

Source I: The breakdown of authority

...at the Viminale, the telephones which linked the prefectures to the Ministry gave no respite and after midnight the news became alarming. In the night I witnessed, in the silence of the great rooms of the Viminale, the disintegration of the authority and power of the State. On the large sheets of paper which I kept in front of me, there grew even thicker the names of the occupied prefectures that I was noting down, the indications of invaded telegraph offices, of military garrisons who had fraternized with the Fascists, providing them with arms, of trains requisitioned by the militia which were directed, loaded with armed men, towards the capital.

Efrem Ferraris, Facta's *chef de cabinet*, night of 27/28 October 1922, quoted in A. Lyttleton, *The Seizure of Power* (1987)

FASCISTS MARCH, UNIMPEDED AT THIS STAGE, TO ROME

Source J: An historian's verdict on the March on Rome

In reality, the March on Rome, in the strict sense, was a colossal bluff. The city was defended by 12,000 men of the regular army under the loyal General Pugliese, who would have been able to disperse the Fascist bands without difficulty. Many of the Fascists failed to arrive at their points of concentration; they were travelling by train and were stopped by the simple expedient of taking up a few yards of track. Those who did arrive were poorly armed and they were short of food. They could do nothing except hang around miserably in the torrential autumn rain. The grandiose 'pincer movement' on Rome could never have been carried out with any chance of success.

A. Lyttleton, *The Seizure of Power* (1987)

Source K

We must now return to Rome, the central government and the King...this was the point of decision. At 8 pm on 27 October, when the King arrived in Rome...he told Facta that the crown must be able to decide in full liberty, and not under the pressure of Fascist rifles. His determination to resist seemed evident...

On the evening of the twenty-seventh (October), he still saw his duty, in plain terms, as resistance. Why did he change his mind? To this central question, whose importance vividly illustrates the role of the individual in historical crisis, the answer cannot be certain...

The excuse that he quite literally ceded to force...convinced that the garrison of Rome was too small and too unreliable to resist the Fascist attack, will not hold. However, these statements may be helpful in understanding the King's state of mind: 'At difficult moments everyone is capable of indecision...few or none are those who can take clear decisions and assume grave responsibilities. In 1922 I had to call "these people" to the Government because all the others in one way or another, had abandoned me'; on other occasions the King spoke of his desire to 'avoid bloodshed given the news from the provinces which were already in the hands of the Fascists,' and said that if he had acted otherwise, 'it would have been civil war.'

A. Lyttleton, *The Seizure of Power* (1987)

Source L: Mussolini is given power

He was still in Milan. His offices were surrounded by units of the Army and the police, and he kept looking out of the window and telephoning constantly for news. He was making a strenuous effort to appear calm and controlled, but his excitement was close to hysteria. When a squadron of tanks rolled through the streets towards Il Popolo d'Italia he ran out of the building with a rifle in his hands shouting incoherently and was nearly shot by a supporter even more excited than he was. In fact there was practically no opposition to the march of Fascism. Both the Army and the police were prepared to stand aside and let it take its course.

C. Hibbert, *Benito Mussolini* (1962)

Source M

'Very urgent. Top Priority. Mussolini - Milan. H.M. the King asks you to proceed immediately to Rome as he wishes to offer your the responsibility of forming a Ministry. With respect - Cittadini, General.'

Telegram from King Emmanuel III to Mussolini, 29 October 1922, quoted in C. Hibbert, *Benito Mussolini* (1962)

Source N

He left by train that evening. As if to make his black shirt more respectable he was wearing, in addition, a journalist delightedly noticed, a bowler hat and spats. When he presented himself to the King he apologised for this unconventional attire. 'Please excuse my appearance,' he said, and then added with a dramatic comment both predictable and unashamedly vainglorious: 'I come from the battlefield.'

C. Hibbert, *Benito Mussolini* (1962)

Source O: Aftermath

It was surprising and significant that he omitted at this point all reference to the role of the Crown...He was intent on showing that he owed his position not to royal investiture but to 'the rights of revolution'. 'I add, so that everyone may know, that I am here to defend and strengthen to the utmost degree the revolution of the blackshirts...with 300,000 young armed men prepared for anything...and ready to execute my demands with religious devotion, I could have castigated all those who defamed and tried to smear fascism. I could have made this grey and gloomy hall into a bivouac for my legions...I could have barred up Parliament and formed an exclusively Fascist government. I could have: but at least for the moment, I did not will it'.

Mussolini's speech to the Chamber of Deputies, 16 November 1922, quoted in A. Lyttleton, *The Seizure of Power* (1987)

Source P

The editor of at least one liberal paper was forced to drink the 'fascist medicine', castor oil; socialist newspapers and bookstores were ransacked and heaps of books burnt in the street; shops were pillaged, houses belonging to political opponents broken into and foreign embassies compelled to fly the Italian flag. A number of private grievances were settled in the turmoil and a dozen people killed...and Mussolini subsequently made the comment that, in those 'radiant days of October' he should have had more people put up against a wall and shot.   D. Mack Smith, *Mussolini* (1981)

Source Q: The myth of the March on Rome

The Fascist leader was not satisfied with something so unspectacular as a royal appointment. He needed to develop the myth of a march on Rome by 300,000 armed fascists to enforce an 'ultimatum' he had given to the King, and eventually a legend was invented of Mussolini on horseback leading his

A GROUP OF FASCIST AVIATORS IN NAPLES, SHORTLY BEFORE THE MARCH ON ROME

legions across the Rubicon. In reality there were fewer than 30,000 fascist militiamen ready to march, many of whom had no arms at all and would have been quite unable to stand up to the garrison troops in Rome with their machine-guns and armoured cars: indeed 400 policemen proved sufficient to hold up the fascist trains long before they reached Rome. Mussolini subsequently admitted this in private with amused satisfaction. His fascist squads did not arrive in Rome until twenty-four hours after he had been asked to form a government and only after General Pugliese had orders to let them through. But the photographers were waiting to picture their arrival and the myth was launched of fascism winning power by an armed insurrection after a civil war and the loss of 3,000 men. These fictitious 3,000 'fascist martyrs' soon took their place in the government sponsored history books.

D. Mack Smith, *Mussolini* (1981)

IN THE AFTERMATH OF THE MARCH ON ROME, THE SOCIALIST NEWSPAPER *AVANTI'S* OFFICES ARE BURNT DOWN

Source R

Mussolini did not really seize power. He did not, by 28 October, need to use force. He won by threatening to use it, and by having the squads ready to obey. Formally, he became prime minister constitutionally, appointed by the King; the 'March on Rome' happened afterwards, when hordes of Blackshirts were allowed to roam around the capital exulting and rampaging in the rain. Mussolini won by being 'brought into the system' by a king and a governing elite that could see no other way of containing organised violence.

M. Clark, *Modern Italy, 1871-1982* (1984)

7.2 March on Rome or national uprising?

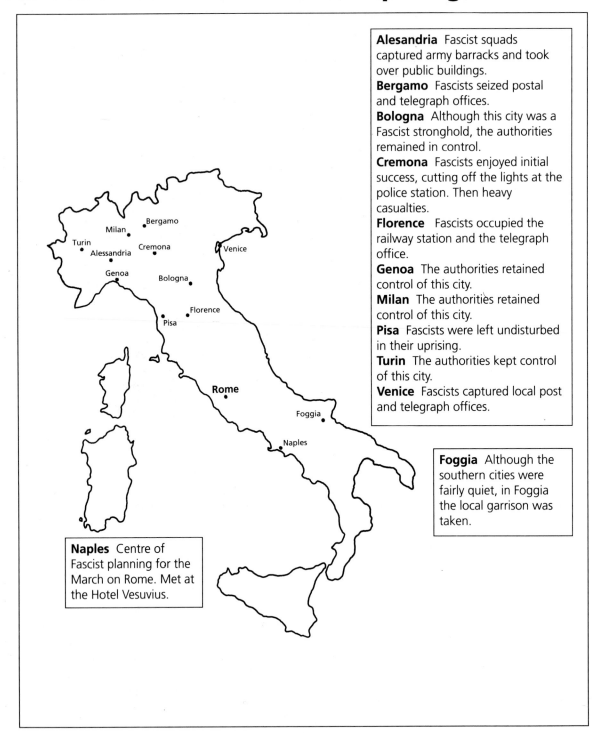

Alesandria Fascist squads captured army barracks and took over public buildings.

Bergamo Fascists seized postal and telegraph offices.

Bologna Although this city was a Fascist stronghold, the authorities remained in control.

Cremona Fascists enjoyed initial success, cutting off the lights at the police station. Then heavy casualties.

Florence Fascists occupied the railway station and the telegraph office.

Genoa The authorities retained control of this city.

Milan The authorities retained control of this city.

Pisa Fascists were left undisturbed in their uprising.

Turin The authorities kept control of this city.

Venice Fascists captured local post and telegraph offices.

Foggia Although the southern cities were fairly quiet, in Foggia the local garrison was taken.

Naples Centre of Fascist planning for the March on Rome. Met at the Hotel Vesuvius.

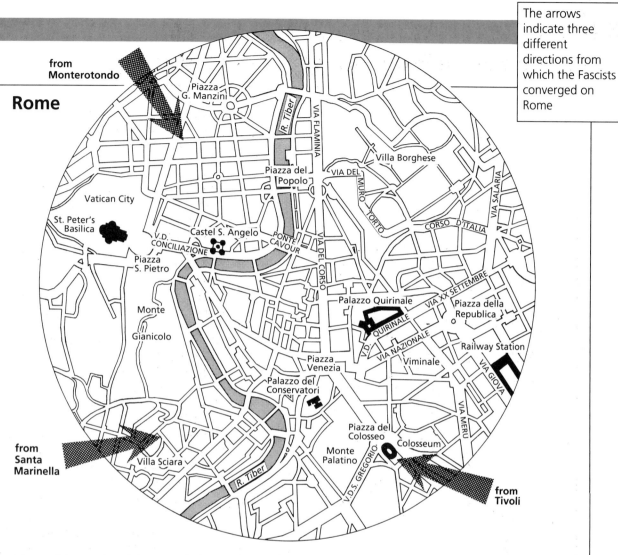

Rome

from Monterotondo

Piazza G. Manzini

R. Tiber

VIA FLAMINIA

Villa Borghese

VIA DEL

Piazza del Popolo

VIA DEL MURO TORTO

VIA SALARIA

Vatican City

CORSO D'ITALIA

St. Peter's Basilica

V.D. CONCILIAZIONE

Castel S. Angelo

PONTE CAVOUR

VIA DEL CORSO

Piazza S. Pietro

Palazzo Quirinale

VIA XX SETTEMBRE

Piazza della Republica

Monte

V.D. QUIRINALE

VIA NAZIONALE

Railway Station

Gianicolo

Piazza Venezia

Viminale

VIA GIOVA

Palazzo del Conservatori

VIA MERU

from Santa Marinella

Villa Sciara

Piazza del Colosseo

Colosseum

Monte Palatino

V.D.S. GREGORIO

from Tivoli

R. Tiber

R. Tiber

Many of the Fascists did not reach their intended destination. Rail tracks were taken up to prevent them from completing their journey. In addition 12,000 troops were deployed by General Pugliese and War Minister Soleri.

QUESTIONS

You will need to have read the written evidence very carefully before you can begin this exercise.

1 Study the maps and the notes.

(a) In which areas did the Fascists seem to achieve fully their objective?
(b) In which areas did they achieve partial success?
(c) In which areas were they unsuccessful?

What tentative conclusions would you now make about the nature of the uprising?

2 Compare the situation in each of the areas with what happened in Rome.

(a) Was Rome a successful part of the overall operation? Give reasons for your answer.
(b) What conclusions would you now make about the 'March on Rome'?

Seizure of power or loss of nerve?

The objective of this task is to enable you to reach a conclusion on the March on Rome. Was it a genuine seizure of power, orchestrated by Mussolini and carried out in accordance with his plans, or could the King have resisted the Fascists' bid for power if only he had kept his nerve?

1 Consider these contrasting viewpoints of Mussolini and the King based on different interpretations of the evidence. Copy out the chart, then place ticks in the boxes which you feel are most appropriate.

Sympathetic viewpoint		Critical viewpoint
Agree	Truth lies somewhere in between	Agree

MUSSOLINI

☐ Mussolini had carefully thought out his tactics and was generally in control of events	☐ Mussolini was an opportunist who responded to the moves of others	☐
☐ Mussolini initiated the March on Rome to forestall criticism from his followers	☐ It was Balbo, not Mussolini, who initiated the March on Rome	☐
☐ There was a clear and well-organised plan of action which succeeded in its objective	☐ The March on Rome was tactically inept and would have ended in disaster if the regime had resisted	☐
☐ Mussolini had behind him thousands of well-organised, highly-motivated and well-armed followers	☐ Mussolini's followers generally found themselves stranded outside Rome, where they played no significant part in events	☐
☐ Mussolini waited patiently to be offered power and arrived triumphantly in Rome to accept it	☐ Mussolini was in Milan, not Rome, at the critical moment, and his mental state was one of near hysteria	☐
☐ Mussolini seized power through force and by the impact of the March on Rome	☐ Mussolini was given a share of power by the King because the King decided that this was the best option open to him	☐

KING VICTOR EMMANUEL

☐ The King made the key decisions in 1922 and others reacted to them	☐ The King was intimidated by Mussolini	☐
☐ The King wanted to resist Mussolini by force but realised that the army and the police were not behind him	☐ The army and the police would have backed the King but he chose not to impose martial law because he lost his nerve	☐
☐ The King was trying to find a peaceful way out of the crisis in the best interests of the country	☐ The King was motivated by the manoeuvres of his cousin, the Duke of Aosta, and his main concern was to retain his own personal position whatever the cost for the country	☐

2 Consider the following conclusions

(a) Mussolini seized power in 1922 thanks to the March on Rome.

(b) It was in the provinces, not the cities, that Mussolini's bid for power succeeded.

(c) The crucial factor in the crisis was the change of mind of the King.

(d) The crucial factor in the crisis was the attitude of the forces of law and order.

(e) The Fascists' lack of success in the big cities underlines the fact that Mussolini could have been effectively resisted.

(f) Mussolini did not seize power, it was handed to him by a regime which had lost its nerve.

Having considered these conclusions very carefully, in small groups discuss which of them:
(i)   You would immediately dismiss;
(ii) You feel contain an element of truth;
(iii) You feel accurately reflect the real circumstances behind Mussolini's rise to power.

Consolidation of power

'Mussolini's designs could not ignore either the limitations posed by established political conventions or, on the other hand, those set by the history and character of his own movement. The ambiguity of the March on Rome, a violent armed movement prepared by political intrigue and legitimized by royal investiture, deeply marked the character of the subsequent period. One cannot use organisations for long without also being used by them; and Mussolini's own personal freedom of action was restricted both by the resistance of the old order, and the State machinery, and by the demands of the new.'

A. Lyttleton, *The Seizure of Power* (1987)

The 39-year-old Fascist leader came face-to-face with the King on the morning of 30 October, dressed extravagantly in a black shirt, bowler hat and spats. Mussolini excused his appearance with the dramatic comment that he had 'come from the battlefield'. In fact, his train journey from Milan to Rome had been distinctly down-to-earth and most of his armed followers were still stranded miles outside the city. As compensation, the squadrismo were given their moment of glory on 31 October when they were allowed into Rome to parade past the royal palace. Nevertheless, as soon as the parades were over, the blackshirts were placed on special trains and packed off back to their home towns. The contrived and empty nature of this ritual seemed to indicate that Mussolini was quickly falling into line and coming to terms with the establishment.

Mussolini's Cabinet, the so-called 'National Government' included himself and three Fascists in key posts, but also included four liberals, two Popolari and three eminent individuals: the philosopher Gentile in education, Marshall Diaz at the war ministry, and Admiral Revel at the Admiralty. The cosmopolitan nature of this Cabinet - which immediately followed an orthodox economic policy and publicly endorsed a return to law and order and normalisation - seemed to support the accepted notion that Mussolini's radical days were over. As one seasoned campaigner observed: 'Once he is at Rome, he will be much more subject to influence.' This apparent process of moderation was taken a stage further through the changing membership of the PNF. In October 1922 the PNF had 300,000 members, but by the end of 1923 the figure exceeded 780,000. Clearly, many of these new members were ambitious opportunists, jumping on the Fascist bandwagon not out of genuine political commitment but because they felt it would further their interests. This dilution was exaggerated by the 'fusion' of the Fascist party with the Nationalist Association, which joined the PNF en bloc in February 1923. Indeed the Nationalists' natural sympathy with the landowning classes enabled them quickly to dominate the southern branches of the party. To what extent would the notion that Mussolini had been absorbed by the state be borne out?

We will now examine some of the key incidents and policies of Mussolini's rule. Here are some of the issues which you should have uppermost in your mind. To what extent did Mussolini establish a totalitarian regime? What gave this government its Fascist character? Was Mussolini able to exert his own personal rule? Finally, were his policies a success or failure?

The Fascist Militia (January 1923)

Mussolini's controversial decision to disperse the squadrismo after the March on Rome opened him up to accusations that he had betrayed his own supporters and that the Fascist revolution was stillborn. The Fascist Militia (MVSN) represented his attempt at countering critics from within his own party, while bringing the wilder elements of the Fascist movement under firmer, central control.

The Militia was funded by public money and its members were usually party members, normally ex-squadristi. Directly responsible to Mussolini, the new organisation in effect became a private army. Mussolini's intention, which the Militia fulfilled, was for this new organisation to resist the local independence of the troublesome Ras and curb the excesses of more extremist members. In practice, the function of the Militia was to give the movement military presence: Militia members provided a bodyguard for Mussolini, paraded at public ceremonies and guarded public buildings. Tactically, Mussolini had given the squadristi visible rewards while denying them real importance.

The Acerbo Electoral Law (1923)

Despite Mussolini's new status, the fact remained that his parliamentary representation was meagre. In the lower chamber, for example, the Fascists had only 7 per cent of the seats. In April 1923 the PPI Congress debated whether to remain in Mussolini's government and Mussolini responded by dismissing the Popolari ministers even though this placed in jeopardy the government's parliamentary majority. Mussolini needed to come up with a plan which would provide the party with a permanent parliamentary majority and remove the possibility of an alternative government taking its place. Fortunately for Mussolini, few people regarded the existing parliamentary system as satisfactory and so his proposals for a 'corrected' parliamentary system were passed without resistance. The new system meant that the party with the largest number of votes - providing that amounted to at least 25 per cent of the valid votes cast - would automatically receive at least two-thirds of the parliamentary seats. Mussolini's justification was that in future Italy would be assured of stable government majorities rather than the wartime and post-war diet of endless coalitions. The bill was passed through its second reading by 235 votes to 139. The real purpose became clear after the elections of April 1924. The government 'bloc' of Fascists, former Nationalists, Agrarians and Right-Wing Liberals won 66.3 per cent of the valid votes and therefore secured two-thirds of the parliamentary seats. Analysis of the bloc's victorious candidates reveals that around 60 per cent were Fascist sympathisers. Mussolini had achieved his objective, a fact which is underlined by the low level of support for the Popolari (9.1 per cent), the reformist Socialists (5.9 per cent) and the Communists (3.8 per cent). The Fascists could point to 4.5 million votes and claim that they now had genuine electoral backing for their policies. Mussolini's next step was to remove the opposition parties altogether. The opportunity presented itself in the summer of 1924.

The Matteotti crisis (1924)

Mussolini's personal satisfaction at his success in the elections of April 1924 was diminished when on 30 May, Giacomo Matteotti made an outspoken speech in parliament condemning the elections as a sham based on corruption and intimidation. To add to Mussolini's discomfort, it was also rumoured that Matteotti had a dossier containing damaging details of Fascist corruption. Mussolini was furious and made several comments to the effect that Matteotti should be 'taught a lesson'. Concrete evidence that Mussolini actually ordered the murder of Matteotti has not been uncovered.

At any rate, on 10 June several eye-witnesses on a busy road in Rome saw the Socialist leader being bundled into a car which then drove off at high speed. Within days the car, with bloodstained upholstery and a broken window, was found abandoned.

MATTEOTTI, IN CHEERFUL MOOD, WITH SOCIALIST COLLEAGUES

MUSSOLINI SITS ON THE COFFIN OF MATTEOTTI

Although Matteotti's body was not discovered until 16 August, the police soon connected his disappearance with Amerigo Dumini - a notorious member of the squadrista from Florence - and Cesare Rossi, head of Mussolini's Press Office. In the Chamber on 12 June, Mussolini's evasive answers to questions about Matteotti fuelled suspicion that he had, at the very least, known about a plan to kill his most outspoken critic. When a Republican denounced Mussolini as an 'accomplice' it was clear that the new government was facing its first major crisis. However, the outcome of this crisis was ultimately to strengthen, not weaken, Mussolini's position.

Crucially, the Crown - conscious of widespread support for Mussolini in conservative circles - refused to act against him. Meanwhile the opposition parties made the courageous but ultimately unwise gesture of walking out of the Chamber and refusing to play any further part in its proceedings. This played into Mussolini's hands. As the impact of the murder and their response wore off, it became clear that Mussolini was actually benefitting from their absence.

For Mussolini, the crisis was most damaging not within parliament but within his own movement. His well-publicised attempts to appear conciliatory, his refusal to admit responsibility for the murder, his willingness to sacrifice other Fascists as scapegoats and his failure to act when a Fascist deputy was murdered in September all combined to fuel unrest among his more radical followers. As late as December 1924, Fascists in Florence, Pisa and Bologna were making it clear in public demonstrations that their patience with their leader had its limits. Pressure was therefore mounting on Mussolini to show his followers that he was prepared to embrace the extremist and authoritarian ideas of his most radical supporters. On New Year's Eve 1924, 33 eminent Fascist Ras called on Mussolini, ostensibly to pay their respects but with the message that 'either you, guided by God, pursue a grandiose programme, as we hope, or we before becoming an object of ridicule will engage in battle.'

TALKING POINT

Elsewhere in this chapter there is ample evidence to suggest that Mussolini was capable of ordering very violent crimes to be committed. Can his record elsewhere be held against him in the case of Matteotti, or should we only use the evidence available?

MATTEOTTI'S BODY BEING TAKEN AWAY AFTER IT WAS DISCOVERED IN A WOOD NEAR ROME

In effect, Mussolini had been given an ultimatum. In an important speech made on 3 January 1925, he made it clear to his followers that he had taken heed of their message.

The shift towards authoritarianism (1925)

Mussolini's speech of 3 January marked a significant change in the regime's direction. To satisfy the conservatives Mussolini repeated his claim that his government had always acted in the best interests of peace and normality. After all, in the last few months the Militia had taken an oath of loyalty to the King, orthodox economic policies had been maintained and a 'democratic' election had been held, based on Mussolini's own electoral reforms. In fact, Mussolini claimed, although he had been accused of terrible crimes it was the opposition - with their unconstitutional and revolutionary act of secession - who had acted illegally. Once again, Mussolini went to great lengths to deny any connection with the murder of Matteotti, and instead condemned the press for the 'slanderous fabrications' which they had published against him. However, the key section of the speech successfully demonstrated to Mussolini's followers that while he continued to deny the murder of Matteotti, he was prepared to accept responsibility for Fascist policies in general. 'I now accept, I alone, full political and moral and historical responsibility for what has happened...if Fascism has been a criminal association, then I am the chief of this criminal association.' In addition, Mussolini made it clear to his opponents that henceforth dissent would be dealt with much more forcefully. It was obviously Mussolini's intention to take steps to curb the freedom of the press and to restrict the activities of the opposition parties. Finally, the advent of this dynamic, 'strong state' meant that government forces - rather than the Ras and the Militia - would be deployed to quell sedition. This measure was designed to satisfy Mussolini's conservative supporters who had been concerned that it was his intention to unleash the squadrista.

Action against the press came swiftly after the 3 January speech. Censorship of it was stepped up and newspapers which had given particular offence to Mussolini were seized. Important independent editors, such as

AFTER THE WALK-OUT OF SOCIALIST DEPUTIES, THE FASCISTS SIT IN AN OTHERWISE DESERTED CHAMBER

Luigi Albertini of the *Corriere della Sera* and Senator Frassati of *La Stampa*, were simply replaced by more compliant journalists. State control became even stronger with the introduction of the Press Law in December 1925. This enforced a closed shop, stating that only registered journalists - and the register was controlled by the Fascists - could write for the press. On a more personal level, Mussolini (still a journalist at heart) personally scrutinised the papers every day.

Beacons of independence remained with the existence of the party newspapers such as the Socialists' *Avanti!* and the Communists' *L'Unita*; however, by 1926 the level of censorship imposed on these papers made their influence negligible.

Denied sympathetic press coverage, the opposition parties now found to their cost that the Aventine Secession had ultimately been misguided. Although, oddly, the Communists had returned to the Chamber in November 1924, the attempts of other deputies to do likewise were fruitless. In October 1925 Matteotti's party - the PSU - was banned completely. In January 1926 the Popolari deputies, receiving no support from the Vatican, attempted to return to Parliament but were driven out by the Fascists. Meanwhile the Nationalists and the Right-Wing Liberals had offered complete support to the Fascists. Finally, after an assassination attempt on Mussolini on 3 October 1926, all opposition parties were suppressed and their reconstitution was forbidden by the euphemistically-named 'law for the defence of the State'. In addition, passports were withdrawn, a 'special tribunal' was set up to repress anti-Fascist activity and, crucially, it was declared that all opposition deputies had expired their electoral mandate and forfeited their parliamentary immunity.

The King's passivity, the impotence of the opposition parties and Mussolini's skilful control of his own extremists meant that by late 1925 Italy had become, to some extent, a totalitarian state. In Mussolini's words, this would mean: 'everything within the State, nothing outside the State, nothing against the State'.

The Aventine Secession

This term, used to describe the walk-out of the opposition parties in 1924, was based on the old Roman expression 'gone to the Aventine Hill' in Rome.

The Concordat (1929)

Although Mussolini had no religious beliefs himself, he realised that the attitude of the church towards his regime was of vital importance. If the Vatican were to come out firmly against Mussolini then it would undermine all his social objectives. Mussolini showed how much importance he placed on this when he made a series of unilateral concessions such as restoring crucifixes to the walls of schools and allowing Catholic priests back into elementary schools.

The Vatican responded to these gestures by signing a Concordat with the Italian state in February 1929. The benefits of this for Mussolini were apparent when the church endorsed Mussolini in the national elections of 1929: 8.5 million voted for the Fascists while only 135,000 expressed dissent. The Concordat seemed to have bridged the gap between support for *il Duce* and allegiance to the Catholic church.

The Ministry for Popular Culture (1937)

This organisation, established in 1937, attempted to place state control of the mass media on a firmer footing. Stemming from this, the government

THE DUCE DECORATES A BALLILA (YOUNG FASCIST) AT A MILITARY REVIEW HELD IN ROME

stepped up its attempts to control radio broadcasting, most notably with a mixture of news and propaganda encapsulated in the programme 'Chronicles of the Regime'. In addition, the government established an 'Experimental Centre of Cinematography' which trained the students destined to become the nation's film-makers. As well as sponsoring films which glorified the achievements of Fascism, the government also ensured that the sporting achievements of famous Fascists were emblazoned across the silver screen. The Fascists were portrayed flying planes and skiing or supporting successful Italian sportsmen such as Primo Carnera (world heavyweight boxing champion from 1933 to 1935) and the football team which won the World Cup in 1934 and 1938.

Economic policies

Between 1922 and 1925 the Fascists achieved some important, if ultimately superficial, economic success. During this period the finance minister, De Stefani, followed orthodox and unspectacular financial policies. De Stefani was fortunate in that the international economy was already showing signs of growth and revival, and by 1924-25 he was able to announce a budget surplus. Richard Overy provides the following summary of Mussolini's economic achievement. 'Economic revival was essential to Fascism's political survival. Mussolini did not gamble with the economy, but used the power of the state to create a secure environment in which orthodox policies could work effectively. Between 1922 and 1929 the budgets were balanced, agriculture expanded, industry more than doubled its output, and the balance of payments deficit was halved.'

Nevertheless, it is fair to say that Mussolini's economic policies were based largely on rhetoric and propaganda rather than clearly thought-out strategies.

AS PART OF THE REDEMPTION OF THE PONTINE MARSHES, MUSSOLINI DRIVES A TRACTOR AT THE 'START' OF THE NEW CITY OF APRILIA

Indeed, the Fascists did not apply a single, consistent theory concerning the economy. Instead, Mussolini applied the totalitarian slogans which he had used to engineer social change to try to stimulate the economy or disguise its shortcomings. Thus Mussolini instigated a 'Battle for Births'. Although

WHAT IMPRESSION IS THIS CARTOON ATTEMPTING TO CONVEY?

1919~Bolscevismo~   *1923~Fascismo~*

some of these schemes enjoyed superficial success they invariably had a significant adverse effect. For example, although grain production - personally endorsed by Mussolini through propaganda pictures of him reaping the crops bare-chested - actually increased by 100 per cent between 1922 and 1939, this was at the expense of other crops which lost land given over to grain. Similarly, Mussolini announced in 1926 that he was determined not to let the lira be undervalued. To ensure that the Italian currency was regarded as prestigious, he set its value at 90 to the pound sterling, as opposed to its then market level of almost 150. This meant that the export boom which occurred between 1922 and 1926 was now placed in jeopardy. Although Mussolini was attempting to keep the lira strong, in practice the new exchange rate meant that many Italian products were now priced too highly for world markets. Italian exports in light-engineering, motor cars and textiles all suffered as a result. The reasoning behind the 'Battle for Births' was to create a sense of national vitality by doubling Italy's population within a generation. Incentives for larger families and penalties imposed on single people failed to achieve the targets set, so that the birth rate between 1936 and 1940 was 23.1 per 1000 compared to 29.9 per 1000 in the period 1921-25.

A significant innovation came in 1931 with the establishment of the *Istituto Mobilaire Italiano* (IMI) to provide industrial credit; and of the *Istituto per la Recostruizione Industriale* (IRI) in 1933, designed to provide finance for important state industries. The IRI came to exert massive control over pig iron, steel, shipping, electricity, the telephone system and machine-tools. In effect, this meant that by 1936 Italian industry had a greater proportion

STRIPPED TO THE WAIST, MUSSOLINI ENCOURAGES THE PEASANTS TO PRODUCE A BUMPER CORN HARVEST AT APRILIA

of state ownership than any other European country, bar Russia. Nevertheless, the regime made little attempt to correct the imbalance between the wealthy North and the poorer South. The dominant industries under Mussolini were mechanical engineering, steelmaking, chemicals and hydro-electric water supply, and these were all centred around the north of Italy.

Finally, it should be noted that Mussolini's policies had a profound effect on both rural and urban workforces. The Fascists easily destroyed the trade unions and replaced them with their own Fascist syndicates. This change was underlined by the law passed in 1926 by the minister of justice, Alfredo Rocco, who emphasised to the chamber that the workers must be disciplined. The Rocco law established syndicates for each major area of economic activity - such as industry, agriculture and transport - and these then came under the control of the ministry of corporations. The ministry settled disputes through negotiations between the syndicates and employers.

Education

Stephen J. Lee provides the following summary of the Fascists' education policy:

'The most important attempt to 'Fascistize' education was initiated by Bottai in 1936. Textbooks became a state monopoly; the number of approved history texts for instance, was reduced from 317 to one, while a junior Italian reader informed the solemn eight-year-olds that "the eyes of the Duce are on every one of you".

From 1938 racism was openly practised and taught in the classroom, while 1939 saw the introduction of the Fascist School Charter. By and large, however, education was not one of the more successful examples of indoctrination. There were too many loopholes and evasions and, in the universities, underground resistance to and contempt for Fascist values.'

The Opera Nazionale Dopolavoro (OND)

The *Dopolavoro* ('after work') represents the biggest attempt by the Fascists to win the goodwill of the Italian people. Its activities are analysed by Martin Clark as follows:

'The OND was easily the largest fascist organisation for adults, and easily the most popular. The Dopolavoro clubs had bars, billiard halls, libraries, radios and sports grounds; they put on concerts and plays; they provided virtually free summer holidays for children...They also handed out welfare relief in poor areas: both circuses and bread. No wonder they were popular. It was the first time in Italian history that mass leisure activities had existed, let alone been encouraged and subsidized by politicians. And it was not too solemn. The Dopolavoro was fun, not propaganda.'

The police and internal security

A new wave of repressive policy was heralded by the latest in a succession of attempts on Mussolini's life, on 3 October 1926. Within a month the Fascists established the 'Special Tribunal for the Defence of the State'. This was given substantial powers to try terrorists and other political offenders. Although the Tribunal was empowered with the death penalty, in practice this measure was rarely applied. Between 1926 and the downfall of the Fascist

TALKING POINT

Should an authoritarian regime like Mussolini's be given credit for the Dopolavoro scheme, or should we be critical of it as a cynical attempt to win favour?

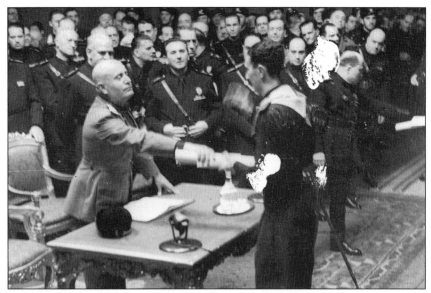

MUSSOLINI REWARDS A PEASANT WHO, ON HIS FARM IN THE RECLAIMED AREAS, RAISED THE FINEST CROP DURING THE YEAR 1936

regime in 1943, only 26 people were executed. Much more widely used was the practice of *confino*, through which those suspected of planning to engage in subversive activity could be sentenced to internal exile and confinement, normally for up to five years. Generally this meant that suspects were sent to the South, or to the Southern islands. Most notoriously, the leader of the Communists, Antonio Gramsci, was banished for 20 years. Despite these measures, the legal system itself was generally unchanged.

Mussolini's policies: success or failure?

Consider carefully the policies followed by Mussolini.

Positive aspects
1 What do you regard as his most positive achievements?
2 Which groups of people in Italian society benefitted from his policies?
3 What innovations did Mussolini introduce?
4 How succcessful were these policies?

Negative aspects
1 What do you regard as the most damaging of Mussolini's policies?
2 Which groups of people in Italian society suffered most as a result of his policies?
3 To what extent were his policies superficial?
4 How damaging, in the long term, were his ideas?

Now answer the following essay question:

To what extent did Italians have cause for satisfaction with Mussolini's regime during the period 1922-40?

FOCUS

7.3 Did Mussolini establish a truly totalitarian State?

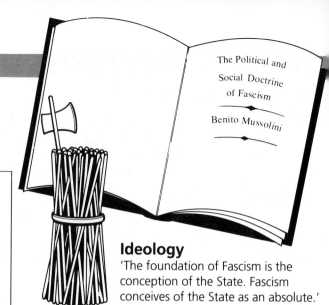

The Political and Social Doctrine of Fascism

Benito Mussolini

Indoctrination

The Opera Nazionale Balilla (established 1926)

Age 6-8	Sons of the She-Wolf	*Note*
Age 8-11	Balilla	Approximately
Age 11-13	Balilla Musketeers	40% of Italian
Age 14-17	Avanguardisti	youth (boys
Age 18	Fascist Levy	*and* girls) did
		not join these
		organisations

Oath taken by the Balilla

'I believe in the genius of Mussolini, in our Holy Father Fascism, in the communion of the martyrs, in the conversion of Italians and in the resurrection of the Empire.'

Ideology

'The foundation of Fascism is the conception of the State. Fascism conceives of the State as an absolute.'

Benito Mussolini, *The Political and Social Doctrine of Fascism* (1932)

Symbolism

The Fasces. The symbol adopted by the Fascist Party. It was a bundle of rods, with a protruding axe-head, carried by magistrates in ancient Rome. These rods were to symbolise the different groups who supported the Fascists; individually weak but bound together by the strength of their Fascist convictions.

Mussolini's oratory

1934 'We are becoming – and shall become so increasingly because this is our desire -— a military nation...To complete the picture, warlike – that is to say, endowed even to a higher degree with the virtues of obedience, sacrifice and dedication to country. This means that the whole life of the nation, political, economic, and spiritual, must be systematically directed towards our military requirements.'

1936 'All knots were cut by our gleaming sword, and the African victory remains in the history of our fatherland entire and unsullied, a victory such as the legionaries that have fallen and those that survived, dreamed of and willed. Italy has her empire at last: a fascist empire.'

1941 'Being anti-individualistic, the Fascist system of life stresses the importance of the state and recognises the individual only in so far as his interests coincide with those of the state...The Fascist conception of the State is all-embracing; outside it no human or spiritual values may exist, much less have any value. Thus understood Fascism is totalitarian.'

Propaganda

'It may well be argued that Fascist Italy was the first state in Western Europe to recognise the political value of the mass media for purposes of political control.'

A SYMBOLIC DISPLAY OF STRENGTH BY THE MUSQUETEERS, MUSSOLINI'S PRIVATE BODYGUARD.

Slogans

MUSSOLINI'S ALWAYS RIGHT BELIEVE! OBEY! FIGHT!

The verdict of historians

Source A

Fascism had aspirations to be 'totalitarian'; Mussolini virtually invented the term. But...it is clear that Mussolini's grip on Italian society was not as firm, his influence so pervasive, as that of a Hitler or a Stalin. Fascism left huge areas of Italian life practically untouched. Nonetheless it would...be mistaken to believe that Fascism did not mark a sharp break in Italy's development. Many men and even institutions from the liberal regime survived, but they had to fit into a new framework.

Adrian Lyttleton

Source B

Until 1936 most people swallowed most of the propaganda most of the time, at a fairly superficial level. Italy was stable, the Duce was popular, open dissenters were rare...But there was little enthusiasm for Fascism...and the regime's claims to 'totalitarianism' were laughable...The Fascists totally failed to arouse warlike zeal among the general population, a failure which became very evident by the late 1930s. In short, there was acceptance but not devotion, consensus but not commitment.

Martin Clark

Source C

Between 1922 and 1943 Mussolini established, at least in theory, all the institutions and devices associated with the totalitarian state. The foundation was the Fascist ideology, upon which was set a one-party system and all the paraphernalia of the personality cult. Popular support was guaranteed by indoctrination and, where necessary, coercion, while the economy was brought under a corporative system and geared to the needs of war.

This is a fairly conventional picture of Fascist Italy. It is not untrue but is incomplete. Below the surface there are indications that the totalitarian state was actually quite precarious. Fascist ideology was a makeshift alliance of different interests, the political institutions retained a surprisingly large number of non-Fascist influences, and the processes of indoctrination, coercion and corporativism were never completed.

Stephen J. Lee

Source D

Although the external elements of Italian Fascism - uniforms, mass parades, grandiloquent architecture - were replicated in Hitler's Germany, there were marked differences between the two totalitarian states...the armed forces remained loyal to the monarchy, and Mussolini never attained the complete grasp of Italian society that Hitler later exercised in Germany. Nor did he have the same undisputed control over the PNF that Hitler achieved over the Nazi party; rivals were pushed to the margins, or sent to the colonies; there was no mass blood-letting like the Night of the Long Knives. Rather that 'seizing power' the Fascists eased themselves into control of the state, and their role was never wholly secure.

Richard Overy

QUESTIONS

1 What evidence is contained here to suggest that Mussolini did establish a totalitarian state?

2 What evidence shown here suggests otherwise?

3 What are your conclusions about the nature of his rule?

FASCISTS MARCH PAST A HOARDING WITH THE SLOGAN: 'TO BELIEVE, OBEY, FIGHT'.

REVIEW

In determining whether Mussolini successfully established a truly totalitarian state it is necessary to consider a broad range of questions. In a genuinely totalitarian regime, one would expect to see almost every aspect of human conduct fall within the control or influence of the State. If the State relied heavily on secret police, the army and the use of terror to restrict its opponents but left many other aspects of day-to-day life untouched, it might be more appropriate to describe that system as authoritarian rather than totalitarian. How widespread, then, was Mussolini's control?

In the 'Checklist for a totalitarian regime' some basic questions have been arranged in three separate categories. Copy out this list and insert in each of the boxes the symbol which you consider to be most appropriate. You should then be in a position to reach some conclusions about the type of regime which Mussolini established.

I To what extent were basic human freedoms eroded under Mussolini?

X = No significant change between Mussolini's regime and the preceeding Liberal regime

✓ = Significant change under Mussolini, to the extent that a substantial number of people in Italian society were denied this right

? = Not significantly changed for the majority of people but called into question for those who were opponents of the regime

- Freedom of speech ☐

- Freedom to stand for political office ☐

- Freedom to vote for the party of your choice ☐

- Freedom of movement ☐

- Religious worship ☐

- Artistic expression ☐

- Freedom to strike ☐

- Add any others here which you consider important ☐

2 To what extent did the institutions associated with the emerging liberal democracy of 1918-22 retain their independence under Mussolini?

X = This group continued to act with independence and was not brought under the control of the State

✓ = This group lost its independence and henceforth followed the line laid down by Mussolini and the State/or was abolished by the State.

? = This group had to fall in line with Mussolini in a superficial sense without coming under rigid Fascist control. This might indicate a kind of informal co-operation.

- The Judiciary ☐
- The Press ☐
- The Catholic Church ☐
- The Trade unions ☐
- Big business ☐
- The Monarchy ☐
- The Army ☐
- The Civil Service ☐
- The Prefect system ☐
- Political parties ☐
- Add any others here which you regard as important ☐

3 To what extent did Mussolini introduce the features associated with a totalitarian regime?

X = This feature did not come to play a significant part in Italian life

✓ = This was imposed on the Italian people in a significant and systematic sense

? = This might indicate a feature which the regime desired or aspired to but which in practice was introduced in a very limited or erratic way

The role of a powerful individual

- Development of personality cult, through state propaganda ☐
- One man making key decisions ☐

- Use of personal decree and accumulation of personal offices by one man ☐

Social control

- State demands active support from citizens not passive acceptance ☐

- Emphasis on law, order and loyalty ☐

- Citizens made to feel grateful for government provision, not to expect it ☐

- Citizens coerced into joining Fascist societies ☐

- Youth organisations as a means of furthering propaganda ☐

- Distortion of economic figures ☐

- Oath of loyalty to secure allegiance of army ☐

- Emphasis on freedom of individual replaced by demands of the State ☐

- Racist ideas urged on population ☐

- Use of aggressive foreign policy to further State propaganda ☐

Political control

- One party system ☐

- Use of coercion to influence voting behaviour ☐

- Use of death penalty/assassination of outspoken opponents ☐

- Use of exile/prison camps for political purposes ☐

- Use of purges to quell dissent within own party/discrediting eminent members of own party to prevent issue of succession ☐

- Opportunity for dissent limited to irregular incidents such as assassination attempts ☐

Answer this question in essay form after you have given careful consideration to the material which comes before it:

How appropriately may Mussolini's Italy between 1922 and 1939 be described as a totalitarian state?

8 The Weimar Republic and the Rise of Hitler 1919-33

PREVIEW

ALL OF HITLER'S SPEAKING ENGAGEMENTS WERE ELABORATELY STAGE- MANAGED AND THEATRICAL

THE NAZIS USED SIMPLE EFFECTIVE SLOGANS: IN THIS CASE: 'A NATION HELPS ITSELF'

THE NATIONALIST SWASTIKA WAS DESIGNED TO BE A CLEAR COUNTERPOINT TO THE MARXIST HAMMER AND SICKLE

THE BLACK, WHITE AND RED COLOURS WERE INTENDED TO EVOKE ASSOCIATION WITH THE OLD IMPERIAL FLAG

THE NAZIS RELIED ON THE LATEST TECHNIQUES IN MASS COMMUNICATION

YOUNG PEOPLE WERE OFTEN PLACED AT THE FRONT AS THE PARTY PLACED GREAT EMPHASIS ON A MODERN, YOUTHFUL IMAGE

Chancellor Adolf Hitler

'They were taken to a red-brick building, which bore the latters "B-a-d", that is to say "bath". There to begin with, they were made to undress and given a towel before they went into the so-called shower room. Later on, at the time of the large convoys, they had no more time to play-act or to pretend; they were brutally undressed, and I know these details as I knew a little Jewess from France who lived with her family at the "Republique" in Paris. She was called "little Marie". Little Marie was the sole survivor of a family of nine. Her mother and her seven brothers and sisters had been gassed on arrival. When I met her she was employed to undress the babies before they were taken into the gas-chamber. Once the people were undressed they took them into a room which was somewhat like a shower room, and gas capsules were thrown, through an opening in the ceiling. An SS man would watch the effect produced, through a porthole. At the end of five or seven minutes, when the gas had completed its work, he gave the signal to open the doors, men with gas masks - they too were internees - went into the room and removed the corpses. They told us that the internees must have suffered before dying, because they were closely clinging to each other and it was very difficult to separate them.'

French survivor of Auschwitz concentration camp, quoted in Martin Gilbert, *The Holocaust* (1986)

TALKING POINT

In this chapter on Hitler's rise to power our starting point has been the holocaust. Does this make it more difficult to view Hitler in a detached, historical way or are our views automatically emotive from the outset?

PERSECUTION OF THE JEWS IN POLAND, AS WOMEN AND CHILDREN ARE ROUNDED UP IN A GHETTO

TALKING POINT

What are your
preconceptions about
Hitler and the National
Socialists? What ideas
about Hitler first come to
mind: are they necessarily
true?

These memories of a survivor of Auschwitz concentration camp serve as a grim reminder that when Adolf Hitler became Germany's 15th post-war chancellor in January 1933, a change had taken place of much greater consequence than the political intriguers who placed him there had bargained for. Within months of his appointment Hitler had brought about the destruction of a modern, civilised society and replaced it with the values of a harsh, totalitarian regime. Justice, freedom of speech, democracy and the rule of law were vanquished. Political parties, the independent press, trade unions and an impartial judiciary passed into history. Germany's parliament, the Reichstag, was reduced to the role of a rubber stamp to endorse Hitler's policies. The police became the instrument of terror rather than the defenders of law and order. All aspects of the media were shaped into the mouthpiece of authoritarianism rather than an outlet for free speech. Ultimately, Germany marched down a path which led to imperialism, total war and genocide.

Why did a country which prided itself on its glorious heritage of fine art, music, literature and political thought come to invest such high office in an ill-educated, racist, demagogue whose earlier years had included time spent in a men's doss house in Austria and in a prison cell in a gothic castle? Why did the conservative élite who controlled the route to the chancellorship hand such power to an Austrian with less than one year's German citizenship, few of the qualities of a traditional politician and a sworn enemy of democracy?

Historians have long since drawn attention to the fact that Hitler was not elected into office. The Nazis never gained more than 37 per cent of the votes in a free election, and it is now accepted that Hitler's installation was more the product of a shoddy 'backstairs intrigue' than any glorious seizure of power. Why did the judgement of such seasoned political manipulators fail them on such a massive scale on this occasion?

Historians have also recognised the significant achievements of the Weimar Republic. In particular the period of stability and recovery under Gustav Stresemann is seen as proof that the Weimar Republic was by no means doomed to failure from its inception, and that the rise to power of Adolf Hitler was not totally irresistible. Yet such were the problems of the Weimar Republic in its early years that on several occasions it appeared that it could not possibly survive.

TALKING POINT

You have just learnt that Hitler never gained more than 37 per cent of the votes in a free election.
(a) How does this fit in with your ideas?
(b) What are the implications of this fact in a discussion of Hitler?

8.1 Years of upheaval: the Weimar Republic 1918-23

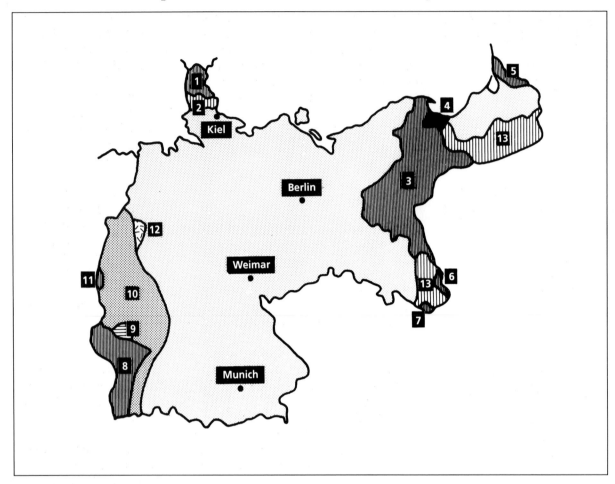

1 Northern Schleswig ceded by Germany to Denmark.

2 Holstein remained part of the German Empire after a plebiscite.

3 Posen and West Prussia were ceded to Poland. This was referred to by Germans as the 'bleeding border'.

4 The important port of Danzig was taken out of German hands and given the status of a free city.

5 The Memel region was ceded to Lithuania.

6 Eastern Upper Silesia was ceded to Poland.

7 Hüttschin territories were ceded to Czechoslovakia.

8 Alsace-Lorraine was ceded to France.

9 Saarland was placed under the control of the League of Nations and was occupied by France.

10 The Rhineland was occupied by Allied troops and became a demilitarised zone for Germany.

11 Eupen-Malmedy was ceded to Belgium.

12 The Ruhr district belonged to Germany but was occupied by France and Belgium in 1923.

13 These areas remained part of the German Empire following a plebiscite.

1918

Kiel

The short-lived German Revolution began in October 1918 when sailors in Wilhelmshaven refused to put to sea. This mutiny quickly spread to Kiel, and as the old political order crumbled in the face of defeat, disorder became nationwide. A key moment came with the establishment under Kurt Eisner of a Socialist Republic in Bavaria. This brought home to Chancellor Prince Max of Baden how serious the situation had become. Against this background of upheaval and street disorder the Kaiser was forced to abdicate, and on 9 November the new Republic was proclaimed with Prince Max giving way to Ebert.

1919

Berlin

Weimar

Although Ebert called for elections to a National Assembly at Weimar, these were boycotted by the new German Communist Party (KPD). Instead, the Spartacist faction of the Communist movement led an armed uprising in Berlin. Significantly, the new chancellor (Ebert) had to rely on the Freikorps, a collection of ex-soldiers and right-wingers, to crush the Spartacists. The brutal murder of Sparticist leaders Luxemburg and Liebknecht highlighted the fact that democracy had relied on brute force to protect itself. This was compounded by the murder of Kurt Eisner and the overthrow of the Bavarian Republic by federal troops.

1920-22

Berlin

Having survived the threat from the extreme Left the Republic was then challenged by the Right. In March 1920, Freikorps officers launched a pro-monarchist coup d'état in Berlin in an attempt to install Wolfgang Kapp as Chancellor. Although troops refused to take action against the Freikorps the success of the putsch was frustrated by the working class who organised a general strike in Berlin. Although the regime had also survived this threat, evidence that extremism still existed was provided by the assassination of Erzberger (leader of the Centre Party) and Rathenau (foreign secretary) in 1921 and 1922.

1923

Munich

The problems of the Weimar Republic reached a peak in 1923. In January, with Germany in default of her reparations payments, French and Belgian troops occupied the Ruhr in order to seize coal deposits. The protracted dispute which followed badly disrupted this key economic region, and this played a part in the hyper-inflation which devastated the German economy in 1923. The trauma of defeat in the First World War was echoed in the humiliation of French occupation. Nowhere was the sense of discontent and rage at the Government's impotence more strongly felt than Munich. It was here that Hitler came to national prominence.

The Munich Putsch (1923)

The trauma of military defeat, revolution, French occupation and hyper-inflation transformed the atmosphere of Munich from its pre-war status as a cosmopolitan, tolerant city, to its post-war reputation as a centre of violent political upheaval. The brutal repression of the Socialist republic had given way to an ultra-right-wing regime which dominated Bavarian politics. By 1923 Adolf Hitler had established himself as the mouthpiece of the numerous right-wing groups which flourished in Munich.

An ex-soldier with artistic ambitions, Hitler had now found his niche as the leader of the National Socialist German Worker's Party (NSDAP). By November 1923 Hitler sensed that the time was ripe to make a stand against the continued prominence of Communist politicians in central Germany. His ambition was to force the Bavarian government to take armed action against the Communists which would leave Hitler poised to seize power in Berlin. However, this attempt was stopped in its tracks and it soon became clear that Hitler had badly misjudged the political situation.

In the so-called 'Beer-hall Putsch', Hitler led his assortment of right-wing followers in a march to the centre of Munich. However, as the following extracts suggest, it took little more than a volley of shots from the well-organised police to scatter the insurgents and ruin Hitler's ambitions.

MEN CARRYING MONEY IN LAUNDRY BASKETS DURING THE HYPERINFLATION OF 1923

EXAMINING THE EVIDENCE

Source A

The column of National Socialists about 2000 strong, nearly all armed, moved on through the Zweibrückenstrasse across the Marienplatz towards the Theatinerstrasse. Here it split up, the majority going down the Perusastrasse to the Residenz, the rest going along the Theatinerstrasse. The police stationed in the Residenz tried to cordon it off as well as the Theatinerstrasse by the Preysingstrasse. Numerous civilians hurried on ahead of the actual column in Residenzstrasse and pushed the police barricade. The ceaseless shouts of 'Stop! Don't go on!' by the state police were not obeyed. Since there was a danger of a breakthrough here, a police section, originally in the Theaterinstrasse, hurried round the Feldherrenalle to give support. They were received with fixed bayonets, guns with the safety catches off, and raised pistols. Several police officers were spat upon, and pistols with the safety catches off were stuck in their chests. The police used rubber truncheons and rifle butts and tried to push back the crowd with rifles held horizontally. Their barricade had already been broken several times. Suddenly a National Socialist fired a pistol at a police officer from close quarters. The shot went past his head and killed Sergeant Hollweg standing behind him. Even before it was possible to give an order, the comrades of the sergeant who had been shot opened fire as the Hitler lot did, and a short gun battle ensued during which the police were also shot at from the Preysingplais and from the house which contains the Café Rottenhoffer. After no more than thirty seconds the Hitler lot fled, some back to the Maxamillienstrasse, some to the Odeonsplatz. General Ludendorff apparently went on towards the

LUDENDORFF, Erich (1865-1937)

1882 Entered Army.
1914 Major-General. Planned deployment of German armies at outbreak of WW1.
1914 Won victory at Tannenberg with Hindenburg.
1916 Transferred to Western Front.
1916 Shared increasing control of government with Hindenburg.
1920 Involved in abortive Kapp Putsch.
1923 Took part in Hitler's Munich Putsch.
1925 Founded extreme nationalist party.
1925 Unsuccessful candidate for Reich Presidency.

Odeonsplatz. There he was seen in the company of a Hitler officer by a police officer barring the Briennerstrasse, who went up to General Ludendorff and said to him: 'Excellency, I must take you into custody.' General Ludendorff replied: 'You have your orders. I'll come with you.' Both gentlemen were then accompanied into the Residenz.

From an official inquiry into the Munich Putsch (1923)

Source B

Hitler's precipitate flight from the Odeonsplatz has often been contrasted unfavourably with Ludendorff's calm and impassive walk through the police cordon to surrender to the officer in charge. It is a matter of taste. One could just as easily argue that Ludendorff behaved in a foolhardy manner, exposing himself to unnecessary risks when bullets were flying whereas Hitler, the seasoned front-line soldier, obeyed the dictates of common prudence and took cover. Actually he was thrown to the ground by the shot that killed Scheubner-Richter (with whom he had linked arms) and dislocated his shoulder. Coward Hitler was not, as his war record proves. But to stay behind with the smell of defeat in the air would have been a romantic gesture out of keeping with his sense of political realism. The 'whiff of grapeshot' was the final incontrovertible proof that the forces of law and order were not on his side and that he could not, therefore, succeed.

W. Carr, *Hitler, a Study in Personality and Politics* (1978)

The events of 1923 were not forgotten by the National Socialists. On the contrary, they commemorated the event and remembered their 'Martyrs'. What does this tell you about their political movement?

1 Prepare, in point form, a thorough defence of Stresemann's actions. Justify his actions and explain his motives.

2 Prepare, in point form, a thorough criticism of Stresemann's actions. You might argue that he concealed his true motives beneath a smokescreen of goodwill.

3 Can you draw, realistically, a one-sided conclusion or is your picture of him balanced? If so, to what extent is the balance in defence of or critical of Stresemann?

1 What light does Source A shed on the chances of Hitler's putsch attempt succeeding?

2 What evidence is there in the extract to suggest that the National Socialists had carefully planned the uprising?

3 How close did the uprising come to succeeding and why, according to Source A, did it ultimately fail?

4 How might Hitler's opponents use the material in Source A against him?

5 How might Hitler's supporters use the same material to present a different picture of events?

6 Read Source B. What reasons does Carr give to explain Hitler's behaviour?

7 What conclusions can you draw from this episode about Hitler's conduct?

The years of stability (1924-29)

Hitler's misguided confrontation with state power led to his subsequent conviction and imprisonment in Landsberg prison. Although the trial brought him national publicity and unprecedented prominence, this marked a period in Hitler's career when his chances of holding real political power seemed increasingly remote. (During his confinement Hitler had the time to write his autobiography, *Mein Kampf*.) Germany was now entering a period of economic recovery and political stability. When Hitler emerged from prison in December 1924 he was to find that the favourable climate in which he had launched his abortive putsch no longer existed. It seemed that the period of political extremism was over. Much of the credit for this was due to the leadership of Gustav Stresemann.

FOCUS

8.2 Biographical study: Gustav Stresemann (1878-1929)

The development of a pragmatic politician (1878-1922)

1878 Born in Berlin, of a modest family background. His father ran a small business bottling beer. Later Gustav established his own business and developed a manufacturers association in the state of Saxony.

1907 Stood for election as a National Liberal candidate in a poor district of Saxony, and at the age of 28 became the youngest member of the Reichstag.

1914 Although physically unfit for military service he adopted an extremist nationalist stance in the First World War. A member of the Navy League, he became a propagandist for a 'Greater Germany' advocating expansion into Belgium and the development of a colonial empire. He also supported the move to unrestricted submarine warfare which, eventually, pushed the United States into the war.

1917 Became leader of the National Liberal Party until its break-up in 1919.

1918 Advocated harsh peace terms in the settlement with Russia.

1919 Stresemann was denied membership of the new Democratic Party even though most of its members were former National Liberals. Written off by his critics, he responded by founding the German People's Party (DVP). Like its founder, the party's attitude towards the embryonic Weimar Republic was ambivalent. Stresemann was emotionally hostile towards the republic but decided that he could only make an effective political contribution within the party system. It was his pragmatic recognition of prevailing circumstance which also led him to advocate acceptance of Germany's commitments under the

CHANCELLOR AUGUST–NOVEMBER 1923
FOREIGN MINISTER 1923–OCTOBER 1929

Treaty of Versailles. Even so, he was strident in his criticism of the Republican leaders, whom he claimed had been duped by Wilson's promises of 'peace without victory'. Stresemann was in favour of submission because he appreciated Germany's military weakness and did not want to risk Allied occupation of the coal-rich mid-Ruhr region. In the long run, it is very clear that Stresemann wanted to see a complete revision of Versailles.

1920 The DVP benefitted from the prevailing anti-Versailles sentiment and obtained 65 seats in the Reichstag.

1921-22 Stresemann led his party in condemning the murders of the Republican politician Mathias Erzberger, leader of the Centre Party (1921) and Walter Rathenau, Foreign Secretary (1922). He advocated firm legislation against the right-wing extremists who carried out these assassinations. Although Stresemann himself was not in office at this time his party was playing an important role in the government. He had come through a turbulent period in Germany's history well placed to offer leadership in Germany's future.

From crisis, through stability, to crisis (1923-29)

'From being a violent nationalist in the First World War, he became the leading statesman of the Weimar Republic. Together with the French Foreign Minister, Aristide Briand, and the British Foreign Secretary, Austen Chamberlain, he negotiated the Locarno Pact in 1925. This held out the promise of peace after the ravages of war and the turmoil of the immediate post-war period. Yet, over this achievement hangs a question mark. Was Stresemann's goal a peaceful Europe in which Germany was a reliable partner, or was his aim rather the step by step revival of Germany as a great power until it had regained a position of dominance?'

Jonathan Wright, *History Today* (1989)

1923 In January 1923, exasperated by Germany's evasiveness and reluctance to pay overdue reparations, France and Belgium sent soldiers into the Ruhr in an attempt to seize direct control of German coal reserves. Chancellor Cuno's policy of passive resistance and non-co-operation succeeded in frustrating the French, but meant that this crucial economic region became a beleaguered and blockaded occupied zone. Germany's fragile currency and delicate economy were devastated by the consequences of the Ruhr occupation. By November, the mark had fallen to the figure of four billion against the US dollar.

Against this traumatic background the leadership of the Republic passed into the hands of a man who was ambivalent about its very fabric. He was unanimously appointed Chancellor in August 1923, placing him at the head of a coalition of the centre parties and the SPD. Stresemann realised that the ensuing deadlock was doing untold damage to the German economy. As Carr has stated (in *A History of Germany 1815-1985* [1987]), 'Chancellor Stresemann acted upon the simple truth that a government which lacks power cannot play power politics'. In September, Stresemann called off passive resistance unconditionally. Although this was domestically unpalatable, Stresemann had laid the foundations for a successful foreign policy grounded in hard-headed realism. He had also created the impression that Germany was at last being led by a reasonable and rational man who would seek compromise and conciliation rather than conflict.

1924 At the end of 1923 the German currency was stabilised by the introduction of the *Rentenmark*, valued at one billion old marks. Further stability came with the Dawes Plan (April 1924) which provided a modified settlement of the reparations issue. Extensive American loans over the next five years boosted German industry and agriculture so that by the start of 1929 its economy was superficially prosperous and stable. Economic prosperity meant that the extremist parties on both the Right and Left floundered. Against this background, Germany was well placed to re-enter the international community on favourable terms.

1925-26 The Locarno Pact of December 1925 signified the readmission of Germany to the international community, and indicated that sympathy for France had been exhausted. It was confirmed that French troops would leave the Ruhr and that future disputes between the two countries would go to an independent ruling. Crucially, Stresemann had convinced the powers that he had no warlike intentions and would accept the limitations of the Versailles Treaty. This trend was underlined when Germany was admitted to the League of Nations in 1926. In the same year Stresemann was awarded the Nobel Prize for Peace.

1927-29 By the end of 1927, although Germany's foreign situation had improved, economic circumstances were beginning to deteriorate. Many farmers, small businessmen and retailers were in trouble while prices and wages were rising. The fact that much German economic growth had been financed by American loans was underlined when the Wall Street Crash of 1929 devastated the German economy. Stresemann died the same year.

'Stresemann's "hundred days" as chancellor marked a real turning-point in the republic's history. He took office when the republic was at its lowest ebb politically and economically; by the time the great coalition collapsed in November 1923, the republic was well on the road to recovery. Stresemann was one of the few really outstanding political figures in the Weimar period. A statesmanlike figure of immense ability and industry, he was a gifted orator and a dynamic and vigorous personality with some of the mental qualities and attitudes of Winston Churchill whom he resembled both in temperament and physique.'

William Carr

Years of crisis (1928-32)

Hitler came within inches of a violent death in November 1923. With this narrow escape came the realisation that the prospect of an armed seizure of power was completely unrealistic. In *Mein Kampf*, his sprawling political monologue, Hitler made it clear that although his intention was still to destroy democracy, the tactics employed by the NSDAP would from now on be very different. Hitler intended to play the system. Between 1924 and 1928 the Nazi structure was reorganised, the SA reformed and the party rallies made more elaborate. Despite these organisational changes, the Reichstag elections of May 1928 - in which the Nazis gained only 2.6 per cent of the votes - showed that Hitler was still a figure of marginal political consequence. The following extract also shows that support for the Nazis was much greater in small towns and villages than it was in the big cities.

'The election results from the rural areas in particular have proved that with a smaller expenditure of energy, money and time, better results can be achieved there than in the big cities. In small towns and villages mass meetings with good speakers are events and are often talked about for weeks, while in the big cities the effects of meetings with even three or four thousand people soon disappear. Local successes in which the National Socialists are running first or second are, surprisingly, almost invariably the result of the activity of the branch leader or of a few energetic members.'

Völkischer Beobachter (Party Newspaper) 31 May 1928

It seems likely that Hitler would have remained on the margins of German politics forever had it not been for the catastrophic events of 1929. The death of Gustav Stresemann in October of that year coincided with the onset of the most severe economic depression in modern world history. As William Carr puts it: 'It is inconceivable that Hitler could ever have come to power had not the Weimar republic been subjected to the unprecedented strain of a world economic crisis.' Memories of 1923 returned as the country was plunged into a crisis which was to be more prolonged and more severe than its drastic predecessor. In the winter of 1929-30, Germany felt the full force of a bitter depression. Unemployment soared from 1.5 million in October 1929 to 4.3 million in December 1930. The extent to which Germany had come to rely on foreign assistance was underlined when these loans were rapidly withdrawn in the winter of 1929. In the urban areas food shortages, poor housing, unemployment, strikes and demonstrations created severe problems. In the countryside, rapidly-accumulating debts, overseas competition, high taxation and bad weather made the lives of many small farmers and fishermen more desperate than ever before. The political repercussions were just as acute.

HITLER, Adolf (1889-1945)

Dictator of Germany. Born in Austria. Lance Corporal in Bavarian Army during WW1, twice decorated with iron cross. 1919 joined German Workers' Party in Munich, reorganising it into the NSDAP/Nazi Party.

HITLER IN PRISON AT LANDSBERG IN 1924

HITLER ADDRESSES AN ELECTION CROWD IN THE 1920s

8.3 The Weimar Republic: economy, reparations and depression

1
Germany's economic difficulties: the view of an historian

'The republic was burdened with intractable economic problems arising out of the war. By 1919 Germany's internal finances were in a parlous state, largely because she had financed her war effort through short-term loans and by inflating the currency in the firm expectation that her enemies would pay the war costs. Defeat left her saddled with a huge internal debt of 144,000 million marks and with a currency which had lost over one-third of its pre-war value. The task of recovery was complicated by other factors. Germany was running a trade deficit; she had little hope of attracting foreign investment when capital was in short supply; her industrial potential was severely crippled by the loss of the Saarland and Upper Silesia, and her pre-war trading pattern was shattered. Faced with the problem of monetary inflation and a falling mark successive governments shied away from the drastic remedies of currency stabilisation and balanced budgets...'

William Carr, *A History of Germany 1915-1985* (1987)

2
Timeline: 1919-29

1919 June The Treaty of Versailles obliged Germany to pay reparations to the victors. However, a total figure was not reached at this conference.

1921 March At the London conference, Germany proposed a significant scaling-down of the reparations figure put forward by the Allies in January 1921. Angered by the additional German conditions that the Rhineland be evacuated and Upper Silesia restored, the Allies occupied three towns in the Ruhr, claiming that Germany was already in breach of the agreement by not making an interim payment of £1000 million.

1921 April The Reparations Commission finally presented its report. It recommended a total bill of £6,600 million (132 billion marks) which was to be delivered in annual payments of £100 million (two billion marks), with additional payments equivalent to the value of 1/4 of all German exports.

1922 By the start of the year it was obvious that Germany was going to have to default on its payments. Consequently, the Reparations Commission granted relief on the first payments of the new year. However, the French felt strongly that Germany could pay but simply did not want to. The Treaty of Rapallo, with its provision for economic co-operation between Germany and Russia, intensified French suspicion.

1923 The Paris Conference in January 1923 tried to resolve the reparations dispute but on 9 January the Reparations Commission announced that Germany had deliberately defaulted over coal deliveries. Two days later French and Belgian troops were sent into the Ruhr, the industrial heartland of Germany. The occupation of the Ruhr devastated the German economy and sparked off the most catastrophic inflation in its history. Early in 1923 the dollar was worth 18,000 marks, by August it was worth 4,600,000 marks and by November it had reached 4 billion marks. By September, interest rates were raised to 90 per cent. Some stability was restored when passive resistance to the occupation was abandoned and the Rentenmark was introduced.

1924 April The Dawes Plan for the settlement of reparations was published after four months' deliberation by the committee led by an American general. Although the total liability figure remained the same, the plan was at least based on a realistic estimation of German capacity to pay. For the first five years Germany would make payments increasing from £50 million to £125 million. After this, payments would be based on an index of German prosperity. Germany also received a loan, designed to stabilise the new currency.

1925-28 Traditionally this period has been depicted as a period of economic 'boom' but many historians now feel that this has been exaggerated. Agriculture and small industry, in particular, did not enjoy a period of growth and prosperity. More generally, growth in economic activity was modest when compared to U.S. growth rates. By 1929, capital investment was already falling and unemployment never fell below 1.3 million (and had risen ominously to 3 million by February 1929). The success of huge industrial trusts (eg, I.G. Farben), the massive influx of foreign capital, and developments in the state welfare system all served to hide the structural problems inherent in the German economy. American loans to Europe abruptly collapsed after the share collapse on the Wall Street Stock Exchange in October. The subsequent contraction in world markets meant that Germany's export trade was drastically reduced. Unemployment, which stood at 900,000 in the summer of 1929, soared to more than three million in December 1930, five-and-a-half million by July 1931, and more than six million by the start of 1932. The consequences of this catastrophe were profound. The Weimar Republic, having overcome the difficulties of 1923, was now placed under intolerable pressure. It was the economic crisis which led to the political upheaval which culminated in the rise to power of Adolf Hitler.

1929 Under the leadership of the U.S. financier Owen Young, the Allied Reparations Commission came up with a new plan to settle German war reparations. Now Germany would pay less than originally intended, although she would still be obliged to make substantial payments until 1988. The German Nationalists, led by Alfred Hugenberg, organised a referendum for a law rejecting the Young Plan out of hand. The nationalist viewpoint was that Germany was being asked to saddle future generations with the burden of debt. To win maximum support for his ideas, Hugenberg invited the co-operation of the Nazis. For Hitler this was a golden opportunity to align himself with the more respectable, conservative and upper-class nationalists. Later, he could abandon them.

3
The verdict of an historian

'Like men and women in a town stricken by an earthquake, millions of Germans saw the apparently solid framework of their existence cracking and crumbling. In such circumstances men are no longer amenable to the arguments of reason. In such circumstances men entertain fantastic fears, extravagant hatreds and extravagant hopes. In such circumstances the extravagant demagogy of Hitler began to attract a mass following as it had never done before.'

Alan Bullock, *Hitler, A Study in Tyranny* (1954)

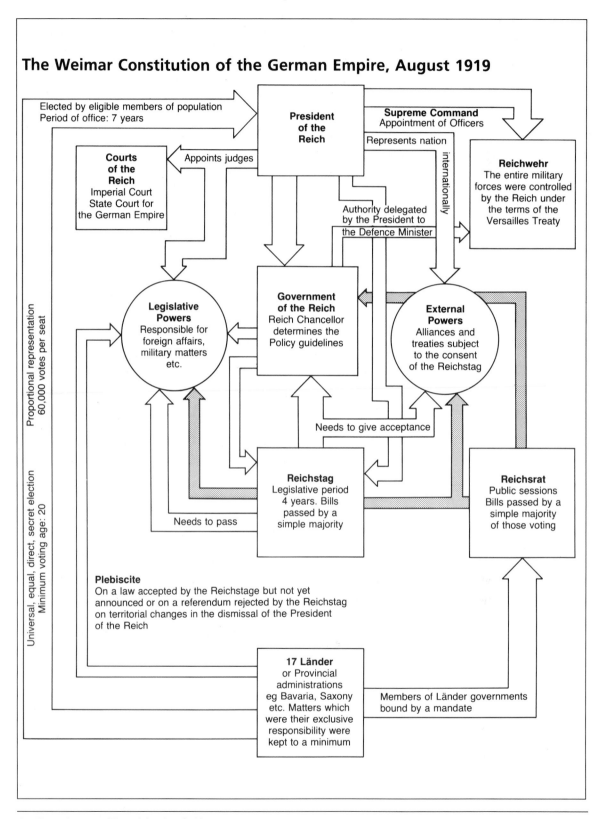

The Weimar Constitution of the German Empire, August 1919

Elected by eligible members of population
Period of office: 7 years

President of the Reich

Supreme Command
Appointment of Officers

Represents nation

internationally

Appoints judges

Courts of the Reich
Imperial Court
State Court for the German Empire

Reichwehr
The entire military forces were controlled by the Reich under the terms of the Versailles Treaty

Authority delegated by the President to the Defence Minister

Legislative Powers
Responsible for foreign affairs, military matters etc.

Government of the Reich
Reich Chancellor determines the Policy guidelines

External Powers
Alliances and treaties subject to the consent of the Reichstag

Needs to give acceptance

Reichstag
Legislative period 4 years. Bills passed by a simple majority

Reichsrat
Public sessions Bills passed by a simple majority of those voting

Needs to pass

Proportional representation
60,000 votes per seat

Universal, equal, direct, secret election
Minimum voting age: 20

Plebiscite
On a law accepted by the Reichstage but not yet announced or on a referendum rejected by the Reichstag on territorial changes in the dismissal of the President of the Reich

17 Länder
or Provincial administrations eg Bavaria, Saxony etc. Matters which were their exclusive responsibility were kept to a minimum

Members of Länder governments bound by a mandate

ERNST THÄLMANN, THE LEADER OF
THE GERMAN COMMUNIST PARTY

Six months after the Wall Street Crash, Germany lost its last parliamentary Cabinet with the resignation of Muller's socialist bloc in March 1930. His successor, Heinrich Bruening, sought to ride the crisis by relying more and more on the emergency powers built into the Weimar constitution. Three years before Hitler came to power, parliamentary democracy was suspended and replaced by an authoritarian system which rested largely on the powers invested in the ageing president, von Hindenburg. Chancellor Bruening, backed by the naturally autocratic President, relied increasingly on Article 48 of the constitution to push through emergency legislation. How long would it be before such substantial powers were taken out of the control of an old and essentially benevolent president and put into the hands of a political extremist?

The answer many Germans feared was that power would soon pass into the hands of the Communists, led by Ernst Thälmann. In the Reichstag elections of September 1930, the Communists received 77 seats but to many anxious middle-class citizens it was the influence of the 'reds' on the streets of the big cities which was most alarming. Fuelled by economic anxiety and influenced by the government's increasingly autocratic stance, political dialogue and debate were replaced by bitter street battles between the extremes of left and right. Ultimately, it may well be that the frightening prospect of Communist rule was the key factor which led so many powerful groups to lend support to the opposite extreme, personified by Adolf Hitler. In retrospect, it is clear that the Communists had little prospect of gaining real political power.

The Communists did succeed in gaining the support of an overwhelming number of the urban workforce, frustrating Hitler's protracted and expensive attempts to secure this vital bloc of votes for himself. But too many powerful groups - including the Army, the Police, the middle classes and the peasantry - felt that they had a great deal to lose if Communists were to win the day in Weimar Germany. The fact that many people came to see the Nazis as the last bulwark in the fight against Communism was of the utmost value to Hitler's campaign. Indeed, the contrast between the spectre of Communist disorder with the Nazis' promises of law and order, economic stability, the curbing of the unions, the endorsement of traditional values and the promise to crush Marxism was at the very centre of Hitler's success.

In addition, the pitched street battles with the Communists furnished Goebbels with the type of propaganda material which he relished. The case study of Berlin which now follows shows that despite unpromising election returns the Nazis were prepared to mount major propaganda campaigns in the very heartland of Communist support.

8.4 A case study in Nazi agitation: Berlin, December 1930

National Socialist disruption of the film 'All Quiet on the Western Front'

Introduction

The film *All Quiet on the Western Front*, based on the anti-war novel by Erich Maria Remarque, was given its German première at the Mozartsaal cinema in Berlin on 4 December 1930. Its realistic portrayal of the horrors of trench warfare and its pacifist message made it a natural target for the Nazis and their patriotic propaganda. Josef Goebbels was the party's propaganda expert and was *Gauleiter* of Berlin.

1 The nature of the film

The metamorphosis of enthusiastic sixth-formers into front soldiers who do their duty because they are forced to; the transformation of an idealistic youth to a steel-helmeted man in field-gray uniform who has seen the most horrific thing a man will ever see...The frightful irrationality of war emerges most clearly in the film's big battle scenes, which belong to the technically most grandiose and most moving which we have experienced in sound-film so far.

Hans Pol, writing in the newspaper *Volkische Zeitung* (6 November 1930.)

2 Disruption of the film

Friday 5 December was to be the evening. Goebbels, a few Nazi MPs and several dozens of SA men and a party members in civilian clothes, in all some 200 of them, had gone to the Mozartsaal and bought seats in different parts of the cinema, especially in the balcony. The film had been screened for no more than ten minutes when the racket began. Loud shouts like 'filthy film', 'pigsty', 'throw the Jews out' could be heard blending with the noise of exploding grenades on the sound-track. Smoke bombs were thrown from the balcony. Paper bags with sneezing power were tossed into the audience. White mice were let loose by Goebbels' men in the stalls. There was pandemonium and the film had to be stopped.

From M Broszat, *Hitler and the Collapse of Weimar Germany* (1987)

A SCENE FROM *ALL QUIET ON THE WESTERN FRONT*, VIVIDLY DEPICTING THE HORRORS OF WAR

CASUALTIES DEPICTED IN THE FILM *ALL QUIET ON THE WESTERN FRONT.*

3 An account from Goebbels' diary

'The Cinema has been turned into a madhouse a mere ten minutes after the start of the film... The jews try to make themselves invisible. Thousands of people enjoy the spectacle in a mood of satisfaction... Afterwards I sit in a café with my lads; experiences are swapped; it is hilariously funny, but everything has worked well... Our action in the Mozartsaal is the topic of the day. The press is teeming with rage or full of enthusiasm once again I have had the right scent... This was a good piece.'

9 Dec 1930

4 *Der Angriff* - Nazi newspaper

STORM OF PROTEST IN THE MOZARTSAAL
When the cowardice of the volunteers was shown on the screen, the audience raised a storm of protest which forced the cinema owner to interrupt the screening. Serious brawls developed which were provoked by Jews and in which the police had to intervene...There is such a blatant tendency in this film to denigrate the German spirit that one must not be surprised, if the Volk takes matters into its own hands.

December 1930

5 A description of events by *The Times* newspaper in London

'A "demonstration" was openly organised by Herr Goebbels, the Berlin Nazi leader with the aid of his newspaper *Der Angriff*...a strong cordon of the police protected the theatre. In spite of a discouraging drizzle, youthful Nazis gathered outside the cordon, shouted "Germany awake", sang Nazi songs and called the police "Bloodhounds" and added their usual embroideries to the *Angriff's* views on "dirty Jews". When Herr Goebbels arrived in a motor car, a mass of hundreds surged across the street and surrounded the car, arms upraised in the Facist salute...Section after section was formed, with "storm detachment leaders" in the front ranks. Behind, in columns of fours, followed a collection of nationally-minded - mostly youths, with a sprinkling of middle-aged men and women, and an occasional dog.'

8 December 1930

TALKING POINT

'A skilful and brilliantly-orchestrated piece of propaganda' or 'A crude, ham-fisted and violent display which would please Nazi supporters but alienate moderate voters and members of the middle class'.

Which is nearer to the truth?

FOCUS

8.5 Who voted for the National Socialists?

It is interesting to note the energetic level of National Socialist agitation which Goebbels mounted in Berlin in December 1930. After all, this was not an area in which the Nazis had enjoyed much success and, furthermore, this intense activity was going on only three months after the demanding Reichstag elections had taken place. Perhaps the Nazis had taken encouragement from the massive increase in their support in the September 1930 ballot. Even though the party's support increased by nine times compared to the 1925 election, they had still failed to make a major breakthrough in Berlin and other large cities. So if the Nazis could not succeed in gaining mass support in the big cities despite their persistent campaigning, where did their support come from?

Reichstag Elections: 1924-33

1 The increase in support for the National Socialists

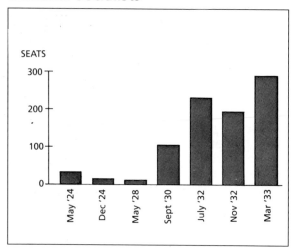

Date	Seats	%	Comments
May 1924	32	6.5	The party was part of an anti-semitic coalition
Dec 1924	14	3.0	Support dwindled due to economic factors
May 1928	12	2.6	The party remained in the margins
Sep 1930	107	18.3	9 fold increase. 6 million votes. Rural landslide. Some villages 100% Nazi
July 1932	230	37.3	With more than 1/3 of votes cast the Nazis became the largest party
Nov 1932	196	33.1	Support dropped
Mar 1933	288	43.9	This election took place against a background of intimidation

2 The limited support for the Communist Party

May 1924	62	Seats
Dec 1924	45	Seats
May 1928	54	Seats
Sep 1930	77	Seats
July 1932	89	Seats
Nov 1932	100	Seats
Mar 1933	81	Seats

3 Unemployment in Germany 1929-33

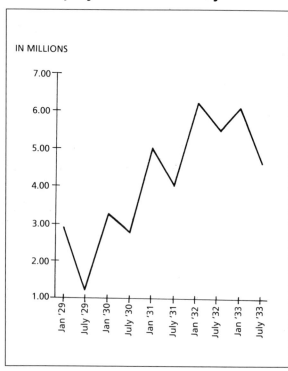

4 Regional variations in support for the National Socialists

	Berlin	Cologne-Aachen	East-Prussia	Koblenz	Lower Bavaria	Schleswig-Holstein
May '24	3.6	1.5	8.6	1.3	10.2	7.4
Dec '24	1.6	0.6	6.2		3.0	2.2
May '28	1.4	1.1	0.8	2.1	3.5	4.0
Sep '30	12.8	14.5	22.5	14.9	12.0	27.0
July '32	24.6	20.2	47.1	28.8	20.4	51.0
Nov '32	22.5	17.4	39.7	26.1	18.5	45.7
Mar '33	31.3	30.1	56.5	38.4	39.2	53.2

Constituency	Characteristics
1 Berlin	Large, cosmopolitan city
2 Cologne-Aachen	Predominantly industrial
3 East Prussia	Largely rural and Protestant
4 Koblenz	Predominantly Catholic and rural
5 Lower-Bavaria	Overwhelmingly Catholic
6 Schleswig-Holstein	Largely rural and Protestant

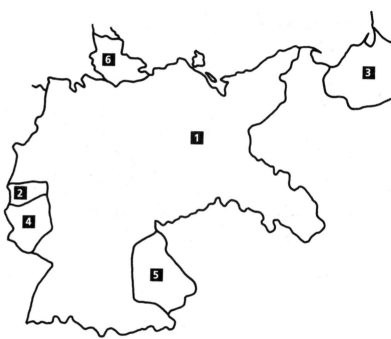

5 Opposition to Nazism in November 1932

Nationally		**Regionally**			
Party	Seats	Region	SPD	Centre BVP	KPD
Communist Party	100	**1** Berlin	20-25%	10%	35%
Social Democrats	125	**2** Cologne-Aachen	10-15%	10-15%	25-30%
German People's Party	11	**3** East Prussia	5-20%	10%	10-15%
Centre Party	70	**4** Koblenz	10%	35%	10%
Bavarian People's Party	20	**5** Lower-Bavaria	10-15%	35%	10%
German National People's Party	52	**6** Schleswig-Holstein	20-25%	10%	10-15%

FOCUS

8.5 Who voted for the National Socialists? (continued)

Social groups	✔	✗
Working-class factory workers	☐	☐
Ex-servicemen	☐	☐
Small businessmen/shopkeepers	☐	☐
Rich industrialists	☐	☐
Small landowners	☐	☐
Poor farm labourers	☐	☐
Junior army officers	☐	☐

Election issues	✔	✗
Economic anxiety	☐	☐
Anti-Semitism	☐	☐
Expansionist foreign policy	☐	☐
Fear of Communism	☐	☐
Anti-trade union	☐	☐
Anti-Versailles	☐	☐
Socialist policies	☐	☐

Geographical variations	✔	✗
Predominantly Catholic	☐	☐
Predominantly Protestant	☐	☐
Big cities	☐	☐
Rural areas	☐	☐
Small towns and villages	☐	☐
North German plain	☐	☐
Schleswig-Holstein	☐	☐

EXERCISE

1 Study all of the information very carefully. Place either a ✔ or an ✗ next to each of the boxes. For example if poor farm labourers were generally National Socialist supporters you would put a tick there. If anti-Semitism was a major vote-winner for the National Socialists you would place a tick there etc.

2 Draw up a detailed profile of a typical National Socialist voter, covering age, sex, status, occupation and most important of all, what their attitudes would be across the range of political issues.

3 Read the historians' accounts. Is there agreement or debate on who voted National Socialist?

4 Essay: Why did the National Socialist rather than the Communists, achieve mass support in the period 1930-33?

7 The verdict of historians

'What was it that drew middle-class audiences to Hitler? Certainly not the content of his speeches, full of vague and woolly phraseology and markedly deficient in detailed, let alone credible policies. Denunciation of the Versailles Treaty, rhetorical talk about Germany's future glory, promises of tax deductions...all this was commonplace stuff at any right-wing meeting...What was compelling about Hitler and what distinguished his party from other right-wing parties were not only the external trappings - the feverish activity, the endless marching, the mass rallies and the ceaseless propaganda drives - important though these were in gathering votes, but above all the ruthless will to victory and the fanatical sense of commitment emanating from the Fuhrer and his followers. When Hitler promised to sweep out 'the old gang' he carried conviction. The old established middle class, frightened by the radicalisation of working-class politics implied in the mounting Communist vote, felt instinctively that this man meant what he said: he would destroy Marxism and restore the old values.'

William Carr

'Until 1928 Nazism was an insignificant political force trying to win factory workers away from Marxism...It was a marginal political movement on the radical right. But under the impact of the slump, the rise of communism and the political stalemate of parliamentary politics the movement began to attract more attention. Nazism became the authentic voice of the small townsman, the anxious officials and small businessmen, the peasant who felt he had had a raw deal from the Republic...The Nazi Party was made up and led by people like this: Nazi leaders articulated their fears and desires, and promised to end the crisis. Nazism gave expression to the latent nationalism of the conservative masses by blaming the Allies and reparations for Germany's ills. Above all, Nazism was violently anti-Marxist. It was the only party demonstrably, visibly combating the threat of communism on the streets. Although the violence alienated many respectable Germans, they hated communism more. Social disorder and disintegration seemed a reality in 1932 with eight million unemployed. In the chaos Nazism promised to restore order, to revive German fortunes, to bring about a moral renewal, to give 'bread and work.'

Richard Overy

'The millions of Germans who voted for Hitler did not do so because they wanted genocide or total war. These aims were by no means in the forefront of Nazi propaganda. For most people, economic anxiety and fear of communism were far more important. However, some social groups were much more likely than others to believe that Hitler and the Nazis could solve their problems. The hard core of Nazi supporters were male, Protestant and broadly speaking, middle class. Women, Catholics and despite strenuous Nazi efforts, industrial workers, were far more resistant, at least until the last, desperate months of the republic when habitual allegiances began to crumble. The NSDAP's youthful, dynamic image attracted young, middle class men. Unlike Weimar's elderly, social democratic and conservative politicians, many Nazi leaders were still in their twenties, when the depression began...But the biggest pool of Nazi voters was in parts of the countryside. In Protestant North Bavaria, the North German Plain and Schleswig-Holstein, debts, foreign competition, high taxes and bad weather caused severe problems for many small farmers and fishermen.'

Robin Lenman

'Between 1928 and 1930 the Nazi Party had concentrated largely on trying to win over sections of the middle class, notably the peasantry, the artisans, and the small retailers. After 1930, while still continuing much of their propaganda for these groups, they revived their pre-1928 efforts to win over the workers. But apart from white collar workers, the majority of workers remained loyal to the Social Democrats and communists and ...if they became more extreme they tended to move to the Communists rather than the Nazis...The main strength of Nazism lay in the Protestant and predominantly rural areas of the North German Plain stretching from East Prussia to Schleswig-Holstein. Eight out of ten districts with the largest Nazi vote in July 1932 are in this area...Nazism was weakest in the big cities (eg Berlin and Leipzig) and in the industrial areas, particulary in predominantly Catholic ones...In the cities it tended to draw most support from upper middle class districts. It was also weakest in overwhelmingly Catholic rural areas.'

Jeremy Noakes

How did Hitler become Chancellor? (1932-33)

'The April sun shone hot like in summer and turned everything into a picture of gay expectation. There was immaculate order and discipline...Aeroplanes above us. Testing of the loudspeakers, buzzing of the cine-cameras. It was nearly 3 pm. "The Fuhrer is coming!" A ripple went through the crowds. Around the speakers' platform one could see hands raised in the Hitler salute. A speaker opened the meeting, nobody listened to him. A second speaker welcomed Hitler and made way for the man who had drawn 120,000 people of all classes and ages. There stood Hitler in a simple black coat and looked over the crowd, waiting - a forest of swastika penants swished up, the jubilation of this moment was given vent in a roaring salute. Main theme, out of parties shall grow a nation, the German nation. He censured the system ("I want to know what there is left to be ruined in this state!"). "On the way here Socialists confronted me with a poster, 'Turn back Adolf Hitler'. Thirteen years ago I was a simple unknown soldier. I went my way. I never turned back. Nor

NAZI RALLY IN THE 1930s

shall I turn back now"...His voice was hoarse after all his speaking during the previous days. When the speech was over, there was roaring enthusiasm and applause. Hitler saluted, gave his thanks, and was helped into his coat. Then he went'.

> Extract from the Diary of Frau Luise Solmitz, a Hamburg school teacher, April 1932

How would Frau Solmitz explain to a critical observer why she supported Adolf Hitler? Devise a brief dialogue that could have taken place after the rally.

The previous extract suggests how polished the Nazi propaganda machine had become, but despite the massive electoral support gained in the July 1932 elections the fact remained that Hitler was still on the outside looking in. He was still without any formal experience of political office. Then, in the elections of November 1932, Nazi support fell significantly and the impression of invincibility which Goebbels had carefully built up was visibly dented. Unrest within the Nazi party began to grow. Would Hitler ever achieve his goal? In understanding why Hitler was finally given political office we must look beyond the propaganda campaigns and the

Why do you think the electoral reverse of November 1932 was so damaging to the party image?

election booths and investigate the period of negotiation and intrigue which took place between August 1932 and January 1933.

Examining the Evidence

Section 1: The period of crisis (August-December 1932)

Source A: Hitler demands power from the President (13 August 1932)

The President of the Reich opened the discussion by declaring to Hitler that he was ready to let the National Socialist Party and their leader Hitler participate in the Reich Government and would welcome their cooperation. He then put the question to Hitler whether he was prepared to participate in the present government of von Papen. Herr Hitler declared that...his taking any part in cooperation with the existing government was out of the question. Considering the importance of the National Socialist movement he must demand full and complete leadership of government and state for himself and his party.

Explain, in your own words, the nature of the conversation between Hitler and Hindenburg. Was the meeting a success for Hitler or not?

The Reich President in reply said firmly that he must answer this demand with a clear, unyielding No. He could not justify before God, before his conscience or before the fatherland the transfer of the whole authority of government to a single party, especially to a party that was biased against people who had different views from their own...

Herr Hitler repeated that any other solution was unacceptable to him.

To this the Reich President replied: 'So you will go into opposition?' Hitler: 'I have no alternative'...The discussion was followed by a short conversation in the corridor between the Reich Chancellor and me, and Herr Hitler and his companions, in which Herr Hitler expressed the view that future developments would lead to the solutions suggested by him and to the overthrow of the Reich President. The Government would get into a difficult position; the opposition would become very sharp and he could assume no responsibility for the consequences.

> Minutes of the second meeting between Hitler and Hindenburg, taken by Otto Meisner, Head of the Presidential Chancellory.

Source B: Goebbels' reaction to the Presidential meeting (13 August 1932)

What signs are there of tension within the Nazi Party in November 1932?

...The Führer is back in under half an hour. So it has ended in failure. He has gained nothing. Papen is to remain Chancellor and the Führer has to content himself with the position of Vice-Chancellor!

A solution leading to no result! It is out of the question to accept such a proposal. There is no alternative but to refuse. The Führer did so immediately. It will mean a hard struggle, but we shall triumph in the end...

In the back room the SA leaders assemble at the command of the Chief of Staff. The Führer and he give them a fairly full outline of events. Their task is the most difficult of all. Who knows if their units will be able to hold together?

Nothing is harder than to tell a troop with victory already in their grasp that their assignment has come to nothing!...Well, the fight goes on! In the end the Wilhelmstrasse will give in...in the long run, despite everything, strength and tenacity will win the day...

Extract from Goebbel's Diary, 13 August 1932

Source C: Goebbels outlines party strategy for the November Reichstag elections

...The struggle against the Papen Cabinet and the reactionary circles behind it must now begin all along the line...The aim is to isolate the Papen regime from the people and prove to the world that it is only a small feudal clique with no other aim than to isolate the National Socialist movement...The NSDAP has no reason whatsoever to spare the Papen regime in any way.

Circular to all Gauleiters and Gau Propaganda Directors from the Reich Propaganda Department, 12 September 1932

Source D: Signs that the campaign against Papen was backfiring

13. vii. 32. Goebbels in the National Socialist *Angriff!* We know this language only too well from the Socialist and Communist papers; we don't want to hear it from Goebbels! This is just what deters many...it alienates the valuable bourgeois element; Hitler, remain master in your own house!

3. xi. 32. EM said, shaking his head, 'One can't possibly vote for Hitler.' He met a Herr von S., whom he knows from the war: 'I voted for Hitler twice; it's no longer the thing to do...Hitler? He is too far to the left!...'

31. xii. 32. This year has robbed us of a great hope - Adolf Hitler. Our reviver and great leader towards national unity...and the man who in the end turns out to be the leader of the party sliding more and more into a dubious future. I still cannot come to terms with this bitter disappointment...

Extracts form the Diary of Frau Luise Solmitz. Autumn 1932

What was the nature of the Papen regime? Explain why this was such a difficult regime for Hitler to criticise. Sources C and D will help you with your answer.

Look back at Frau Solmitz's diary account of April 1932. Why was her criticism of Autumn 1932 so damaging for the party?

Source E: Problems in the party's organisation

The organisation has naturally become a bit on edge through these everlasting elections. It is as jaded as a batallion which has been too long in the front trenches, and just as nervy.

Goebbels' Diary, October 1932

What practical problems would you imagine lay behind the difficulties mentioined by Goebbels in his diary entry in October 1932?

Source F: The role of Schleicher

It was then (2 December 1932) Schleicher's turn. He said he had a plan which would absolve the President from taking his last drastic step (suspending the Reichstag). If he took over the government himself, he thought he could bring about a split in the National Socialist Party which would ensure a parliamentary majority in the present Reichstag. He then gave a detailed explanation of the differences of opinion within the Nazi movement which made it more likely that he would be able to attract the support or Gregor Strasser and about sixty members of the Reichstag. Strasser and one of two of his close supporters would be offered posts in the government, which would be based upon the support of the trade

According to Papen, what was the nature of Schleicher's plan?

unions, the Social Democrats and the burgeois parties. This would provide a majority which would make it possible to put through the economic and social programme of the Papen government.

The memoirs of Franz von Papen

Source G: Strasser's defection from the party (December 1932)

The Führer has not been following a clear line of policy in his endeavour to achieve power. He is only clear about one thing - he wishes to become Reich Chancellor. He should, however, have become aware of the fact that he is being consistently refused this post by everybody and that in the foreseeable future there is no prospect of his attaining this goal. As a result of this situation, the movement is being put under considerable stress which is undermining its unity and may expose it to splits and disintegration...

There are two paths which can lead to a solution of this serious crisis and if the collapse of the movement is to be avoided one of them must be followed: the legal or the illegal path. I would be prepared to follow either path. But I refuse to wait until the Führer is made Reich Chancellor, for by then the collapse will have occurred. If the legal path was to be followed, the Führer should have accepted Hindenburg's offer in August to make him Vice-Chancellor. From this basis the attempt should have been made to secure new positions...

The second method is the illegal path. I would have been prepared to folllow this path as well. The National Socialist stormtroops of the SA and SS are still intact; they are prepared for the final march and will be at the ready the moment the order comes...But this path has also been rejected and for my part I no longer see any possibility of future activity.

Strassers's resignation speech to the Senior Gauleiters (the Party's regional inspectors), 8 December 1932

What criticisms does Strasser make of Hitler? How did he justify his decision to leave the Party?

Source H: Hitler refutes Strasser's charges, speaking to the same audience

'I thought Gregor Strasser was much cleverer than that; I am shocked by the position he adopts...I will answer...point by point.

1 ...He spoke to you about the legal path to the conquest of power and declared that it was my duty in August to accept the office of Vice-Chancellor. Herr Strasser knows quite well that Herr von Papen and Herr von Schleicher are not National Socialists and therefore are not willing to follow National Socialist policies. Judging by the measures introduced by, and the results of, the policy of Reich Chancellor von Papen, as Vice-Chancellor I would have had serious differences with him within the first week...I would have had to protest against policies...Herr von Papen would have declared to me with a smile, 'Forgive me, Herr Hitler, but I am Chancellor and head of the Cabinet. If my political course and the measures which result from it do not suit you, I am not forcing you to stay. You can resign your office.'

Herr von Papen and his backers...would have achieved their goal - the proof of the incapacity of Hitler and his subordinates would have apparently been provided...I reject this path and intend to wait until I am

GREGOR STRASSER, DISSIDENT MEMBER OF THE NAZI PARTY

offered the post of Chancellor. That day will come - it is probably nearer than we think...

2 The illegal path to the conquest of power is even more dangerous and more fatal. It cannot be said that I do not have the courage to carry out a coup by force and, if necessary, by a bloody revolution, I tried it once in Munich in 1923. Herr Strasser knows that; he was there.

But what was the result and what would the result be now? Our formations are without weapons and...they would have no effect against the united action of the police and the Reichswehr which are armed with the most modern weapons. You surely do not believe that they would stand by. The police will shoot at the command of Herr von Papen and the Reichswehr at the command of its Supreme Commander, Reich President Hindenburg, for they have taken their oath to him and not to me...

Hitler became quieter and more personal, more amiable and appealing. At the end of the two-hour long interview he had found that comradely tone which those present knew and found completely convincing. Now he was their friend, their comrade, their leader, who has shown them the way out of the hopeless situation which Strasser had portrayed...Those present once more sealed their old bond with him with a handshake.

Notes on Hitler's speech to the Gauleiter, 8 December 1932

What light does Hitler's response to Strasser's resignation shed on his political ability?

According to Hitler, why was a seizure of power out of the question? What does this tell you about the political situation at the end of 1932?

---

1 Produce a chronology of the Nazis and Hitler's fortunes for the autumn of 1932 based on the evidence in Section 1.

Highlight in your chronology: successes, failures, turning points, the role played by Hitler and the importance of other individuals.

Was this a successful period for the Nazis or not?

Section 2: From intrigue to chancellory (January 1933)

TALKING POINT

This meeting is now regarded by historians as being of vital importance. Why do you think the meeting is regarded as so significant?

Source A: A crucial meeting (4 January 1933)

On 4 January 1933 Hitler, von Papen, Hess, Himmler and Keppler arrived at my house in Cologne. Hitler, von Papen and I went into my study where a two-hour discussion took place. Hess, Himmler and Keppler did not take part but were in the adjoining room...The negotiations took place exclusively between Hitler and Papen...Papen went on to say that he thought it best to form a government in which conservative and nationalist elements that had supported him were represented together with the Nazis. He suggested that this new government should, if possible, be led by Hitler and himself together. Then Hitler made a long speech in which he said that, if he were elected Chancellor, Papen's followers could participate in his (Hitler's) Government as Ministers if they were willing to support his policy which was planning many alterations in the existing state of affairs. He outlined these alterations, including the removal of all Social Democrats, Communists and Jews from leading positions in Germany and the restoration of order in public life. Von Papen and Hitler reached agreement in principle...It was agreed that further details could be worked out later...This happened, as I learned later, at a meeting with Ribbentrop. This meeting between Hitler and Papen on 4 January 1933 in my house in Cologne was arranged by me after Papen had asked me for it on about 10 December 1932. Before I took this step I talked to a number of businessmen and informed myself generally on how the business world viewed a collaboration between the two men. The general desire of businessmen was to see a strong man come to power in Germany who would form a government that would stay in power for a long time...'

Kurt von Schroeder, evidence given at the Nuremburg Trial

Source B: From Papen to Schleicher

Explain why

(a) Papen was dismissed
(b) Schleicher's policy failed.

Explain the role played in these negotiations by

a) Hindenburg
b) Hindenburg's son.

...Papen was dismissed because he wanted to fight the National Socialists and did not find in the Reichswehr the necessary support for such a policy, and...Schleicher came to power because he believed he could form a government which would have the support of the National Socialists. When it became clear that Hitler was not willing to enter Schleicher's Cabinet and that Schleicher on his part was unable to split the National Socialist Party, as he had hoped to do with the help of Gregor Strasser, the policy for which Schleicher had been appointed Chancellor was shipwrecked. Schleicher was aware that Hitler was particularly embittered against him because of his attempt to break up the Party, and would never agree to cooperate with him. So he now changed his mind and decided to fight against the Nazis - which meant that he now wanted to pursue the policy which he had sharply opposed when Papen had suggested it a few weeks before. Schleicher came to Hindenburg therefore with a demand for emergency powers as a prerequisite of action against the Nazis. Furthermore, he believed it to be necessary to dissolve, and even temporarily eliminate, the Reichstag, and this was to be done by

Presidential decrees on the basis of article 48 - the transformation of his government into a military dictatorship...

Schleicher first made these suggestions to Hindenburg in the middle of January 1933, but Hindenburg at once evinced grave doubts as to its constitutionality. In the meantime Papen had returned to Berlin, and by an arrangement with Hindenburg's son had had several interviews with the President. When Schleicher renewed his demand for emergency powers, Hindenburg declared that he was unable to give him such a blank cheque and must reserve to himself decisions on every individual case. Schleicher for his part said that under these circumstances he was unable to stay in office and tendered his resignation on 28 January.

In the middle of January, when Schleicher was first asking for emergency powers, Hindenburg was not aware of the contact between Papen and Hitler - particularly, of the meeting which had taken place in the house of the Cologne banker, Kurt von Schroeder. In the latter part of January, Papen played an increasingly important role in the house of the Reich president, but despite Papen's persuasions, Hindenburg was extremely hesitant, until the end of January, to make Hitler Chancellor. He wanted to have Papen again as Chancellor. Papen finally won him over to Hitler with the argument that the representatives of the other right-wing parties which would belong to the Government would restrict Hitler's freedom of action...

Many of Hindenburg's personal friends, such as Oldenburg-Januschau, worked in the same direction as Papen, also General von Blomberg. The President's son and adjutant, Oskar von Hindenburg, was opposed to the Nazis up to the last moment. The turning-point at which his views changed came at the end of January. At Papen's suggestion, a meeting had been arranged between Hitler and Oskar von Hindenburg in the house of Ribbentrop. Oskar von Hindenburg asked me to accompany him: we took a taxi, in order to keep the appointment secret, and drove out to Ribbentrop's home...

Oskar von Hindenburg was told that Hitler wanted to talk to him *tête à*

GENERAL KURT VON SCHLEICHER, GERMAN CHANCELLOR IN 1932. HE WAS MURDERED DURING THE NIGHT OF THE LONG KNIVES (30 JUNE 1934)

PRESIDENT HINDENBURG, 1925

Summarise in point form the important evidence provided by Meissner at the Nuremburg Trial

tête; as Hindenburg had asked me to accompany him, I was somewhat surprised at his accepting this suggestion and vanishing into another room for a talk which lasted quite a while - about an hour. What Hitler and Oskar von Hindenburg discussed during this talk I do not know.

In the taxi on the way back, Oskar von Hindenburg was very silent; the only remark he made was that there was no help for it, the Nazis had to be taken into the Government. My impression was that Hitler had succeeded in getting him under his spell.

Otto Meisner, evidence given at the Nuremburg Trial

Source C

From about 20 January 1933 onwards, rumours grew that the position of the Reich Chancellor von Schleicher was thoroughly shaken, because Reich President von Hindenburg, acting under the influence of Papen, Hugenberg's backstairs men and Hindenburg's son, wished to withdraw his confidence in him. There was talk of a Papen-Hugenberg cabinet with National Socialist participation. General von Stülpnagel or Herr Schmidt-Hannover were mentioned as possible war ministers, with the rider that the National Socialists might possibly demand and be given the War Ministry.

All this was improbable, as the National Socialists would on no account have entered a Papen-Hugenberg Cabinet. However, the rumours persisted and became stronger still.

On the morning of 26 January I went to see Schleicher and asked him what was true in the rumours about a change in government. Schleicher confirmed that the Reich President would almost certainly withdraw his confidence either today or tomorrow, and that he would resign. I went from Schleicher to State Secretary Meissner, asked him what was to happen after Schleicher's resignation, and told him clearly and unmistakably that the National Socialists would never enter a Papen-Hugenberg cabinet. Such a cabinet would have as enemies the National Socialists on the one hand and the Left from Dingeldey (DVP) to Thälmann on the other. It would thus rest on a tiny base. The army would then have to support this 7 per cent base against 93 per cent of the German people. That would be dangerous to the highest degree; could such a situation be avoided?

Meissner evidently judged the situation similarly and arranged for me to report my concern to the Reich President immediately. This I did. Hindenburg angrily forbade me to intervene in political matters, but then said, apparently to reassure me, 'that he had no intention of making the Austrian lance-corporal War Minister or Reich Chancellor.' Hindenburg failed to understand my fear that the army might become involved or be misused in a fight between Papen-Hugenberg on the one hand and the National Socialists and the entire Left on the other. I departed with my fears increased, for Schleicher's dismissal was already settled. What was to follow was obviously completely unclear.

On 29 January a discussion took place in my office between Schleicher and myself. We were both convinced that only Hitler was possible as future Reich Chancellor. Any other choice would lead to a general strike, if not a civil war, and thus to a totally undesirable use of the army against the National Socialists as well as against the Left. We considered whether we knew of any other way to influence the situation to avoid this misfortune. The result of our considerations was negative. We saw no possibility of exercising any further influence on the Reich President. Finally I decided, in agreement with Schleicher, to seek a meeting with Hitler.

General von Hammerstein, Army Commander-in-Chief
(from notes made in 1935)

Source D: Intrigue bears fruit

Wednesday, 18th January: In Dahlem at noon; Hitler, Röhm, Himmler, Papen.

Hitler insists on being Chancellor. Papen again considers this impossible. His influence with Hindenburg was not strong enough to effect this. Hitler makes no further arrangements for talks. Joachim tentatively suggests a meeting between Hitler and Hindenburg's son.

Sunday, 22nd January: Meeting at Dahlem at 10 pm. Papen arrives alone at nine o'clock. Present: Hitler, Frick, Göring, Körner, Meissner, young Hindenburg, Papen and Joachim. Hitler talks alone to young Hindenburg for two hours, followed by Hitler-Papen talk. Papen will now press for Hitler as Chancellor, but tells Hitler that he will withdraw from these negotiations forthwith if Hitler has no confidence in him.

Monday, 23rd January: In the morning Papen saw Hindenburg, who refused everything. Joachim goes to Hitler to explain this. Long talk about the possibility of a Schacht Cabinet. Hitler rejects everything.

Friday, 27th January: Hitler back in Berlin. Long talk with him at Göring's flat. Hitler wants to leave Berlin forthwith...New meeting with old Hindenburg arranged. Hitler declares that he has said all there is to say to the Field Marshal, and does not know what to add. Joachim

GENERAL VON HAMMERSTEIN

Summarise, again in point form, the evidence provided by General von Hammerstein.

FRANZ VON PAPEN WITH LEADERS OF THE 'STAHLHELM' ORGANISATION

The Stahlhelm (or 'Steel Helmet') was a vociferous ex-servicemen's organisation. In 1929 they joined Hugenberg in forming a national committee to oppose the Young Plan. Hitler temporarily lent this group his support, but only for his own purposes.

RIBBENTROP, PHOTOGRAPHED IN THE STUDY OF HIS DAHLEM VILLA, IN BERLIN'S FASHIONABLE SUBURB

persuades Hitler that this last attempt should be made, and that the situation is by no means hopeless.   Notes taken by Ribbentrop's wife

Source E

I have never seen Hitler in such a state; I proposed to him and Göring that I should see Papen alone that evening and explain the whole situation to him. In the evening I saw Papen and convinced him eventually that the only thing that made sense was Hitler's Chancellorship, and that he must do what he can to bring this about...Papen is now absolutely certain that he must achieve Hitler's Chancellorship at all costs, and that he must abandon his belief that it is his duty to remain at Hindenburg's disposal. This recognition by Papen is, I believe, the turning point. Papen has an appointment with Hindenburg for Saturday 10 am.

Saturday, 28th January: About 11 am I went to see Papen who received me with the question: 'Where is Hitler?' I told him that he had probably left, but could perhaps be contacted in Weimar. Papen said the he had to be got back without delay, because the turning point had been reached; after a long talk with Hindenburg he, Papen, considered Hitler's Chancellorship possible. I went to see Göring immediately and heard that Hitler was still at the Kaiserhof. Göering telephoned him, Hitler will remain in Berlin...Göring and I went to see Hitler. Long talk with Hitler alone explaining that a solution depended entirely on trust and that his Chancellorship did not now appear to be impossible...

Sunday, 29th January: At 11 am long Hitler-Papen talk. Hitler declared that on the whole everything was clear. But there would have to be general elections and an Enabling Law. Papen saw Hindenburg immediately. I lunched with Hitler at the Kaiserhof. We discussed the elections. As Hindenburg does not want these, Hitler asked me to tell the President that these would be the last elections. In the afternoon Göring and I went to Papen. Papen declared that all obstacles are removed and that Hindenburg expects Hitler tomorrow at 11 am.

Monday 30th January: Hitler appointed Chancellor.

Notes taken by Ribbentrop

HITLER AND HIS FIRST CABINET

REVIEW

How did Hitler come to power in January 1933?
1 Popular support

Gather notes under the following headings:

(a) Electoral support. Details of various elections. The limitations in support.

(b) Exact nature of support. Who voted for Hitler? Who resisted Hitler?

(c) Nature of Nazi propaganda. The role of Goebbels.

(d) The personal influence of Hitler. The limits of his influence.

(e) Problems faced by Weimar Republic. Unemployment, economy, political instability, failure of moderate parties, increased reliance on emergency powers.

(f) In contrast to (e), highlight successes of Weimar Republic, especially those achieved under Stresemann. Why were these short-lived?

(g) Was the Republic itself doomed before the accession of Hitler became inevitable?

(h) Other factors connected with popular support.

GENERAL VON BLOMBERG, MINISTER OF WAR AND SUPREME COMMANDER OF THE WEHRMACHT

2 Political intrigue

(a) Highlight the fact that Hitler's support was limited and that in November 1932 he suffered a major reverse. He was still not in power.

(b) Role of powerful individuals – Hindenburg.

(c) Schleicher

(d) Papen

(e) Hindenburg's son

(f) Resignation of Strasser

(g) Role of Reichswehr-Army

(h) Role of businessmen - eg, Kurt von Schroeder

(i) Why did these individuals deal with Hitler? What did they offer him? What did they gain in return? Did they control Hitler or did they lose control while Hitler manipulated them?

3 Other factors

(a) The whole nature of German society

(b) Problems inherent since 1918; eg, Versailles, economic problems.

Question

Essay How did Hitler come to power in January 1933?

9 Lenin's Russia 1917-24

PREVIEW

AN EARLY PHOTOGRAPH OF LENIN WHEN HE WAS A MEMBER OF THE 'UNION OF STRUGGLE FOR LIBERATION OF THE WORKING PEOPLE'

LENIN'S FORGED PASSPORT WITH A PICTURE OF HIMSELF IN DISGUISE

It is clear from these photographs that Lenin could easily change his appearance. Did he also change his policies when the moment suited?

Prelude to a second revolution

Continuation of the struggle

The master of disguise had used his talents well. The scene appeared mundane: a steam train following the regular, timetabled route from Petrograd to Finland. Beyond the billowing black smoke a bleak landscape with huge areas of marshland. Searing summer temperatures meant that voracious mosquitoes were out in force. Aboard the train on the night of 21 August 1917 the passengers and crew did not seem to warrant a second glance. They were all allowed through the border security into Finland without delay. Yet closer examination would have revealed the wanted man. A professional revolutionary who had sworn his opposition to the Provisional Government and would soon return to destroy it. He had escaped their grasp and made his way to a rural hideout. When he arrived at the safehouse he was able to relax. Vladimir Ilyich Lenin discarded the railway stoker's uniform which he had worn for the journey and carried on with his plans for the second revolution of 1917.

Meanwhile problems were mounting for the Provisional Government which had appointed itself to govern after the demise of the Tsar. Led at first by Prince Lvov and subsequently by Kerensky, this small group of liberal middle-class politicians had made the crucial decision to continue with the war. Kerensky personally toured the trenches urging the soldiers to fight for 'war till a victorious end' and moving men to tears with his brilliant oratory. Yet when a major Russian offensive in June turned into a headlong retreat in July it became clear that words were not enough and that the war was becoming increasingly unpopular. In the towns and cities, power was passing into the hands of newly-elected councils (soviets) which represented the views of the workers, soldiers and sailors. Dominated initially by the

LENIN, Vladimir Ilyich (1870-1924)
Russian revolutionary leader and architect of Soviet State
Expelled from Kazan University as a result of political activity, then studied writings of Marx
In St Petersburg, organised League for the Liberation of the Working Class
1897 Exiled to Siberia
1903 in London when Russian Social Democratic Labour Party split into Bolsheviks + Mensheviks. Led Bolshevik wing and published newspaper, 'The Spark'
1905 involved in abortive revolution. Controlled revolutionary movement from exile in Switzerland
1917 Smuggled into Russia by Germans

ALEXANDER KERENSKY REVIEWING THE TROOPS IN 1917

Social Revolutionaries and the Mensheviks, these soviets offered tentative support for the war but demanded immediate improvements in social conditions and food supplies. When the government failed to deliver these improvements, it faced a major demonstration by sailors and workers in July. The Bolsheviks initially supported this July uprising but then withdrew their backing in the face of fierce government suppression. Having temporarily overcome the threat from the left the Provisional Government then had to stave off a revolt from the right led by Kornilov, the commander in chief of the armed forces.

Even though Kornilov's attempted coup came to nothing, Kerensky had no room for comfort. Peasant conscripts were deserting the army en masse, seizing land from the nobility when they returned. The soviets were becoming more radical and by September the Bolsheviks enjoyed a majority on both the Petrograd and Moscow soviets. With the German army close to Petrograd, food shortages in the capital city became more acute than ever. Still Kerensky refused to abandon the war effort. Co-operation between the soviets and the Provisional Government was breaking down but the Mensheviks and the Social Revolutionaries were reluctant actually to take power for themselves. Only one party had its sights firmly fixed on power and that was the Bolsheviks. Their radical policies and powerful slogans of 'Peace, Bread and Land' and 'All Power to the Soviets' seemed increasingly to coincide with the aspirations of the soldiers, the peasants and the urban masses. After his long years in exile, Lenin was now convinced that his party could successfully carry out a coup in the capital city. First of all he had to get back from Finland and persuade his Bolshevik colleagues that the time for an uprising was ripe. At the start of October, Lenin donned a wig and returned to the capital. Having begun 1917 with its leaders in exile and a membership of around 25,000 the Bolshevik party was now on the brink of power. Why was this party more successful in 1917 than its rivals?

GENERAL KORNILOV ADDRESSING RUSSIAN SOLDIERS IN
THE SUMMER OF 1917

9.1 The growth in popularity of the Bolshevik Party: February-October 1917

Front line troops
* The soldiers initially supported continuation of the war, providing it was fought on defensive not expansionist lines.
■ Said they'd continue the war for the protection of Russia. April - said to Allies they'd stand by full commitment. June offensive ended in retreat.
☐ Their line, criticised by opponents, was always consistent; and promised an immediate, just peace without annexations.

Peasantry
* Although countryside was fairly calm in February, they became impatient for land. July - major peasant disturbances.
■ Promised land reform but said it would have to wait until the Constituent Assembly was elected.
☐ They promised nationalisation of land, distribution to the peasants without compensation to landowners.

Factory workers
* Supported democracy and elections to Constituent Assembly. They wanted better wages, conditions and a 9-8 hour working day.
■ Did not bring about real change in the factories. Urged workers to show restraint in relations with employers.
☐ Promised to hold Constituent Assembly elections as soon as possible. Called for 'greater workers' control' and began to pick up support from skilled craftsmen in metallurgical factories.

Urban masses
* Wanted democracy and improvement in food supply. Mass enthusiasm for elections, councils, soviets and radical ideas.
■ Unable to bring about any immediate improvement in food supplies. Indeed, the government was associated with shortages.
☐ Lenin said that the masses were often more radical than the Bolsheviks. Slogan 'Peace, Bread and Land' tried to bridge the gap.

Soviets
* Dominated until summer by Mensheviks and SRs. Content to offer conditional support to the provisional government, not seek power.
■ Perhaps they regarded the soviets as a convenient

> **Key**
> * Represents the expectations of these groups from the government
> ■ What the Provisional government offered these groups
> ☐ What the Bolsheviks offered these groups

mechanism to exercise control over the radical Left.
☐ Campaigned under the slogan 'All power to the soviets'. During the summer, Bolshevik representation on the soviets increased dramatically.

Middle classes
* These groups generally supported the Kadets who formed basis of provisional government.
■ Sought to preserve and enhance the status and power of these groups and agreed that the elections to the Assembly would be delayed.
☐ Although some Bolsheviks were from middle-class backgrounds themselves, they totally opposed 'bourgeois' groups.

The programme of the Provisional Government
• Freedom of speech, assembly and association.
• Elections based on a universal adult franchise to be held for a Constituent Assembly.
• To keep Russia in the war and defend the motherland.
• A complete amnesty for all political and religious offences and abolition of the death penalty.
• The confiscation of Crown lands.

• Abolition of tsarist governors: local authority to regional zemstvos

The programme of the Bolshevik Party

Made clear in Lenin's *April Theses*. Lenin urged no co-operation with the Provisional Government. All power to the soviets. An end to the war. Nationalisation of land, banks; abolition of the police force, the Army and the bureaucracy.

The Bolshevik Party changed almost beyond recognition during 1917. In February the party leaders were in exile and presided over a factious, unpopular, minority party with less than 25,000 members. It is estimated by some historians that by November the membership figure exceeded 250,000. They were the only party which really welcomed the instability and upheaval of 1917 and - more importantly - were the only party really trying to gain power.

Profile of the Social Revolutionaries

The SRs were particularly powerful in the countryside because for a long time they had advocated major land reform for the peasants. They claimed to have a membership of more than one million. Although they were strongly represented in the soviets, they were inhibited by what they saw as the major risks inherent in holding power.

Profile of the Mensheviks

Like the SRs, the Mensheviks were reluctant to translate

MEETING OF THE COUNCIL OF WORKERS, SOLDIERS AND PEASANTS

representation in the soviet into a full-blooded bid for power. They believed that the Provisional Government represented an essential 'bourgeois' transitional period which had to precede Communism. In February 1917 they numbered their membership only in thousands but by the autumn they had 200,000 members.

The Kadets

Unlike the other parties, the Kadets represented the professional and middle classes. Backed by civil servants and industrialists, it was the Kadets who formed the core of the Provisional Government and who made certain that the state bureaucracy remained largely intact after February 1917.

TALKING POINT

'A small, unpopular party whose success was due solely to the determination of its leader to seize power.'
How far would you agree with this statement?

EXAMINING THE EVIDENCE

The role of Lenin in the October Revolution

Source A: Lenin's attitude towards the war (September 1914)

Lenin had no doubt about the party attitude to the war...to 'utilize the economic and political crisis caused by the war in order to...hasten the destruction of the class domination of the capitalist class'. The defection of the Socialists and Social Democrats of western Europe who, almost to a man, supported their respective national governments in August 1914 was the blackest treason. It in no way shook Lenin's convictions. He reached Berne on 5 September 1914; and on the following day he assembled the small group of available Bolsheviks and read them a set of theses on the war, in which he explicitly declared that 'from the point of view of the working class and of the toiling masses of all the peoples of Russia the defeat of the Tsarist monarchy and its armies would be the least evil'.

E.H. Carr, *The Bolshevik Revolution*, Vol. 1 (1950)

What characteristics would you say that Lenin displayed in his leadership of the Bolshevik Party in 1914?

Source B

The dimensions of his personal influence, like everything else about him, are not open to easy assessment. It is becoming accepted that his organisational position in the party before 1917 was often fragile; it can now also be shown that he suffered numerous defeats on matters of political and economic policy in the same period.

R. Service, *Lenin* Vol. 1 (1985)

Source C: Lenin's response to the February Revolution and the Provisional Government (February 1917)

His eagerness to return to Russia turned into a frenzy at the news of what was happening to the Bolshevik organisation at home...To Lenin's dismay (even though he himself had not worked out fully an alternative policy), the new arrivals [Stalin and Kamenev had just returned from Siberia] adopted a conciliatory policy towards the Mensheviks, and even, o horror! towards the Provisional Government...He was supremely confident that once in Russia he could redirect his straying cohorts, but he had to get there and fast. But how?...

Ever since the beginning of the war the German Imperial Government and the General Staff had been conscious of the great help they might derive from the Russian revolutionary movement. Internal subversion of the enemy was already recognised as a legitimate weapon of warfare. And in the case of Russia the opportunities for its use appeared limitless...

Adam B. Ulam, *Lenin and the Bolsheviks* (1978)

Source D: German intervention (April 1917)

...We must now definitely try to create the utmost chaos in Russia. To this end we must avoid any discernible influence in the course of the Russian revolution. But we must secretly do all we can to aggravate the contradictions between the moderate and the extreme parties, since we are extremely interested in the victory of the latter, for another upheaval will then be inevitable, and will take forms which will shake the Russian state to its foundations.

Count von Brockdorff-Rantzau, German Ambassador in Copenhagen, to the ministry of foreign affairs. Top secret, 2 April

Source E: April Theses

3. No support for the Provisional Government; the utter falsity of all its promises should be explained, particularly those relating to the renunciation of annexations. Exposure in place of the impermissible, illusion-breeding 'demand' that this Government, a Government of capitalists, should cease to be an imperialist Government.

4. ...as long as we are in the minority we carry on the work of criticising and exposing errors and at the same time we preach the necessity of transferring the entire state power to the Soviets.

Lenin, extract from April Theses (1917)

Source F: Lenin's return to Russia (April 1917)

Granted Lenin's premises, his decision to accept German help was perfectly natural. It was not to affect his position an iota: he was working to bring about a new revolution in Russia, but that government in turn was to over-throw the German government and bring about the victory of revolutionary socialism in all Europe...Thus on 9 April [1917] Lenin, his wife, and more than twenty leading members of his Swiss group...set out for home. After Germany they travelled through Sweden, then Finland...At 11.10 the night of April 3 the train pulled in at the Finland Station of Petrograd. Vladimir Ilyich was home...Lenin descended from his car and was engulfed by the greeters.

Adam B. Ulam, Lenin and the Bolsheviks (1978)

Source G: PAINTING SHOWING LENIN MAKING A SPEECH FROM AN ARMOURED CAR TO A CROWD OF WORKERS, SAILORS AND SOLDIERS ON HIS ARRIVAL AT THE FINLAND STATION (3 APRIL 1917) HOW RELIABLE DO YOU FIND THIS SOURCE TO BE?

Source H: A description of Lenin in October 1917

...Dressed in shabby clothes, his trousers much too long for him. Unimpressive, to be the idol of a mob, loved and revered as perhaps few leaders in history have been. A strange popular leader - a leader purely by virtue of intellect; colourless, humourless, uncompromising and detached, without picturesque idiosyncracies - but with the power of explaining profound ideas in simple terms, of analysing a concrete situation. And combined with shrewdness, the greatest intellectual audacity.

John Reed, *Ten Days That Shook The World* (1926)

Source I: The role of Lenin in the build-up to the Revolution

Lenin, from the time of his return to Russia in April 1917, was the overall strategist of the revolution: he also dealt with internal divisions within the party and provided an authoritarian base which promoted a degree of discipline and unity which the other parties lacked. Above all, he was entirely responsible for the timing of the October Revolution. He had realised that the rising of July 1917 was premature and therefore urged restraint on that occasion. But by October he calculated that circumstances had changed sufficiently to warrant immediate action, and he urged: 'We must not wait! We may lose everything!'

S.J. Lee, *The European Dictatorships* (1987)

Source J: 10 October 1917

He had limitless capacity to persuade, cajole and goad. On 10 October, the Central Committee debated the question of state power. Lenin returned clandestinely from Finland to participate, and the consequent decision came from his pen. Still he had to be restrained. He wanted power seized immediately. Trotski's view was preferred, that the uprising would be timed to allow state authority to be grasped on the opening day of the Second All-Russian Congress of Soviets. Thus 'soviet power' would be established.

Robert Service, *The Russian Revolution* (1986)

Source K: 24 October 1917

On the evening of the 24th Lenin, still heavily disguised, arrived in the Smolny...He still suspected that the rising was being bungled. As he made his way stealthily from the Vyborg suburb, where he had been hiding for the last few days, to the Smolny, he did not realise that the city he walked through was virtually in his party's hands. He bombarded Trotsky and the other leaders with questions...Why was the city so calm? But as he listened to the answers, as he watched the tense staff work in the room of the Military Revolutionary Committee, the reports coming in ceaselessly and the instructions going out, as he eyed the leaders of the rising themselves, almost exhausted, unshaven, dirty, with eyes inflamed from sleeplessness, yet confident and composed, he realised that they had crossed the Rubicon without him, and his suspicion melted away.

I. Deutscher, *The Prophet Armed, Trotsky 1879-1921* (1954)

Analysis of the individual

Here are two views of Lenin's leadership of the Bolshevik Party.

Critical view

In exile for most of the time.
Pursued unpopular policies.
Other Bolshevik leaders often disagreed with him.
Led a small, divided party.
Lived in fear of arrest.
Had to accept the views of others on the timing of the revolution.
Left the actual organisation of the uprising to Trotsky.

Sympathetic view

He established the Party's opposition to the war and the Provisional Government.
Intellectually dominant within the party.
Persuaded colleagues to accept his views.
Responsible for the timing of the revolution.
No other figure exerted as much influence.

The purpose of examining these documents has been to try to reach some conclusions about the extent of Lenin's personal control over the Bolshevik Party.

1 What impression of Lenin's leadership is given in Sources A and B? Are these two sources in agreement?

2 Source C shows that Lenin's colleagues disagreed with him. Would you conclude from this that Lenin's position within the party at this time was rather weak?

3 What evidence is contained in Sources D-F to suggest that Lenin's policies were sometimes unpopular?

4 Source G was obviously produced after the event. What appears to have been the intention of the artist? Is the impression given in this source supported by the evidence in Source F? Does the preceding text give the same impression?

ANOTHER PAINTING PURPORTING TO SHOW LENIN'S ARRIVAL AT THE FINLAND STATION IN APRIL 1917

5 Is the writer of Source H impressed by Lenin's personality?

6 Read Source I to K.

(a) Which aspects of the October Revolution appear to have been controlled by Lenin?

(b) Over which aspects of the October Revolution does his influence appear to have been more limited?

7 Read the two views of Lenin shown on the previous page.

(a) Write a paragraph in support of each view.

(b) Explain which view you find ultimately more convincing.

EXAMINING THE EVIDENCE

Myth and reality in the October Revolution

Traditional Soviet accounts of the October Revolution have emphasised the role of Lenin and have tended to ignore the actions of Trotsky. In addition, Russian historians have presented the revolution as an heroic popular uprising, bravely led by the Bolsheviks and supported by the workers, soldiers and sailors of Petrograd. What really happened?

Source A

Portrayal by the artist Deshalyt of the storming of the Winter Palace. How convincing is this picture?

TALKING POINT

Look very carefully at Source A. it comes from a famous film on the October Revolution. What are the advantages and disadvantages of using this type of film as historical evidence?

Source B

The twelfth hour of the revolution was near. The Smolny was being transformed into a fortress. In its garret there were a dozen or two machine guns...

November 6, a grey morning, early. I roamed about the building from one floor to another...to make sure that everything was in order and to encourage those who needed it. Along the stone floors of the interminable and still half-dark corridors of the Smolny the soldiers were dragging their machine guns...On the third floor of the Smolny, in a small corner room,

Read Trotsky's comments on the revolution in Sources B and C.

1 Which phrases would you say are designed to give the impression of a heroic uprising?

2 What comments does Trotsky make which undermine the impression of a heroic uprising and make it sound more down to earth?

3 What impression of the uprising is provided by the painting? How valuable is this type of evidence to the historian?

the Committee was in continuous session. All reports about the movement of the troops, the attitude of soldiers and workers, the agitation of the barracks...the happenings in the Winter Palace - all these came to this centre.

All that week I had hardly stepped out of the Smolny: I spent the nights on a leather couch without undressing, sleeping in snatches, and constantly being roused by couriers, scouts, messenger-cyclists, telegraphists, and ceaseless telephone calls.

L.D. Trotsky, *History of the Russian Revolution* (1965)

Source C

The Ministers, who had sought refuge in the Winter Palace...were guarded only by a company of the Women's Battalion and a few of the cadets from the Military Schools. At six in the evening a message was sent into them calling on them to surrender immediately, but as no answer was received the attack on the Palace was opened by a few blank rounds being fired from the Fortress as a preliminary warning. This was also followed by a massed onslaught from both sides, armoured cars and machine guns firing at the Palace from under the archway on the square, while now and then the guns of the fortress or of the cruiser *Aurora* thundered and crashed above the din. Actually, however, a good many of the shots were only gun-cotton, and the firing in all cases was so inaccurate that the Palace was only hit three times from the river, though on the other sides the walls were riddled with innumerable bullet marks, and a good many of the windows were broken.

L.D. Trotsky, *History of the Russian Revolution* (1965)

Source D

A painting by the artist Sokolov-Skalya from 1937 gives a retrospective picture of the storming of the Winter Palace

Source E: Ultimatum

The Winter Palace is surrounded by revolutionary forces, the guns of the Peter-Paul Fortress and the cruisers *Aurora* and *Amur* are trained on the Winter Palace and GHQ, and members of the supreme command will be arrested. The junior officers, soldiers and clerks will be disarmed and, after examination, released. You have twenty minutes to reply. This ultimatum expires at 7.10 after which we shall open fire. Antonov, president of the PVRK; commissioner of the Peter-Paul Fortress.

Quoted in Marc Ferro, *The Bolshevik Revolution* (1953)

Source F

There was considerable disorder among the attackers. At 7.10 the searchlight of the Peter-Paul Fortress, which should have given *Aurora* the signal to fire, failed to work. Antonov and Blagondarov went off towards Peter-Paul Fortress to find out what was happening there. There was thick fog over the bridges, the Neva and the fortress. Antonov, who was short-sighted, stumbled around in his wanderings, and then Blagondarov got lost. The nervousness was extreme, and time went by with neither a signal nor the *Aurora's* guns showing themselves. Finally, at 9.35, the signal beam was repaired, and at 9.40 the salvo from the *Aurora* rent the night. It was blank shot, 'so as to avoid damage to an historical monument', but the noise was vast, and was remembered by several eye-witnesses. A little later, machine-gunnery and rifle-fire crackled around the Palace. The government members were terrified, though, not knowing the full extent of the disaster, they did not give in like the cadets, who did. The women's volunteer unit refused to follow, and even wished to attack, for honour's sake. Around 10.00 pm the attackers had reformed, and all was ready for a final assault, if need be, in an hour's time. At Smolny, Podvoysky said, 'Lenin was like a caged beast: he had to preside at the second congress and so had to have the Winter Palace, at whatever cost. The palace was the last barrier on the soviet's road to power, and Vladimir Ilyich screamed and yelled, ready to have us all shot.'

Marc Ferro, *The Bolshevik Revolution* (1985)

1 What similarities are there in the historian's account given in Source F and Trotsky's description provided in Sources B and C?

2 What are the key differences in these two accounts?

Source G

About 11.00 we broke in the doors and filtered up the stairway one by one or in little bunches. When we got to the top of the stairs the officer-cadets took away our guns. Still our fellows kept coming up, little by little until we had a majority. Then we turned around and took away the cadets' guns.

A revolutionary's account in John Reed, *Ten Days That Shook the World* (1926)

Source H

On 23 October, the very day on which Trotskii's personal appeal had won over the garrison of the fortress of Saints Peter and Paul whose cannons commanded the Neva River and the Winter Palace, Kerenskii came inadvertently to Lenin's aid. He prevailed upon the cabinet to authorise the removal of the MRC's commissars, the arrest of leading Bolsheviks, the closing of two of their newspapers, and the calling of loyal troops from the suburbs. Early the next morning, a Tuesday, detachments of government soldiers seized the presses and premises of the Bolshevik papers, leading the MRC to declare that the Petrograd Soviet was in danger. The MRC put all units on battle alert, gained the adherence of the crew of the cruiser *Aurora* which was anchored in the Neva, by countermanding a government order that put it to sea, and sent pro-Bolshevik units to reopen the closed printing shops. Later that day and the next, soldiers, sailors, and Red Guards occupied the central telegraph and post offices, the telephone exchange, railway stations, and other strategic points. At ten o'clock on Wednesday morning the 25th, the MRC proclaimed that power had passed to the Petrograd Soviet and before that body Trotskii, in the afternoon, announced that the Provisional Government had been overthrown. The final assault on the Winter Palace, where the cabinet refused to surrender, came during the night; it was taken with surprising ease and few casualties. The ministers were arrested at 2 am on the 26th.

Hans Rogger, *Russia in the Age of Modernisation and Revolution 1881-1917* (1987)

Source I

It would, however, be idle to consider that the Bolsheviks' planning for revolution was efficient, co-ordinated or thoroughly considered. It succeeded by default rather than design. On Trotsky's own admission, the events of 24-26 October were marked by confusion, apprehension, uncertainty and opportunism...After hours of indecision and ignored ultimata punctuated by sporadic and innocuous shell-fire, the palace was infiltrated (not 'stormed') during the night of the 25/26th by a squadron of revolutionary guards who arrested the remaining members of the Provisional Government. Kerensky was not among them. He had earlier fled in a car placed at his disposal by the United States Embassy.'

Alan Wood, *The Origins of the Russian Revolution 1861-1917* (1987)

Source J

The October Revolution marked the beginning not the end of the Bolsheviks...The myth is that the October Revolution gave the Bolsheviks power. The reality is that they had to fight a bloody civil war to win it afterwards. The reality of the October Revolution was an armed rising by a revolutionary minority inspired by the political genius of Lenin against a government that had already lost control. Once in power the Bolsheviks replaced that reality with the propaganda myth of a revolution of all workers, soldiers and peasants under their leadership.

Christopher Andrew, *Timewatch*, BBC TV (1987)

Source K

Contrary to the dramatic scenes in Eisenstein's famous film, the provisional government was not overthrown by a mass attack on the Winter Palace. A few Red Guards climbed in through the servants' entrance, found the provisional government in session and arrested the ministers in the name of the people.

That was the Bolshevik revolution. Six people, five of them Red Guards, were casualties of bad shooting by their own comrades.

A.J.P. Taylor, *Revolutions and Revolutionaries* (1980)

Source L

How had it come about that the Bolsheviks could seize power in October? The answer widely proposed at the time and endorsed by countless commentators in our own day was unambiguous. The Bolshevik party manipulated an untutored public opinion among workers, soldiers and peasants. They grabbed governmental authority through conspiracy. They were disciplined and centralised and they served their dictatorial leader Lenin with blind devotion. Thus the Russian 'masses' were highjacked into acceptance of the coup of October by a tiny intellectual elite of megalomaniacs.

Robert Service, *The Russian Revolution* (1986)

TALKING POINT

Was it Trotsky rather than Lenin who was really responsible for carrying out the October Revolution?

Myth and reality in the October Revolution
Assignment

Soviet historians have interpreted the events of October 1917 very differently from their Western counterparts. The premise for this task is that a post-glasnost history conference to commemorate 1917 is being held at Leningrad University. Historians from the West have been invited for the first time. The following tasks have to be completed in preparation.

1 Devise two titles for the conference.
(a) Reflecting the Soviet view.
(b) The Western view.

2 (a) Select two pieces of evidence which the Soviet historians would most want to emphasise.
(b) Select two pieces of evidence which the Soviet historians would choose to leave out.
Repeat this exercise from the Western viewpoint.

3 On which aspects of the Revolution and the evidence might the historians be in agreement?

4 The most important part of the conference will be the Keynote papers. You have to prepare two of these. The first paper will briefly outline and justify the sympathetic Soviet view - endorsing the picture of a popular, heroic uprising. The second paper seeks to present the Western viewpoint, without offending the Soviet hosts!

5 The Western historian has three questions which he can ask of the Soviet historian. Devise three questions and the answers that might be provided.

6 Summarise the roles played by Lenin and Trotsky in the October Revolution, again from the two different points of view.

The consolidation of power

'To depose a government which could barely be said to exist or govern proved to be the easiest part of the Bolsheviks' task. To carry out their programme and hold together a country whose disintegration had created the conditions of their rise and triumph was vastly more difficult. The editors of *Izvestia*, the Soviet's newspaper, pointed out, just before they were replaced, that the Bolsheviks had only seized Petrograd, not the rest of

Russia, and warned prophetically of the threat of civil war. 'Bloodshed and pogroms - this is what we must prepare ourselves for.'

Hans Rogger, *Russia in the Age of Modernisation and Revolution 1881-1912* (1983)

The Bolsheviks' tentative hold on power was put to the test after only five days. While the one-time revolutionaries were still getting used to the idea that they were now in power, the counter-revolution began. For the first time Lenin must have appreciated what it was like to belong to an unpopular government. Roles were reversed as Kerensky attempted to topple the new government. During the revolution he had escaped from Petrograd in a fast car and made his way to the northern front. Such was the state of uncertainty that an astonished Kerensky noted that some soldiers of the Red Army who recognised him still offered this despised figure of authority their salute! Kerensky contacted General Krasnov and they agreed to march together on Petrograd. Their efforts were short-lived. They reached the outskirts of Petrograd but there Krasnov's army wilted in the face of a furious onslaught from the combined forces of the Red Army and the Bolshevik sailors. Krasnov's men deserted him and once again, Kerensky was obliged to flee the city. Yet the Bolsheviks' struggle for control of Russia had only just begun.

The Bolsheviks had retained control of Petrograd but in Moscow the struggle was more intense. Army officers and military cadets based in Moscow now offered stiff resistance. The fighting was severe with heavy casualties on both sides. The Kremlin itself was shelled during the struggle but after five days of bloody street fighting Moscow too came firmly under Bolshevik control. The possession of these two key cities was to be a vital factor in deciding the outcome of the Civil War itself. Other major cities soon followed suit.

Meanwhile Lenin transferred his embryonic government to Moscow. What did it consist of? The government was to be known as the Council of the People's Commissars (*Sovnarkom*). Headed by Lenin, other key posts included Trotsky as Commissar for Foreign Affairs and Stalin as Commissar of Nationalities. Apart from Trotsky, Jews - like Zinoviev and Kamenev - were excluded, as were any socialist politicians who were not members of the Bolshevik party. When the Mensheviks complained that the principles of the Revolution were being disgraced, Trotsky retorted: 'You are pitiful, isolated individuals, you are bankrupts: your role is played out. Go where you belong from now on - onto the rubbish heap of history.'

Many opponents of the Bolsheviks felt that their 'mad experiment' would not last. Indeed, Lenin's position within the Central Committee of the Bolshevik Party placed him close to the actual seat of power, but his position was still very far from that of a dictator. He could rely on obedience neither from the rank and file nor the leadership of the party. For the next few months, until he became completely indispensible, he had to rely on his powers of persuasion rather than coercion.

We will now examine the politics pursued by Lenin and the Communists between 1917 and 1924. You should have the following questions uppermost in your mind. To what extent were these policies determined solely by Lenin? Did the Bolsheviks succeed in bringing about a genuine Communist society? Did they betray their Communist principles? To what extent did Lenin's policies initiate totalitarian principles which were later taken to their logical conclusion by Stalin? Were these policies successful?

The land issue (November 1917)

The Decree on Land, proclaimed by the Bolsheviks immediately after the Revolution, abolished all private property in land and placed it at the disposal of peasant committees which were to ensure order and prevent wilful damage. Local peasant soviets were to oversee the redistribution of the estates of crown, church and nobility. All non-peasant land was expropriated without compensation. In effect this decree simply gave approval to a movement which was already well under way and over which the Bolsheviks exerted little control. Since September, returning peasant soldiers had taken part in the destruction of country houses, the seizure of land and timber and in some cases, the murder of landlords. In Lenin's view a class war between peasants and the wealthier Kulaks was taking place. He hoped that the largest estates would take the form of model collective farms but this was short lived: where land was retained for this purpose, looting and the destruction of machinery were commonplace.

Although the Bolsheviks claimed great credit for their land policy (which in effect was simply appropriated from the SR's), many historians now contend that the peasants acted independently and treated Bolshevik intervention with hostility and violence. Indeed such was the antagonism that within three months of the revolution, Bolshevik officials were being sent into the countryside to seize grain hoarded by the peasants.

The press (November 1917)

Lenin's toleration of dissent was extremely limited. In November 1917 he stated that 'to tolerate the existence of bourgeois papers means to cease being a socialist.' The newspapers of the Kadet Party were quickly suppressed and this was followed by the closure of each of the socialist parties' presses.

LENIN READING A COPY OF *PRAVDA* IN HIS KREMLIN STUDY. HE TOOK FIRM ACTION AGAINST THE PUBLISHERS OF OTHER NEWSPAPERS

'In the trying initial period of the revolution and the days that immediately followed it the Provisional Revolutionary Committee was compelled to take a number of measures against the counter-revolutionary press of different shades. Immediately outcries were heard from all sides that the new, socialist power had violated a fundamental principle of its programme by encroaching upon the freedom of the press.

The Workers' and Peasants' Government calls the attention of the population to the fact that what this liberal facade actually conceals is freedom for the propertied classes, having taken hold of the lion's share of the entire press, to poison, unhindered, the minds and obscure the consciousness of the masses...'

Chairman of the Council of People's Commissars, Vladimir Ulyanov (Lenin), *Decree on the Press* (9 November 1917)

National self-determination (1917-40)

Lenin had always condemned the tsarist empire as a 'prison of the nations'. He said that he detested Russian chauvinism and nationalism and believed that the subordinated states should be given national self-determination. Amid the upheaval of the Revolution and the Civil War that followed many of the non-Russian nations of the empire took the opportunity to escape from Russian control and establish national states of their own. Lenin and Trotsky firmly believed that further revolutions in Europe were imminent and so they were able to shrug off the loss of Finland, the Baltic States and Poland (which was already occupied by Germany in any case). Even after victory in the Civil War, Lenin's rule was generally confined to the old Muscovite heartland of Soviet Russia. However, once the Red Army had established its control in the heartland there ensued a piecemeal reconstruction of the old Russian empire which, by 1940, was virtually complete.

LITHUANIA
A Baltic and largely Catholic nation, united with Poland 1386-1795. Annexed by Russia 1795. Independent 1918-40.

FINLAND
Originally in union with Sweden. Annexed by Russia in 1808. Independent since 1918.

ESTONIA
Historically and ethnically close to Finland. Annexed by Russia from Sweden 1808. Independent 1918-40.

LATVIA
Historically Livonia and the Duchy of Courland. Annexed by Russia from Sweden 1808. Independent 1918-40.

BYELORUSSIA
Properly 'White Ruthenia', an East Slav nation closely related to the Ukrainians. Historically part of the Grand Duchy of Lithuania, to 1793. Nominally independent 1918.

DON COSSACKS
An autonomous community, briefly independent during the Russian Civil War.

—··—·· Frontier of tsarist empire in 1914

POLAND
Once, in union with Lithuania, the largest state in Europe. Largely annexed by Russia, 1773-1795. Independent from 1918.

UKRAINE
A nation of East Slavs formerly known as Ruthenians, and renamed as 'Little Russians' by the tsars. Annexed by Russia in stages from Poland, 1662-1795. The Western Ukraine as 'East Galicia' ruled by Austria and Poland to 1939. Independent 1918-20. Reconquered by the Red Army.

0   miles   200

TRANSCAUCASIA
Annexed by Russia 1801-28. Georgia and Armenia are historic, Christian nations. Western Armenia was part of the Ottoman Empire. Muslim Azerbaijan was part of Persia. Independent 1918-21.

THE MOVE TO INDEPENDENCE IN THE RUSSIAN EMPIRE 1918-21 (ADAPTED FROM *THE INDEPENDENT* 7 APRIL 1988)

The Cheka (December 1917)

The 'Extraordinary Commission to Combat Counter-Revolution and Sabotage' was set up as a political police force in December 1917. Its brief was to combat counter-revolution but as its leader, Felix Dzerzhinsky, exclaimed with some enthusiasm: 'We stand for organized terror - this should be frankly stated.' Western authorities now estimate that by 1924 the Cheka had executed more than 250,000 people.

FELIX DZERZHINSKY

Examining the Evidence

Source A: Legalisation of terror

The Soviet of People's Commissars, after having heard the report of the Chairman of the Extraordinary Commission, finds that in the present situation, the protection of the rear by terror is an urgent necessity...All those involved in White Guard organisations, plots and revolts are to be shot.

People's Commissar of Justice Kursky (5 September 1918)

Source B: Criticism of weakness

Tell us why you did not subject this Lockhart to the most refined tortures, in order to get the information and addresses which this 'goose' must be full of? In that way you could have easily discovered a whole number of counter-revolutionary organisations...

Tell us why, instead of subjecting him to such tortures, the mere description of which would have sent a thrill of cold horror through the counter-revolutionaries, you allowed him to leave the Extraordinary Commission.

Letter from Nolim Soviet (1919)

Source C: Description of Dzerzhinsky

Dzerzhinsky was a silent, gloomy man. Tall, spare, with grey shifty eyes. He spoke in monosyllables...When Scheglovitov inquired of him the reason of his trial, he answered, 'Simply because you were one of the Tsar's ministers,' and to the same question of Diestler, a Right Socialist Revolutionary, 'Why, because you are a Socialist Revolutionary'. A few minutes later he signed their death warrants. He signed scores of such warrants every day whilst sipping glasses of tea, always with the same gloomy air and casting anguished glances abroad.

From Russian Press Bureau (2 October 1919)

Source D: The methods used by the Cheka

The Cheka freed from all legal constraints, became a fearful organ of Bolshevik power. Each provincial section of the Cheka developed its own favourite methods of torture. In Kharkov Chekists scalped their prisoners and took the skin, like 'gloves', off their hands. In Voronezh they placed the naked prisoner in a barrel punctured with nails and then set it in motion. They burnt a five pointed star into the forehead and placed a crown of barbed wire around the neck of priests. In Tsaritsyn and Kamyshin they severed bones with a saw. In Poltava they impaled eighteen monks and burnt at the stake peasants who had rebelled. In Ekaterinoslav they crucified priests and stoned them. In Odessa they boiled officers and ripped them in half. In

Talking Point

Why do you think the Cheka resorted to such dreadful policies?

Kiev they placed them in a coffin with a decomposing corpse, buried them alive and then after half an hour dug them out.

Martin McCauley, The Soviet Union Since 1917 (1981)

The Civil War (1918-21)

In the Treaty of Brest-Litovsk (March 1918) Lenin accepted stringent terms from Germany in order to concentrate on the danger within from the forces of the right. The offensive Lenin anticipated was launched by the Whites, with the assistance of the Allied powers, in the summer of 1918. The key White generals were Kornilov, Krasnov, Denikin and Yudenich. Their forces were swelled by Allied troops and Finnish Whites. A further problem came from around 30,000 Czech activists who, ironically, had been released from Russian prisons in May 1918. In the summer of 1918 they gained control of a large area west of the Urals. As these soldiers advanced on Ekaterinburg the Bolsheviks took the decision to murder The Tsar and his family.

Initially the Whites enjoyed considerable success. Kulchak was victorious in Perm and Ufa and Denikin in Kharkov and Kiev. Indeed Denikin and Yudenich came close to Moscow and Petrograd respectively. The situation was so grave that at one stage the Bolsheviks seriously considered a retreat from Petrograd.

Trotsky's role in reversing the situation was absolutely crucial. It was Trotsky, as commissar for war, who created the new Red Army. Following the introduction of conscription in May 1918, the army comprised 500,000 men in April 1919 and 5 million by June 1920. This was rigidly controlled from Moscow. Trotsky astutely recruited almost 50,000 ex-tsarist officers to serve in the Red Army. Strict discipline and the use of firing squads encouraged the army to be cohesive and well-organised. Trotsky was given a free hand in running the Red Army; this can be seen in the way he prevailed upon Lenin to recall Stalin to Moscow following a personal dispute. The Bolsheviks' unity of purpose, clear ideological motivation and Trotsky's dynamic leadership meant that by 1920 the three main White offensives had been repelled. In the face of impending defeat the war-weary Allies withdrew their support and resources. The Civil War was over. Why had the Bolsheviks been successful?

● The states of Latvia, Estonia and Finland would have lent their support to the counter revolutionary forces but they were deterred by the Whites' refusal to recognise their independence.

● The White forces lacked a cohesive base. They were scattered all over Russia and this made concerted action difficult. By contrast, the Bolsheviks never lost control of Moscow and Petrograd.

● The Allied powers were weak and war-weary, and once the Whites suffered reverses they were reluctant to carry on.

● The Whites had no single leader with a force of personality equal to that of Lenin or Trotsky. They did not have a unified set of aims and were politically divided.

● The peasantry supported the Reds: a vital factor.

The Constituent Assembly (January 1918)

Although Lenin had often poured scorn on the notion of 'parliamentarianism', since April 1917 his party had noisily supported proposals for a democratically-elected Constituent Assembly. When it became clear after the elections that they could not control the Assembly, the Bolsheviks decided to close it down. Trotsky announced that 'we have trampled underfoot the principles of democracy for the sake of the loftier principles of a social revolution'. The SRs, the majority party in the Assembly, demonstrated against the closure but were crushed by the power of the Kronstadt sailors. An important postscript is that town soviet elections held in central Russia in Spring 1918 were also ruled invalid when it became clear that the Communists had been defeated.

Source A: The election results for the Constituent Assembly

Political party	Votes cast (millions)	Seats won
PSR	15.80	299
Ukrainian SRs	4.9	81
Other national minority SRs	1.0	19
Mensheviks	1.36	18
Popular Socialists	0.5	4
Ukrainian SPs	–	2
Kadets	3.2	17
Other National parties	2.5	56
Left SRs	–	39
Bolsheviks	9.8	168
Total	41.68	703

Source B: The dissolution of the Constituent Assembly

At its very inception, the Russian revolution produced the Soviet Workers', Soldiers' and Peasants' Deputies as the only mass organisation of all the working and exploited classes capable of giving leadership to the struggle of these classes for their complete political and economic emancipation...

The Constituent Assembly, elected on the basis of lists drawn up before the October Revolution, was expressive of the old correlation of political forces, when the conciliators and Constitutional-Democrats were in power...Outside the Constituent Assembly, the parties which have the majority there, the Right-Wing Socialist-Revolutionaries and the Mensheviks, are waging an open struggle against Soviet power, calling in their press for its overthrow...

Obviously, under such circumstances the remaining part of the Constituent Assembly can only serve as a cover for the struggle of the bourgeois counter-revolution to overthrow the power of the Soviets.

In view of this, the Central Executive Committee resolves: The Constituent Assembly is hereby dissolved.

Quoted in Martin McCauley, *The Russian Revolution and the Soviet State 1917-1921 Documents* (1975)

War Communism (1918-21)

The Bolsheviks inherited massive economic problems in 1917. The impact of the war, the breakdown of the transport system, inadequate supplies of raw materials, rampant inflation and the withdrawal of foreign capital led to a major economic crisis. War Communism was introduced as the government's response to this, in the spring of 1918. This policy was characterised by extensive nationalisation, the forceful requisition of grain from the countryside, harsh direction of labour and the temporary abolition of money as a measure of value. Labour discipline was draconian and lateness and absenteeism were punished severely. All workers were subjected to army style control and a state of war was extended to virtually every sphere of life. Everything was subordinated to victory in the Civil War.

By 1921, the people were increasingly unhappy with the economic chaos, harsh discipline, food shortages and hardship which seemed to be associated with War Communism.

Many historians are critical of the economic virtues of War Communism. Factory output in 1920 was approximately one seventh of what it had been in 1913. The area of farmland sown to grain in 1921 was down by at least 16 per cent compared to 1913. The level of popular dissent was intense and in 1921 the government embarked upon a radically different New Economic Policy.

In this extract from his book, *The Russian Civil War*, Evan Mawdsley indicates some of the controversy surrounding the policy of War Communism:

'The nature of the Bolsheviks' radical economic policies is a matter of controversy. The name usually given to them, "War Communism" is wrong on several counts. It is an anachronism; the term "War Communism" was first used - in Lenin's notes - only in 1921. It suggests that the policy was a wartime stopgap. (It is often said that the policy was provoked by the supposed "outbreak" of the Civil War in the summer of 1918.) My view is that while this fighting deepened an existing crisis, the economic policies later called War Communism - food detachments, nationalisation of industry, restrictions of trade - had been developing at the center and in the grass roots since the early winter of 1917-1918. There was no "normal" period followed by crisis; the crisis began with the start of the Bolsheviks' Civil War in October 1917..."War Communism" was essentially the policy of victorious communism.'

The Kronstadt Rising (March 1921)

The revolutionary credentials of the sailors of the Baltic Fleet were regarded as second to none. Trotsky described the sailors as 'the pride and joy of the revolution'. In October 1917 they had trained the guns of the cruiser *Aurora* on the Winter Palace in Petrograd. When protestors objected to the dissolution of the Constituent Assembly it was the Baltic sailors armed with rifles and bayonets who crushed the dissent. In 1921 they were still regarded by many people as an important barometer of radical opinion. Their links with the workers of Petrograd were very close. From their headquarters at Kronstadt on Kotlin Island the sailors controlled the vital sea approach to Petrograd. In the winter months there was easy access across the frozen sea from their base to the city. In February 1921 they responded sympathetically when thousands of workers in Petrograd went out on strike. Although the Petrograd workers were chiefly on strike for economic reasons, the repressive way in which the government treated them aroused great concern among the Baltic sailors. In particular they objected to Trotsky's use of strikebreakers selected from the Red Army. In a meeting held at the end of February the sailors expressed their support for the striking workers and also made it clear that they were concerned about a whole range of Communist Party policies.

EXAMINING THE EVIDENCE

Source A: Extracts from the demands of the Kronstadt sailors

1. New elections should be held...preceded by free electoral propaganda among workers and peasants.
2. Freedom of speech and press to be granted to workers and peasants, to Anarchists and left-wing socialist parties.
3. Also freedom of assembly and of trade union and peasants' associations.
5. All political prisoners belonging to socialist parties...to be set free.
7....No one party can be allowed to possess privileges in propagating its ideas and to receive government money for that purpose.

Source B

THE KRONSTADT SAILORS PATROLLING IN PETROGRAD, OCTOBER 1917

Source C: A description of the battle between the Red Army and the Kronstadt sailors

On 5th March an ultimatum from Trotsky was delivered composed in menacing terms. On 7th March Tukhachevsky, the hero of the Red Army's Polish Campaign, acting on Trotsky's orders, launched an infantry assault across the ice. This failed, because the troops sympathised with the rebels. Trotsky realised that Kronstadt had to be taken before the thaw...On 16th March the preliminary bombardment began and at dawn on the 17th the assault troops, dressed in white, advanced across the ice in two columns. One column was almost totally destroyed or drowned when it marched in close formation into a minefield laid on the ice. However, the other column, after hours of bitter fighting, entered the streets of Kronstadt. By this time the rebels were disorganised and the street fighting assumed the character of a massacre. On the 18th the battleships were captured and the Kronstadt rising was over.

J.N. Westwood, *Purnell's History of the 20th Century* (1968)

Famine (1921)

Although food shortages and rationing were common throughout this period, it was the poor harvest of 1921 which plunged Russia into a famine of massive proportions.

Source A
STARVING CHILDREN AT THE SAMARA CAMP, OCTOBER 1921

Source B

By the spring of 1922, a million had died of starvation...From all parts of the country, food and money poured into the stricken areas. Voluntary offerings alone provided nearly 150,000 tons of food. The general staff in the war on hunger - the Central Commission for Aid to the Famine Stricken - poured in thousands of tons of bread, potatoes and other foods to the starving people, and provided the peasants with grain fodder for their livestock

By the summer of 1922, some 30,000 field-kitchens were operating in the areas of crop-failure, feeding 12,500,000 people.

Y.A. Polyakov, *History of the Twentieth Century* (1969)

The New Economic Policy (1921-27)

In February 1921 amid a range of pressing economic problems and an alarming level of popular dissent from among the peasants and the working class, the politburo agreed upon a series of major reforms known collectively as the New Economic Policy (NEP). This represented a partial return to the capitalist system and was aimed at restoring the Russian economy and quelling the demands of the peasantry. These measures, approved at the 10th Party Congress in March 1921, are examined below.

Key features of the NEP

1. Grain requisitioning was abolished. This was replaced by a graduated tax with modest targets set for grain collection. Peasants could now sell off surplus grain for profit whereas previously these extra amounts would have been handed over to the state.

2. Private enterprises was also restored in industry. Many small factories were leased back to their former owners by the state. Again private profit was now made legal.

3. The government renewed efforts to open up trade with foreign countries.

Impact of the NEP

Agriculture   Generally agriculture picked up under the NEP. By 1926 grain output was at the same level as the average for the years 1909-13. Agriculture became more intensive and wider-ranging. Improvements were made in production of sugar-beet, potatoes and cotton. Use of horse-drawn machinery and crop-rotation also became widespread. There were few rural disturbances in the mid-1920s.

Industry   By 1926-27 output from small-scale businesses and handicrafts had returned to the pre-war level. Some experts estimate that in large-scale industry there may have been an increase in output by 1926 of up to 6 per cent compared to 1913. Engineering capacity, production of luxury goods and the level of investment were all comparable with performance under the tsarist regime. By 1924 trading links with some of the great powers had been renewed.

Assessment   It is clear that the NEP helped to revive Russia's industrial and agricultural sectors and boost economic development. Crucially the NEP

Debate the following
motion: Lenin's policies
were a betrayal of his
Communist principles.

had demonstrated that the government could be flexible. The achievements of the mid-1920s seemed to underline the substantial economic progress made before the First World War. However, there were still problems: armaments output was inadequate, there was a huge technological gap between Russia and the West in machine tools, and the use of tractors was still limited. Collective farms had not developed and urban employment was still high. In 1928, with a new leader at the helm, the NEP gave way to new, more radical economic policies.

TALKING POINT

In early 1990 it emerged that Trotsky had refused Lenin's offer of leadership on account of his Jewish origins. Why do you think he did this, and what light does it shed on Russian and international politics of the time?

LENIN IN HIS COFFIN AT GORKY, 1924

The struggle for power (1922-24)

In March 1923 Lenin suffered his third stroke in less than a year. His right side was paralysed and he was deprived of the power of speech. He had effectively been removed from the political scene but the question of who would succeed him now assumed crucial importance. The notion of an election to decide democratically on a successor to Lenin was not considered. Within the higher echelons of the Communist Party four candidates - Trotsky, Zinoviev, Kamenev and Bukharin - were regarded as worthy of consideration. The same élite group regarded a fifth candidate, Stalin, as the least able and the least likely to succeed.

Although the succession was in doubt, it was clear to each of the candidates that Lenin's political influence had been snuffed out at a crucial stage. Privately, Lenin was becoming increasingly convinced that Stalin's aggressive personality rendered him unfit for high office. His preference was for Trotsky, perhaps as the cornerstone of a new collective style of leadership. Yet Lenin's illness meant that at this stage his views were not made public.

On 21 January 1924 Lenin died. Who would prove to be the strongest of the five candidates? Begin the chapter on Russia 1924-41 by reading the biographies of each of the contenders and then move on to examine the evidence concerning the struggle that developed between two deadly rivals: Trotsky and Stalin.

10 Stalin's Russia 1924-41

PREVIEW

'We are fifty to a hundred years behind the advanced countries. We must make good this distance in ten years. Either we do it, or they crush us.'
                                                                        Stalin, 1931

Stalin's stated objective was to modernise Russia at all costs. This was achieved but with great human suffering.
Can such measures ever be justified?.

INDUSTRIAL PROGRESS. A SCENE FROM THE MIKOYAN CANNING FACTORY

10.1 The struggle for power: who would succeed Lenin?

On 21 January 1924 Lenin's struggle finally came to an end. He died at 6.50 that evening, his last act being to express concern for his personal physician whom he did not want to have to travel home after dark. Such acts of kindness from the Russian leadership were soon to be a thing of the past. Why was it that Stalin succeeded Lenin rather than Trotsky? What happened to the other candidates? Read the biographies of each of the contenders and then move on to examine the evidence concerning the struggle between the two most deadly rivals, Trotsky and Stalin.

Nikol Ivanovich Bukharin

1888 Born in Moscow. Parents were teachers. **1905** As student already taking part in illegal political meetings. Drawn to militant Bolshevism and joined party in 1906. Meteoric rise through party organisation in Moscow as organiser and propagandist. **1908** Seat on Moscow Committee. **1909** First arrest, subsequently arrested and released several times. **1912** First meeting with Lenin. Running dispute with leader over Malinovski – a Bolshevik whom Bukharin correctly claimed was a spy. After further arrests he escaped to Germany and remained an emigré until 1917. He now became a major figure in the party. Now the 'leading theorist' and a 'close comrade' of Lenin although their personal contact between 1912 and 1917 was infrequent. An unorthodox thinker, he was especially interested in non-Marxist ideas. **1917** Working on radical paper in New York, alongside Trotsky. Sailed back by April. Joined in rejection of Lenin's September 'uprising' letter. Based in Moscow he was appalled at the bloodshed in the revolution. Did not become a full member of Politburo in 1922. Prestige rested not on posts but as theoretician. Very popular in party. Lenin said he 'should…be considered the favourite of the whole party' in his testament.

Lev Borisvich 'Kamenev'

1883 Born in Moscow. Brief spell spent in higher education, soon abandoned. **1905** By now a full-time revolutionary and committed Bolshevik. Thereafter remained a fairly close associate of Lenin, although prone to open disagreement with him. **1907** Attended important Bolshevik conference in London with Stalin also present. By now Lenin regarded him as able and reliable. Therefore classified later as an 'Old Bolshevik'. Long period of study followed in which Kamenev established a reputation as an important contributor to party doctrine. **1913** Exiled and sent to Siberia. Now married to Trotsky's sister. **1917** Returned from exile after downfall of Tsar. *March* – friction between Kamenev and local leadership of Petrograd Bolsheviks who were more radical. Denied seat on Russian Bureau of Central Committee but slowly reasserted himself. With Zinoviev he rejected Lenin's proposals for an armed uprising. *October* – openly opposing uprising; Lenin outraged. Close to expulsion. Stalin defended him. Not given formal office in October, but served as Moscow Party Secretary and later Commissar for Foreign Trade.

Grigorii 'Zinoviev'

1883 Born at Elisavetgrad in the Ukraine. His name is usually linked with 'Kamenev', though it is generally felt that he overshadowed the latter. **1903** Already an active Bolshevik. Soon established a reputation as outstanding orator and a lively contributor to party doctrine. He worked closely with Lenin and was on good personal terms with him. A critical moment came in 1917 when, along with Kamenev, he took a different line to Lenin on the Provisional Government and then came out in total opposition to Lenin's plans for an armed uprising. Lenin reacted angrily but Stalin came to their defence. Kept a low profile when it came to physical action. Overlooked for a post in October 1917 he did serve as Leningrad Party Secretary. By **1923** he was seen as the leader of the Triumvirate (with 'Kamenev' and Stalin) which took up collective leadership when Lenin fell ill. Historian E.H. Carr describes him as 'hesitant and not a talented organiser' (*The Bolshevik Revolution*).

Josef Visarionovitch Djugashvili ('Koba' then 'Stalin')

1879 Born in utter poverty at Gori in Georgia **1894-99** Attends seminary school – expelled. **1902** First of many periods of arrest/exile. **1905** Absorbing Marx/Engels. Staunchly Leninist line, but *not* an associate. Meets Lenin for first time in Finland. **1906** Dispute with Lenin over agrarian issues. Maintains militant line in Georgia and opposes Mensheviks. **1908-1911** Various arrests and escapes. **1912** Career takes off after Prague conference. Assumes some seniority in party after Lenin appoints him to Party Central Committee and underground Russian Bureau. Becomes chief political adviser to *Pravda* newspaper. Uses name K. Stalin first time. **1912-17** Exiled to frozen wastes. Moved. Abortive rescue attempt. **1917** Petrograd. Opposes Lenin. Takes moderate line, later more radical. *April* – Castigated by Lenin but by August, with Lenin in exile, virtually at helm. *October* – not active operationally but kept informed. Key posts in government include: People's Commissar for Nationalities (1917), Workers and Peasants Inspectorate (1919), General Secretary of Party (1922).

Lev Davidovich Bronstein 'Trotsky'

1879 Born on a farm at Yanovka; fairly comfortable upbringing. Had been associated in early political career with Lenin but moved towards Mensheviks in 1905. Established his reputation taking the Menshevik line on the St Petersburg soviet which was prominent in the aftermath of the 1905 Revolution. As with others, he spent four-and-a-half years of his early life in prison or exile. Political activities enabled him to establish a reputation as an outstanding writer and intellectual. In the summer of 1917 he was still outside the Bolshevik movement and had a past record of outstpoken criticism of Lenin's ideas. However, his increasingly radical line enabled him to fit in smoothly when he joined the Bolsheviks in late July/early August. *October* – acknowledged as key strategist in uprising of October 1917, leading Military Revolutionary Committee. Appointed Commissar for War, he created the Red Army, inspired the Reds to victory in the Civil War and was chief negotiator at Brest-Litovsk. Lenin said 'the ablest man in the Central committee but…too far-reaching self confidence'.

QUESTIONS

1 Consider each of the five candidates using the following criteria:
(a) Extent of political experience
(b) Relationship with Lenin
(c) Position within the Bolshevik movement
(d) Strengths and qualities
(e) Weaknesses
(f) Role in the revolution.

2 Consider the links and relationships between each of the five candidates.

3 Place the candidates in rank order on the basis of:
(a) Their suitability as a new leader
(b) Their prospects of victory in a struggle for power.

EXAMINING THE EVIDENCE

Why did Stalin rather than Trotsky succeed Lenin?

Source A: The character of Stalin

He's not an intellectual like the other people you will meet. He's not even particularly well informed, but he knows what he wants. He's got willpower, and he's going to be on top of the pile some day.

John Reed, quoted in Alex de Jonge, *Stalin and the Shaping of the Soviet Union* (1986)

(John Reed was an American journalist noted for his coverage of the Russian Revolution.)

Source B

A strongly built man with a sallow face, black moustache, heavy eyebrows and black hair...I paid little attention to him. He himself said nothing. He did not seem of sufficient importance to include, in my gallery of Bolshevik portraits.

Robert Bruce Lockhart, quoted in Alex de Jonge, *Stalin and the Shaping of the Soviet Union* (1986)

(Lockhart was a Scottish writer who met many of the Bolshevik leaders.)

Source C

'Comrade Stalin, having become general secretary has immeasurable power concentrated in his hands, and I am not sure that he always knows how to use that power with sufficient control' (29 December, 1922)

This was later followed by an even more damaging postscript...

'Stalin is too rude, and this fault, entirely acceptable in relations between communists, becomes completely unacceptable in the office of General Secretary. Therefore I propose to the comrades that a way be found to remove Stalin from that post and replace him with someone else who differs from Stalin in all respects, someone more patient, more loyal, more polite, more considerate.' (4 January 1923)   Lenin's political testament

LENIN'S FUNERAL TRAIN ARRIVES IN MOSCOW

STALIN ALONGSIDE LENIN

Source D

I saw straight through Stalin swearing public oaths of loyalty to his genius mentor and actually sincerely hating Lenin because Lenin had become the major obstacle on his road to power. Stalin did not bother to pretend in front of his secretaries, and I could clearly tell from individual remarks, phrases, tone of voice, what he really thought of Lenin.

Bazhanov, quoted in Alex de Jonge, *Stalin and the Shaping of the Soviet Union* (1986)

(Bazhanov was a private secretary to Stalin.)

Source E: Why was Trotsky unable to take advantage of Lenin's criticisms?

On 18 January, Trotsky set off on a slow journey to the south. Three days later his train halted at Tiflis. There, while the train was being shunted, he received a coded message from Stalin informing him of Lenin's death...

(The telegram from Stalin informed him that)...the funeral would be held on the 26th; since he would be unable to return in time, he should continue travelling south. The telegram lied: the funeral was to be held a day later, on the 27th, giving Trotsky ample time to attend it as one of the pallbearers. But only the triumvirate featured in the ceremony; Trotsky, it was widely felt, had not bothered to turn up. It was a political error of the first magnitude and dealt a fatal blow to Trotsky's prestige.

I. Deutscher; *The Prophet Unarmed; Trotsky 1921-1929* (1959)

LENIN ADDRESSING A MEETING IN MOSCOW. ON THE RIGHT IS TROTSKY. LATER, STALIN HAD TROTSKY REMOVED FROM THE PHOTOGRAPH

Source F

Hindsight makes Trotsky's behaviour appear incredibly foolish...years later he remarked wistfully that if he had spoken up at the twelfth congress, with Lenin's authority behind him, he would have defeated Stalin there and then...The truth is that Trotsky refrained from attacking Stalin because he felt secure. No contemporary, and he least of all, saw in the Stalin of 1923 the menacing and towering figure he was to become. It seemed to Trotsky almost a bad joke that Stalin, the wilful and sly but shabby and inarticulate man in the background, should be his rival.

I. Deutscher, *The Prophet Unarmed; Trotsky 1921-1929* (1959)

TROTSKY, THE PEOPLE'S COMMISSAR FOR MILITARY AND NAVAL AFFAIRS, SUPERVISING A MILITARY PARADE IN MOSCOW

Source G

Stalin, sitting on the steps of the rostrum looked small and miserable. I studied him closely; in spite of his self-control and show of calm it was clearly evident that his fate was at stake.

Finally, with Trotsky silent, it fell to Zinoviev to announce that no action would be taken.

But we are happy to say that on one point Lenin's fears have proved baseless. I have in mind the point about our General Secretary. You have witnessed our harmonious cooperation in the last few months; and like myself, you will be happy to say that Lenin's fears have proved baseless.

The reading of Lenin's political testament at the Central Committee, described in
I. Deutscher, *Stalin* (1949)

Source H

In the autumn of 1923 Trotsky finally began to put together a series of challenging and effective criticisms of the Triumvirate. On 15 October, forty-six prominent party members issued a major statement formally criticising on ideological grounds the new party leadership. As matters came to a head Trotsky fell ill at the vital moment. At the end of October he picked up a malarial infection on a hunting expedition in the marshy country outside Moscow. Later, Trotsky himself ruefully noted that his illness could hardly have come at a worse time. 'One can foresee a revolution or a war but it is impossible to foresee the consequences of an autumn shooting trip for wild ducks.'

Trotsky's wife later recalled the strain he was under at this time. 'Those were hard days of tense fighting for Lev...at the Politburo against the rest of its members. He was alone and ill and had to fight them all. Because of his illness the Politburo held its meetings in our apartment...after each of these meetings L.D.'s temperature rose. He came out of his study soaked through, and undressed and went to bed. His linen and clothes had to be dried as if drenched in a rain storm.'

I. Deutscher, *The Prophet Unarmed, Trotsky 1921-1929* (1959)

The years 1924-28 marked a painful fall from grace for Trotsky, who was systematically stripped of all his ties with the party. On 16 January 1925 he was dismissed from the post of war commissar. At the 14th Party Conference in April 1925 Stalin's policy of 'Socialism in One Country' was formally adopted. This represented a complete rejection of Trotsky's ideas of 'permanent revolution' which envisaged Bolshevik involvement in working-class struggle throughout Europe, not just in Russia. In October 1926 Trotsky was expelled from the Politburo and in November 1927 he lost his place in the party. Finally, Trotsky was formally banished to the provinces in January 1928 and to Turkey a year later. His attempts to lead the Revolution in a different direction to that intended by Stalin were at an end.

The struggle for power (1924)

Read this list carefully, and attempt the exercises with reference to all the evidence up to 1924.

Careless/ Arrogant/ Determined/ Sincere/ Cunning/ Intelligent/ Gullible/ Isolated/ Out of touch/ Reticent/ Ill/ Impatient/ Ruthless/ Loyal/ Co-operative/ Self-controlled/ Naïve/ Temperamental/ Experienced Bolshevik/ Strong ideological background/ Rude/ Strong leader/ Friendly with Lenin/ Well informed/ Powerful orator/ Excellent writer/ Healthy/ Inconsiderate/ Popular with the party/ Popular with the people/ Inarticulate.

1 Under the headings *Stalin* and *Trotsky*, assign as many points as you can to each individual. Leave out any points which you feel do not apply.

2 Working in pairs, discuss which you feel to be the most important strengths and weaknesses of each individual.

3 Now consider these questions in relation first to Stalin and then to Trotsky.
(a) How well suited was this individual to succeed Lenin as leader of the Party?
(b) How well suited was he to come out on top in a political power struggle?

4 To what extent would you now conclude that the outcome of the power struggle was determined by the personality of the two main candidates?

Stalin's industrial policy (1928-38)

1928 can be seen in retrospect as a watershed year in Russia's history. It had taken Stalin four years to destroy the prospect of collective leadership which Lenin had envisaged. Stalin immediately embarked upon a range of policies which were to transform the country, modernise its industry and agriculture, and traumatise the Russian population.

At the 15th Congress in 1928, Stalin announced dramatic changes in Russia's industrial and agricultural policies. His intention was to transform the Soviet Union into a superpower by equipping the country with a formidable industrial base. Lenin's economic planning institution, Gosplan, was retained and the Five Year Plans which it drew up were at the centre of the super-industrialisation policy which was launched in 1928.

How successful was the policy and what were its drawbacks? Study the section which now follows to determine whether the achievements of Stalin's industrial policy outweighed the cost.

BUILDING THE FINAL STAGE OF VOLKHOV HYDROPOWER STATION IN 1926

EXAMINING THE EVIDENCE

Before you begin reading through the evidence, look at the task which you will need to complete at the end of the section.

In reading through the sources, you should be aware that they are a combination of primary evidence, secondary evidence, material compiled by the author, and the views of historians. Your objective is to take the raw material and use it to prepare a piece of propaganda in favour of Stalin's industrial policies.

Source A: Industrial performance under the tsarist regime in 1914

Industrial growth rate 1880-1914 (average per annum)
Russia 3.5%   USA 2.75%
Germany 3.75%   UK 1%

Industrial production in millions of tons 1914

	Russia	France	Germany	USA	Great Britain	Russian ranking
Coal	36	40	190	517	292.0	5th
Pig Iron	4.6	5.2	16.8	31	10.4	5th
Steel	4.8	4.6	18.3	31.8	7.9	4th

Russia also ranked 2nd in world oil production, 4th in goldmining

Source B: General objectives of the industrialisation drive

1. To enable Russia to catch up with Western industrial output.
2. To give Russia a strong economic base which would enable the country to equip and defend itself against foreign invasion.
3. To exploit Russia's latent mineral resources more fully than ever before.
4. To develop towns and industry in some of Russia's more remote areas.
5. To develop to a maximum extent the regime's degree of personal control over each and every worker.
6. To link industrial growth with the rapid development of collective farming by making full use of machinery such as tractors.

Source C: The First Five Year Plan (1928-32)

This called for the maximum possible development of heavy industry based on the complete dedication of all workers, One of the most controversial aspects of the plan was the decision to move away from the ideal of equal pay for all. Included were plans for the development of industry, agriculture, transport, electrification, housing and education.

Achievements
- Machinery output up 4.5%
- Electricity output up 2.5%
- 1,500 new industrial plants
- More than 100 new towns, eg Magnitogorsk
Population 1929 = 1,157   Population 1933 = 100,000
At least 50,000 of these consisted of forced labour

Production	1928	1933
Pig iron (approximate millions of tons)	3.3	6.2
Steel (approximate millions of tons)	4.0	5.9
Coal (approximate millions of tons)	31	73

Major industrial development in Urals, Kuzbass, Volga River. Expansion of rail and canal links. Europe's largest Hydroelectric Dam constructed at River Dneiper.

Source D: The Second Five Year Plan (1933-37)

This was redrafted in January 1934 and generally set more realistic targets than the First Five Year Plan. Again the emphasis was entirely on heavy industry at the expense of consumer goods and living standards. Steel output trebled. Engineering industry grew rapidly as did electricity generation. Oil production was the main disappointment, falling below expectation. Real wages increased but were still lower in 1937 than in 1928. Free market food prices were high and bread shortages were common.

Source E: The Third Five Year Plan (1938-41)

Cut short by the German invasion but always set against a background of international tension, this plan again placed emphasis on heavy industry. Living standards deteriorated as by 1940 defence expenditure took up 32.6 per cent of the total budget. R. Hutchings maintains: 'One can hardly doubt that if there had been a slower build up of industry, the (German) attack would have been successful and world history would have evolved quite differently.'

Source F: Progress achieved by 1939

Between 1929 and 1939, Russia's gross national product grew by just under 12 per cent a year. By 1939 4/5 of Russian industrial production come from plant which had only come on-stream during the previous ten years, although

CHEAP WIRELESS SETS DEMONSTRATED WITH THE BROADCASTING OF PROPAGANDA TO WORKMEN AT THE CENTROSHAMOT FACTORY

AT THE MAGNITOGORSK IRON AND STEEL WORKS IN 1937, TECHNICAL COLLEGE STUDENTS RECEIVE INSTRUCTIONS CONCERNING BLAST FURNACES

much of this was a consequence of pre-1928 investment. Between 1928 and 1941 steel output increased fourfold.

Production	1927	1939
Coal (millions of tons)	35	145
Oil (millions of tons)	12	40
Iron (millions of tons)	6	32

The Soviet Union was now the second largest manufacturer of heavy vehicles in the world. Industrial progress also brought improvements in social conditions. For example, by 1939 Magnitogorsk had 50 schools, 2 colleges, 17 libraries and 18 clinics.

Source G: Stakhanov movement

Alexei Stakhanov, a 29-year-old former shepherd, had by himself shifted 102 tonnes of coal - nearly 15 times the norm - in a single six-hour shift on the night of 30-31 August 1935, in a mine in the Donbas...Newspapers duly proclaimed the feat as proof that 'there are no fortresses Bolshevism cannot storm'.

Rupert Cornwell, *The Independent* newspaper, October 1988

Source H: Stakhanov movement in perspective

Alexei Stakhanov did not perform his feat alone, in fact he had two helpers ...(who) shored up the tunnel and removed the coal while Stakhanov worked at the face with hammer and pick. The event was, moreover, deliberately organised by the local party to meet Stalin's request for 'heroes', and provide a fitting achievement to mark international youth day...

Rupert Cornwell, *The Independent* newspaper, October 1988

Source I

Moscow is encircled by a broad ring of new factories, and housing estates. Eight miles from the heart of the city stands the Freezer Cutting Tool Plant finished in 1931. In sight of it are six new factories...From the outside it looks like a modern European or American factory, but on its walls, in large letters, slogans have been painted, 'Long Live the World Revolution.'

Louis Fischer, *Soviet Journey* (1935)

Source J: Working conditions

Jan 1931 – Work record books monitoring individual output were introduced.

Aug 1932 – Death sentence introduced for the theft of state or collective farm property.

Nov 1932 – Missing a day's work could mean instant dismissal. By 1940 the free labour market no longer existed. No worker could change jobs without permission. Absenteeism became a crime and social benefits were cut.

The verdict of historians

Source A

The industrialisation drive was an heroic exploit of all Soviet people, an expression of their enthusiasm born of the revolution and victory in the Civil War and of an understanding of the perspectives of the country's development...These perspectives were defined by five-year plans...evoking hope and joy...The whole world intently followed the progress of industrial construction in the USSR, a gigantic drive to do away with backwardness.

From *The Illustrated History of the USSR* (1982)

Source B

At tremendous human cost Soviet society was propelled within a few years, 1928-34, into the industrial age. To some, this is the greatest crime of modern history. To others it is a grandiose feat of social engineering, ruthless in conception, cruel in its effects on millions of human beings, but still it laid the foundations of a richer and more rational economy, enabling Russia to withstand a foreign invasion and become a superpower.

A. Ulam, *Stalin* (1973)

Source C

Stalin had made three vital contributions to industrialisation. First, he accelerated the whole process, breaking away from the more cautious mentality of Bukharin and perhaps even of Lenin. Second, he extended the range of industrial centres by equipping the Urals and Siberia with plants and factories. Third, he found the resources to transform Russia's economic base without having to seek investment. In using agriculture to subsidize industry and in squeezing every drop of money from the ordinary consumer, Stalin devised a ruthless but effective method of accumulating capital.

S.J. Lee, *The European Dictatorships 1918-1945* (1987)

Source D

There is evidence that he exaggerated Russia's industrial deficiency in 1929. The Tsars had developed a considerable industrial capacity, based on five main centres: Moscow (textiles), Petrograd (heavy industry), the Donetz region (coal fields), Baku (oil) and the Ukraine (iron and steel). In a sense the spadework had already been done and it is not altogether surprising that Stalin should have achieved such rapid results. He was also reluctant to acknowledge that most of his plans for widespread electrification were inherited from Lenin. Worst of all was the severe deprivation which accompanied industrial growth.

S.J. Lee, *The European Dictatorships 1918-1945* (1987)

The role of propaganda in Stalin's industrialisation programme

Historians are generally agreed that Stalin's industrialisation programme brought about considerable economic progress at the expense of the Russian people's comfort. Rather than simply going over the issue again, the following exercise will ask you to consider the importance of propaganda and of a particular viewpoint in evaluating the notion of success.

The premise for this exercise is that it is 1938 and the Russian government has opened a major exhibition in Moscow celebrating '10 years of Industrial Growth'. Western journalists have been invited and there will be limited opportunities for them to ask questions. With reference to the source material and careful consideration of the propaganda employed, try to complete the tasks as convincingly as possible.

THE POSTER DEFINES SIX CONDITIONS FOR VICTORY AND SAYS 'THE REALITY OF OUR PROGRAMME IS LIVING PEOPLE'

1 You have been asked to help prepare a speech which will be given by Stalin to declare the exhibition open. Write a draft of this speech, outlining the reasons why drastic changes were necessary and highlighting what you consider to be the key achievements of the industrialisation programme.

2 Devise short propaganda slogans which could have been used to accompany posters and photographs celebrating:

(a) The First Five Year Plan
(b) The Second Five Year Plan
(c) The creation of Magnitogorsk
(d) The achievements of Stakhanov
(e) Stalin's role in the programme
(f) The overall progress made.

3 A Western journalist has been given the opportunity to interview the director of the exhibition. Write down five questions that the journalist might have wished to ask, then try to formulate the kind of replies that the director would have given.

Stalin's agricultural policy

If Russia's industry was backward its agriculture was positively primitive. Eighty per cent of Russia's population were peasants, engaged in the bleak task of survival in often formidably hostile conditions. They were equipped with ploughs and tools the design of which had not changed in hundreds of years. Stalin realised that his industrialisation initiative would be jeopardised by the inadequacy of grain supplies needed to feed the urban workforce. The peasants tended to hold on to their grain rather than sell it, to the extent that only 17 per cent of the 1926 harvest was marketed. The agricultural problems were compounded by the fact that most farming plots were far too small to accommodate any large farming equipment such as tractors.

PEASANTS IN THE MAGNITOGORSK AREA

Stalin's proposals, announced at the 15th Party Congress in 1928, went as follows: 'The solution lies in the transformation of the small scattered peasants' plots into large consolidated farms based on the joint cultivation of land using superior techniques.' Stalin elaborated on this policy in 1929: 'We are beginning seriously to re-equip agriculture. For this we must expand the development of collective state farms, employ on a mass scale the contract system and machine and tractor stations as a means of establishing a bond between industry and agriculture along the lines of production. We must reinforce the support of the middle and poor peasant masses, as one of the means of breaking the resistance of the Kulaks.'

The Kulaks owned land, hired workers, and exerted considerable influence over each village. Under Stalin they were depicted as an 'exploiting class' and in 1929 the Politburo announced 'the policy of liquidation of the Kulaks as a class.'

The North Caucasus and the Volga region, two key grain-growing areas, witnessed the first wave of collectivisation which was almost complete by the spring of 1931. To 'assist' the process, 25,000 workers - the notorious 'twenty-five thousanders' - poured into the countryside. The war against the Kulaks which was to result in the mass deportation of 10 million people had just begun. Virtually all Kulaks were expelled from their holdings and their livestock and implements handed over to the collective farms (the *Kolkhoz*). Stalin showed no signs of remorse: 'It is ridiculous and foolish to talk at length about dekulakisation...When the head is cut off, one does not grieve for the hair. There is another question no less ridiculous: whether Kulaks should be allowed to join the collective farms? Of course not, for they are the sworn enemies of the collective farm movement!' (quoted in M. McCauley, *Stalin and Stalinism* [1983]).

The following account was only made public in 1988, 60 years after the liquidation of the Kulaks began. 'Even now I have that day before my eyes. Winter, the bitter cold, and us six children - myself aged seven. We walked 15 kilometres to the railway station at Kurgun. There we had to spend several

KULAKS FACE DEPORTATION FROM THEIR VILLAGE (MARCH 1930)

days in the open. Finally, a train of cattle trucks came, and they loaded us up...We weren't hoarding any surpluses, but in winter 1929 they came to dispossess us. They took away everything. Our furniture, all our belongings. They took the boots off my grandmother's feet. They even took the shawl and blankets from the cradle in which my little sister Frosya was lying,'

Quoted by R. Cornwell in *The Independent* newspaper (23 February 1988)

Despite such brutality, the Kulaks offered massive resistance to Stalin. They now resorted to killing their livestock rather than having it confiscated and handed over to the communes. The scale of this protest was staggering. Out of 34 million horses, 16 million were slaughtered; 30 out of 60 million cattle and 100 million sheep and goats suffered the same fate.

The regime's response was brutal. Stalin sent out groups who seized grain on a massive scale in the Ukraine area and then left the peasants to starve. The scenes which followed were horrendous. The starving peasants had to resort to eating cats, dogs, mice and even tree bark. Altogether the famine probably cost six million lives in the Ukraine, Kazakhstan, the North Caucasus and the Volga region.

The severe human cost of the collectivisation programme represents one of the worst aspects of Stalin's regime. How successful were the collective farms which had been at the centre of all this upheaval? The figures for the grain harvest are shown below:

1913	1928	1940	1945
76	69	75	47 (million tonnes)

The move to collective farms began smoothly but the brutal methods used by Stalin's officials led to severe problems. Despite this, by 1932 60 per cent of all farmland had been collectivised. By 1940 almost 97 per cent had been brought into line. Within individual Kolkhoz there can be no doubt that farming techniques were improved. After 1932 there was much more substantial use of tractors, mechanised equipment and modern fertilizers.

In 1931 Stalin made clear, in a speech which has since become famous, that he would not diminish the pace of change in Russia's industry and agriculture. While it may provide a rationale for Russia's drastic modernisation programme it cannot diminish the scale of the human sacrifice which Stalin demanded from his own people:

'To slacken the tempo would mean falling behind. And those who fall behind get beaten. But we do not want to be beaten. No, we refuse to be beaten! One feature of the history of old Russia was the continual beatings she suffered for falling behind, for her backwardness...

We are fifty to a hundred years behind the advanced countries. We must make good this distance in ten years. Either we do it, or they crush us.'

Debate: Were Stalin's agricultural reforms a success?

Divide the class into small groups:
(a) Supporting the reforms;
(b) Opposing the reforms;
(c) Acting as an independent jury.

Preparation
Groups A and B should discuss how they intend to present their cases and equip themselves with sufficient information to be able to ask and answer searching questions.

Group C members are to look for weaknesses on both sides and prepare their questions.

Presentation
Allow each group 10 minutes to present its arguments in whichever way it chooses and without any interruption.

Question time
Group A to be questioned for 10 minutes by B and then by C. Repeat the process for Group B.

Summary
One person from groups A and B to give a one-minute summary of their argument.

Verdict
The jury then decides which side it supports and gives detailed reasons for the decision.

Domestic repression (1928-40)

'As usual at five o'clock that morning reveille was sounded by the blows of a hammer on a length of rail hanging up near the staff quarters. The intermittent sound barely penetrated the window-panes on which the frost lay two fingers thick, and they ended almost as soon as they'd begun. It was

POLITICAL PRISONERS CARRYING OUT HARD LABOUR IN A CAMP IN THE DNIEPER REGION

cold outside and the camp-guard was reluctant to go on beating out the reveille for long. The clanging ceased, but everything outside still looked like the middle of the night when Ivan Denisovich Shukhov got up to go to the bucket. It was pitch dark except for the yellow light cast on the window by three lamps - two in the outer zone, one inside the camp itself.'

Alexander Solzhenitsyn, *One Day in the Life of Ivan Denisovich* (1963)

While a great deal is now known about the conditions endured by many victims of the Great Terror, there is a lot less information available to historians concerning the decision-making process which led to so many arrests and executions. The most basic questions remain unanswered. Both Soviet and Western historians remain divided and uncertain about exactly how many people were imprisoned or killed as a direct result of Stalin's policies. Recent Russian analysts have estimated that approximately 12 million people died while some Western authorities claim that at least 20 million people were killed; millions more were deported or arrested but survived. Some experts maintain that while the archives of key bodies such as the Military Tribunal of the Soviet Supreme Court, local military courts and - above all - the KGB remain closed, we may never know how many people were affected.

The sheer scale of these events has led many Western historians to assume that the victims of the purges had suffered at the hands of a supremely efficient and well-organised secret police system. Supporters of this viewpoint have depicted a ruthless and monolithic organisation with Stalin personally at the helm, issuing orders and directives which were instantly and efficiently carried out. They see the purges, trials, mass deportations and executions as all part of a systematically escalating programme of terror and violence, beginning with the purging of industrial experts in 1928 and being turned off like a tap after the cold-blooded execution of Bukharin in 1938. The orthodox Stalin-centred model has now been brought into question by a revisionist approach which does not seek to diminish Stalin's personal responsibility but does question the degree of personal control he exerted.

A strong proponent of this revisionist viewpoint is the American historian J. Arch Getty who, in his book, *Origins of the Great Purges: The Soviet Communist Party Reconsidered, 1933-38*, presents a rather different picture. He sees the purges as an ad hoc process, careering along in an anarchic and spontaneous fashion. Arch Getty contends that Stalin did not receive constant acquiescent support for his policies in the 1930s. The secret police, far from being a united and monolithic organisation was in fact riddled with factions and court intrigue. Therefore Stalin had to maintain his personal rule by constantly shifting his support from one group to the next and playing off one faction against another. The brief job tenure of many leading figures both in the Communist Party and in the secret police, who themselves fell victim to accusation and imprisonment, reinforced an anarchic rather than a clearly thought-out progression from one victim to the next. Accusation and counter-accusation, trials and confessions led to a system marked by spontaneous changes in direction which were very difficult for any individual to control. Arch Getty maintains that the secret police were, at times, very inefficient. Important files on key suspects were often misplaced, lost or not kept up to date. Stalin himself had little clear idea of who would be next and how events would progress.

The Great Terror (1928-40)

1928 **The 'Wrecking Scare'**	In April 1928 Stalin claimed that 'class enemies' were 'trying to act against Soviet power'. It was announced that a massive conspiracy had been uncovered among expert engineers in the industrial Shakhty areas of the Donbass. Stalin claimed that these experts had deliberately wrecked machinery in an attempt to sabotage the regime's attempt to improve industrial output.
1931 **The 'Industrial Party' Trial**	At this trial it was alleged that a well organised group with members in top industrial and planning posts - and in the pay of foreign enemies of the Soviet Union - were sabotaging the First Five Year Plan.
1931 **The Menshevik Trial**	Leading figures in the earlier drawing-up of the First Five Year Plan and the prosecution of the wreckers now found themselves on trial because of their Menshevik background.
1933 **Secret trials**	These took place in March 1933 and led to the execution of around 70 officials from the State Farm and People's Commissariat of Agriculture. These trials helped to set up the structure employed in the great show trials which were to follow.
1934 **Murder of Kirov**	The murder of Stalin's second-in-command - the party secretary in Leningrad - is seen by some historians as setting in motion a train of events which led directly to the arrest and execution of hundreds of thousands of people.
1936 **Show Trial of Zinoviev and Kamenev**	At this, the first of the infamous show trials, Zinoviev and Kamenev confessed to a catalogue of crimes against the Stalinist regime. Kamenev said: 'I together with Zinoviev and Trotsky, organised and guided this terrorist conspiracy....we were actuated by boundless hatred and by lust for power.' State Prosecutor Vyshinsky concluded, 'I demand that the mad dogs be shot! Every one of them!'
1937 **Show Trial of Piatakov, Radek and Sokolnikov**	These leading party functionaries confessed to conspiring together to form an 'Anti-Soviet Trotskyist Centre.' Like the other victims of the show trials they had been subjected to sustained torture in the Lubianka prison.
1937 **The Military Trial**	Marshal Tukhachevsky, Soviet war hero and deputy Commissar for Defence was tried alongside many other top military leaders. After their execution for 'treason', all 11 deputy Commissars of Defence and 75 of the 80 members of the Supreme Military Council were executed. All eight admirals were shot; altogether, 35,000 - half of the officer corps - were either killed or imprisoned on charges which were later proved baseless.
1938 **Show Trial of Bukharin, Yagoda and Rykov**	The last and most famous show trial. As well as the execution of the party's leading theorist and intellectual, Nikolai Bukharin, the trial also signified the downfall of the notorious Yagoda. The former head of the NKVD was now given a taste of his own medicine.
1940 **Murder of Trotsky**	Trotsky, the great enemy of Stalin, had escaped trial and in 1940 was living in exile in Mexico where he was working on a history of Stalin's regime. On 21 August Stalin's agents burst into his study and struck Trotsky over the head with an ice pick, shattering his skull.

EXAMINING THE EVIDENCE

The assassination of Kirov: was it planned by Stalin?

The evidence you are about to consider is divided into two sections. The first section contains evidence of a factual nature over which historians are in broad agreement. The second section deals with the views of two leading historians who have written recently on this issue and yet arrived at very different conclusions.

Section 1: the background

Source A: The victim - S.M. Kirov

Kirov was shot dead on 1 December 1934 at 4.30 pm. The murder took place outside his office in the Smolny Institute.

Kirov was the Communist Party Secretary in Leningrad and a senior member of the Politburo. Five years younger than Stalin, he was regarded by many as his most likely successor. He had been associated with Stalin since 1920 and there is no written evidence of personal animosity between the two.

KIROV : DID STALIN ORDER HIS ASSASSINATION?

Source B: The assassin - Nikolaev

Nikolaev was on his own when arrested and it has always been accepted that he alone carried out the murder. Nikolaev had been a member of the Communist Party before he was dismissed on grounds of incompetence. His ex-wife was employed by Kirov as a secretary and Nikolaev may have suspected that they were having an affair. Nikolaev had been arrested and released by the secret police twice before: they had confiscated a revolver and a map showing Kirov's route to work. His diary was taken from him after the murder but it contained no details or allegations of any plot. He then claimed that the N.K.V.D. had forced him to kill Kirov. He was tried in secret on 28-29 December with 13 alleged 'accomplices' and then shot.

Source C: Stalin - the real culprit?

While there is no direct evidence of a quarrel between them we do know that Kirov declined Stalin's offer of a move from Leningrad to Moscow. When Stalin heard the news of the murder he immediately took the night train from Moscow to Leningrad accompanied by other leading figures.

Upon arrival in Leningrad, Stalin personally interrogated Nikolaev who maintained that the N.K.V.D. had forced him to kill Kirov and stuck by his story even after he had been beaten.

Stalin was a prominent figure at Kirov's funeral.

Source D: Kirov's bodyguard - Borisov

Kirov's personal bodyguard was regarded as loyal and reliable. Although he had arrested Nikolaev twice he had been forced to release him by Zaporozhets. On 1 December he had been taken off bodyguard duty to attend to 'N.K.V.D. business'. On his way to be questioned after Kirov's murder, Borisov died in a mysterious car crash.

TALKING POINT

Should we assume Stalin's innocence of this crime, until he is proved guilty? Or can we go by his previous and subsequent acts of terror?

Source E: The secret police - Medved
Medved was head of the Leningrad N.K.V.D. and a close friend of Kirov. Stalin had tried to remove him from his post but Kirov objected so strongly that he was kept on. After the murder, Medved was removed from the enquiry and sent to the Far East as a punishment for 'negligence'.

Source F: The police - Zaporozhets
Zaporozhets was a policeman installed as Medved's second-in-command shortly before Kirov's death. It is alleged that Zaporozhets had secret dealings with Nikolaev in 1934. It was he who ordered Nikolaev's release after he was twice picked up by Borisov. He too was dismissed for 'negligence' after the murder, and was sent to the Far East where he remained in security.

Section 2: Opposing interpretations of the Kirov affair

Source A: Stalin was to blame

Summary of the argument
Stalin could have been behind it all. The probabilities favour the most obvious explanation. Kirov had emerged as a possible rival to Stalin, the only beneficiary of his death. Besides, an assassination that unleashed terror after a breathing space was a favourite technique of Stalin. It seems unlikely that the local N.K.V.D. acted on its own initiative, for it could not expect Stalin to thank it...

Evidence
(a) Those close to Kirov who might have told the truth were killed or exiled - suggesting a conspiracy.
(b) Stalin immediately acted against a range of enemies as though he were using Kirov's death as an excuse.
(c) Stalin must have planned the murder of Kirov. If he had really believed that the murder of Kirov was the first part of a plot against him he would surely have remained safe in the Kremlin, rather than travelling to Leningrad where he might also have been killed in a larger conspiracy.

Alex de Jonge, *Stalin and the Shaping of the Soviet Union* (1986)

Extract B: Stalin was not responsible

Summary of the argument
It is widely asserted that Stalin conspired in the assassination of Serge Kirov in December 1934. Yet the evidence for Stalin's complicity is complicated and at least secondhand...Neither the sources, circumstances, nor consequences of the crime suggest Stalin's complicity. The lack of any evidence of political dispute between Stalin and Kirov...would appear to refute any motive for Stalin to kill his ally...all one can say with any certainty is that Leonid Nikolaev, a rank-and-file dissident, pulled the trigger.

Evidence
(a) No one at the time, even the exiled Trotsky, accused Stalin of being the murderer.
(b) Stalin regarded the assassination of Kirov as the first part of a plot against

him and reacted in panic against 'enemies' of the regime.

(c) The head ot the N.K.V.D. - Yagoda - later confessed in open court to planning the death of Kirov but before the microphones of the world press he made no attempt to implicate Stalin.

J.Arch Getty, *Origins of the Great Purges* (1985)

Who killed Kirov?

Theory 1:

Nikolaev was solely responsible for the murder. He was motivated by personal jealousy and resentment. His claim that the N.K.V.D. forced him to murder Kirov was simply an excuse.

Theory 2:

A faction within the N.K.V.D., perhaps opposed to Medved, planned the murder independently of Stalin. They used Kirov to carry out the murder and face the consequences. Zaporozhets deliberately exposed Kirov to the assassin. Stalin had no quarrel with Kirov.

Theory 3:

Stalin was at the centre of events, ordering the murder and using it as as excuse to instigate a wave of terror against a range of opponents. Stalin's personality and conduct throughout the 1930s show him to be more than capable of the murder even though no written evidence of a quarrel exists.

---

1 Divide into three groups. Each group must argue a case, answer questions on its theory, and then move to a conclusion.

2 Carefully assess the implications of these theories for the role of Stalin in the terror as a whole. Was Stalin exerting firm day-to-day control over events or was he merely reacting to events which were sometimes outside his personal control?

EXAMINING THE EVIDENCE

Stalin: an assessment

Source A

It is my belief that Stalin was a very skilled, indeed gifted politician, and one of the great political figures of the twentieth century. This does not mean that he was a good man. He had a dark, even evil side to his nature.

Martin McCauley, *Stalin and Stalinism* (1983)

Source B

Stalin, the shoemaker's son, was spectacularly successful in his reaching out after power, in the way he outflanked and destroyed his apparently brilliant rivals...

He showed an instinctive grasp of the principles of machine politics and was always working to create an organisation within an organisation.

It was not a question of one evil man dominating a country of the oppressed. He employed nationwide support at every level because he and his style of government were popular; he was truly a dictator of the people. The party followed him because it saw him as a winner.

Alex de Jonge, *Stalin and the Shaping of the Soviet Union* (1986)

TALKING POINT

The evidence available to historians concerning Kirov's murder is clearly patchy and, at times, unreliable. Should we attempt to reach a conclusion based on incomplete evidence, or would it be more advisable not to try?

Source C

Wielding limitless power, Stalin changed the face of the Soviet Union as no man in history ever changed the face of such a vast country.

Gradually he became a virtual deity. No Russian town was without its Stalin Square or Avenue, its Stalin statue. Poets and musicians paid their tributes; the top literary award was the Stalin Prize. The worship was undoubtedly orchestrated, but in many hearts it was sincere.

R. Cornwell, The *Independent* newspaper (7 November 1987)

Source D

In the purges of the 1930s, Stalin was systematically slaughtering anyone who incurred his displeasure or his suspicion. The dark record, which still awaits full disclosure in the Soviet Union, has been carefully analysed by western scholars. On a sober estimate, about 700,000 people were executed and 12 million died in the camps, where the average survival was two years.

R. Cornwell, The *Independent* newspaper (7 November 1987)

REVIEW

Essay

'The Soviet state was established at the expense of the Soviet people.'

Examine the nature of the policies adopted towards agriculture and heavy industry between 1928 and 1939 in the light of this statement.

Prepare for this essay as follows.

(a) What was the nature of the agricultural policy? What were its successes and failures?
(b) What was the nature of the industrial policy? What were its successes and failures?
(c) What was the nature of the Soviet state which Stalin established?
(d) In what sense was (i) Agriculture (ii) Industry (iii) the Soviet state changed at the expense of the Soviet people?
(e) What were the benefits of the changes adopted by Stalin?
(f) To what extent were these benefits outweighed by the cost?
(g) What are your own conclusions about Stalin's policies?

11 Hitler's Germany 1933-39

PREVIEW

View put forward by the Nazis
- The Nazis were swept into office on a wave of popular support.
- The Nazis were supported by the vast majority of the German people.
- Nazi newsreel and films show fervent enthusiasm for the Nazi leadership.
- The Nazi party was closely knit and unified behind the leadership of Adolf Hitler.
- Hitler was the supreme dictator, taking all the key decisions and controlling events closely.
- The Nazis brought about an economic miracle after 1933.
- The Nazis spoke of their desire to bring about a classless society.
- The Nazi regime always intended to bring about the extermination of the Jewish race in Europe. This stemmed from Hitler's personal hatred of the Jews.

Challenging the Nazi view
- Hitler was offered the position of Chancellor in a 'backstairs intrigue'.
- The Nazis never obtained more than 37% of the votes in a free election.
- The lack of opportunity to express discontent/criticism of the regime makes it hard to assess popular opinion.
- The party was riddled with personal faction and intrigue.
- Hitler was often lax and indecisive,and spent much time away from Berlin.
- By 1933 the European economy was already recovering. In 1937 the Nazis faced a major economic crisis of their own.
- The Nazis did very little to promote genuine social change.
- A whole range of factors beyond Hitler's control contributed to the demise of the Jews.

TALKING POINT

Dictators distort the truth. Is it possible in examining the regime of a dictator for the real truth to emerge?

Power is handed to Hitler

By 10.00am on the morning of 30 January 1933 a large crowd had gathered in the massive square called the Wilhelmstrasse in the centre of Berlin. Largely silent, the atmosphere they created was one of tension and anticipation. Meanwhile, a smaller group had gathered in the entrance lobby of the Hotel Kaiserhof which overlooked the square. Inside the opulent building the smell of freshly-brewed coffee and the haze of cigarette smoke seemed to confirm that for many people in Berlin that morning, time was passing exceptionally slowly. One of the group, Ernst Röhm - a small stocky man dressed in the brown-shirted uniform of Hitler's stormtroopers - paced backwards and forwards between his colleagues and the window which overlooked the square. Through his binoculars he was able to look beyond the

THE NEW CHANCELLOR, ADOLF HITLER, WAVES TO ADORING CROWDS (JANUARY 1933)

TALKING POINT

President Hindenburg: A doddery old man or a wise political schemer?

crowds and focus his attention on the centre of all the anticipation. The crowds had assembled outside the gates of the Chancellory, the very centre of German political power.

At approximately 11.45 am the Chancellory gates were opened and tension gave way to excitement. The crowd roared their approval as a car carrying the new Chancellor of Germany sped down the driveway and into the square. Standing in the back of the car to receive the crowd's good wishes was Adolf Hitler who, at the age of 43, had just become the fifteenth German Chancellor since 1918.

Shaking with emotion and with tears in his eyes, Hitler swept into the Hotel Kaiserhof so that he could share his good news with his closest associates. He told the leading Nazis that at his first Cabinet meeting that afternoon he would insist that the Reichstag be dissolved once again and that in March the German people be asked to vote in the third major election in nine months. Hitler's objective was to gain sufficient control of the Reichstag to render obsolete his earlier need to co-operate with the conservative parties.

That night the Nazis celebrated with a massive torchlight parade through the centre of Berlin. From 7.00 pm until after midnight, more than 25,000 of Hitler's most fanatical supporters took part in a uniformed march through the Brandenburg Gate and past the Chancellory. In an illuminated window, Hitler stood with his arm outstretched towards his followers. The Nazi salutes, demonstrations, the uniforms and the flags which for so long had been the symbols of protest had in the space of one long day come to represent a new and fearsome authority. A few windows along from Hitler, President Hindenburg - 84 years old and one of the few representatives of continuity that Germany had left - tapped his cane in time to the music of the bands that marched past below. Earlier that day, he had given his consent to the dissolution of the Reichstag and the calling of a new election. The scene had been set for the most dramatic election campaign in Germany's short history. While the old man might have wondered whether he would live to see another election, he cannot have imagined that he had witnessed the first stage in the destruction of German democracy or that the opportunity for the German people to vote freely for the party of their choice was about to come to an end.

Over the next two months the Nazis mounted an election campaign which surpassed in its intensity even the frenzied efforts of July 1932. In a diary entry of January 1933 Goebbels anticipated a 'masterpiece of agitation'. This was launched by Hitler himself late in the evening of 1 February when, on the radio network, he read his inflammatory 'Proclamation to the German People'. In a vitriolic speech Hitler once again raised the spectre of Communism:

'Fourteen years of Marxism have ruined Germany; one year of Bolshevism could destroy her. The richest and fairest territories of the world would be turned into a smoking heap of ruins. Even the sufferings of the last decade and a half could not be compared to the misery of a Europe in which the red flag of destruction had been hoisted.'

Hitler claimed that the objective of the election would be to 'revive in the nation the spirit of unity and co-operation'. It was now apparent that the Communist Party and the Socialists would be the target of a massive programme of intimidation. At the start of February the Reich press agency announced that Hitler would be keeping his humble apartment in Munich and that he would not be drawing the new salary he was entitled to as Chancellor. However, beneath the smokescreen of virtuous words, the Nazis' actions towards their political opponents soon revealed that they were prepared to go to any lengths to ensure a massive victory in the forthcoming

HINDENBURG, Paul von (1847-1934)

German soldier and President.
1866 Fought at Königgratz.
1870-71 in Franco-Prussian War.
1903 Became general.
1911 Retired, but recalled at outbreak of WW1.
1914 Won victory at Tannenberg with Ludendorff.
1916 Became Chief of General Staff.
1918 Organised withdrawal from Western Front.
1919 Advised Kaiser to abdicate and arranged Armistice.
1925-34 Elected as President of the Weimar Republic.
1932 Defeated Hitler in presidential election.
1933 Appointed Hitler Chancellor.

HITLER WITH PRESIDENT HINDENBURG IN 1933. THE AGEING PRESIDENT DESPISED HITLER AND HIS 'VULGAR MANNERISMS'

JOSEF GOEBBELS, HITLER'S BRILLIANT PROPAGANDA MINISTER. SECRETLY RIDICULED FOR HIS PHYSICAL DISABILITY, HE WAS ALSO FEARED BY MANY

election. On 4 February the decree 'For the protection of the German people' was issued, allowing the government - on the vaguest of grounds - to prohibit political meetings and to ban the newspapers and publications of other political parties.

Perhaps the most important tactic in the election build-up was the effective subordination of the Prussian police force to the authority of Hermann Goering, a leading Nazi and member of the Cabinet. Within a week of Hitler's appointment as Chancellor, Goering had drawn up a list of police officers and government officials to be purged. On 11 February, auxiliary police were brought into the Rhineland area with instructions to back up the ordinary police in their campaign against left-wing subversive elements in the Ruhr cities. By the middle of February, key police chiefs had been ousted and replaced by high-ranking SA leaders. The brutal simplicity of the takeover was revealed in the astonishingly frank advice by Goering to his new 'police officers'. In their dealings with the Left the police were told to 'make free use of their weapons whenever necessary'. If they had still not appreciated what Goering had in mind, his subsequent instructions left no room for doubt: 'Every bullet that is now fired from the barrel of a police pistol is my bullet. If that is called murder, then I have committed murder, for I have ordered it all; I take the responsibility for it'.

It was against this well-organised campaign of intimidation that the left-wing parties had to fight for their political survival. However, their prospects were sorely diminished when on the night of 27 February 1933 the Reichstag building was burned down. The swift manner in which the Nazis blamed and then punished the Communists for the fire has led many historians to assume that the fire was actually instigated by the Nazis to provide them with the excuse they desperately needed for moving against their arch enemies. Analyse carefully the evidence which follows, and try to determine whether the Nazis' control over these events was as complete as was once assumed.

Examining the evidence

The Reichstag Fire

Source A: The traditional view

Goering and Goebbels were looking for some pretext to smash the Communist Party. After rejecting various plans - such as an attack on Hitler - they hit on the notion of setting fire to the Reichstag building.

An underground passage linked Goering's Palace of the President of the Reichstag with the main building across the street. Through this a small group of S.A. men under the command of Karl Ernst, the leader of the Berlin S.A., entered the deserted building on the evening of the 27th and scattered a chemical preparation with a delayed-action effect over carpet, curtains and chairs. After doing this they made their way back to safety by the underground tunnel. As they were leaving, a half-crazed young Dutchman, who had been picked up by the S.A. after attempting to set fire to other buildings, and carefully groomed for the dupe, climbed into the Reichstag from the outside and proceeded to start fires at a number of points. By the time the police and the fire-brigades arrived the fire was out of control and rapidly engulfed the building.

A. Bullock, *Hitler, A Study in Tyranny* (1952)

GOERING IN HEROIC POSE. HE MADE A GOOD DEAL OF HIS RECORD AS A FIRST WORLD WAR ACE

Source B: The revisionist view

Goering seems to have been utterly thunderstruck; he went at once to the burning building. His first thought was to save the tapestries and the library. He arrived at about 9.30 pm shortly after the main hall had gone up in flames and the fire had reached ten-alarm proportions. It cannot be inferred from Goering's behaviour that he welcomed the fire. He...spoke to Fire Chief Gempp, and inquired after Councillor Galle, the president of the Reichstag. Assistant Secretary Gravert, who was with him, inquired at once into the origin of the fire, learned of grounds for suspecting Ernst Torgler and Wilhelm Koenen (2 senior members of the KPD) and was convinced from that moment on that the Communists were behind the fire.

Goering later said that the moment he heard the word 'incendiary' the idea that the Communist Party was to blame had come to him spontaneously. But it seems more likely that the idea was first suggested by the information he obtained from Gravert.

Hans Mommsen, *Aspects of the Third Reich* (1985)

Extract C: The role of Goering

(i) 'This is the beginning of the Communist uprising. They are about to strike. There is not a moment to lose!'

(ii) 'When I heard the word "arson" it was as if the curtain had risen at one stroke and I saw the play clearly before me. The moment the word "arson"

TALKING POINT

This account shows Goering showing concern for saving fine art, and then anxiety for the safety of the president of the Reichstag

(a) How does your view of Goering change as a result of this?

(b) Are you now convinced that Goering was genuinely surprised by the fire?

THE BLAZING REICHSTAG BUILDING. THE QUESTION OF RESPONSIBILITY FOR THE FIRE REMAINS CONTROVERSIAL. COULD ONE MAN HAVE SET SUCH A LARGE BUILDING ALIGHT?

fell, I knew that the Communist Party was guilty and had set the Reichstag on fire.'

(iii) 'On the day of the Reichstag fire, I who was then his only aide-de-camp, reported the incident to Goering, I was convinced that his surprise was authentic.'

Sources i-iii quoted in Hans Mommsen, *Aspects of the Third Reich* (1985)

(iv) On the occasion of a luncheon on the Fuhrer's birthday in 1943, the people round the Fuhrer turned the conversation to the Reichstag and its artistic value. I heard with my own ears how Goering broke into the conversation and shouted 'The only one who really knows the Reichstag is I, for I set fire to it'.

(v) What the General says is not true. I should very much like to see him here so that he can say it to my face. The whole thing is preposterous. Even if I had started the fire, I would most certainly not have boasted about it.

Sources iv-v quoted in F. Tobias, *The Reichstag Fire* (1963)

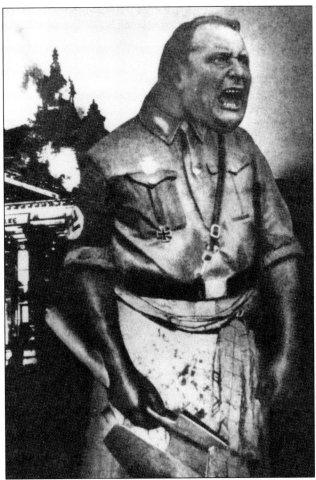

GOERING - 'THE EXECUTIONER OF THE THIRD REICH'

Source D: Goebbel's account

At nine the Fuhrer came for supper. We had a little music and talked. Suddenly the telephone rang. The Reichstag is burning. I thought the news was pure fantasy and wouldn't even tell the Fuhrer about it. After a few more calls I got the terrible confirmation it was true...I informed the Fuhrer, and we raced downtown at 70 m.p.h. The whole building was in flames...Goering met us, and soon von Papen arrived. It had already been established that the fire was due to arson.

Quoted in C. Reiss, *Joseph Goebbels* (1949)

Source E: Hitler's role

i)'I hope to God that this is the work of the Communists. You are now witnessing the outbreak of a great epoch in German History.'

Hitler's words to Sefton Delmer, Berlin correspondent of the *Daily Mail.*

ii) I saw that his face had turned quite scarlet, both with excitement and with the heat...Suddenly he started screaming at the top of his voice - 'Now we'll show them. Anyone who stands in our way will be shot, mown down. The German people have been too soft too long. Every Communist official must be shot. All Communist M.P.s must be hanged this very night.

Eye-witness quoted in F. Tobias, *The Reichstag Fire* (1963)

Source F: The head of the Berlin political police

When I pushed my way into the burning building with Schneider, we had to climb over the bulging hoses of the Berlin fire brigade, although as yet, there were few onlookers. A few officers of my department were already engaged in interrogating van der Lubbe. Naked from the waist upwards, smeared with dirt and sweating, he sat in front of them breathing heavily. He panted as if he had completed a tremendous task. There was a wild triumphant gleam in the burning eyes of his pale young face...

The voluntary confessions of Marinus van der Lubbe prevented me from thinking that an arsonist who was such an expert in his folly needed any helpers. Why should not a single match be enough to set fire to the cold yet inflammable splendour of the Chamber, the old upholstered furniture, the heavy curtains, and the bone-dry wooden panelling! But this specialist had used a whole knapsack full of inflammable material. He had been so active that he laid several dozen fires. With a firelighter, the 'Industrious Housewife', he had set the chamber aflame. Then he had rushed through the big corridors with his burning shirt which he brandished in his right hand like a torch to lay more fires under the old leather sofas. During this hectic activity he was overpowered by Reichstag officials.

Rudolf Diels, Head of the Prussian political police, quoted in Noakes and Pridham, *Nazism 1919-45* (vol II) (1983)

Source G: van der Lubbe

As to the question whether I acted alone. I declare emphatically that this was the case. No one at all helped me, nor did I meet a single person in the Reichstag.

Statement to the police of 3 March 1933

VAN DER LUBBE ON TRIAL IN BERLIN, ACCUSED OF STARTING THE REICHSTAG FIRE

The Reichstag fire: who was to blame?

Theory 1
- The fire was planned by Goering and Goebbels with the approval of Hitler.
- The fire was started by the SA who then set up van der Lubbe as a scapegoat.
- The motive was to use the fire as 'proof' that the Communists were planning an uprising. Therefore the Nazis could clamp down on them before the election in March.

Theory 2
- The fire was planned by the Communist Party as part of an armed uprising.
- The fire was started by several people including van der Lubbe.
- The Nazi leadership were taken by surprise but then quickly set about containing the Communist uprising.

Theory 3
- van der Lubbe acted on his own.
- He did not meet anyone else in the Reichstag and the fire was not part of a wider Communist plot.
- However, the Nazi leadership were so alarmed that they imagined the Communists were trying to overthrow the Government.

Before you attempt to make a judgment on who started the fire you should also consider the additional information. These points are not intended to support one viewpoint only, so you may come across points which seem to be contradictory.

TALKING POINT
It does not matter much who set fire to the Reichstag. What really counts is the use Hitler made of the episode. Discuss this view.

HITLER ADDRESSING THE REICHSTAG FOR THE FIRST TIME IN 1933. BEFORE THE YEAR WAS OVER IT HAD BEEN REDUCED TO THE ROLE OF A RUBBER STAMP

Other factors

The Nazis

1 If the fire was planned by Goering and Goebbels, Hitler would surely have known about it.

2 Goering and Goebbels disliked each other intensely. Could they have co-operated in something as important as this?

3 Goering's love of fine art was well known. Could he have approved a plan which would lead to the destruction of priceless works of art?

4 Hitler's personal reaction seemed to be one of surprise and outrage. Was this genuine or feigned?

5 Would the Nazis have allowed the election campaign to take place without planning some sort of action – such as the fire - which would enable them to clamp down on the Communists?

van der Lubbe

1 van der Lubbe's physical and mental health were regarded as below average.

2 Could one man have started a fire in so many different places and on such a wide scale?

3 van der Lubbe remained adamant that he had acted alone. He never qualified his statement at any time up to his execution.

4 If he had been part of a wider plot, would van der Lubbe have kept quiet or would he have implicated others?

Task

You will need to divide yourselves into four groups.

(a) Planning The first group will support Theory 1 and will argue that the Reichstag Fire was planned by Goering and Goebbels. To defend Theory 1 members must extract as much useful information as possible from the evidence, the additional points and their own background knowledge of the Third Reich.

Group 1 should then prepare a written statement supporting their theory, as well as anticipating questions which may be put to them and making themselves aware of weaknesses in the argument. The group should also try to pinpoint weaknesses in the Theories 2 and 3.

The second and third groups will at the same time perform similar tasks in support of Theories 2 and 3 respectively.

(b) Hearing Group 4 are to act as independent judges of all the evidence put forward. Each submission should be carefully listened to, with time allotted for questions and answers.

(c) Verdict When all the Theories have been discussed, votes will be cast as follows. Each individual in Groups 1-3 can cast one vote for the theory which they now find most persuasive. Each individual in Group 4 also has to decide which theory is most credible, but their decision is worth two votes.

Finally, consider your verdict: was it unanimous? Has the group really reached a conclusive decision about who started the Reichstag Fire?

Many historians now argue that the real importance of the Reichstag Fire lies not so much in the continuing mystery of who started it but rather in the political use made of it by the Nazis. While the building was still smouldering, Hitler confronted a shocked and disorientated Hindenburg and persuaded him to authorise an emergency 'Decree for the Protection of the People and State'. This gave Hitler massive powers of repression and control, backed by the fact that he was able to claim that he had obtained these extra powers constitutionally. In the Reichstag elections on 5 March 1933, the Nazis won 288 seats compared with 196 in the November 1932 election. They had increased their percentage of the vote from 33.1 per cent to 43.9 per cent. They had still failed to gain an absolute majority. However, events now moved with an inexorable force as one after another of Germany's democratic safeguards was brushed aside with shocking simplicity.

The consolidation of power
February-July 1933

Date/Legislation	Details
4 Feb 1933 Curtailment of freedom of speech	The decree, sanctioned by President Hindenburg, authorised the prohibition of newspapers and of political meetings that 'abused or treated with contempt, institutions, bureaus or leading officials of state' or broadcast 'false information'. The phrasing of the decree was deliberately vague so that action could be taken against a wide range of political opponents
28 Feb 1933 The Emergency Laws for the Protection of People and State	Taking advantage of the Reichstag Fire, this decree: suspended all basic rights of the citizen for the duration of the emergency; authorised the Reich Government to take charge of law, order and security when the situation demanded it; and ordered death or imprisonment for a series of political offences.
1 March 1933 First law directed at aligning the Länder	The independence of the Federal States or Länder was curtailed. Germany's system of federal government had been diminished and power now passed towards the central government.
23 March 1933 The Enabling Law	This bill brought about the destruction of parliamentary democracy and handed all legislative powers over from the Reichstag to the government. The law was passed by 444 votes to 44. Only the Social Democrats opposed it. The other opposition parties hoped to restrain Hitler with limiting provisions within the bill. Henceforth the Reichstag was merely a rubber stamp for Nazi legislation and a sounding board for Hitler's speeches.

TALKING POINT

We live in a centralised state. Does a federal system serve to strengthen or undermine democracy?

THE JUDICIARY FALL INTO LINE

THE ARREST OF POLITICAL OPPONENTS (1933)

7 April 1933 The Law of the Restoration of the Professional Civil Service	This enabled the government to dismiss any civil servants who were 'unsuitable' or not of 'Aryan descent' (initially with the exception of war veterans). The civil service was to be purged of Jews and political opponents.
7 April 1933 Law on the Admission to the Practice of Law	Restricted Jews from joining the legal profession.
1-2 May 1933 Destruction of the Trade Unions	For several years the union leadership had demanded a May Day holiday for the workers. At Goebbels' initiative, Hitler declared 1 May the Day of National Labour, a paid national holiday. The Nazis had assumed the guise of the true champions of the workers and the holiday was duly observed. When they returned to work the next day, the Nazis had occupied union offices throughout the country. Key union officials were arrested and taken to labour camps. The Nazis announced that henceforth there would be only one union, the German Labour Front (DAF). The Nazis' act of force against the union leadership took place without any legal sanction.
June-July 1933 Disbanding of political parties apart from the NSDAP	The Communist Party was curtailed after the Reichstag Fire. The Socialists had made a vigorous protest against the Enabling Act and were suppressed on 22 June. The Centre Party was the last party to fold. It dissolved itself on 5 July. On 14 July 1933 a new law was declared that the NSDAP was the only legal party in Germany and that any separate political activity would result in imprisonment for up to three years.

The Night of the Long Knives

Although Hitler had to a large extent succeeded in removing external domestic opposition by 1934, he still had to contend with powerful forces inside his own party which wanted to see him lead German society in a more radical, socialist direction. In the spring of 1934, powerful members of the party such as Gregor Strasser and Ernst Röhm (the leader of the SA) repeatedly criticised Hitler and urged him to reconsider the whole nature of his social policies. Meanwhile powerful Nazis like Goering, Goebbels and Himmler viewed Röhm – now at the head of more than two million stormtroopers - with concern and disdain. Each of these individuals was primarily concerned with the extension of his own power base. Himmler, for example, was eager to extend the authority of the SS which, technically, was still subservient to the SA. Goering's attempts to establish himself at the helm of economic policy were being obstructed by the economics minister, Schacht, who in turn was being backed by Röhm.

By June, it was clear that the ageing President von Hindenburg did not have long to live. If, as many anticipated, Hitler wished to then combine the offices of Chancellor and President he would need the full support of the Army. His concern was that the army might persuade Hindenburg to nominate an alternative successor before he died. Hitler knew that the power of the SA was a big worry to the Army, and realised that decisive action against Röhm would bring him greater support from the leading generals. Set against this was Hitler's personal sense of loyalty to Röhm who had been at his side in the Munich Putsch. Throughout June, Hitler received warnings of imminent danger from enemies of Röhm but he remained indecisive and uncertain.

Just before midnight on 28 June 1934, Hitler received a message of the utmost importance from Himmler in Berlin. Himmler convinced his leader that the Berlin SA had finalised its preparations to unseat the Fuhrer in a desperate coup d'etat. The SA, he told Hitler, would be ready to move by 4.00 pm and would begin the occupation of government buildings at 5.00 pm. Hitler was unable to contain his rage, and his natural tendency to hesitate now gave way to furious action. At 2.00 am, still shaking with anger and agitation, he climbed aboard a three-engined aircraft with his closest companions and set off for Munich. When the plane touched down at Oberwiesenfeld airport dawn had just broken. Three fast cars were ready to take Hitler and his heavily-armed entourage to the small spa town of Bad Wiessee. Hitler tersely informed a Reichwehr officer that he was going to 'pass severe judgement' on his former ally. Meanwhile Röhm slept on oblivious to the events which he was alleged to have set in motion and which were soon to consume him. Use the evidence that follows to assess whether you think Röhm was intending to rise up against Hitler.

ERNST ROHM (LEFT), LEADER OF THE SA. AT HIS SIDE IS FRANZ PAPEN. PERHAPS THEY BOTH UNDERESTIMATED HITLER IN DIFFERENT WAYS

Examining the evidence

The Night of the Long Knives

Source A: An account by Hitler's chauffeur, Eric Kempka

Just before Wiessee, Hitler suddenly breaks his silence: 'Kempka,' he says, 'drive carefully when we come to the Hotel Hanselbauer. You must drive up without making any noise. If you see an SA guard in the front of the hotel, don't wait for them to report to me; drive on and stop at the hotel entrance.' Then, after a moment of deathly silence: 'Röhm wants to carry out a coup.'

An icy shiver runs down my back. I could have believed anything, but not a coup by Röhm!

I drive up carefully to the hotel entrance as Hitler had ordered. Hitler jumps out of the car and after him Goebbels, Lutze and the adjutants. Right behind us another car stops with a squad of detectives which had been raised in Munich.

As soon as I have turned the car so that it is ready to leave in a moment, I rush into the hotel with my gun at the ready...

I run quickly up to the first floor where Hitler is just coming out of Röhm's bedroom. Two detectives come out of the room opposite. One of them reports to Hitler: 'My Fuhrer...the Police-President of Breslau is refusing to get dressed!'

Taking no notice of me, Hitler enters the room where Heines is remaining. I hear him shout 'Heines, if you are not dressed in five minutes I'll have you shot on the spot!"...

Meanwhile, Röhm comes out of his room in a blue suit and with a cigar in the corner of his mouth. Hitler glares at him but says nothing. Two detectives take Röhm to the vestibule of the hotel where he throws himself into an armchair and orders coffee from the waiter.

I stay in the corridor a little to one side and a detective tells me about Röhm's arrest. 'Hitler entered Röhm's bedroom with a whip in his hand. Behind him were two detectives with pistols at the ready. He spat out the words "Röhm, you are under arrest." Röhm looked up sleepily from his pillow: "Heil, my Fuhrer." "You are under arrest," bawled Hitler for the second time, turned on his heel and left the room.'

[The bewildered SA men were bundled into the hotel's laundry room but it was at this stage, as Kempka now describes, that things could have gone badly wrong for Hitler.]

Suddenly...there is the sound of a car arriving!...to my horror, a lorry full of heavily armed SA men rattles into the yard. Now there'll be some shooting, I think to myself. I can see Bruckner negotiating with the Sturmfuhrer of the SA. The man seems to be refusing. Walking backwards, he tries to get to his lorry...At this moment Hitler goes up to him: 'Drive back to Munich immediately!' he tells the puzzled fellow. 'If you are stopped by SS on the way, you must let yourselves be disarmed without resistance.'

The Sturmfuhrer salutes and jumps into the lorry, and the SA men leave again. No shot, no sign of resistance. All this time, Röhm is sitting unsuspectingly drinking his third cup of coffee. Only a single word from him, and the whole thing would have worked out differently...

Now the bus arrives which has been ordered by Schreck. Quickly the SA leaders are collected from the laundry room and walk past Röhm under police guard. Röhm looks up from his coffee sadly and waves to them in a melancholy way...

At last Röhm too is led from the hotel. He walks past Hitler with his head bowed, completely apathetic. Now Hitler gives the order to leave...our column, which in the meantime has grown to about twenty cars starts moving...

Quoted in Noakes & Pridham, *Nazism, A Documentary Reader Vol 1* (1983)

Are there any aspects of Source A which you find unreliable?

Source B: The governor of Stadelheim prison, Munich

Two SS men asked at the reception desk to be taken to Röhm...There they handed over a Browning to Röhm, who once again asked to speak to Hitler. They ordered him to shoot himself. If he did not comply, they would come back in ten minutes and kill him...When the time was up, the two SS men re-entered the cell and found Röhm standing with his chest bared. Immediately one of them from the door shot him in the throat, and Röhm collapsed on the floor. Since he was still alive, he was killed with a shot point-blank through the temple.

From Noakes & Pridham, *Nazism, A Documentary Reader, Vol 1* (1983)

Source C: Defence Minister General von Blomberg

The Fuhrer with soldierly decision and exemplary courage has himself attacked and crushed the traitors and murderers. The Army, as the bearers of arms of the entire people, far removed from the conflicts of domestic politics, will show its gratitude through devotion and loyalty.

General von Blomberg, July 1934

Source D: Reich President von Hindenburg

I note from the reports I have received that through your decisive intervention and your courageous personal commitment you have nipped all the treasonable intrigues in the bud. You have saved the German nation from serious danger and for this I express to you my deeply felt gratitude and my sincere appreciation.

Reich President von Hindenburg, 2 July 1934

Source E: The Reich Cabinet

At the meeting of the Reich Cabinet on Tuesday 3 July, the Reich Chancellor, Adolf Hitler, began by giving a detailed account of the origin and suppression of the high treason plot. The Reich Chancellor stressed that lightning action had been necessary, otherwise many thousands of people would have been in danger of being wiped out.

Extract from the minutes of the Reich Cabinet Meeting, 3 July 1934

Source F: The verdict of a German historian

The smoothness with which the murders of 30 June were carried out is eloquent proof that no Röhm putsch was imminent. There was no resistance encountered anywhere, not even among the armed elite formations of the SA; many victims unsuspectingly surrendered of their own accord, having faith in their Fuhrer and in the eventual clarification of an obvious mistake. The only shots fired were those of the executioners...The number of victims, officially set at 77, is estimated to have been between 150 and 200.

Karl Dietrich Bracher, *The German Dictatorship* (1971)

---

1 Examine Hitler's conduct as described in Source A. To what extent did Hitler seem to believe that Röhm was planning a coup?

2 To what extent is this picture contradicted by Röhm's behaviour as described in the same source?

---

3 Does the conduct of the SA men suggest that Röhm was planning a coup?

4 Are the actions of Hitler, Röhm and the SA supported or contradicted in the other sources?

5 Many Germans, before and after this incident, regarded Röhm as an 'extremist' and Hitler as a 'moderate'. Why do you think this was the case? In what ways does this viewpoint alter your perceptions of the whole affair?

6 Look carefully at Source C. Blomberg evidently approved of the completely lawless massacre of political opponents. Why do you think he took this stance? What does this tell you about the attitude of the army towards (a) Röhm and the SA; (b) Hitler?

7 What conclusions would you now reach about Nazi-military relations?

8 Many historians are emphatic in their belief that Röhm was *not* planning any sort of revolt against Hitler. Would you dissent from this view in any way?

9 Would you now conclude that the Röhm purge was instigated, controlled and executed by Hitler?

The extension of power

With the SA removed, Hitler's next opportunity to extend his personal power base presented itself only a month later. On 2 August 1934 President Hindenburg died aged 85. His heart was still beating when it was announced that, from now on, the office of Reich President would be combined with that of Reich Chancellor and that both posts would be held by Adolf Hitler. Still grateful to Hitler for his action against the SA, the Army accepted this extension of his authority without question. The degree to which Hitler had become the dictator of Germany was reflected in the oath of loyalty which all soldiers in the German Army were now forced to take.

'I swear by God this sacred oath: I will render unconditional obedience to Adolf Hitler, the Fuhrer of the German nation and people, Supreme Commander of the Armed Forces, and will be ready as a brave soldier to risk my life at any time for this oath.'

Hitler's political judgement seemed unerring. The oath of loyalty constituted an almost physical bond which no honourable soldier, particularly those in the officer corps, would contemplate compromising. Hitler's conquest of his main opponents and his consolidation of power among his own party were complete, but the support of the ordinary people towards the regime was not something he could afford to take for granted. To what extent then was the Nazi regime a popular one?

The policies which Hitler adopted towards key groups in Nazi Germany are explored in Focus sections 11.1, 11.2, 11.3.

Berlin ißt heute sein Eintopfgericht

FOCUS

11.1 How popular were the Nazis in the years 1933-39?

Background to the Plebiscite Campaign of August 1934

1 Before the election. The verdict of a Social Democrat

a) Hitler's portrait hanging from every window, every car, public loudspeakers to broadcast the speeches on the radio.

(b) The moral pressure: those who said 'no' were branded as traitors, rogues, saboteurs of national reconstruction.

2 During the voting

a) The uniformed SA people and Party members in the polling stations created an atmosphere of terror in the polling room right from the start.

b) In many cases there were no polling booths at all, in others it was made virtually impossible to enter them. Either the booth was put in a far corner, or SA men barred the way to it or there were posters to put people off.

(Eg. Every German Votes publicly, who votes otherwise? or 'Only Traitors go in here.')

Jeremy Noakes, *Nazism-state, Economy and Society* (1984)

A party ceremony (1935)

The 'Day of Potsdam'. A sea of flags in all the streets. We too couldn't opt out...In the morning a broadcast of the ceremonies in Potsdam. All cleverly done, impressive, spellbinding even, at any rate for the masses...How marvellously it's been staged by that master producer Goebbels.

Observation of a liberal whose general outlook was anti-Nazi (1935)

TOP: THE NAZIS'S WINTER RELIEF CAMPAIGN AN APPEAL FOR NATIONAL SOLIDARITY. THE MONEY IS GOING TO THE ARMAMENTS INDUSTRY AND THE SLOGAN SAYS 'BERLIN IS CASTING ITS HOTPOT TODAY'.

RIGHT: A MAJOR NAZI RALLY. WHAT IMPRESSION OF THE REGIME IS CREATED IN PHOTOGRAPHS SUCH AS THIS?

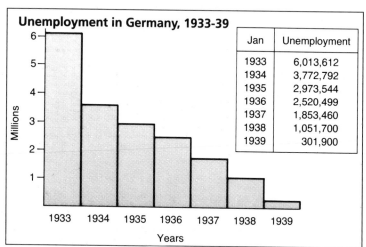

Unemployment in Germany, 1933-39

Jan	Unemployment
1933	6,013,612
1934	3,772,792
1935	2,973,544
1936	2,520,499
1937	1,853,460
1938	1,051,700
1939	301,900

Popularity or propaganda?

The Fuhrer's birthday (1939)

'The Fuhrer's fiftieth birthday. Berlin puts on its finery, makes the last preparations for this twentieth of April 1939, which is to become a unique day of thanks giving. The Filmwochenschau has a specific assignment in this..it must create an historic document for the future, to capture in pictures the greatness of this day...Under a bright shining sky the birthday itself begins. Cheerful marching tunes resound...Hitler receives the homage...A gigantic crowd in front of the Reich Chancellory swells in a song of jubilation for Hitler. Now Hitler appears on the balcony before the crowd, which breaks out into a repeated ovation.'

From an official account of the making of a weekly newsreel (1939)

'Hitler is still outside the line of fire of criticism but the messianic belief in him has more or less died out, whereas for example Goebbels is almost universally despised.'

Comment by a Socialist in 1936

The verdict of an historian

'Although the regime deployed a formidable apparatus of terror, it is clear that it was also based on a large measure of consent from broad sections of the population. The fact that Hitler was associated with the solving of the unemployment problem and with the restoration of Germany's position as a European power appeared to many to confirm the message of Goebbel's propaganda...

'A crucial element in popular consent to the regime was the fact that Nazism embodied, albeit in an extreme form, many of the basic attitudes of a very large section of the German people...Such people approved of the regime's hostility towards unpopular minorities, not just Jews but also gypsies, and of its harsh attitude towards deviant groups - homosexuals, tramps, habitual criminals, the so-called asocials and "workshy". They welcomed the fact that such people were now being locked up in concentration camps.

Jeremy Noakes, *Nazism – State, Economy and Society* (1984)

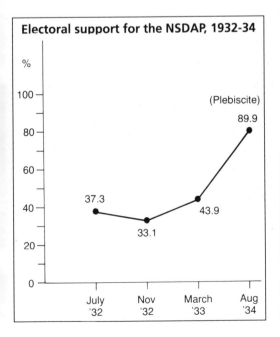

TIME: MAY DAY
PLACE: ANY FASCIST COUNTRY.
" ACH ! NO ONE CAN SAY THE LEADER
DOES NOT DO HIS BEST TO MAKE THE PEOPLE HAPPY."

COMPULSORY SPONTANEOUS DEMONSTRATION

Electoral support for the NSDAP, 1932-34

%

100 —

80 —

(Plebiscite)

89.9

60 —

40 —

37.3

43.9

33.1

20 —

0 —

July '32   Nov '32   March '33   Aug '34

QUESTIONS

1 What difficulties are faced by an historian in attempting to assess the popularity of the Nazis?

2 Can you find any genuine evidence here either of Hitler's personal popularity or of successful party policies which may have won popularity for the Nazis?

3 Are there any examples here to suggest that Hitler was less popular than the propaganda might suggest?

4 Was Hitler genuinely popular or is that a propaganda myth?

11.2 The role of women in Hitler's Germany

1 Hitler outlines the Nazi party attitude to women

...The slogan 'Emancipation of women' was invented by Jewish intellectuals and its content was formed by the same spirit. In the really good times of German life the German woman had no need to emancipate herself. She possessed exactly what nature had necessarily given her to administer and preserve...

If the man's world is said to be the State, his struggle, his readiness to devote his powers to the service of the community, then it may perhaps be said that the woman's is a smaller world. For her world is her husband, her family, her children and her home. But what would become of the greater world if there were no one to tend and care for the smaller one?...

The sacrifices which the man makes in the struggle of his nation, the woman makes in the preservation of that nation in individual cases. What the man gives in courage on the battlefield, the woman gives in eternal self-sacrifice, in eternal pain and suffering. Every child that a woman brings into the world is a battle, a battle waged for the existence of her people...

So our women's movement is for us not something which inscribes on its banner as its programme the fight against men, but something which has as its programme the common fight together with men.

Extracts from speech by Hitler to the National Socialist Women's Section (NSF), 8 September 1934. Quoted in Noakes and Pridham, *Nazism, A Documentary Reader, vol II* (1984)

2 The party attitude towards marriage

The Reich encourages marriage in accordance with the following regulations.

Marriage loans, section 1

1 People of German nationality who marry one another after this law has come into force can on application be granted a marriage loan of up to 1000 Reichsmarks. The application for the marriage loan can be made before marriage...The conditions which must be fulfilled before the grant of a marriage loan are as follows:

(a) That the future wife has spent at least six months in employment in Germany between 11 June 1931 and 31 May 1933.

(b) That banns has been issued by the Registry Office and that the future wife gives up her job at the latest at the time of the wedding...

(c) That the future wife pledges herself not to take up employment so long as her future husband receives an income (within the meaning of the Income Tax Law) of more than 125 Reichsmarks a month.

From Section 5 of the Law for the Reduction of Unemployment of 1 June 1933.

3 'Ten Commandments for the Choice of a Spouse' (1934)

1 Remember that you are a German.

2 If you are genetically healthy you should not remain unmarried.

3 Keep your body pure.

4 You should keep your mind and spirit pure.

5 As a German choose only a spouse of the same or Nordic blood.

6 In choosing a spouse ask about his ancestors.

7 Health is also a precondition for physical beauty.

8 Marry only for love.

9 Don't look for a playmate but for a companion for marriage.

10 You should want to have as many children as possible.

4 Incentives for women to have more children

May 1939: The Mother's Cross

Gold: for those with 8 children.

Silver: for those with 6 children

Bronze: for those with 4 children.

Taken from Noakes and Pridham, *Nazism, A Documentary Reader vol II* (1984)

TALKING POINT

What differences are there in the demands which a totalitarian state makes of women, compared to the expectations in a democratic state?

---

5 Population statistics 1919-39

Year	Marriages	Marriages per 1,000 inhabitants	Divorces per 10,000 existing marriages	Live births	Deaths	Surplus of births over deaths
1929	589,600					
1931				1,047,775	734,165	313,610
1932	516,793			993,126	707,642	285,484
1933	638,573	9.7	29.7	971,174	737,877	233,297
1934	740,165	11.1	37.0	1,198,350	724,758	473,592
1935	651,435	9.7	33.0	1,263,976	792,018	471,958
1936	609,631	9.1	32.6	1,277,052	795,203	481,849
1937	620,265	9.1	29.8	1,277,046	794,367	482,679
1938	645,062	9.4	31.1	1,348,534	799,220	549,314
1939	772,106	11.1	38.3	1,407,490	853,410[1]	554,080

Year	Per 1,000 inhabitants		Illegitimate Births per 100 births	Loans per 1,000 marriages	Loan remissions per 100 births
	Births	*Deaths*			
1932	16.0	4.8			
1933	15.1	4.3			
1934	14.7	3.5	10.7	33.0	8.7
1935	18.0	7.1	8.6		
1936	18.9	7.1	7.8	24.1	12.3
1937	19.0	7.2	7.8	28.1	14.6
1938	18.8	7.1	7.7	29.7	17.5
1939	19.6	7.9	7.7	35.2	19.0
1940	20.3	8.0	7.8	33.0	20.5

[1] Deaths excluding those killed in action.

6 Population control: the Law for the Prevention of Hereditarily Diseased Offspring

1) Anyone who has a hereditary illness can be rendered sterile by a surgical operation if, according to the experience of medical science, there is a strong probability that his/her offspring will suffer from serious hereditary defects of a physical or mental nature.

2) Anyone is hereditarily ill within the meaning of this law who suffers from one of the following illnesses:

(a) Congenital feeble mindedness
(b) Schizophrenia
(c) Manic depression
(d) Hereditary epilepsy
(e) Huntington's chorea
(f) Hereditary blindness
(g) Hereditary deafness
(h) Serious physical deformities.

Law issued on 14 July 1933. Quoted in Noakes and Pridham, *Nazism, A Documentary Reader vol II* (1984)

11.3 Education and youth in Nazi Germany

Aspects of the education system

1 An historian's view of Nazi education policy

For a regime bent on indoctrinating youth with a new set of values, education was clearly a vital area. The Nazis used various methods to try and control the education system and use it for their purposes.

'In the first place, they tried to ensure that the teaching profession was both politically reliable and ideologically sound. The weeks following the Nazi take-over saw a number of ad hoc measures by the various states to purge the profession of unreliable teachers, which were then superceded by the application of the Law for the Re-establishment of a Professional Civil Service of 7 April 1933.

Noakes and Pridham, *Nazism, A Documentary Reader,* vol II (1984)

2 Controlling the curriculum: the teaching of history in secondary schools

The German nation in its essence and greatness, in its fateful struggle for internal and external identity is the subject of the teaching of history. It is based on the natural bond of the child with his nation and, by interpreting history as the fateful struggle for existence between the nations, has the particular task of educating young people to respect the great German past and to have faith in the mission and future of their own nation and to respect the right of existence of other nations. The teaching of history must bring the past alive for the young German in such a way that it enables him to understand the present, makes him feel the responsibility of every individual for the nation as a whole and gives him encouragement for his own political activity.

Guidelines for the teaching of history issued in 1938 by the German Central Institute of Education

3 Distorting the curriculum: extracts from maths textbooks

(a) The construction of a lunatic asylum costs 6 million RM. How many houses at 15,000 RM each could have been built for that amount?

(b) To keep a mentally ill person costs approx 4 RM per day, a cripple 5.50 RM, a criminal 3.50 RM. Many civil servants receive only 4 RM per day...unskilled workers not even 2 RM per head for their families. (a) Illustrate these figures with a curriculum - according to conservative estimates, there are 300,000 mentally ill, epileptics etc, in care. (b) How much do these people cost to keep in total, at a cost of 4 RM per head? (c) How many marriage loans at 1000 RM each...could be granted from this money?

(c) A modern night bomber can carry 1,800 incendiaries. How long (in kilometres) is the path along which it can distribute these bombs if it drops a bomb every second at a speed of 250 km per hour? How far apart are the craters from one another? How many kilometres can 10 such planes set alight if they fly 50 metres apart from one another? How many fires are caused if 1/3 of the bombs hit their targets and of these 1/3 ignite?

4 Aspects of youth policy

Hitler outlines his youth policy

The ideal of manhood has not always been the same even for our own people. There were times which now seem to us very far off and almost incomprehensible, when the ideal of the young man was the chap who could hold his beer and was good for a drink. But now his day is past and we like to see not the man who can hold his drink, but the young man who can stand all weathers, the hardened young man. Because what matters is not how many glasses of beer he can drink, but how many blows he can stand; not how many nights he can stand on the spree, but how many kilometres he can march.

We no longer see in the boorish beer-drinker the ideal of the German people: we find it in men and girls who are sound to the core, and sturdy.

What we look for from our German youth is different from what people wanted in the past. In our eyes the German youth of the future must be slim and slender, swift as the greyhound, tough as leather, and hard as Krupp steel. We must educate a new type of man so that our people is not ruined by the symptoms of degeneracy of our day.

Speech at Nuremberg (14 September 1935), quoted in Noakes and Pridham, *Nazism, A Documentary Reader, vol II* (1984)

5 Membership figures of the Hitler Youth

	HJ (boys aged 14-18)	DJ (boys aged 10-14)	BDM (girls aged 14-18)	JM (girls aged 10-14)	Total	Total population of 10-18 year olds
End 1932	55,365	28,691	19,244	4,656	107,956	
End 1933	568,288	1,130,521	243,750	349,482	2,292,041	7,529,000
End 1934	786,000	1,457,304	471,944	862,317	3,577,565	7,682,000
End 1935	829,361	1,498,209	569,599	1,046,134	3,943,303	8,172,000
End 1936	1,168,734	1,785,424	873,127	1,610,316	5,437,601	8,656,000
End 1937	1,237,078	1,884,883	1,035,804	1,722,190	5,879,955	9,060,000
End 1938	1,663,305	2,064,538	1,448,264	1,855,119	7,031,226	9,109,000
Beg. 1939	1,723,886	2,137,594	1,502,571	1,923,419	7,287,470	8,870,000

and the BDM Werk (girls aged 18-21): 440,189

Abbreviations: HJ Hitler-Jugend (Hitler Youth); DJ Deutsches Jungvolk (German Young People); BDM Bund Deutscher Mädel (League of German Girls); JM Jungmädelbund (League of Young Girls).

6 Indoctrination of youth: extracts from the Reich Youth Leadership Handbook, 1937

Guidelines for activities for a fortnight's camp (extracts)

Friday 10 July:
Password: Adolf Hitler
Motto for the day: Hitler is Germany and Germany is Hitler.
Words: We owe to our leader Adolf Hitler the fact that we can open our camp today.
Song: Onward, onward.
Community hour: is omitted since the group is still very tired.

Saturday 18 July:
Password: Schlageter
Motto for the day: Let struggle be the highest aim of youth!
Words: The camp leader speaks about the fact that we all have to become fighters...
Song: Unroll the blood-red flags.
Community hour: Germans in the world – Versailles is a burden on us.

(Reich Youth Leadership folders)Taken from Noakes and Pridham, *Nazism, A Documentary Reader, vol. II* (1984).

While there are obvious difficulties for the historian in assessing popular opinion in the Third Reich it seems fair to say that the attitude of most Germans towards the Nazis' anti-semitic programme was one of indifference or acquiescence rather than enthusiasm. The motivation and drive behind the anti-Jewish campaign came very much from within the party. To what extent, though, was it personally instigated by Adolf Hitler?

EXAMINING THE EVIDENCE

Hitler's role in the persecution of the Jews (1933-39)

Source A

If I am ever really in power the destruction of the Jews will be my first and most important job. As soon as I have the power, I shall have gallows after gallows erected...Then the Jews will be hanged one after another and they will stay hanging until they stink. They will stay hanging as long as hygienically possible. As soon as they are untied, then the next group will follow and that will continue until the last Jew in Munich is exterminated. Exactly the same procedure will be followed in other cities until Germany is cleansed of the last Jew.

From a letter written by Hitler to Josef Hell in 1922

Source B:

People grow tired of the controversy about Hitler's intentions towards the Jews - whether he always planned their extermination, or decided upon the 'Final solution' at the last moment. They complain that this is biographical niggling, that it diverts attention away from the proper subject of study which is the deed itself.

But the critics are wrong. What is at stake here is the role of Hitler in history, the question of whether there are 'exceptional human beings' who can spend 30 years preparing and then carrying out the genocide of a portion of the species...or whether Hitler, after all, was nudged into the solution-by-murder by particular circumstances.'

Neal Ascherson, The Observer (20 January 1985)

Source C:

It is sometimes supposed even today that Nazi policy towards the Jews had from beginning to end only one objective in view, and that it moved with relentless logic from the first anti-Jewish demonstrations in April 1933 to the 'Final Solution' in the death camps of Poland. The very enormity of the holocaust encouraged men to search for a 'master plan' which could be attributed to Hitler's personal predilections. Closer examination suggests a rather different pattern. It seems much more likely that the pressure of external events, internal power configurations and the influence of powerful individuals were just as important as Hitler's personal inclinations.

William Carr, Hitler, A Study in Personality and Politics (1978)

1 What does Source A tell you about Hitler and the extent of his anti-semitism?

2 What does Source A tell us about Hitler's personality? Can we really hope to establish what sort of person he was?

3 What are the two points of view concerning Hitler's role in the holocaust, outlined by the journalists in Source B?

4 Which of these two viewpoints is endorsed by the historian in Source C?

5 Look again at Source A after you have looked at the three case studies. What conclusion would you now draw concerning the connection between Hitler's personality and the persecution of Jews in Germany?

The boycott of Jewish shops and businesses (April 1933)

Between 1933 and 1938, three key moments marked the deterioration in the position of Jews within German Society:

a) The boycott of Jewish shops and businesses
b) The Nuremberg Laws
c) Reichkristalnacht.

The virulence of Hitler's own anti-semitic beliefs has never been in doubt. On the eve of power he spoke privately of a wave of pogroms which he claimed would 'hit the Jews harder than those described in their biblical past'. These brutal sentiments encouraged the most rabid anti-semites in the party to believe that violent action against the Jews would ensue almost as soon as Hitler became chancellor. They were to be disappointed. Hitler was a highly astute politician and he realised that for most Germans economic recovery was the priority. For the time being, pressing economic issues closed in on Hitler and for the first time in his political career the prospect of disruptive anti-semitic campaigns became an unwelcome distraction. Nevertheless, by the end of March the hard-liners in the party were demanding that Hitler should take action soon. On 28 March the party press demanded an organised boycott of Jewish shops and businesses. It was only then that Hitler somewhat reluctantly gave his consent and asked Julius Streicher, a notoriously violent anti-semite, to set up a central committee in Munich. Within 24 hours the committee had issued the following order:

'Action committees in every local branch and subdivision of the NSDAP organisation are to be formed for putting into effect the planned boycott of Jewish shops, Jewish goods, Jewish doctors and Jewish lawyers. The action committees are responsible for making sure that the boycott affects those who are guilty and not those who are innocent...

The action committees must at once popularise the boycott by means of propaganda and enlightenment.'

It was on Saturday 1 April that the new government launched its first action against the Jews. The boycott began at ten in the morning with stormtroopers standing outside Jewish-owned shops and businesses carrying placards urging 'Germans' not to enter. Swastikas and anti-semitic slogans were daubed across shop windows leading Goebbels to enthuse in his diary about the 'imposing spectacle' that this had created.

Yet it soon became apparent to more objective observers that the campaign, despite the massive level of intimidation, had been a disaster. Many Germans regarded the demand to change the shopping habits of a lifetime as a pointless and inconvenient imposition. Similarly, the prospect of having to change banks simply because the new regime said so carried little appeal.

Finally, many Jewish firms were controlled by foreign creditors or German banks. The boycott simply brought further upheaval to an already fragile economy.

The boycott was abandoned after one day and on 2 April Hess announced a ban on further boycotts of department stores. At a cabinet meeting on 14 July it was agreed that government contracts would not be withheld from Jewish firms. Ironically, Hitler personally authorised loans of government money to Jewish firms rather than letting them face bankruptcy, closure and massive job losses. It was clear that for the time being at least harsh economic realities carried more urgency than ideological prejudices. Therefore the general economic recovery of 1933-35 was bound to worsen the position of the Jews.

The Nuremberg Laws (1935)

On the face of it, Hitler's personal initiative in the production of the notorious anti-semitic legislation known as the Nuremberg Laws was clear-cut. In the middle of the massive party rally in September 1935, without consulting anyone else, he ordered Bernhard Losener - a civil servant in the Ministry of the Interior - to come to Nuremberg and receive his orders. The urgent brief was to draw up a new package of anti-semitic laws in time for Hitler to present them for ratification at a specially-convened Reichstag session on the last day of the party rally on 15 September. Four draft laws were presented to Hitler who, still anxious to present himself as a moderate, opted for the least severe one. The hasty and haphazard manner in which the legislation was being produced is indicated by the fact that the finishing touches to the legislation were drawn up on the back of a menu at 2.00 am on the morning of 15 September. Later that morning Hitler took a pencil to the draft Law for the Protection of German Blood and struck out the moderating clause 'This law is only valid for full Jews'. As usual, Hitler's ability to present himself as a man of moderation while satisfying his gut feelings of anti-semitism was remarkable.

It is important to recognise that many other factors played a part in these developments and Hitler's personal role should be placed in context. For example, there is no doubt that the party rank and file were desperate for Hitler to resume the initiative against the Jews. Secondly, other individuals

Law for the Protection of German Blood and German Honour (extracts)

1. Marriages between Jews and citizens of German or kindred blood are forbidden...
2. Sexual relations outside marriage between Jews and nationals of German or kindred blood are forbidden...
3. Jews are forbidden to display The Reich and national flag or the national colours.

THE ANTI-JEWISH BOYCOTT OF SHOPS IN APRIL 1933. IS IT POSSIBLE TO DISCERN FROM THIS PHOTOGRAPH WHAT THE PUBLIC'S ATTITUDE TOWARDS THIS WAS?

like Goebbels and Wagner were pressing for action. Crucially, Hitler was determined to stave off pressure for a 'Jew free economy' but realised that this would make him vulnerable to criticism; he was therefore eager to present his racial laws as an acceptable and less damaging initiative. Hitler had got what he wanted and boosted his own position with the party faithful.

As the successful rally drew to a close and with the legislation approved by the Reichstag, Hitler lifted the veil on his personal views with these chilling private remarks to some close colleagues. 'Out with them from all the professions and into the ghettos with them! Fence then in somewhere where they can finish as they deserve while the German people look on the way people stare at wild animals.'

Reichkristalnacht (November 1938)

The awful scenario envisaged by Hitler in his virulent comments of 1935 came near to fruition in the winter of 1938 when the position of the Jews deteriorated dramatically. Closer examination of the circumstances does not reveal a picture of a carefully-controlled programme instigated by Hitler. Indeed, in the autumn of 1938 he was completely preoccupied with problems of foreign policy and went to the trouble of reminding the party that further anti-semitic initiative would be unwelcome. However, a series of chance factors came together so that the plight of the Jews worsened in spite of the Fuhrer's instructions.

In the autumn of 1938, Josef Goebbels - party propaganda chief and virulent anti-semite - was desperate to restore his position of favour with the Fuhrer. Hitler had made it clear that he thoroughly disapproved of Goebbels' well-publicised affair with a famous actress. The chance Goebbels was waiting for presented itself when a German diplomat in Paris was murdered by a Jewish youth. Goebbels ensured that the party press gave massive coverage to the 'Jewish outrage' and waited for Hitler's enthusiastic response. In a major speech the next day, Hitler did not even mention the incident.

READ THE POSTER SHOWN IN THIS PHOTOGRAPH CAREFULLY. HOW WAS THE BOYCOTT JUSTIFIED? WAS THE CAMPAIGN SUCCESSFUL?

SYMBOLS OF NAZI STRENGTH AT THE NUREMBERG PARTY RALLY. AT THE 1935 RALLY, THE POSITION OF JEWS DETERIORATED DRAMATICALLY

Goebbels dashed to Munich and urged Hitler to give his seal of approval to a 'spontaneous' reprisal. Hitler told Goebbels that 'the SA should be allowed its last fling' and the awful reprisals began.

In 24 hours of frenzied street violence, 91 Jews were murdered and more than 30,000 arrested and sent to camps. In his monumental study of the Holocaust, Martin Gilbert gives a frightening picture of the scene in Leipzig on the night of 9-10 November 1938. According to the US consul in Leipzig David H. Buffurn: 'The Nazis practised "tactics which approached the ghoulish", uprooting tombstones and violating graves...Having demolished dwellings and hurled most of the effects to the streets, the insatiably sadistic perpetrators threw many of the trembling inmates into a small stream that flows through the Zoological Park, commanding horrified spectators to spit at them, defile them with mud and jeer at their plight."'

Another observer, Dr Arthur Flehinger, 'recalls that all Jewish men in the town were marched through the streets to the synagogue. Once inside, they were confronted by exuberant Nazi officers and SS men. Dr Flehinger himself was ordered to read out passages from *Mein Kampf* to his fellow Jews. "I read the passage...so quietly that the SS men posted behind me repeatedly hit me in the neck...after these readings there was a pause. Those Jews who wanted to relieve themselves were forced to do so against the synagogue walls, not in the toilets, and they were physically abused while doing so."'

Martin Gilbert, *The Holocaust* (1986)

The initiative now passed to Goering who, with his combined responsibilities for the economy and rearmament saw the opportunity to exploit the latent wealth of the Jewish community. On 12 November he issued the following decree.

'All damage which was inflicted on Jewish businesses and dwellings on 9 and 10 November 1938 as a result of the national indignation about the rab-

TALKING POINT

Look critically at the language employed by the Nazis in their anti-semitic propaganda. What does it actually mean? Which terms do you find most shocking?

ble-rousing propaganda of international Jewry against National Socialist Germany must at once be repaired by the Jewish proprietors or Jewish traders...

The hostile attitude of the Jews towards the German people and Reich which does not shrink even from cowardly murders, demands decisive resistance and heavy reparation...The Jews of German nationality are required communally to pay a contribution of RM 1 billion to the German Reich.'

In April 1938 there were still 39,532 Jewish businesses in operation. Twelve months later 14,803 had been liquidated, 5,976 'dejewified', 4,136 were in the process of being 'dejewified' and 7,127 were under investigation. In the wake of *Reichkristalnacht* it was made illegal for Jews to attend German schools and universities, and they were even excluded from cinemas, theatres and swimming pools. Having resisted the campaign for a 'Jew free economy' for so long, Hitler had become an enthusiastic onlooker at the initiatives initially of Goebbels and subsequently Goering.

In conclusion, we will now try to analyse Hitler's personal influence in the Third Reich.

THE WRECKED WINDOWS OF A JEWISH SHOP IN THE FRIEDRICHSTRASSE, BERLIN. LOOK AT THE EXPRESSIONS OF THE PASSERS-BY

11.4 Hitler: master in the Third Reich or weak dictator?

'Master'?

'The point cannot be stressed too strongly, Hitler was master in the Third Reich.'

N. Rich, *Hitler's War Aims* (1980)

'Weak dictator'?

'Unwilling to take decisions, frequently uncertain, exclusively concerned with upholding his personal prestige and personal authority, influenced in the strongest fashion by his current entourage, in some respects a weak dictator.'

H. Mommsen, *National Socialism, Continuity and Change* (1979)

The nature of Hitler's government

'The popular picture of the Third Reich as a monolithic unity with all parts of the well-oiled machine responsive to the Fuhrer's will has long been discredited. A more exact parallel would be with feudal society, where vassals great and small struggled endlessly with each other and with their overlords to establish themselves as the king's chief adviser. The administrative structure formed a complex mosaic of state and party agencies with ill-defined and overlapping jurisdictions...often mutually antagonistic.'

William Carr, *Hitler, A Study in Personality and Politics* (1978)

Who influenced Hitler?

Hitler's private staff

This group included his chauffeur and adjutant.

Old friends

This group included
Eva Braun - mistress
Morell - doctor
Speer - architect

The leading agencies of state

Foreign Office (Neurath)
Economics (Schacht)
Interior (Frick)
Propaganda (Goebbels)
Armed Forces (Blomberg - Army)
(Raeder - Navy)
(Goering - Airforce)

Hitler's personal entourage

This consisted of around 12 individuals, all long-standing party members with easy access to Hitler. They included Goering, Himmler, Hess, Goebbels and Bormann

The major industrial combines

They had financed Hitler's electioneering in 1931-32 and now exerted some influence in foreign and economic policy

ONE OF THE PEOPLE CLOSEST TO HITLER - HIS MISTRESS, EVA BRAUN

How did the Fuhrer spend his time?

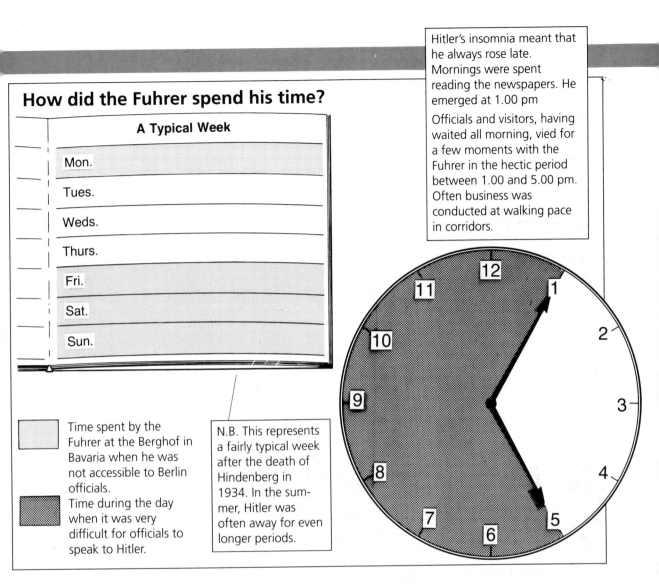

A Typical Week

Mon.	
Tues.	
Weds.	
Thurs.	
Fri.	
Sat.	
Sun.	

Time spent by the Fuhrer at the Berghof in Bavaria when he was not accessible to Berlin officials.

Time during the day when it was very difficult for officials to speak to Hitler.

N.B. This represents a fairly typical week after the death of Hindenberg in 1934. In the summer, Hitler was often away for even longer periods.

Hitler's insomnia meant that he always rose late. Mornings were spent reading the newspapers. He emerged at 1.00 pm

Officials and visitors, having waited all morning, vied for a few moments with the Fuhrer in the hectic period between 1.00 and 5.00 pm. Often business was conducted at walking pace in corridors.

REVIEW

Hitler: master in the Third Reich or weak dictator?

We will now review certain key aspects of Hitler's regime

	Details
The consolidation of power, January–July 1933	
The Reichstag Fire, February 1933	
The Night of the Long Knives	
The 'popularity' of the regime	
The persecution of the Jews	
The style of government	

1 Copy out the chart indicating in each case the extent of personal control exercised by Hitler.

2 What conclusions would you now draw about the nature of Hitler's rule?

12 The Foreign Policy of the Third Reich 1933-39

PREVIEW

Hitler's war?

'The Second World War was Hitler's personal war in many senses. He intended it, he prepared for it, he chose the moment for launching it.'

Hugh Trevor Roper (1953)

'Little can be discovered so long as we go on attributing everything that happened to Hitler.'

A.J.P. Taylor, *The Origins of the Second World War* (1961)

'While Adolf Hitler was a powerful and relentless military commander, the war years saw him as a lax and indecisive political leader who allowed affairs of state to rot. In fact he was probably the weakest *leader* Germany has known this century.'

David Irving, *Hitler's War* (1977)

'Hitler was in some respects a weak dictator.'

Hans Mommsen, *National Socialism: Continuity and Change* (1979)

'The point cannot be stressed too strongly: Hitler was master in the Third Reich.'

Norman Rich, *Hitler's War Aims* (1980)

HITLER IN CONSULTATION WITH GENERALS BLOMBERG AND FRITSCH. DID HITLER CONTROL GERMAN FOREIGN POLICY AND DICTATE THE PACE OF CHANGE TO HIS GENERALS?

Introduction

On the afternoon of Monday 30 April 1945, a handful of Adolf Hitler's most faithful followers entered his underground study in Berlin and saw their Fuhrer for the last time. His body, slumped on a couch, was still warm. Blood oozed from his mouth and from a gunshot wound in the right temple. Next to Hitler was the body of Eva Braun, who had crunched a poison capsule as her part in one of history's most notorious suicide pacts and shortest marriages. The newly-weds were wrapped in gray army blankets and carried into the shell-torn Chancellory garden. A large quantity of gasoline was poured over the couple and ignited. The two corpses were enveloped in a sheet of flame. On 1 May, Hamburg Radio interrupted a performance of Bruckner's Seventh Symphony with a roll of drums and a sombre announcement that Adolf Hitler:

'Fighting to the last breath against Bolshevism, fell for Germany this afternoon in his operational headquarters in the Reich Chancellory.'

The thousand-year Reich dreamt of by Hitler had ended with the charred remains of its creator after only 12 years. Hitler's war was over. How did it begin? More than half a century has elapsed since Germany's invasion of Poland in September 1939 triggered the Second World War. Yet Hitler's foreign policy has remained the most controversial aspect of the Third Reich's history. Historians remain divided on the central issue: to what extent was German foreign policy instigated and controlled by one man - Adolf Hitler?

At first the answer seemed all too obvious. At the Nuremberg Trials (1945-46) of the Nazi war criminals, almost every testimony referred to the hypnotic grip which Hitler had exerted over his followers; to the extent that they had blindly followed him in provoking the Second World War and annihilating the Jewish race in Europe. This was not enough to save them. The Nazi leadership was finally wiped out by a combination of the hangman's noose, sordid suicides and massive prison sentences. Yet the public felt that the real villain of the piece was the man who could now never be brought to trial. In a curious way, Hitler still dominated the proceedings at Nuremberg.

In turn, he has continued to dominate the thoughts of historians of the Third Reich. For many years the verdict that Hitler was solely responsible for the Second World War remained completely unchallenged. Ironically, it was at the Nuremberg Trials that there was just a hint that this outlook was not perfectly valid. With Hitler dead, Hermann Goering was the leading Nazi who remained. At the Nuremberg Trials, Goering seemed to relish being in this position and made no attempt to evade responsibility. On the contrary, he emphasised that he was proud of the key role he had played in foreign affairs:

'I was responsible for the rearmament, the training and the morale of the Luftwaffe. Not so much the Fuhrer as I, personally bear the full and entire responsibility for everything that happened.'

More specifically, Goering claimed that it was he who had engineered the German annexation of Austria in March 1938, 'fulfilling an old, old longing of the German people to become a unified Reich.'

Goering claimed that important military leaders such as General Keitel had exerted little influence on the decision-making process because they 'came between the millstones of stronger personalities'. According to Goering, the attitude of the German General Staff to Hitler was reticent and timid. The Reich Cabinet hardly met after 1937 because 'The Fuhrer did not think much of Cabinet meetings.' Goering's conclusion was that 'at best, only the Fuhrer and I could have conspired.' Most observers were unconvinced by this testimony and attributed it more to personal vanity than to actual fact.

Yet Goering had provided his last clues to the mystery of how the Third Reich was governed. Sentenced to death by the Nuremberg Tribunal for his part in the Nazi War crimes, he chose suicide rather than the hangman's noose. On the evening of 15 October 1946:

'The guard at Goering's door had just glanced through the hatch. Goering who had previously seemed to be sleeping peacefully, was now moaning and twitching. The guard...found Goering lying as if in a convulsion, froth on his lips, right hand flung over the side of the bed and fist tightly clenched...Goering was turning blue...There was a quick rattle in his throat. Then he was dead...In Goering's mouth...there were slivers of glass. Goering had crushed a phial of cyanide.'

In committing suicide Goering had followed Hitler's example for the last time. Who made the decisions when they were both alive?

LEADING NAZIS ON TRIAL AT NUREMBERG. IN THE FRONT ROW ON THE LEFT ARE GOERING, HESS AND RIBBENTROP

RUSSIAN CARTOON ON THE NUREMBERG TRIALS STATES: 'YOU STOOD FOR FASCISM, YOU SAT FOR FASCISM, NOW YOU'LL HANG FOR FASCISM.'

GOERING IN THE DOCK AT NUREMBERG. HOW MUCH INFLUENCE DID HE EXERT ON GERMAN FOREIGN POLICY?

TALKING POINT

Goering's enforced withdrawal from his morphine addiction brought about massive weight loss. Did it also influence his reliability as a source for Third Reich historians?

EXAMINING THE EVIDENCE

The ideological background

Source A

'For who wants to read documents? And what are they to prove? Is evidence needed to show that Hitler was a gangster who broke his word whenever it suited him.'

Sir Lewis Namier (historian)

Hitler disliked putting pen to paper. he wrote few letters, made no marginal notes on official documents and kept no diary. For these reasons his first book, *Mein Kampf*, published in 1925, has assumed considerable significance for those who seek to understand the mind of this enigmatic man. The book was an attempt by Hitler to establish himself as the dominant theorist as well as the best speaker in the party. For the most part it reveals his obsession with questions of race in general and anti-semitism in particular. Hitler linked his anti-semitism - in which he fervently believed - to questions of foreign policy, in which he advocated German expansion to the east. The following extract has received a great deal of attention.

Source B

'We National Socialists must hold unflinchingly to our aim in foreign policy, namely to secure for the German people the land and soil to which they are entitled on this earth...

Much as all of us today recognise the necessity of a reckoning with France, it would remain ineffectual in the long run if it represented the whole of our aim in foreign policy. It can and will achieve meaning only if it offers the rear cover for an enlargement of our people's living space in Europe. For it is not in colonial acquisition that we must see the solution of this problem, but exclusively in the acquisition of a territory for settlement.

And so we National Socialists consciously draw a line beneath the foreign policy tendency of our pre-war period. We stop the endless German movement to the south and west, and turn our gaze towards the land in the east. At long last we break off the colonial and commercial policy of the pre-war period and shift to the soil policy of the future.

If we speak of soil in Europe today, we can primarily have in mind only Russia and her vassal border states.

Adolf Hitler, Mein Kampf, (1925, trans. 1939)

To what extent did Hitler reveal his true intentions in this work? Over the years opinions have been sharply divided.

Source C:

'Was Hitler really just a more violent Mr Micawber sitting in Berlin and waiting for something to turn up: Something which, thanks to historic necessity, he could then turn to advantage? Certainly Hitler himself did not think so. He regarded himself as a thinker, a practical philosopher...And since he published a blueprint of the policy which he carried out, ought we not at least to look at this blueprint?'

H.R. Trevor-Roper in The Origins of the Second World War (ed. E.M. Robertson, 1976)

Source D

'Was Lebensraum Hitler's sole idea or indeed the one which dominated his mind? To judge from *Mein Kampf*, he was obsessed by anti-semitism, which occupies most of the book. Lebensraum gets only seven of the seven hundred pages. Then and thereafter it was thrown in as a final rationalisation, a sort of 'pie in the sky' to justify what Hitler was supposed to be up to. Perhaps the difference between me and the believers in Hitler's constant plan for Lebensraum is over words. By 'plan' I understand something which is prepared and worked out in detail. They seem to take 'plan' as a pious...wish.'

A.J.P. Taylor, *The Origins of the Second World War* (1961)

Source E

'The policy in *Mein Kampf*...has little connection with the actual policy followed by Hitler in the 1930s. It is a character statement, a creed of violence; but it is only a guide book to Hitler's diplomacy in 1933 to 1939 by way of a very long stretch of imagination.'

H.W. Koch, *Hitler and the Origins of the Second World War* (1971)

Hitler viewed the generals with a mixture of contempt, awe and respect. He despised their aristocratic pretensions but he had to be sure of the Army's support. So, when the new Minister of War, General von Blomberg, extended an invitation to the new Chancellor to address local commanders he accepted straight away.

Hitler made it clear that he had maintained his radical outlook in an after dinner speech, behind closed doors.

1 Give a precis of Hitler's intentions regarding foreign policy as set out in the extract from *Mein Kampf*.

'How should political power be used when it has been gained? That is impossible to say yet. Perhaps fighting for new export possibilities, perhaps - and probably better - the conquest of new living space in the east and its ruthless Germanisation.'

Notes on Hitler's speech, 3 February 1933

2 How do the three historians differ in their interpretations of Hitler's book?

3 In which areas do these historians find agreement?

4 *Mein Kampf* was written long before Hitler came to power. Should historians therefore look elsewhere for evidence of his intentions when he was in power?

While some generals were disturbed by the tone of Hitler's speech, most took encouragement from his firm commitment to rearm on a massive scale, re-introduce conscription and restore the military to their old, privileged position. Hitler left the building pleased with his reception and certain that he need not fear opposition from the Army.

Hitler now decided that rearmament was to proceed on the basis of a plan drawn up by the previous chancellor, Schleicher. This so-called immediate programme incorporated two four-year plans; the first designed to provide relief for farmers, the second to reduce unemployment. Where Hitler's programme departed from Schleicher's was in its emphasis on military projects. A typical multi-purpose measure was the *Reichsautobahnen* programme, which employed thousands of young men on the construction of 7,000 kilometres of new roads over six years. Not only did this have a major impact on unemployment, it also made an important contribution to the Nazis' military preparations.

HITLER AND HIS MINISTERS AT THE HOTEL KAISERHOF IN BERLIN (31 JANUARY 1933)

Rearmament

The strict limitations imposed by the Treaty of Versailles on Germany's armed forces were clear for all to see. Germany was allowed a token professional army of 100,000 men but was expressly forbidden to manufacture tanks, military aircraft or submarines. At the start of 1933 the Reichswehr consisted of a mere ten divisions. With Russian help, Germany had carried out a small level of rearmament since 1920 but her military position in 1933 was extremely weak. Germany possessed only about 80 aircraft and 450 trained flying personnel. The pilots who would one day form the German Luftwaffe practised on gliders belonging to the euphemistically-named League of Air Sports. More significantly, the regulations limiting the size of the German Army were flagrantly ignored; it trebled between 1933 and 1935.

Any foreign diplomat could have seen what was going on but the reaction of Britain and France was invariably one of anxiety rather than anger. On 9 March 1935 Goering revealed the existence of a German airforce in an interview with the *Daily Mail*. The news caused so little surprise that Britain and France did not even take the trouble to register a formal protest. One week later Germany announced that it had conscripted a peace-time army of 500,000.

The casual manner in which the Nazis ignored the terms of the Versailles Treaty might have been taken by Britain as a sound indication of Hitler's unreliability. Instead, Germany's rearmament was excused by many as an understandable security measure.

The manner in which the Anglo-German Naval Pact was reached, reflects the rather unconventional manner in which Nazi diplomacy operated. The agreement was drawn up with the British government through the hard bargaining of Joachim von Ribbentrop. In the spring of 1935 he had set up the Dienstelle Ribbentrop, an agency which soon became a rival to the more orthodox German Foreign Office. The successful conclusion of the Naval Pact - the first major agreement between the Nazis and a democracy - was a major coup for Ribbentrop and served to undermine the authority of the conservative old guard in Germany's Foreign Office.

By 1936 the increasingly anarchic structure of Germany's foreign policy

AN OPENING CEREMONY FOR AN AUTOBAHN. THE CONSTRUCTION OF THESE MOTORWAYS HAD A DYNAMIC IMPACT ON THE ECONOMY

administration was complemented by an economy which, though outwardly successful, was becoming dangerously imbalanced. The large-scale rearmament which Hitler desired could not be financed out of the budget. (He had inherited a deficit for 1932 of RM 900 million.) Hitler's appointment of Hjalmar Schacht as president of the Reichsbank, in March 1933, marks a significant turning point in the way armaments were funded.

Schacht's major innovation was the Mefo bill. This acted as a form of short-term credit for up to five years. The idea was that industry would produce armaments for the government on a massive scale but payment would be deferred for five years on the basis of 4 per cent interest. Unfortunately for Schacht, when the time came for the bills to be redeemed his influence with the Fuhrer was clearly on the wane. Hitler combined a marked reluctance to honour his old debts with a strong desire to open some new ones. An acceleration in the pace of rearmament in 1936, masterminded by Goering through a four-year plan, only increased the imbalance in the economy. It became clear by 1937 that Germany was moving towards a serious internal crisis. The sense of urgency which Hitler invariably brought to foreign policy stemmed from his awareness that the so-called Nazi economic miracle of 1933-36 was coming to an end.

By the spring of 1936 however, the process of rearmament had gone far enough for Hitler to try his hand at tampering with the hated Versailles system. Like a murderer in a detective story, he now possessed the motive and the weapon. The world waited to see where he would strike.

Risk! The reoccupation of the Rhineland (March 1936)

In the summer of 1935, French secret agents in Berlin reported back to Paris with some astonishing news. Hitler had instructed his generals to prepare for the military reoccupation of the Rhineland. It would be Germany's most daring foreign policy move so far. The international situation could hardly have been more favourable.

Italy's invasion of Abyssinia (1935) had many short-term repercussions, all of them seemingly favourable to Hitler. The clear failure of the League of Nations to take effective sanctions against the aggressor state delivered a mortal blow to the democracies' chief instrument for keeping the peace.

Despite their ideological affinities, Italy's opposition to *Anschluss* had kept the two dictators apart during the first three years of Hitler's rule. In the winter of 1936, with Italy at last feeling the pinch of economic sanctions, Mussolini informed Berlin that he was not opposed to Austria becoming 'a German satellite'.

Hitler's behaviour over the next crucial month followed a pattern which was to be repeated during subsequent critical stages of foreign policy later in his career. The following pattern can be clearly identified:

(a) Cautious and thorough diplomatic preparation;
(b) Astute and opportunistic exploitation of chances as they arose;
(c) Last-minute doubt and hesitation;
(d) Ruthless action.

In February 1936 Hitler consulted his military advisers about the Rhineland. They urged caution. This did not satisfy Hitler, who argued that: 'Passivity was, in the long run, no policy...Attack in this case...was the better strategy'.

At the eleventh hour Hitler wavered and a postponement was considered but then rejected. The troops moved back into the Rhineland at dawn.

NAZI BANNERS AND GARLANDS DISPLAYED BY NAZI MEMBERS IN SAARBRUCKEN, PRIOR TO THE PLEBISCITE OF JANUARY 1935

Examining the Evidence

The reoccupation of the Rhineland - could Hitler have been stopped?

Source A: The German forces
- 19 battalions of infantry: total strength = 22,000.
- 13 Artillery groups. Many of the soldiers were on bicycles.
- 54 Single-seater planes
- One French report had estimated that the Germans would call upon 265,000 troops in the Rhineland.

Source B: Inside Germany
An American journalist, William Shirer, was in Germany at the time of the reoccupation. The following are extracts from his diary.

March 7 1936: The Reichstag, more tense than I have ever felt it, began promptly at noon...Hitler began with a long harangue about the injustice of the Versailles Treaty and the peacefulness of Germans. Then...'In the interests of the primitive rights of its people to the security of their defence, the German government has re-established, as from today, the absolute and unrestricted sovereignty of the Reich in the de-militarised zone...First we swear to yield to no force whatever in restoration of the honour of our people...Secondly, we pledge that now, more than ever, we shall strive for an understanding between the European peoples...We have no territorial demands to make in Europe...Germany will never break the peace.'

March 8 1936: Hilter has got away with it, France is not marching...No wonder the faces of Hitler and Goering and Blomberg...were all smiles this noon...Oh the stupidity (or is it a paralysis?) of the French. I learned today on absolute authority that the German troops who marched into the de-militarised zone of the Rhineland yesterday had strict orders to beat a hasty retreat if the French army opposed them in any way.

Source C

THE GOOSE-STEP.

"GOOSEY GOOSEY GANDER,
WHITHER DOST THOU WANDER?"
"ONLY THROUGH THE RHINELAND—
PRAY EXCUSE MY BLUNDER!"

Source D: Hitler's view
This was revealed in the memoirs of his interpreter, Paul Schmidt, published in 1951.

'More than once, even during the war, I heard Hitler say: "The 48 hours after the march into the Rhineland were the most nerve-racking of my life." He always added; " If the French had then marched into the Rhineland, we would have had to withdraw with our tails between our legs."'

Source E: Opinion in Britain

'I suppose Jerry can do what he likes in his own back garden.'

Taxi-driver's comment to Anthony Eden (Foreign Secretary) on the morning of 9 March.

1(a) How did Hitler justify the German move into the Rhineland?
(b) What tactics did Hitler employ in his speech to pacify the foreign powers?

2(a) What evidence is contained in these sources to suggest that Hitler had taken a major risk in reoccupying the Rhineland?
(b) What factors appeared to prevent the British from acting on France's behalf?
(c) The Reoccupation of the Rhineland is seen as a major turning point in Hitler's foreign policy. Why do you think this is the case?

The road to expansion (1937)

The successful reoccupation of the Rhineland provided a massive boost to Hitler's own position. Crucially, Germany's western frontier was now heavily fortified, giving Hitler much more freedom to act in the east. The only cloud

TALKING POINT

'Hitler could have been stopped in 1936.' Do you agree?

THE REOCCUPATION OF THE RHINELAND (MARCH 1936). DOES THIS APPEAR TO HAVE BEEN A POPULAR MOVE?

on the horizon at the end of 1937 was the economic situation.

It is against this background of impending financial crisis that the controversial Hossbach conference of 5 November 1937 must be viewed. At the Nuremberg Trials, the meeting which Colonel Hossbach recorded assumed enormous significance. The British prosecuting counsel spoke of 'the plot...divulged at the Hossbach meeting'. An American attorney claimed that 'as early as 5 November 1937 the plan to attack had begun to take definiteness as to time and victim'. It is therefore worth looking at this text in some detail.

Examining the evidence
The Hossbach Memorandum

Source A: The memorandum itself (5 November 1937)
Minutes of the Conference in the Reich Chancellory, Berlin, 5 November, 1937. From 4:15 to 8:30 pm.

Present: The Fuhrer and Chancellor,
Field Marshal von Blomberg, War Minister,
Colonel General Baron von Fritsch, Commander in Chief, Army
Admiral Dr. H.C. Raeder, Commander in Chief, Navy
Colonel General Goering, Commander in Chief, Luftwaffe,
Baron von Neurath, Foreign Minister,
Colonel Hossbach.

The Fuhrer began by stating that the subject of the present conference was of such importance that its discussion would, in other countries, certainly be a matter for a full Cabinet meeting, but he - the Fuhrer - had rejected the idea of making it a subject of discussion before the wider circle of the Reich Cabinet just because of the importance of the matter. His exposition to follow was the fruit of thorough deliberation and the experiences of his four-and-a-half years of power, and he asked, in the interests of a long-term German policy, that his exposition be regarded, in the event of his death, as his last will and testament.

The Fuhrer continued:

The aim of German policy was to make secure and to preserve the racial community and to enlarge it...There remain still to be answered the questions 'when' and 'how'.

Case 1: Period 1943-45
After this date only a change for the worse, from our point of view, could be expected.

The equipment of the army, navy, and Luftwaffe, as well as the formation of the officer corps, was nearly completed. Equipment and armament were modern; in further delay there lay the danger of their obsolescence...

If the Fuhrer was still living, it was his unalterable resolve to solve Germany's problem of space at the latest by 1943-45. The necessity for action before 1943-45 would arise in cases 2 and 3.

Case 2

If internal strife in France should develop into such a domestic crisis as to absorb the French Army completely...then the time for action against the Czechs had come.

Case 3

If France is so embroiled by a war with another state that she cannot 'proceed' against Germany.

Our first objective, in the event of our being embroiled in war, must be to overthrow Czechoslovakia and Austria simultaneously.

The second part of the conference was concerned with concrete questions of armament.

Certified correct.   Colonel (General Staff) Hossbach

---

1 What aims in foreign policy does Hitler describe in this document?

2 Compare these aims with those described earlier in *Mein Kampf*. Do Hitler's aims appear to have changed or have they remained constant?

3 Hitler showed no interest in retaining Hossbach's record of this meeting. Can you draw any conclusions from this?

While few historians would go along with the interpretation offered at Nuremberg, historians remain divided on the significance of the Hossbach meeting. The position of two leading historians is set out below. Which view do you find the more convincing?

Source B: The Taylor thesis

Who first raised the storm and launched the march of events? The accepted answer is clear: it was Hitler. The moment of his doing so is also accepted: it was on 5 November 1937. We have a record of the statements which he made that day. It is called 'the Hossbach memorandum', after the man who made it. This record is supposed to reveal Hitler's plans. Much play was made with it at Nuremberg: perhaps we shall find in it the explanation of the Second World War; or perhaps we shall find only the source of a legend.

Hitler's exposition was in large part day-dreaming, unrelated to what followed in real life. Even if seriously meant, it was not a call to action, at any rate not to the action of a great war.

Why then did Hitler hold this conference? This question was not asked at Nuremberg; it has not been asked by historians...The conference of 5 November 1937 was a curious gathering: only Goering was a Nazi. The others were old-style Conservatives...dismissed from their posts within 3 months. Hitler knew that all except Goering were his opponents; and he did not trust Goering much. Why did he reveal his inmost thoughts to men whom he distrusted and whom he was shortly to discharge? This question has an easy answer: He did not reveal his inmost thoughts. The conference was a manoeuvre in domestic affairs.

...The second part of the conference was concerned with questions of armament. This no doubt was why it had been called.

From A.J.P. Taylor, *The Origins of the Second World War* (1961)

Source C: The Adamthwaite thesis

The document is not a full and accurate record of the 5 November meeting. It is not the original record...but a copy of a copy...moreover, the conference was not called to discuss foreign policy but to decide on priorities in the allocation of armaments between the three armed services. This said, there is no reason why the memorandum should not be accepted as a guide to Hitler's ideas on foreign policy.

The Hossbach Memorandum confirms the continuity of Hitler's thinking: the primacy of force in world politics, conquest of living space in the east, anti-Bolshevism, hostility to France. Hitler's warlike intentions were now explicit.

From Anthony P. Adamthwaite, *The Making of the Second World War* (1977)

---

1 Try to summarise, in point form
(a) Taylor's argument
(b) Adamthwaite's argument

2 On which aspects of the meeting are the sources in agreement?
Do they just agree on matters of fact - such as who was present - or is there also agreement on questions of interpretation - such as why the meeting was held?

3 When the two historians are in agreement, is it then safe to say that their conclusions must be correct? Give reasons.

4 In what ways do the two sources disagree?

5 Now explain which of the arguments you find the more convincing. If you now had to present the opposite case, what arguments would you put forward?

6 What are your own conclusions about the significance of the meeting?

Anschluss with Austria (1938)

Anschluss - the political union of Germany and Austria - was forbidden under article 80 of the Versailles Treaty. However, as an Austrian by birth, Hitler had a personal as well as political commitment to breaking this rule. Indeed, on the very first page of *Mein Kampf*, Hitler declared that Anschluss was 'a task to be furthered with every means'.

Inside Austria there was a flourishing Nazi movement determined to promote Anschluss and disrupt the democratic government . However, Dolfuss - Chancellor of Austria since May 1932 - was determined to stamp out the Nazi movement in his country. Political assemblies and parades were forbidden and, on 19 June 1933, the Nazi party in Austria was declared illegal.

In normal times these measures might have been successful, but in Hitler Dolfuss faced an exceptionally formidable opponent. In retaliation, Hitler announced in May that all German tourists going to Austria would have to pay a 1000 mark fee. The action inflicted a crippling blow on the Austrian tourist industry, a major source of government revenue.

Within months the Austrian Nazis were planning the violent overthrow of the Austrian government. There is every reason to believe that Hitler knew details of these plans and gave the go-ahead to the conspirators. On 25 July 1934 the Nazis seized the Austrian chancellory and murdered Dolfuss.

This putsch was quickly suppressed by Austrian forces and President Miklas called upon Kurt von Schuschnigg to form a new government. Although the German Nazi party denied any knowledge of the assassination plot, the murder of Dolfuss was a damaging blow to Hitler's reputation abroad. It also prompted Mussolini to mobilise his troops, ready to come to Austria's defence if the assassination were followed by an invasion attempt. Hitler was forced to re-think his tactics, and it was clear that a change in Italy's attitude was needed before Germany could act.

The crucial shift in the international situation came with Italy's invasion of Abysinnia in October 1935. Ostracised by the rest of Europe, Mussolini increasingly came to look upon Hitler as his natural ally. In February 1936 Mussolini told the German ambassador to Italy: 'It would now be possible to achieve a fundamental improvement in German-Italian relations and to dispose of the only dispute, namely, the Austrian problem.'

In the winter of 1937, the Austrian chancellor, Kurt von Schuschnigg, came under increasing pressure to find some sort of agreement with Hitler. It was with this in mind that he made his fateful decision to accept an invitation to meet Hitler. On 12 February 1938 Schuschnigg made the short car journey to the Fuhrer's picturesque mountain retreat at Berchtesgaden close to the Austrian border. It was not a meeting which Schuschnigg was likely to forget, and his account is generally regarded by historians as a reliable piece of evidence.

Hitler was waiting on the steps at the Berghof, and invited the Austrian chancellor into his study for a private conversation before lunch. Schuschnigg's polite remarks about the beautiful view from the window were swept aside as Hitler launched into a vitriolic attack on Austrian policy. 'The whole history of Austria is just one uninterrupted act of high treason...And I can tell you here and now, Herr Schuschnigg, that I am absolutely determined to make an end of all this'.

Hitler let Schuschnigg know of his fury that Austria had begun to conduct defence works on the border. 'Listen. You don't really think that you can move a single stone in Austria without my hearing about it the very next day do you? You don't seriously believe that you can stop me or even delay me for half an hour do you?'

Finally, the Austrian chancellor was told that unless he gave his agreement to a package of changes proposed by Hitler, the Germans would have no alternative but to use force. 'Think it over, Herr Schuschnigg, think it over well. I can only wait until this afternoon. If I tell you that, you will do well to take my words literally. I don't believe in bluffing. All my past is proof of that.'

Hitler's demands to Schuschnigg

1. The Austrian Government was to recognise that National Socialism was perfectly compatible with loyalty to Austria.
2. Seyss-Inquart, a known Nazi sympathiser, was to be appointed Minister of the interior with control of the police.
3. An amnesty for all imprisoned Nazis was to be proclaimed within three days.
4. Nazi officials who had been dismissed were to be reinstated in their posts.

Schuschnigg desperately tried to secure changes in the draft but Hitler refused to budge. Eventually Schuschnigg told Hitler that he was willing personally to accept the terms but there was no guarantee that these changes would be ratified by the Austrian government under a free constitution.

Hitler threw open the door ushering Schuschnigg out and shouting for General Keitel, the Chief of the German High Command. Von Papen later described what Hitler was up to: '...Hitler could be heard shouting behind the open door: "Where is General Keitel? Tell him to come here at once." Keitel told us later that when he presented himself and asked for orders, Hitler grinned and said: "There are no orders. I just wanted you here."'

Now Hitler told Schuschnigg that: 'I have decided to change my mind for the first time in my life. But I warn you - this is your very last chance. I have given you three more days before the Agreement goes into effect.'

The agreement seemed to have secured for Hitler the close co-ordination of Austria's foreign policy and economic development with that of Nazi Germany. It was now that the initiative passed briefly into the hands of Schuschnigg. On 9 March he announced his plan to hold a referendum for his fellow countrymen to express their support for 'A free and German, independent and social, Christian and united Austria'.

It was a brave move, but Schuschnigg's stand against Hitler collapsed in the absence of any signs of support, either from within his own Cabinet or from interested parties like Italy and Britain. On 11 March Schuschnigg announced that Austria would give in without a struggle. No plebiscite would be held and Seyss-Inquart would take over as Chancellor.

The next day, German soldiers entered Austria. Signs that the operation was hastily improvised rather than planned were everywhere. Panzer tanks had to refuel at petrol stations along the road to Vienna, and tank drivers had to use tourist maps to plan their route. Only after Hitler himself received a rapturous reception in his home town of Linz, did he turn his initial plan of assimilation into a full-scale invasion. Who was responsible for this?

EXAMINING THE EVIDENCE

Decision-making in Nazi Germany

Source A

It was Goering rather than Hitler who pushed the pace along - probably because of his interest in seizing Austrian economic assets and avoiding the flight of capital which a prolonged crisis would have provoked.

Ian Kershaw, *The Nazi Dictatorship* (1985)

Source B

(i) If other measures prove unsuccessful, I intend to invade Austria with armed forces to prevent further outrages against the pro-German population.

(ii) The behaviour of our troops must give the impression that we do not want to wage war against our Austrian brothers.

If, however, resistance is offered, it must be broken ruthlessly by force of arms.   Extract from Operation Otto: Hitler's Plans for Austria

Source C

Listen carefully. The following telegram should be sent here by Seyss-Inquart. He does not have to send the telegram. He has only to say that he did. You get me? Take the notes.

'The provisional Austrian government, which after the resignation of the Schuschnigg government considers it its task to establish peace and order in Austria, sends to the German government the urgent request to support it in its task and to help it prevent bloodshed. For this purpose, it asks the German government to send German troops as soon as possible.'

Goering's instructions to Keppler, Austrian Nazi Party Director

Source D

On Tuesday 8th March, the first statements reached me about a plan for a plebiscite, Through a truly astounding speech, we were informed of an attack upon the majority of the Austrian people...Herr Schuschnigg sought through an unexampled election fraud to create for himself the moral justification for an open violation of the obligations to which he had agreed.

Speech by Adolf Hitler, 18 March 1938

GERMAN TROOPS MOVE THROUGH THE CROWDED STREETS OF KUFATEIN, THE AUSTRIAN FRONTIER TOWN (MARCH 1938). HOW WOULD YOU DESCRIBE THE REACTION?

Source E

1 What evidence is contained in these sources to support the thesis that the whole operation was hastily improvised?

2 Explain the significance of Source B.

3 Read Source C very carefully. Why did Goering say that the telegram did not have to be sent?

4 Look at Source D. How did Hitler justify his actions in Austria?

5 Anschluss: who was responsible?

	Responsible	Not responsible
(a) Hitler		
(b) Goering		
(c) Schuschnigg		

Use the sources and background information to fill in the table above. Write a clear statement about each figure, affirming or denying their responsibility.

The policy of appeasement (1937-39)

'Neville Chamberlain was in the years 1937-1939, a Prime Minister with a mission. The mission was somehow to arrive at a general settlement of differences with an increasingly agressive Germany. The policy he developed, partly on the precedents of his predecessors and partly anew, was called appeasement. It has since become one of the most controversial policies in the history of international relations.'

William R. Rock, *British Appeasement in the 1930s* (1977)

When Neville Chamberlain succeeded Stanley Baldwin as prime minister in May 1937 he was determined to place Britain's foreign policy on a more positive footing. Chamberlain had served five years (1932-37) as Chancellor of the Exchequer and was acutely aware of the mounting expense of rearmament. When he came face to face with Hitler in September 1938 he told him that armaments were, 'eating up the capital which ought to be employed on building houses, on better food and on improving the health of the people.' For these reasons, Chamberlain regarded the pacification of Hitler as a positive policy with economic, diplomatic and economic virtues.

Unable to accept the new prime minister's policy, Foreign Secretary Anthony Eden resigned on 20 February 1938, to be replaced by Lord Halifax, a man whose ideas were far more sympathetic to those of Chamberlain.

Halifax had hardly taken office when Hitler annexed Austria on 12 March 1938. That evening a press photographer asked for a smile from War Minister Hore-Belisha as he left 10 Downing Street. 'Why should I smile?' he answered. Like many others, the minister feared that having consumed Austria, Germany would now hunger for Czechoslovakia. Chamberlain's sense of personal mission and his desire to appease Hitler had never been greater. He proposed to leave for Germany at once to talk with Hitler. It set in motion a dramatic trilogy - three visits by Chamberlain to Hitler over the course of two weeks - which came to symbolise the cause of appeasement.

On 15 September, the two protagonists came face to face for the first

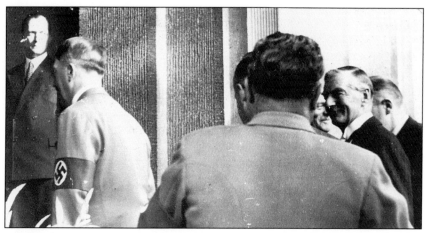

CHAMBERLAIN AND HITLER MEET FOR THE SECOND TIME, AT BAD GODESBERG IN SEPTEMBER 1938.
HITLER IS SHOWN FOLLOWED BY THE BRITISH PREMIER

time at Hitler's Alpine retreat in Berchtesgaden. In a polite but firm manner, Hitler informed the Prime Minister of his insistence upon the transfer of the Sudetenland to Germany. Chamberlain told Hitler that while he was personally prepared to accept this outcome, he would have to return home to secure government approval and then return to Germany to see Hitler again and confirm this. Hitler agreed to this but refused to discuss the broader issue of peace until the Czechoslovak issue was settled.

On 22 September Chamberlain arrived in scenic Godesberg on the Rhine, ready to do business with Hitler and bring the Czech crisis to an end. The Prime Minister was stunned to encounter an aggressive and petulant Fuhrer who now demanded the immediate German military occupation of the Sudetenland. Thirty-six hours of tense bargaining followed but Hitler's only concession was to defer the timetable for military occupation by a few days. With Hitler grumbling that Chamberlain was the first man to whom he had ever made such concessions, the Prime Minister returned to London. He was not the first politician to find a meeting with Hitler both bewildering and depressing.

Broadcasting to the nation on the night of 27 September, the Prime Minister announced his readiness 'to pay even a third visit to Germany' given the 'horrible, fantastic, incredible fact that Britain was preparing for war because of a quarrel in a far-away country between people of whom we know nothing'.

The conference in Munich on 29 September 1938 was virtually a non-event since the details were cut and dried before the leading statesmen arrived. The Agreement, signed on 30 September, provided for: German occupation of the Sudetenland in ten days from 1 October, with an international commission from Britain, France, Germany, Italy and Czechoslovakia to supervise the operation. The emotional sense of relief shown by the general public in Germany and Great Britain disguised the fact that once again Hitler had got his way. The Czechs, their country dismembered and left wide open to subsequent German aggression, were not even invited to the conference and would never trust the Allies again.

Before he left Munich, and acting entirely on his own initiative, Chamberlain sought out Hitler at his apartment. He asked Hitler to sign a short declaration drawn up by Chamberlain himself, which expressed the two statesmen's determination to continue to strive to resolve their differences through consultation and negotiation.

It was the slip of paper bearing this declaration that Chamberlain waved in the air when he arrived back in London. He was given a hero's reception by a relieved public. Chamberlain was convinced that he had pacified Hitler and that war had been avoided. Yet on 21 October, Hitler gave instructions to his armed forces to prepare 'to smash the remainder of the Czech state, should it pursue an anti-German policy'. Chamberlain's hopes of peace did not survive the winter.

AT HESTON AIRPORT, CHAMBERLAIN HOLDS ALOFT THE ANGLO-GERMAN AGREEMENT WHICH SEEMED TO PROMISE A PEACEFUL FUTURE FOR EUROPE

A POSTER DISTRIBUTED THROUGHOUT CZECHOSLOVAKIA IN 1938. ITS DEFIANT CAPTION READ 'WE WILL ALL BECOME SOLDIERS IF NECESSARY'

HITLER, HENDERSON, CHAMBERLAIN AND RIBBENTROP WALK PAST THE GUARD OF HONOUR AT MUNICH AIRPORT AFTER THE FATEFUL CONFERENCE

Examining the Evidence

Did Hitler fool Chamberlain?

Source A: Chamberlain

(i) 'I got the impression that here was a man who could be relied upon when he had given his word.'

> Written shortly after the meeting with Hitler at Berchtesgaden.

(ii) 'Before saying farewell to Herr Hitler I had a few words with him in private, which I do not think are without importance. He repeated to me with great earnestness, that this was the last of his territorial ambitions in Europe...he said again very earnestly, that he wanted to be friends with England.'

> Extract from Chamberlain's statement to the House of Commons, 28 September 1938.

Source B: The role of Lord Halifax

(i) Lord Halifax travelled to Germany in November 1937. He described Hitler as 'very sincere' and 'liked all the Nazi leaders'.

(ii) In September 1938, at the height of the Czechoslovak crisis, Lord Halifax was persuaded to oppose the terms laid down by Hitler at Godesberg and felt very differently to Chamberlain on this issue. His change of mind is described in the diary of an adviser, Sir Alexander Cadogan.

'Saturday 24 September. Meeting of "Inner Cabinet" at 3.30 and P.M. made his report to us. I was completely horrified - he was quite calmly for total surrender. More horrified still to find that Hitler had evidently hypnotised him to a point. Still more horrified to find P.M. has hypnotised H. who capitulates totally. P.M. took nearly an hour to make his report, and there was practically no discussion...I gave H. a note of what I thought.

Sunday 25 September: Cabinet up about 6. H. sent for me. He said "Alec, I'm very angry with you. You gave me a sleepless night. I woke at 1 and never got to sleep again. But I came to the conclusion you were right, and at the Cabinet, when P.M. asked me to lead off, I plumped for refusal of Hitler's terms."'

> From the diaries of Sir Alexander Cadogan, 1938-45

Source C: Hitler

TOP SECRET, MILITARY   Berlin, May 30 1938

It is my unalterable decision to smash Czechoslovakia by military action in the near future.

Source D: An expression of dissent

'The Prime Minister has believed in addressing Herr Hitler through the language of sweet reasonableness. I have believed that he was more open to the language of the mailed fist.'

> Extract from resignation speech of Duff Cooper (member of Chamberlain's Cabinet)

1 What impression of Hitler is given by Chamberlain in Source A? Pick out the key words and phrases to back up your argument. These sources are all in agreement: is it therefore safe to draw any conclusions about whether Hitler fooled Chamberlain?

2 Which other sources contained here could you use to check the impression created in Source A? Do these support or negate the views put forward in Source A?

3 What light does Source C shed on Hitler's character? Why was Hitler so concerned that Chamberlain might come up with some kind of compromise over Czechoslovakia?

4 What were the consequences of the policy of appeasement for:
(a) Hitler
(b) Chamberlain
(c) Czechoslovakia
(d) Stability in Europe?

From Munich to Poland

Apart from its substantial German minority, Czechoslovakia also contained large numbers of Slovaks and smaller numbers of Hungarians and Poles. At the start of 1939 Hitler intensified pressure on the remainder of the Czech state by encouraging these groups to press their separatist claims. At the same time, pressure was exerted on the Poles to force them to agree to the construction of a major road and railway across the Polish corridor, and for the return of Danzig to Germany. On 15 March Hitler took matters into his own hands when German troops occupied the remainder of the Czechoslovak state. A week later the Germans took control of the Lithuanian port of Memel. The position of Poland had now become a matter of grave concern.

In Britain, the public was appalled by Hitler's callous disregard for the promises he had made to Chamberlain at Munich. Amid rumours that German troops were about to march into Poland, Britain finally took a decisive step against Hitler, On 31 March, the British stated that if Poland were the victim of an unprovoked attack, Britain would come to her aid. France quickly gave the Poles a similar guarantee. Despite this collective pressure, on 23 May 1939 Hitler made it clear to senior army commanders that Poland was definitely the next item on his agenda. He told the generals that 'the problem "Poland" cannot be dissociated from the showdown with the West...There is therefore no question of sparing Poland and we are left with the decision: To attack Poland at the first suitable opportunity.'

Hitler made it clear in the same speech that the success of the enterprise would rest on the extent to which it was possible to isolate Poland. On the eve of the meeting Hitler had concluded the Pact of Steel with Mussolini. Despite the grandiose name given to the agreement, Hitler knew that Italy was ill-prepared for a major war. However, Germany's position was dramatically improved on 23 August by the conclusion of a non-aggression pact with Russia. (Details of how this agreement was concluded are contained in Chapter 6.) These developments made Hitler confident that France and Britain would now try to withdraw from their undertakings to Poland, and he went ahead with his plans for invasion at the start of September. However, on 25 August, Britain signed a Treaty of Alliance with Poland and it became clear that France would also stand by her Polish guarantees. Once again, Hitler hesitated at a critical moment in German foreign policy and European history. Yet again, he overcame his doubts and on 1 September German troops marched into Poland. On 3 September Britain and France declared war on Germany. Poland offered brave resistance but this was quickly overcome.

In Britain, the lack of military action led to the use of the term 'phoney war'. However, Hitler was now planning measures against Western Europe which were implemented in 1940. In April Germany invaded Norway and Denmark and the following month, Holland, France and Belgium were attacked. Before the year was out the Battle of Britain, the Blitz and the initial planning stages for the German invasion of Russia had all taken place. In 1941 the European conflict escalated into world war with the German invasion of Russia in June and the Japanese attack on the American navy in Pearl Harbor in December. It was in this context that the holocaust - the murder of approximately six million Jews - took place. Four years later, in a bunker in Berlin, Hitler went about his plans to commit suicide and restated, for the last time, his hatred of the Jews. By then, the quest for peace was once again underway. What problems would this present?

12.1 Hitler's foreign policy (1935-39): the road to war

RIGHT: GERMAN TROOPS, WITH FULL EQUIPMENT, MARCH THROUGH THE CROWD IN SALZBURG, AUSTRIA (MARCH 1938)

BELOW RIGHT: BRITISH PEOPLE POSE FOR A PHOTOGRAPH, HOLDING OPEN A NEWSPAPER CONFIRMING THE OCCUPATION OF POLAND

BELOW: MAP SHOWING NAZI DESTRUCTION OF THE PEACE OF VERSAILLES

BELOW RIGHT: MOBILISATION OF POLISH CAVALRY

1935 Dates of German action

MEMEL
1939

• Berlin

POLAND
1939

SUDETENLAND
1938

RHINELAND
1936

Prague

SAAR
1935

CZECHOSLOVAKIA
1939

Munich

Vienna

AUSTRIA
1938

POLAND INVADED
Several Towns Bombed

Chronology

1935 *13 Jan* Saar Plebiscite favours reabsorption into Germany
16 Mar Germany repudiates disarmament clauses in Treaty of Versailles, restores conscription and announces expansion of the peace-time army to over half a million men.
18 June By Anglo-German Naval Agreement, Germany agrees that her naval tonnage shall not exceed a third of that of the Royal Navy

1936 *7 Mar* German troops reoccupy demilitarised Rhineland, violating Treaty of Versailles
24 Aug Germany adopts two-year compulsory military service.
1 Nov Rome-Berlin Axis proclaimed between Hitler and Mussolini

1937 *Nov* Hossbach Conference

1938 *4 Feb* Hitler appoints Joachim von Ribbentrop to be foreign minster. Fritsch is relieved of his duties as commander-in-chief of the army. Hitler takes over personal control of the armed forces. The War Ministry is abolished and OKW (High Command of the Armed Forces) is set up.
11 Mar German troops enter Austria which is declared part of the Reich.
23 Apr Sudeten Germans demand autonomy
18 Aug Beck resigns as Chief of the Army General Staff
Aug Germany mobilises over Czech crisis
30 Sept Munich Agreement gives Sudetenland to Germany
9-10 Nov Anti-Jewish program, the 'Kristallnacht'.

1939 *15 Mar* German troops occupy remaining part of Czechoslovakia
23 Aug Nazi-Soviet pact signed
1 Sept Germany invades Poland
3 Sept Great Britain and France declare war on Germany
27 Sept Warsaw surrenders, end of Polish Campaign.
8 Oct Western Poland incorporated into the Reich.
12 Oct Austrian Jews deported to east.
23 Nov Polish Jews ordered to wear the Yellow Star of David.

GERMAN TROOPS MOVE INTO POLAND

TALKING POINT
At what point did Hitler's foreign policy become too ambitious?

13 Formation of the UN and Origins of the Cold War 1941-45

Preview

Casualty figures of the Second World War (1939-45)

	Total mobilised	Killed or died of wounds	Civilians killed
Belgium	625,000	8,000	101,000
Britain	5,896,000	265,000	91,000
Bulgaria	450,000	10,000	N.A.
Czechoslovakia	150,000	10,000	490,000
Denmark	25,000	4,000	N.A.
Finland	500,000	79,000	N.A.
France	5,000,000	202,000	108,000
Germany	10,200,000	3,250,000	500,000
Greece	414,000	73,000	400,000
Hungary	350,000	147,000	N.A.
Italy	3,100,000	149,000	783,000
Netherlands	410,000	7,000	242,000
Norway	75,000	2,000	2,000
Poland	1,000,000	64,000	2,000,000
Romania	1,136,000	520,000	N.A.
Soviet Union	22,000,000	7,500,000	6-8,000,000 (approx)
Yugoslavia	3,741,000	410,000	1,275,000

N.A.= not available.

Talking Point

Compare these figures with those for the First World War shown at the start of Chapter 5.

BOMB DAMAGE TO THE GERMAN CITY OF DRESDEN (1945)

Planning for peace: Yalta

The *Sacred Cow* touched down on the icy runway at Saki airport on the Crimean peninsula shortly after noon on 3 February 1945. President Roosevelt waited on board for 20 minutes before a plane carrying Prime Minister Winston Churchill also arrived. Then the crippled President, who had recently celebrated his sixty-third birthday, was lifted out of the plane

MEETING BETWEEN PRESIDENT ROOSEVELT AND CHURCHILL IN NORTH AFRICA

Briefly recall the problems which President Wilson had faced in 1919. Why had his country entered a period of isolationism?

in his wheelchair. A blanket was wrapped around his shoulders and he looked thin and haggard. Churchill's doctor was shocked by the President's appearance. Later he noted in his diary that 'the President appears to be a very sick man. He has all the symptoms of hardening of the arteries of the brain in an advanced stage, so that I give him only a few months to live.'

The strain of leading the US through four years of war had taken its toll on the man who, since 1932, had been elected President a record four times. Like Woodrow Wilson before him, Roosevelt was to discover that the task of leading the American nation *out* of a war was exceptionally difficult. In 1919 Wilson had failed to persuade Congress and the American people to back his vision of a League of Nations fortified by US membership. Wilson's health had collapsed and his country had embarked upon a long period of isolationism. To what extent was Roosevelt able to avoid making the same mistakes as Wilson? How much did American policy change when Roosevelt was replaced by Truman? Why did the 'Grand Alliance' - which gave the Allies victory over Germany and Japan - collapse when peace was achieved? Why was there a Cold War?

Following his long flight, Roosevelt faced a tiring car journey through tortuous mountain terrain which the Red Army had only recently liberated from the Germans. Both leaders were able to appreciate at first hand the scale of the suffering endured by the Russian people during the German invasion. Perhaps this provided a reminder - if one were needed - that in the European conflict the Soviet Union was bearing the major military and civilian burden. It would be many years before the Kremlin revealed the full scale of the destruction: it would eventually emerge that 20 million Russians had been

RUSSIAN CASUALTIES IN THE FIGHTING WITH FINLAND (FEBRUARY 1940)

TALKING POINT

What do we mean by the term Cold War? What are its characteristics?

killed; 25 million people were made homeless; 7 million horses were killed and 20 out of 23 million pigs; 65,000 kilometres of railway tracks had been destroyed.

They now knew that after the latest Red Army offensive the Russian troops were only 40 miles from Berlin. While publicly Roosevelt often referred to his 'gallant Russian ally', privately he was very concerned about the extent of Russian ambition, especially as far as Eastern Europe was concerned. Meanwhile the Allied forces were on the German borders with Belgium, Luxemburg and France. They were about to launch an offensive that would take them into Germany and across the Rhine. What would hap-

GERMAN CIVILIANS ATTEMPT TO CLEAR UP BOMB DAMAGE IN BERLIN (1940)

pen when their armies joined up? How would the vanquished Germans be treated? What form would post-war Germany take?

After more than five hours they reached their destination at the Soviet seaside town of Yalta. They were relieved to find that in contrast to the chilly, snow-covered mountains they had just driven through, the weather in this genteel resort was unseasonably mild. The dying president had travelled more than 6,000 miles at considerable risk to his own health and safety to attend what would be the second and - as it turned out - final meeting of the 'Big Three'. Ironically, although Stalin had readily agreed to a conference he had stubbornly refused to have a meeting outside Russia on grounds of 'ill health'. Roosevelt's advisers considered that this was really an excuse to cover for Stalin's notorious aversion to flying - he flew for the only time in his life to the first meeting of the Big Three at Tehran in 1943 - or perhaps, a crude attempt to establish the upper-hand psychologically.

Roosevelt agreed to make this last, supreme effort because, as Churchill put it, 'the whole shape and structure of post-war Europe clamoured for review'. Important samplings of public opinion conducted in January made it clear to the administration that the American people were very sceptical about the post-war intentions of Britain, and to a greater extent, Russia. Many Americans still felt strongly that their country would be safer if she once again isolated herself from the dangerous power politics of troublesome Europe. Roosevelt was concerned that he would preside over another damaging swing towards American isolationism from Europe's affairs. One of his priorities at the start of 1945 was to bolster public support for American participation in post-war world affairs, and in particular US menbership of a new peacekeeping organisation: the United Nations. Even before the Yalta Conference, a series of meetings had taken place at which the details of a new peacekeeping organisation were hammered out.

THE BIG THREE: STALIN, ROOSEVELT AND CHURCHILL AT THE TEHRAN CONFERENCE

13.1 The Origins of the United Nations

Name	Date and Location	Those Present	Details
The Atlantic Charter	August 1941 'somewhere at sea'	Roosevelt (USA) Churchill (G.B)	The agreement referred to the establishment of 'a wider and more permanent system of general security.'
Declaration by the United Nations	New Year's Day 1942 Washington D.C.	Representatives of 26 nations that were fighting against Germany, Italy and Japan	This declaration used the term 'United Nations' for the first time, but only to describe the countries that had joined together in a 'common struggle against savage and brutal forces.'
The Moscow Declaration	October 1943 The Soviet Union	Representatives from USA, Great Britain, China and the USSR	The declaration recognised the need to establish as soon as possible an international organisation, open to all states, for the maintenance of international peace and security.
The Tehran Conference	December 1943 Iran	Roosevelt (USA) Churchill (GB) Stalin (USSR)	'The big three' were mainly concerned with ending the war in Europe and ensuring that the UN could command the support of all the peoples of the world in pursuing peace. Stalin still had doubts about this.
The Dumbarton Oaks Conference	Late Summer 1944 Washington D.C.	Representatives from USA, GB, USSR. (China were present at the second stage of negotiations)	Detailed plans for the organisation and aims of the UN were drawn up. The Security Council was to act on behalf of all the members of the UN to preserve peace. Its role was to look into major disputes and to act accordingly.
The Yalta Conference	February 1945 A holiday resort in the Crimean Coast in the Soviet Union	'The big three' Roosevelt, Churchill and Stalin	The Russians were warned that they would be isolated in the Security Council, so the Americans introduced the idea of a veto vote. Any permanent member of the Security Council could reject any motion with which they disagreed.
The San Francisco Conference	April–June 1945 The United States	Representatives from the USA, GB, China and USSR. Plus smaller nations	Plans for the UN were presented to the smaller nations. It was agreed that the UN should have as wide a membership as possible. The UN Charter of 111 points was drawn up and signed on 26 June 1945 by all participating members in the Veterans Memorial Hall in San Francisco.

The structure of the United Nations

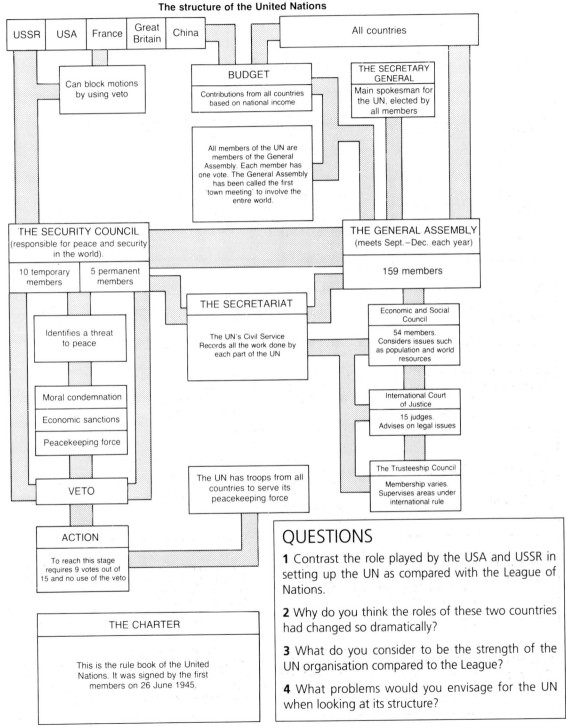

USSR	USA	France	Great Britain	China

All countries

Can block motions by using veto

BUDGET
Contributions from all countries based on national income

THE SECRETARY GENERAL
Main spokesman for the UN, elected by all members

All members of the UN are members of the General Assembly. Each member has one vote. The General Assembly has been called the first 'town meeting' to involve the entire world.

THE SECURITY COUNCIL
(responsible for peace and security in the world).

10 temporary members | 5 permanent members

THE GENERAL ASSEMBLY
(meets Sept.–Dec. each year)

159 members

Identifies a threat to peace

THE SECRETARIAT
The UN's Civil Service. Records all the work done by each part of the UN

Economic and Social Council
54 members. Considers issues such as population and world resources

Moral condemnation

Economic sanctions

Peacekeeping force

International Court of Justice
15 judges. Advises on legal issues

VETO

The UN has troops from all countries to serve its peacekeeping force

The Trusteeship Council
Membership varies. Supervises areas under international rule

ACTION
To reach this stage requires 9 votes out of 15 and no use of the veto

THE CHARTER
This is the rule book of the United Nations. It was signed by the first members on 26 June 1945.

QUESTIONS

1 Contrast the role played by the USA and USSR in setting up the UN as compared with the League of Nations.

2 Why do you think the roles of these two countries had changed so dramatically?

3 What do you consider to be the strength of the UN organisation compared to the League?

4 What problems would you envisage for the UN when looking at its structure?

In his State of the Union Address in January 1945, Roosevelt stated: 'In our disillusionment after the last war we gave up the hope of achieving a better peace because we had not the courage to fulfill our responsiblities in an admittedly imperfect world. We must not let that happen again, or we shall follow the same tragic road again - the road to a third world war.' Roosevelt urged the American people not to allow 'the many specific and immediate problems of adjustment connected with the liberation of Europe to delay the establishment of permanent machinery for the maintenance of peace'. The President knew that when he returned from Yalta he would have to reassure the American people that the Allies were united and Russian ambition was limited. A major split amongst the Allies at this stage might do untold damage to Roosevelt's plans for a new United Nations organisation. More immediately, in response to urgent requests form his chiefs of general staff, he was desperate to secure from Russia a pledge to join in the war against Japan.

On the evening of 3 February, Roosevelt took much needed rest in the quarters provided for him in the Lavadia Palace, the former summer residence of Tsar Nicholas II. The Big Three came together when Stalin arrived from Moscow the following morning, having completed most of his journey by train. He would prove to be a perplexing combination of ally and adversary. A man who often began meetings at ten in the evening and who unnerved seasoned diplomats when he doodled wolves in the margins of state papers, he could also be a cordial if rather drunken host. He was a short, stocky man whose stiff, severely brushed-back hairstyle reminded one senior British diplomat of a porcupine. Now he was with his war-time allies for the last time. For a week, in the palace ballroom, the fate of the post-war world rested in the hands of these three ageing statesmen. How successful was their final meeting?

EXAMINING THE EVIDENCE

The conference at Yalta

TALKING POINT

What were the major weaknesses of the League of Nations which had to be avoided when setting up the United Nations?

THE BIG THREE AT YALTA (1945). COMPARE ROOSEVELT'S APPEARANCE WITH THE PHOTOGRAPH OF HIM AT TEHRAN

Source A: An historian's view of the conference atmosphere

The Big Three gathered for their final wartime conference, between February 4 and 11, under bright, clear skies that seemed a harbinger of victory, not only in the war but also over the unfamiliar terrain of postwar international politics. FDR brought his practicality to bear, in an effort to make firm the foundation of his Grand Design. The pleasant days and nights matched the climate of the conference itself - auguring victory for Roosevelt's foreign policy [and] marking the high tide of allied unity.

D. Yergin, *Shattered Peace* (1977)

Look carefully at Source B. What appears to be Roosevelt's intention in dealing with Stalin?

Source B: Roosevelt's relationship with Stalin

i) F.D.R. hoped Stalin:
'Would again propose a toast to the execution of 50,000 officers of the German army.'

ii) The President wanted to tell Stalin:
'Something indiscreet', that Britain wanted to make France strong again because 'The British were a peculiar people and wished to have their cake and eat it too.'

iii) He confided to Stalin that he and Churchill called him 'Uncle Joe'.

Look carefully at Source C. What tactics were employed by Stalin in dealing with
(a) Churchill?
(b) Roosevelt?

What motives might he have for dealing with them differently?

Source C: Stalin's relationship with Roosevelt - an historian's assessment

Whereas he emphasised Soviet military advances to Churchill in their first conversation, he made much less of these in his first talk with FDR. He apparently believed that an emphasis on points of agreement rather than on Soviet power would make Roosevelt more receptive to Soviet claims. 'In all probability,' historian Diane Shaver Clemens contends, 'Stalin played down his military hand in an effort to avert suspicion, discord, lack of co-operation, and, at worst, military retaliation."

R. Dallek, *Franklin D. Roosevelt and American Foreign Policy, 1932-1945* (1979)

Source D: The issue of Germany

Why would Roosevelt express the view that American troops would be unlikely to remain in Europe for more than two years after the war?

A casual remark by Roosevelt that he doubted that the American people would allow American troops in occupation of Germany for more that two years after the war, and the obvious lack of any carefully thought out American proposal for the future of Germany, may have convinced Stalin that the United States was not greatly concerned about the fate of Central and Eastern Europe. The three powers merely accepted the agreements their officials had reached in 1944 on the military zones the three allies would occupy in Germany after her surrender - although, on Churchill's insistence, France was also given a small zone. A four power military council for Germany was set up in Berlin, which was also to be divided into four Allied military sectors. The future of Germany was left for determination by a future peace conference...

Why was reparation likely to be such a thorny issue at the conference?
Is this an area where you would expect agreement or conflict between America and Russia?

Neither did Stalin appear to have any definite policy about Germany, except to insist that the Russians should extract as much compensation as possible from the German economy for the damage the Nazis had inflicted on the Soviet Union. At Yalta the Soviets put forward figures of from $10 to $20 billion...The conference postponed a decision on this issue by setting up a Reparation Commission to determine how much Germany would pay and in what form she should pay it - although the Soviet claim was accepted as the basis for discussion.

M. Dockrill, *The Cold War 1945-63* (1988)

Extract E: The Polish question

(i) Poland, the emblem of the early Cold War, took up more time than any other issue at the conference. The Allies did agree that the Russian-Polish border should be moved westward, to the Curzon Line and, though not in very precise terms, further consented to compensation for Poland in the form of what had been German territory on its west.

More difficult was the nature of Poland's new government, that is, whether to install the Western-supported London exile government, bitterly anti-Soviet, or the Lublin government, little more than a Soviet puppet.

Britain went to war so 'that Poland should be free and sovereign,' said Churchill. Britain's only interest, he assured the other leaders, was 'one of honour because we drew the sword for Poland against Hitler's brutal attack'...

Stalin, however, was still interested in practical arithmetic. 'For Russia it is not only a question of honour but of security...Not only because we are on Poland's frontier but also because throughout history Poland has always been a corridor for attack on Russia.' Twice in the last thirty years 'our German enemy had passed through this corridor...'

A British diplomat commented, 'Uncle Joe's masterly exposition of the Russian attitude over Poland sounded sincere, and as always was hyper-realistic.'

At last, the Allies agreed to 'recognise' the Lublin government with some men from London and from the Polish underground, but details were left to Molotov and the two Allied ambassadors in Moscow to work out.

D. Yergin, *Shattered Peace* (1977)

(ii) On Poland provision was made at Yalta for the establishment of a new government based on the existing Soviet-backed 'Lublin' government but with the addition of 'democratic leaders from Poland and from Poles abroad.' Free elections were to follow as soon as the military situation would permit. Even before FDR's death on 8 April, 1945 wrangles had developed over observance of the agreement, as the Soviet Union made it clear that it was unprepared either to accord non-Communists any real role or to conduct the kind of elections which would satisfy the West.

R. Crockatt, *The United States and the Cold War 1941-1953* (1989)

(iii) A disagreement over Poland could: 'only lead our people to think that there is a breach between us, which is not the case...Our people at home look with a critical eye on what they consider a disagreement between us...They, in effect, say that if we cannot get a meeting of minds now...how can we get an understanding on even more vital things in the future?'

Letter from President Roosevelt to Stalin at Potsdam, February 1945.

Source F: The United Nations

The Russians, remembering their difficulties in the League of Nations, which culminated in their expulsion, were worried that they would find themselves

To what extent would you agree with Churchill's claim that Britain went to war so 'that Poland should be free and sovereign'.

TALKING POINT

'By granting the use of the veto to each of the Great Powers, the makers of the UN had ensured that it would rarely make a decision.' Discuss.

isolated in a new international organisation controlled by the United States and the United Kingdom through their Allies, clients, dominions and 'Good Neighbors'. The Russians accepted an American compromise, whereby the Great Powers retained a veto in the Security Council, and the Western leaders agreed to support the admission of two or three constituent Soviet republics.   D. Yergin, *Shattered Peace* (1977)

Source G: The American viewpoint
i) *Roosevelt's personal performance at Yalta*
Much had been made of the idea that Roosevelt was a dying man at Yalta who lacked the physical strength and mental alertness to deal effectively with Stalin. Without question, his physical condition had greatly declined by the time of the conference...

[Yet] the men closest to him at Yalta thought the President performed effectively. 'I always found him to be mentally alert and fully capable of dealing with each situation as it developed,' Stettinius said...A review of the agreements reached at Yalta confirms his point. On all the central issues - the United Nations, Germany, Poland, Eastern Europe, and the Far East - Roosevelt largely followed through on earlier plans, and gained most of what he wished: the world body, the division of Germany, the pronouncement on Poland, and the Declaration on Liberated Europe promised to encourage American involvement abroad and possible long-term accommodation with the U.S.S.R.

R. Dallek, *Franklin D. Roosevelt and American Foreign Policy, 1932-1945* (1979)

(ii) *The view of Harry Hopkins, Roosevelt's closest aide*
We really believed in our hearts that this was the dawn of the new day we had all been praying for. The Russians had proved that they could be reasonable and farseeing and there wasn't any doubt in the minds of the President or any of us that we could live with them and get along with them peacefully for as far into the future as any of us could imagine.

(iii) *Roosevelt's viewpoint*
We have wound up the conference - successfully I think...I'm a bit exhausted but really all right.'   Note from F.D.R. to his wife, 12 February 1945

(iv) *Roosevelt's message to Congress*
The President apologised to the House for sitting during his speech. 'I know that you will realise that it makes it a lot easier for me not to have to carry about ten pounds of steel around the bottom of my legs; and also because of the fact that that I have just completed a fourteen-thousand-mile-trip...the question of whether it is entirely fruitful or not lies to a great extent in your hands. For unless you here in the halls of the American Congress - with the support of the American people - concur in the general conclusions reached at Yalta, and give them your active support, the meeting will not have produced lasting results...We shall have to take the responsibility for world collaboration, or we shall have to bear the responsibility for another world conflict!'   1 March 1945

Source H: The Russian performance
i) I think Uncle Joe much the most impressive. The President flapped about and the P.M. boomed, but Joe just sat taking it all in and being rather amused.

When he did chip in, he never used a superfluous word, and spoke very much to the point.

> Alexander Cadogan, Permanent Undersecretary of the British Foreign Office.
> From a letter written to his wife at the end of the conference.

(ii) I have never known the Russians so easy and accommodating. In particular Joe has been extremely good. He is a great man, and shows up impressively against the background of the other two ageing statesmen.

> Alexander Cadogan, letter from the conference.

(iii) I am talking as an old man, that is why I am talking so much, but I want to drink to our alliance, that it should not lose its character of intimacy, its free expression of views. In the history of diplomacy I know of no such close alliance of three Great Powers as this, when allies had the opportunity of so frankly expressing their views...I propose a toast to the frankness of our Three Power Alliance. May it be strong and stable, may we be as frank as possible.

> Stalin's personal toast to Churchill and Roosevelt, quoted in A. de Jonge,
> *Stalin and the Shaping of the Soviet Union* (1986)

Source I: The verdict of an historian

Roosevelt came away from Yalta with a feeling of triumph. Stalin quickly began to shatter the American illusion. He refused to reorganise the Polish government in any significant way, suppressed freedom of speech, assembly, religion, and the press in Poland, and made no move to hold the promised free elections. To a greater or lesser extent the Soviets followed this pattern in the rest of East Europe, making it perfectly clear that now that they held the region they would not give it up. They shut the West out completely. By any standard the Soviet actions were high-handed, their suppressions brutal.
> S. Ambrose, *Rise to Globalism* (1980)

US report on the Yalta conference

Imagining yourself to be an American diplomat, prepare the following briefing:

(a) Summary of the main issues which were discussed
(b) The Soviet stance on the key issues
(c) Successes gained at Yalta by the US team
(d) Aspects of the talks which did not go so well
(e) Recommendations for the future
(f) Summary of US/Soviet relations at this time.

The Atomic Age

The experiment took place while most of the people of New Mexico were still fast asleep. It was 5.29 in the morning on 16 July 1945. Across the state, buildings shook and windows were shattered. Some people got up to investigate and inspect the damage but they could find no obvious explanation for what had happened. Others slept on, oblivious to what had taken place. That was what the scientists had wanted. They had carried out their experiment at Alamogordo Air Force Base in a remote part of the New Mexico

SCIENTISTS MEASURE RADIOACTIVITY AT ALAMOGORDO IN NEW MEXICO AFTER THE EXPLOSION OF THE FIRST ATOMIC BOMB IN 1945

desert. There they had witnessed a spectacle which some of them likened to Armageddon. George Kistiakowsky, a scientist who had worked on the 'Manhattan Project' for some time, described it as 'the nearest thing to doomsday that one could possibly imagine. I am sure that at the end of the world in the last millisecond of the earth's existence - the last man will see what we have just seen.' They had unleashed the awesome power of the atomic bomb for the first time in the history of mankind and its force had shocked them. Through their protective goggles they witnessed an enormous fire ball brighter than several midday suns. At the centre of the explosion - Ground Zero - they estimated that the temperature reached 100 million degrees fahrenheit, three times hotter than the interior of the Sun and ten thousand times the heat on its surface: it was as though man had pre-empted nature's sunrise. This was followed by a mushroom-shaped cloud which extended up to 41,000 feet. Within a mile radius of Ground Zero the plant and animal life which normally thrived in the harsh desert sun simply disappeared. A crater 1,200 feet in diameter had taken its place. The project - often referred to simply as 'S-1' - was declared a complete success. The Manhattan Project had equipped the United States with the most destructive weapon in history. The awesome responsibility of deciding whether to use

PRESIDENT ROOSEVELT'S FUNERAL (APRIL 1945)

this weapon passed into the hands of a president who had only been in office for three months.

On 12 April 1945 the four-time President, Franklin D. Roosevelt, suffered a massive cerebral haemorrhage and died. The presidency automatically passed to the vice-president - a former haberdashery salesman, and senator from Missouri - Harry S. Truman. A senior figure in the Roosevelt administration noted that he 'knows absolutely nothing of world affairs'. During the 82 days in which he had served office as Roosevelt's vice-president he conferred with the President only twice. Indeed one of the most telling criticisms of Roosevelt's presidency is the lack of thought he had given to the grooming and briefing of his successor. Roosevelt had not even seen fit to inform Truman of the Manhattan Project. The sudden death of Roosevelt meant that Truman was given the responsibility of leading the Western world without any preparation or experience in foreign policy. Immediately he was surrounded by issues of the greatest complexity and urgency.

In Europe the war was almost at an end. On 25 April, Russian and American soldiers came together for the first time on the banks of the River Elbe. On 30 April Hitler committed suicide in his Berlin bunker, leaving Admiral Doenitz to surrender on behalf of the German nation on 7 May. With Russian and American troops on German soil, the question of the future resettlement of Germany and the rest of war-torn Europe was of vital importance. The common desire to defeat Hitler and the forces of fascism had served to unite together Russia, Great Britain and America in a powerful wartime alliance. Would it be possible to preserve this alliance now that their common enemy was vanquished? As Stalin himself remarked: 'That tie no longer exists, and we shall have to find a new basis for our close relations in the future.'

The international political system was entering a period of painful transition from a European-led model to a global system, at the same time that Truman was presiding over his own abrupt inheritance. The first months were difficult. In May he told an aide: 'You don't know how difficult the thing has been for me. Everybody around here that should know anything about foreign affairs is out.' On one occasion, Truman told his early morning staff conference 'I'm one American who didn't expect to be President.'

HARRY TRUMAN BECOMES PRESIDENT IN THE WHITE HOUSE (APRIL 1945)

Isolated by his new importance, Truman lamented 'I am the lonesomest man in Washington. I have nothing to do but walk around all by myself.' After a bewildering succession of high-level briefings, Truman remained 'not up on all details' and trying to 'catch the intricacies of our foreign affairs'. One hostile observer - Roosevelt's secretary of commerce, Henry Wallace - anticipated that Truman would be moulded 'like putty' by his new advisers. To whom did the President turn in these first difficult months, and what was the nature of their advice?

Within weeks of Roosevelt's funeral, Truman made it clear that things had changed. On 23 April the Russian foreign secretary, Molotov, came to Washington to meet with the President. It was a blistering encounter which he would never forget. Truman told the dismayed diplomat in 'plain American language' that he was very unhappy with Soviet conduct in Poland and that in future the Russians would be well advised to stick by their agreements. Molotov's face turned ashen and he told Truman, 'I have never been talked to like that in my life'. Truman's blunt advice was to 'Carry out your agreements and you won't get talked to like that.' Those who had urged the President to 'get tough' with the Soviets were delighted by his performance. To others, his actions came to symbolise the fact that the Russians and the Americans were finding it increasingly difficult to find agreement. Within weeks Truman had established a reputation among his staff and advisers for selecting crisp and decisive policy options. Not everyone was impressed: even a sympathetic observer like House Speaker Tom Rayburn noted, 'I am afraid one of these days he will make a decision based on inadequate information.'

Yet surprisingly, by the start of May, Truman was already formulating serious doubts about the 'get tough' policy. He noted that Churchill was in some respects even more difficult to deal with than Stalin, and that in any case: 'Each of them was trying to make me the paw of the cat that pulled the chestnuts out of the fire.' Truman's private recollection of his recent encounter with Molotov reflects the new uncertainty in his thinking towards the Russians. He told his close friend and former ambassador to the Soviet Union, Joe Davis, 'I gave it to him straight. I let him have it. It was the straight one-two to the jaw.' Yet he then sought reassurance asking 'Did I do right?' The opportunity for Truman to find out what dealing with the Russians was really like came when it was decided that he would meet with Stalin and Churchill in July 1945. The Americans had deliberately delayed the timing of the meeting to enable the scientists to complete their atomic experiment. This time the venue was on the outskirts of the war-torn city of Berlin. In the suburb of Potsdam, which had miraculously escaped major damage, Truman came face-to-face with Stalin for the first and last time. Would they be able to find agreement or had the Cold War already set in?

Examining the Evidence

The Conference at Potsdam

Source A

Roosevelt's successor, Harry Truman, introduced a more abrasive style in relations with the Soviet Union, but in substance he sought to continue Roosevelt's preference for dealing independently with Stalin rather than

THE ALLIED LEADERS AT POTSDAM (1945)

tying America to British policy and arousing Stalin's suspicions of a Western allied bloc against him.

R. Crockatt, *The United States and the Cold War 1941-53* (1989)

Source B

Perhaps more important then the agreements and arguments at Potsdam was the attitude Truman took back to the White House. At Potsdam, he later recorded, he learned that the only thing the Russians understood was force. He decided he would no longer 'take chances in a joint set up with the Russians,' since they were impossible to get along with. The immediate

A MORE INFORMAL PHOTOGRAPH TAKEN AT POTSDAM IN 1945

result of this decision was Truman's determination 'that I would not allow the Russians any part in the control of Japan.'

S. Ambrose, Rise to Globalism (1980)

Source C

The Potsdam Conference of the Three Great Powers (17 July-1 August 1945) did not produce any major constructive agreements but it did conceal temporarily the growing divergence between East and West. A reparations agreement was reached designed to reduce Soviet claims to German industrial capital in the three Western zones. Each occupying power was allowed to extract reparations freely from its own zone, while the Soviet Union was authorised to take 10 per cent from the Western zones, and a further 15 per cent provided that this was matched by supplies of food and raw materials from the Soviet zone. The Soviets again promised free elections in Poland. The United States finally accepted the Oder-Western Neisse line as Poland's future Western frontier. Substantive issues such as the long-term future of Germany and peace treaties with Germany's former European allies (eventually signed in 1946) were referred to future meetings of the foreign ministers of the great powers.   M. Dockrill, *The Cold War 1945-63* (1988)

Source D

Admiral Leahy noted that the British and Americans had been forced to accept many unilateral actions taken by the Russians since Yalta, but rejoiced that Truman had 'stood up to Stalin in a manner calculated to warm the heart of every patriotic American' by refusing to be 'bulldozed into any reparations agreement that would repeat the history of World War 1.' Byrnes believed that the concessions that had been made reflected the realities of the situation in Europe, and that this 'horsetrade' on reparations and the Polish boundary question had left the way open for further negotiations at the foreign ministers' level.'

J.L. Gaddis, The United States and the Origins of the Cold War 1941-47 (1972)

Source E

Joseph E. Davies, always a sensitive barometer of anti-Russian sentiment, noted that 'the hostility to Russia is bitter and surprisingly open - considering that we are here to compose and secure peace. There is a constant repetition of the whispered suggestions of how ruthless the Russian Army had been in looting and shipping back vast quantities of everything from cattle to plumbing fixtures...The atmosphere is poisoned with it. The French are carrying everything, including the kitchen stove, out of their territory. Our own soldiers and even some members of this delegation are "liberating" things from this area. But the criticisms are levelled only at the Soviets.'

Davies worried that the President was 'surrounded by forces actively hostile to the Russians, even to the point of destroying the Big Three Unity.'

J.L. Gaddis, The United States and the Origins of the Cold War 1941-1947 (1972)

Source F

But Truman took a more balanced view than many of his advisers. 'Joe,' he explained to Davies, 'I am trying my best to save peace and to follow Roosevelt's plans...Jim Byrnes knows that, too, and is doing all he possibly can.' The President found the tenacious bargaining tactics of the Russians frustrating - 'on a number of occasions I felt like blowing the roof off the place' - but thought he understood and could deal with the Soviet dictator...The Russians were negotiating from weakness rather than strength. Truman believed, because 'a dictatorship is the hardest thing in God's world to hold together.'...Stalin was 'an S.O.B.,' the President told his startled companions on the voyage home, but then he added affably: 'I guess he thinks I'm one too.'

J.L. Gaddis, *The United States and the Origins of the Cold War 1941-1947* (1972)

Source G

Even at Potsdam (16 July-2 August, 1945), the contradictions between American and Soviet concepts of post-war planning had such a forceful effect on the course of the conference that the delegates were on the brink of an open crisis on more than one occasion. A rift discernible even from the outside could only be avoided after two weeks of extensive, but unproductive negotiation by Byrnes putting together a provisional compromise package: with the proviso of a conclusive settlement in the future peace treaty with Germany, the Western powers recognised Polish administration of the former eastern territories of Germany as far as the Oder-Neisse line. In return for this, the Soviet leadership was provisionally to reduce its reparation demands with regard to Germany.

W. Loth, *The Division of the World 1941-1955* (1988)

Source H

It was at the Potsdam Conference of July 1945 that the remaining scales fell from most Allied eyes, as Stalin, feeling further pretence to be unnecessary, abandoned the role of benign Uncle Joe...Newsreel footage of his first meeting with Churchill and Truman is revealing. Stalin strides into the conference room carrying a briefcase, which he tosses onto the table with an unmistakably dominant air, making it clear that he is the strong man of the trio...The finest example of Stalin's sense of humour is the practical joke he played on President Truman. Truman had invited Stalin to dinner. Wishing to provide appropriate entertainment, he inquired who Stalin's favourite composer was. Stalin let it be known that it was Chopin. Truman arranged to have a pianist play mazurkas and polonaises to Stalin as he dined. Stalin, who had never displayed the slightest interest in Chopin, must have enjoyed listening to him during the conference which finally extinguished any flicker of hope for a free Poland. Yet he kept the joke to himself; his sense of humour was never flamboyant.

A. de Jonge, *Stalin and the Shaping of the Soviet Union* (1987)

Source I

For President Truman it was the moment when he first understood what he was up against:
'Anxious as we were to have Russia in the war against Japan the experience ot Potsdam now made me determined that I would not allow the Russians any part in the control of Japan. Our experience with them in Germany, Bulgaria, Rumania, Hungary and Poland was such that I intended to take no chances...Force is the only thing the Russians understand. And while I

was hopeful that Russia might some day be persuaded to work for peace, I knew that the Russians should not be allowed to get into...control of Japan.'

Truman quoted in A. de Jonge, *Stalin and the Shaping of the Soviet Union* (1987)

Source J

As President Truman put it, 'On July 24th I casually mentioned to Stalin that we had a new weapon of special destructive force. The Russian Premier showed no unusual interest. All he said was that he was glad to hear it and hoped we would make good use of it against the Japanese. Although his reaction has been interpreted as a failure to grasp the importance of Truman's communication, it is more likely that Stalin was playing his cards close to his chest.'

A. de Jonge, *Stalin and the Shaping of the Soviet Union* (1987)

Source K

The British decided that Truman was 'quick and businesslike'. This was an image Truman deliberately fostered. 'I took 'em on a ride when I got down to presiding,' Truman wrote his mother after the first meeting. 'It was a nerve-wracking experience but it had to be done.'...Before the conference, three of Truman's top aides had advised him, 'As a well known Missouri horse trader, the American people expect you to bring something home to them.' But the give-and-take, the manipulation, the drawing and redrawing of the maps of the world - all this only made him restless and uncomfortable. He prefered draw poker to the wrangling of high diplomacy. What he wanted most, at the beginning, was a Soviet commitment to enter the war in the Far East; Stalin so promised the first day. 'Could go home now,' Truman said. Frustrated at the slowness of subsequent proceedings, he whispered to Byrnes during a plenary session, 'Why, in ten days, you can decide anything!' He departed Potsdam with the vow, 'I'll never have another.'

D. Yergin, *Shattered Peace* (1977)

Source L

On July 21, Truman learned that the weapon was far more destructive than expected, and that the bomb would be ready for combat use very soon. 'He was a changed man,' Churchill noted of Truman after the July 21 plenary session. 'He told the Russians just where they got on and off and generally bossed the whole meeting.'

D. Yergin, *Shattered Peace* (1977)

Source M

Churchill...was distracted by the upcoming British general election, which, he said, 'hovers over me like a vulture of uncertainty.' The Prime Minister's long, rhetorical digressions annoyed not only Truman and Stalin but even the Englishman's own subordinates. 'He butts in on every occasion and talks the most irrelevant rubbish, and risks giving away our case at every point,' Cadogan wrote. 'Every mention of a topic started Winston off on a wild rampage.'

D. Yergin, *Shattered Peace* (1977)

US report on the Potsdam Conference

Look back at the report which you prepared for the Yalta Conference. This time provide:

(a) Summary of the main issues which were discussed
(b) Comparison of President Truman with President Roosevelt
(c) Any changes in Soviet attitude or behaviour
(d) Successes gained at Potsdam
(e) Aspects of the talks which did not go so well
(f) Summary of US/Soviet relations at this time.

THE CREW OF THE *ENOLA GAY*, THE PLANE WHICH DROPPED THE ATOMIC BOMB ON HIROSHIMA IN 1945

The dropping of the bomb

The news of the readiness of the bomb increased President Truman's impatience to get away from Potsdam and return to the United States, and on 21 July the conference came to a close. As the American delegation prepared to leave, a massive dust storm swept through the wrecked streets of Berlin carrying dust and rubble from the capital and showering the diplomatic enclave in Potsdam. The sky was dark even though it was the middle of a summer's day. On the same afternoon the President wrote out in longhand the order to use the atomic bomb on Japan. The grim scene in Potsdam on that day would be mild in comparison with the destruction which was shortly to be visited upon the Japanese.

At the beginning of August, Colonel F. Tibbets and the crew of his B 29 bomber were ordered to stand by for the order to fly to Japan and deliver the single most powerful blow in the history of human warfare. On 5 August American meteorologists reported that clear skies over the selected target cities would provide ideal conditions for the atomic explosion. The next day the *Enola Gay* set off for Japan with its twelve-man crew and a missile known as 'Little Boy'. As the plane neared Japan, the Captain was told that weather conditions dictated that the target should be Hiroshima. On the intercom Tibbets told the crew, 'It's Hiroshima' and for the first time he gave them

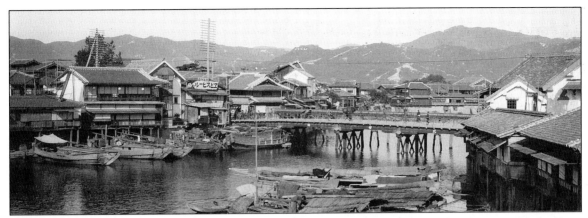

A VIEW OF HIROSHIMA BEFORE
THE ATOMIC EXPLOSION

some idea of just how powerful the new bomb was.

At 8.05 am *Enola Gay* came in towards Hiroshima at just over 9,000 metres. Down below in the city - population 340,000 - the rush hour was in full swing. At 8.15 the crew donned their protective goggles and the bomb bay doors were opened. Upon release, 'Little Boy' wobbled for a moment and then began to pick up speed. The detonating mechanism was triggered when the device was exactly 548 metres above Hiroshima. Down below, the rush hour was about to come to an end. Within a few minutes more than 130,000 people were dead.

A statement from the White House warned the Japanese that if they did not now surrender they might 'expect a rain of ruin from the air, the like of which has never been seen on this earth'. Still the Japanese refused to surrender, and on the morning of 9 August a plutonium bomb - 'Fat Man' - was dropped on Nagasaki. The city centre was destroyed and more than 35,000 people were killed. Finally, on 14 August 1945 the Japanese people heard the voice of their Emperor for the first time. In a radio broadcast to the entire nation, Hirohito told his people that 'the enemy has begun to employ a new and most cruel bomb' and 'we have ordered the acceptance of the provisions of the Joint Declaration of the Powers'. The war in the Pacific was at an end. To some observers, however, the weapon which had ended one war simply presented Mankind with the prospect of a further war: possibly the last that would ever be waged.

EMPEROR HIROHITO.

A DEVASTATED HIROSHIMA AFTER THE EXPLOSION

14 Europe 1945-90

This is the nightmare. At 07.00 hours GMT a fleet of 2000 rockets rise from their silos in the Soviet Union. Four minutes later the ICBMs (Intercontinental ballistic missiles) are out in space, above the earth's atmosphere, heading for the United States. Their paths curve. Suddenly each rocket drops away, leaving a "bus" – a container loaded with warheads and decoys. The bus is left just above the North Pole. At 07.11 the bus unloads.

The warheads, each carrying a computer that directs it to its own target, are released. So are a much larger number of decoys. All are still travelling in space. Three minutes later they aren't. The decoys are doing whatever they will and the warheads are falling through the earth's atmosphere to their targets. We are now in the "terminal phase". The entire process, the first half of a nuclear war, has taken 29 minutes, a breakfast time for man but at 07.29 the beginning of the end for mankind. Or is it?

From an article by Tony Osman in the *Sunday Times* (17 November 1985)

TALKING POINT

Are the arms race and the threat of nuclear war a thing of the past?

CLOUD FORMATION AFTER THE DETONATION OF A HYDROGEN BOMB. PICTURE TAKEN AT A HEIGHT OF APPROXIMATELY 12,000 FEET, 50 MILES FROM THE DETONATION SITE

Technological developments in the arms race

USA	1945	Atomic bomb	1949	USSR
USA	1948	Intercontinental bomber	1955	USSR
USA	1952	Thermonuclear bomb	1953	USR
USSR	1957	Intercontinental ballistic missile (ICBM)	1958	USA
USA	1966	Multiple warhead	1968	USSR
USSR	1968	Anti-ballistic missile	1972	USA
USA	1982	Long-range cruise missile	1984	USSR
USA	1983	Neutron bomb	?	USSR
USA	1986	Strategic defence initiative (research)	?	USSR

Estimates of nuclear weapons held by the superpowers in 1985

An historical perspective on the Cold War.

In the autumn of 1949, American scientists picked up a message which was literally carried on the wind. On 3 September a B 29 aircraft on a routine reconnaissance mission picked up a radiation count that was slightly higher than normal. High radioactive readings continued over the next seven days. The Americans drew an alarming conclusion from this: it appeared that at some time in the last days of August (it was later thought to be the 29th), the Russians had tested an atomic device of their own. The awful possibility of a nuclear exchange between the two superpowers has dominated world politics ever since. At the core of this possibility has been the poor state of relations between the USA and the Soviet Union.

The historian Michael Dockrill provides the following definition of this period:

'The Cold War has been defined as a state of extreme tension between the superpowers, stopping short of all-out war but characterised by mutual hostility and involvement in covert warfare and war by proxy as a means of upholding the interests of one against the other. The Cold War remained "cold" because the development of nuclear weapons had made resort to war a suicidal enterprise: both sides would be totally destroyed by such an eventuality. The struggle between the two sides has accordingly been carried out by indirect means, very often at considerable risk, and the resulting tensions have ensured that both sides have maintained a high and continuous state of readiness for war. The massive expenditures by both sides on research and development of nuclear arsenals and delivery vehicles has led to a spiralling arms race which could, in turn, as a result of miscalculation by one side or the other, have led to a holocaust.'

Historians have discerned three key stages in the historiography of the Cold War.

Stage 1: The orthodox view

This developed among the Western historians in the late 1940s and early 1950s. The view developed that the Soviet Union bore primary responsibility for the outbreak and the continuation of the Cold War. The Soviet State was seen as cold, malevolent and expansionist. This evil, Communist regime – led by the harsh ruler, Stalin, and not content with the establishment of totalitarian rule amongst its own people – was regarded as intent on spreading the gospel of Communism as far as possible. The wartime co-operation shown by Stalin and the sacrifice made by the Soviet people tended to be forgotten. Instead, the regime was presented as a threatening, antagonistic force, and anti-Communist sentiment reached widespread and at times hysterical proportions in the US.

Stage 2: The revisionist view

The revisionist view represented a major shift in the historiography of the Cold War. This school of historians – mainly American – took the view that the United States had initiated and sustained the Cold War. They claimed that America had misunderstood, and over-reacted to, Soviet actions. They said that the Soviets were motivated not by expansionist aims but by priorities of defence and security. This view was sustained by the contemporary situation which saw America stepping up its ill-fated intervention in Vietnam.

TALKING POINT

Which country would you say was responsible for the Cold War?

Stage 3: The post-revisionist view

American historians who formulated the post-revisionist view based their research on the archives which were newly available under the *Freedom of Information Act*. For the first time a view emerged which did not seek to ascribe blame to one party. The more sophisticated notion that the Cold War was the product of mutual suspicion and over-reaction now emerged. In addition, for the first time American historians also called into question the accepted orthodoxy that Stalin had ruled Russia single-handedly.

Stage 4: The Cold War as history

In his study of *The United States and the Cold War*, Richard Crockatt indicates how the historical view of the Cold War is constantly shifting entity:

After a generation and more of intensive research, historians are no nearer agreement on the causes of the Cold War than they are on other subjects of major importance. To the familiar problem of all historical inquiry – the susceptibility of evidence to multiple interpretations – must be added the decisive fact that the Cold War is a going concern. Total detachment in these circumstances is a sheer impossibility...Americans as a whole have been less inclined to echo recent Soviet views that in the era of "glasnost" the Cold War is over. Nevertheless, for most American historians, if not for the officials in the administration, the beginnings of the Cold War are by now in a real sense "history".

In examining the two long evidence sections which now follow, consider which of the above views of the Cold War you feel to be most appropriate.

Examining the Evidence

The Cold War (1945–60)

Source A

At Potsdam we were faced with an accomplished fact and were by circumstances almost forced to agree to Russian occupation of Eastern Poland and the occupation of that part of Germany east of the Oder River by Poland. It was high-handed outrage.

At the time we were anxious for Russian entry into the Japanese War. Of course we found later that we didn't need Russia there and that the Russians have been a headache to us ever since...

Unless Russia is faced with an iron fist and strong language another war is in the making. Only one language do they understand – 'How many divisions have you?'...

I'm tired babying the Soviets.

> Extract from a letter sent to Secretary of State Byrnes by President Truman, 5 January 1946

Source B

A shadow has fallen upon the scenes so lately lighted by the Allied victory. Nobody knows what Soviet Russia and its Communist international organisation intends to do in the immediate future, or what are the limits, if any, to their expansive...tendencies...

TALKING POINT

Refer back to Truman's conduct as detailed in Chapter 13.

Do you find the tone of the Presidential letter in keeping with his view of the Soviets, or does this letter represent a deterioration in relations?

TALKING POINT

Why do you think Churchill's speech is regarded as a landmark in the history of the Cold War?

From Stettin, in the Baltic, to Trieste, in the Adriatic, an iron curtain has descended across the continent. Behind that line lie all the capitals of the ancient states of Central and Eastern Europe – Warsaw, Berlin, Prague, Vienna, Budapest, Belgrade, Bucharest and Sofia. All these famous cities, and the populations around them, lie in the Soviet sphere, and all are subject to a very high and increasing measure of control from Moscow...The Communist parties, which were very small in all these Eastern States of Europe, have been raised to pre-eminence and power far beyond their numbers, and are seeking everywhere to obtain totalitarian control. Police governments are prevailing in nearly every case...

From a speech by Winston Churchill at Fulton, Missouri, USA, 5 March 1946

WINSTON CHURCHILL DELIVERING HIS SPEECH AT FULTON, MISSOURI (MARCH 1946)

Source C: The Marshall Plan

(i) Marshall and his advisers feared that unless generous American aid to Europe was provided soon, the deterioration in the economic life of Western Europe would lead to a severe slump which would have dire effects on the American economy. An economic crisis of such magnitude might encourage the peoples of Western Europe to turn to communism and the Soviet Union for their salvation – the communist parties in France and Italy had already attracted considerable electoral support and communists occupied ministerial posts in their coalition governments.

In a speech at Harvard University on 5 June 1947 Marshall called for a determined United States effort to promote the economic revival of Europe and thus ensure the continued prosperity of the American economy...An additional invitation was extended to the Soviet Union and the Central and East European states, although the State Department hoped that it would be refused. In view of the growing hostility in the United States towards the Soviet Union it was not likely that Congress would have approved the vast sums the shattered Soviet economy required, or indeed would have passed the programme at all if it had been linked to massive aid to the Soviet Union.

'PEEP UNDER THE IRON CURTAIN'

What was the Marshall Plan? Why did Russia not avail itself of the help which might have been forthcoming from the US?

Molotov and a team of 89 Soviet economic experts turned up at the preliminary conference of the European powers in Paris on 26 June 1947, called to draw up Marshall Plan requirements, in order to discover the terms on which the United States' aid to the Soviet Union might be available. However, he soon abandoned the meeting, refusing to supply the economic data on which Washington insisted before credits could be extended.

The episode does suggest, however, that Stalin – who had assured a visiting American politician in April 1947 that he was still willing to do business with the United States – had not finally determined on a breach with the United States at this time. Yet he could not afford to open the Soviet Union to the prying eyes of Marshall Aid planners.

The Western European powers drew up their Marshall Plan requirements, and after complicated negotiations they were accepted by the United States. In 1948 Truman was able to persuade Congress to provide the necessary funds under the *European Recovery Act*, a task assisted by a complete communist take-over of power in Czechoslovakia in February 1948, which further fuelled anti-Soviet feelings in Congress.

Michael Dockrill, *The Cold War 1945–1963*

(ii) It is logical that the United States should do whatever it is able to do to assist in the return of normal economic health in the world, without which there can be no political stability and no assured peace. Our policy is directed not against any country or doctrine but against hunger, poverty, desperation, and chaos. Its purpose should be the revival of a working economy in the world so as to permit the emergence of political and social conditions in which free institutions can exist...

Secretary of State, George C. Marshall – at Harvard University on 5 June 1947

A RURAL FAMILY IN FRANCE BENEFIT FROM AMERICAN ECONOMIC AID

WHAT IS THIS CARTOON TRYING TO CONVEY?

NEIGHBOURS: "COME ON SAM! IT'S UP TO US AGAIN."

Source D: The Formation of the North Atlantic Treaty Organisation (1949)

The Parties to this Treaty reaffirm their faith in the purposes and principles of the Charter of the United Nations and their desire to live in peace with all peoples and all Governments.

They are determined to safeguard the freedom, common heritage and civilisation of their peoples, founded on the principles of democracy, individual liberty and the rule of law.

They seek to promote stability and well-being in the North Atlantic area.

They are resolved to unite their efforts for collective defence and for the preservation of peace and security.

They therefore agree to this North Atlantic Treaty:

Article 1:

The Parties undertake, as set forth in the Charter of the United Nations, to settle any international dispute in which they may be involved by peaceful means in such a manner that international peace and security and justice are not endangered...

Article 3:

In order more effectively to achieve the objectives of this Treaty, the Parties, separately and jointly, by means of continuous and effective self-help and mutual aid, will maintain and develop their individual and collective capacity to resist armed attack.

Article 5:

The Parties agree that an armed attack against one or more of them in Europe or North America shall be considered an attack against them all...

Extract from the Preamble to the North Atlantic Treaty, signed in April 1949 and implemented in August 1949

SIGNING THE NORTH ATLANTIC DEFENCE TREATY IN 1949

SENATOR McCARTHY AT THE
COMMITTEE OF UN-AMERICAN
ACTIVITIES

Consider Source E
carefully. How did
domestic events influence
the nature of the Cold
War?

Source E: Domestic Pressures on US foreign Policy (1950)

(i) And ladies and gentlemen, while I cannot take the time to name all the men in the State Department who have been named as active members of the Communist Party and members of a spy ring, I have here in my hand a list of 205 – a list of names that were known to the Secretary of State as being members of the Communist Party and who nevertheless are still working and shaping policy in the State Department.

> Extract from speech at Wheeling, Missouri, by Joe McCarthy
> (9 February 1950)

(ii) 'McCarthyism, is America with its sleeves rolled up.'

> Chairman of the House Committee on Un-American Activities

Source F: The Korean War (1950–53)

The Truman administration showed little hesitation in revising its assumptions about involvement in a land war in Asia. Within a few days of the North Korean attack on 25 June, 1950 it had committed ground troops to the defence of South Korea, pushed a resolution through the UN labelling North Korea as the aggressor, and interposed the 7th Fleet between Formosa and the mainland to prevent an attack by the People's Republic of China. Militarily the course of the war fluctuated wildly in the first few months. The initial push by the North Koreans took them deep into the South by the middle of September and left only a corner of the peninsula beyond their reach. General MacArthur, seconded from his post as occupation commander in Japan, responded with an outflanking amphibious attack at Inchon, a port half way up the west coast, and within a month had retaken Seoul and driven the North Koreans back to the line dividing North and South Korea at the 38th parallel. MacArthur's military success raised the question of America's political aims in Korea – to reestablish the *status quo* or to revise it by reunifying Korea?

PRISONERS BROUGHT IN BY JEEP TRAILER IN NORTH KOREA

...The initial UN resolution on the Korean War envisaged only the restoration of the 38th parallel but the success of MacArthur's northward drive held out the inviting prospect of reunification by force of arms. Containment, it appeared, was giving way to 'roll-back' as Truman endorsed military operations north of the 38th parallel and gained UN approval for it. Ignoring China's warnings that they would intervene if the Americans continued north, MacArthur pushed deep into the North, reaching the North Korean border with China at the Yalu river at the end of October. As promised, the Chinese entered the war and by the end of the year had forced the UN forces into a headlong retreat down the peninsula to a point south of the 38th parallel.

Truman's response was a combination of strident verbal aggression against China – including a hint that the United States reserved the option of using the atomic bomb – and a strategic retreat to the initial goal of restoring the 38th parallel...The British Prime Minister, Attlee, rushed to Washington in early December to express his anxiety about the direction of American policy...

In practice, however, Truman was as concerned as Attlee to avoid war with China...A serious obstacle in the way of this policy was General MacArthur, whose bellicose pronouncements and evident desire to extend the war into China became a serious embarrassment to Truman...By April 1951, with MacArthur now back at the 38th parallel, eager to cross it once again into the North, and demanding unconditional surrender from the Chinese, Truman ordered his recall. Containment was re-established as the reigning orthodoxy...

MacArthur returned to the United States as a conquering hero denied his booty, to be fêted by Congress and public opinion...As the front stabilised around the 38th parallel, military stalemate ensued, though at enormous cost in casualties. It was two years before negotiations, continually stalled over the issue of the return of prisoners of war, brought a conclusion to the conflict...The geostrategic and ideological assumptions which had led to the original formulation of containment in Europe were now firmly adopted in Asia. These included the 'domino theory' – that a loss of one country to communism would set up a chain reaction in its neighbours – and the belief that by whatever devious route all manifestations of communism were to be traced to the activities of the Kremlin.

From Richard Crockatt, *The United States and the Cold War 1941–1953* (1989)

Source G: The impact of the Korean War

The United Nations suffered 142,000 casualties in the war to save South Korea from communist domination. The Koreans themselves lost at least a million people. United States losses in three years were only narrowly outstripped by those suffered in Vietnam over more than ten years later...Since 1945, only the Cuban missile crisis had created a greater risk of nuclear war between East and West...in Korea the American military displayed a far greater private enthusiasm for using atomic weapons against the Chinese than the Western world perceived...Korea remains the only conflict since 1945 in which the armies of two great powers – for surely China's size confers that title – have met on the battlefield.

Max Hastings, *The Korean War* (1987)

Summarise the events of the Korean War. Explain why the war is seen as such a significant landmark in the Cold War.

What evidence is there that atomic weapons were almost used in the Korean War?

Source H: The Formation of the Warsaw Pact (1955)

The Contracting Parties, reaffirming their desire for the establishment of a system of European collective security based on the participation of all European states irrespective of their social and political systems, which would make it possible to unite their efforts in safeguarding the peace of Europe...

Article 111: The Contracting Parties shall consult with one another on all important international issues affecting their common interests guided by the desire to strengthen international peace and security.

They shall immediately consult with one another whenever, in the opinion of any one of them, a threat of armed attack on one or more of the parties to the Treaty has arisen, in order to ensure joint defence and the maintenance of peace and security.

Extract from the text of the Warsaw Pact Treaty, signed in May 1955

Source I: The Suez Crisis (1956)

SIGNING THE DECLARATION OF THE WARSAW TREATY (1956)

Although Dulles had broken with Truman's policy of support for Israel and was trying to improve relations with the Arabs, he was either unable or unwilling to match Communist aid programs for the area. In late 1955 he had a 'conniption fit' when he learned that the Egyptians had negotiated an arms deal with the Czechs. Dulles' initial response was to offer the Egyptian leader, Colonel Gamal Abdel Nasser, American aid for the Aswan Dam, a gigantic project designed to harness the power of the lower Nile. Technical experts then studied the project and pronounced it feasible. By February 1956 Nasser was ready to conclude the deal...

Then on July 19, 1956, at the moment the Egyptian Foreign Minister was arriving in Washington to discuss the project, Dulles announced that America was withdrawing its support from the Aswan Dam. Nasser's immediate response was to seize the Suez Canal, which restored his loss of prestige at a stroke and gave him $25 million annual profit from the canal operation. Now it was the British and French who were furious. They were dependent on the canal for oil, they were certain that the Arabs did not have the skills to run the canal properly, they feared that Nasser would close it to their ships, and their self-esteem had suffered a serious blow. Long complicated negotiations ensued. They got nowhere...The Middle East contained 64 percent of the world's then-known oil reserves...The Suez remained necessary

SCENE FROM THE SUEZ CRISIS (1956)

to move the oil. Dulles began a complex series of negotiations designed to help Nasser run the canal without the British or the French. The Europeans thereupon decided to take matters into their own hands. In conjunction with Israel, the British and the French began plans for an invasion of Egypt. They did not inform the United States...

At the decisive moment, however, just as it seemed that the European balance of power was about to be drastically altered, the Israeli Army struck Egypt. In a matter of hours it nearly destroyed Nasser's army and took most of the Sinai Peninsula. Britain and France then issued an ultimatum, arranged in advance with the Israelis, warning the Jews and the Egyptians to stay away from the Suez Canal. When Nasser rejected the note, the Europeans began bombing Egyptian military targets and prepared to move troops into Suez, on the pretext of keeping the Israelis and Arabs apart...

In Egypt, meanwhile, the British and the French had bungled. They blew their cover story almost immediately. Their advance was so rapid that they could not pretend that their invasion was one by a disinterested third party designed to keep the Israelis and Egyptians apart. Ike was upset at their use of nineteenth-century colonial tactics; he was livid at their failure to inform him of their intentions. The Americans backed a resolution in the UN General Assembly urging a truce, then imposed an oil embargo on Britain and France, the first use of oil as a political weapon in international diplomacy. Khrushchev, meanwhile, rattled his rockets, warning the British and the French on 5 November to withdraw before he destroyed them. Although they were only hours away from taking the Suez Canal, the Anglo-French governments agreed to a ceasefire and pullback.

Stephen E. Ambrose, *Rise to Globalism* (1980)

Source J: De-Stalinisation and the Soviet Invasion of Hungary

At the 20th Party Congress in February 1956 Khrushchev shocked the party by denouncing Stalin for his crimes, confessing that there could be several roads to communism, and indicating that Stalinist restrictions would be loosened. Two months later the Russians dissolved the Cominform...Ferment

Summarise the events of the Suez Crisis. Is it possible to attribute responsibility for the crisis to any individual country or would you attribute collective responsibility?

immediately swept through East Europe. Riots in Poland forced Khrushchev to disband the old Stalinist Politburo in Warsaw and allow Wladyslaw Gomulka, an independent Communist, to take power (October 20, 1956). Poland remained Communist and a member of the Warsaw Pact, but it won substantial independence and set an example for the other satellites.

The excitement spread to Hungary, before the war the most Fascist of the East European states and the one where Stalin's imposition of Communism had been most alien. On October 23 Hungarian students took to the streets to demand that the Stalinist puppets be replaced with Imre Nagy. Workers joined the students and the riot spread. Khrushchev agreed to give power to Nagy, but that was no longer enough. The Hungarians demanded the removal of the Red Army from Hungary and the creation of an anti-Communist political party. By October 28 the Russians had given in and begun to withdraw their tanks from around Budapest...

How would the events of 1956 in Hungary have been interpreted

(a) In Russia?
(b) In America?

On October 31, the day after the bombing of Egypt began and less than a week before the U.S. Presidential elections, Nagy announced that Hungary was withdrawing from the Warsaw Pact. The Russians, hoping that events in Egypt and the American Presidential campaign would paralyze the United States, and unwilling in any event to let the Warsaw Pact disintegrate, decided to move. Russian tanks crushed the Hungarian rebels, who fought back with Molotov cocktails. Bitter street fighting left seven thousand Russians and thirty thousand Hungarians dead. Radio pleas from Hungary made the tragedy even more painful: 'Any news about help? Quickly, quickly, quickly!' And the last, desperate cry, on a teletype message to the Associated Press: 'Help!–Help!–Help!–SOS!–SOS!–SOS! They just brought us a rumour that the American troops will be here within one or two hours...We are well and fighting.' There never would be any American troops. Eisenhower did not even consider giving military support to the Hungarians and he would not have done so even had there been no concurrent Middle Eastern crisis. Under no conceivable circumstances would he risk World War III for East Europe. Liberation was a sham; it had always been a sham. All Hungary did was to expose it to the world. However deep Eisenhower's hatred of Communism, his fear of nuclear war was deeper.

Explain why America was so reluctant to become involved in the Hungarian crisis?

Stephen E. Ambrose, *Rise to Globalism* (1980)

RUSSIAN TANKS MOVE INTO BUDAPEST, HUNGARY (1956)

Source K: The Russian Stance (1958)

Is it not time for us to draw appropriate conclusions from the fact that the key items of the Potsdam Agreement concerning the maintenance of peace in Europe, and consequently, throughout the world, have been violated, and that certain forces continue to nurture German militarism, prompting it in the direction in which it was pushed before the Second World War, that is, against the East?

Extract from speech by Khrushchev, 10 November 1953

Source L: The U2 Incident (May 1960)

Just as the superpowers appeared to be moving toward a comprehensive test ban, an event occurred with fatal impact on the agreement. On May 7 Khrushchev announced that six days earlier the Soviet Union had shot down an American U–2 aircraft deep inside Soviet territory. The aircraft's pilot, Francis Gary Powers, survived the crash and was being held in Soviet captivity. The incident seemed to confirm Eisenhower's earlier prediction that 'some day one of these machines [the U–2] is going to be caught, and we're going to have a storm'. Khrushchev, at first, tried to give the President a face-saving way out of the administration's embarrassment. He stated that he was prepared to accept that Eisenhower knew nothing about the U–2's mission, but he also wanted the President's assurance that similar flights would not be repeated. Eisenhower, however, refused to evade responsibility for the incident. To do so, he believed, would be an admission on his part that he was not fully aware of his nation's military activities, especially one as sensitive as the U–2 flights over Soviet territory. Turned down by the President, Khrushchev then demanded an apology. Eisenhower angrily refused...Khrushchev responded by angrily denouncing the President and by cancelling the invitation he had extended to him to visit the Soviet Union.

Ronald E. Powaski, March to Armageddon (1987)

What does the U2 incident reveal to you about the nature of the Cold War?

THE AMERICAN U–2 PILOT, FRANCIS GARY POWERS, BEING CHARGED WITH ESPIONAGE IN MOSCOW

Produce a chronology of the events described in this evidence section:

(a) Include brief details on each of the major events

(b) Indicate what appeared to be the motivation of the superpowers in each case

(c) Explain whether their objectives were achieved

(d) Explain what the contribution of these events was to the continuation of the Cold War

(e) Which interpretation of the Cold War would you subscribe to at this stage: orthodox; revisionist; post-revisionist?

By 1960 the people of the world had become used to the division of the world into two armed camps. However, the prospect of a nuclear holocaust seemed – to the public at least – an unthinkable scenario. However, events in Cuba in the early 1960s were to bring the world to the brink of oblivion. As both countries recovered from their close encounter, the US found itself involved in a war which was to traumatise the nation. The Cold War, it seemed, was never-ending.

EXAMINING THE EVIDENCE

The Cold War (1961–75)

Source A: Cuba (1961–63)

Why was the Bay of Pigs expedition launched in 1961?

Why did America object so strongly to the positioning of nuclear missiles on Cuban soil?

(i) By the time Eisenhower left office, official Washington was convinced that Cuba had become an intolerable affront, a communist state, a Russian satellite in the heart of the American sphere of influence. An expeditionary force of Cuban exiles had been prepared for dispatch against it. Kennedy ordered the enterprise to go ahead. It met total, humiliating disaster at the Bay of Pigs on the Cuban coast on 17 April 1961. This defeat enraged American public opinion and encouraged Khrushchev's adventurism: eighteen months later he secretly began to install nuclear missiles on Cuban soil, an operation which, if successful, would bring the heartland of the United States into danger. Thanks to the CIA Washington discovered this threat in time, and Kennedy ordered a blockade of Cuba. For a moment the world held its breath; but then the Soviet ships which were carrying the missiles sheered away rather than challenge the blockade.

Hugh Brogan, *Longman History of the United States of America* (1985)

TALKING POINT

Cuba: the worst moment in the Cold War? Would you agree, or can you suggest an alternative?

(ii) The characteristics of these new missile sites indicate two distinct types of installations. Several of them include medium range ballistic missiles, capable of carrying a nuclear warhead for a distance of more than 1,000 nautical miles. Each of these missiles, in short, is capable of striking Washington D.C....or any other city in the southeastern part of the United States...To halt this offensive buildup, a strict quarantine on all offensive military equipment under shipment to Cuba is being initiated. All ships of any kind bound for Cuba from whatever nation or port will, if found to contain cargoes of offensive weapons, be turned back...

President John F. Kennedy, radio and television broadcast (22 October 1962)

(iii) Your rockets are stationed in Turkey. You are worried over Cuba. You say that it worries you because it lies at a distance of ninety miles

How convincing do you find President Kennedy's speech? What risks did it contain?

across the sea from the shores of the United States. However, Turkey lies next to us.

Nikita Khrushchev, extract from letter to President Kennedy (26 October 1962)

(iv) The Soviet Government has consistently striven, and is striving, to strengthen the United Nations...We therefore accept your proposal, and have ordered the masters of Soviet vessels bound for Cuba but not yet within the area of the American warships' piratical activities to stay out of the interception area, as you recommend.

Nikita Khrushchev, letter to U Thant, Secretary General of the United Nations (26 October 1962)

As a member of the American public, do you think you would have found Khrushchev's answer to Kennedy convincing?

Source B: The Prague Spring and the subsequent Soviet invasion of Czechoslovakia (1968)

(i) The Soviet decision to invade Czechoslovakia on 21 August 1968 was slow in coming and was only taken as a last resort...The crisis had been brewing since the spring and one explanation for Soviet slowness to make up their minds would be that the situation was novel for everyone...What were the limits beyond which a socialist state could not go without ceasing to be socialist?...the Czechoslovakians reiterated time and again their loyalty to the Pact. They just did not accept that the Soviets had the right to define socialism on their own...The Czechoslovaks were idealistic, they were convinced that they were contributing to the creative development of socialism. Socialism with a human face was an expression of faith in its future...Censorship was effectively abolished and plans to re-examine the sentences passed on political undesirables after 1948 forced those who felt threatened into active opposition to the 'Prague Spring'...

The Czechoslovak tragedy can be seen as a failure to communicate. Had the Soviets spelled out clearly the limits beyond which the Czechoslovaks

Summarise in your own words what the Czechs meant by the Prague Spring

What reasons can you give to explain why the Soviet Union decided to take such firm action

RUSSIAN INVASION OF CZECHOSLOVAKIA (AUGUST 1968)

A YOUNG CZECH CARRIES A BLOODY NATIONAL FLAG AS A DEMONSTRATION AGAINST THE INVASION

could not go then it is likely that the whole episode would never have occurred. It was the slow Soviet response to the developing situation, compounded by poor intelligence reporting from the Soviet embassy in Prague, that exacerbated the situation on the road they were taking. The Soviets were reluctant invaders ...

Over 400,000 troops, overwhelmingly Soviet, occupied the country quickly leaving seventy-two Czechoslovaks dead. The Romanians refused to join the march on Prague and let it be known that they would fight if offered similar 'fraternal help' by Moscow. As an earnest of their intent Romanian border guards destroyed a Soviet tank. President Tito, who had visited Dubcek shortly before the invasion, also had his people behind him.

The Czechoslovak episode gave rise to the Brezhnev Doctrine: the socialist commonwealth was duty bound to intervene whenever socialism was under threat in a member country. This was not new, but is as old as the October Revolution. However, it changed the mood of optimism in Czechoslovakia to one of despair and turned a country which had been pro-Soviet into one resentful of the Soviet connection. It soured relations with the outside world, halted any political or economic reforms in Eastern Europe and slowed down economic reform in the USSR.

Martin McCauley, *The Soviet Union Since 1917* (1981)

Source C: Vietnam

(i) *The Domino Theory:* By early 1950, America policymakers had firmly embraced what would become known as the 'domino theory', the belief that the fall of Indochina would bring about in rapid succession the collapse of the other nations of southeast Asia.

George C. Herring, *America's Longest War, The United States and Vietnam, 1950–1975* (1979)

(ii) *America's stake in Vietnam*: The fundamental tenets of this nation's foreign policy depend in considerable measure upon a strong and free Vietnamese nation. Vietnam represents the cornerstone of the Free World in Southeast Asia, the keystone in the arch, the finger in the dike.

Senator John F. Kennedy (1 August 1956)

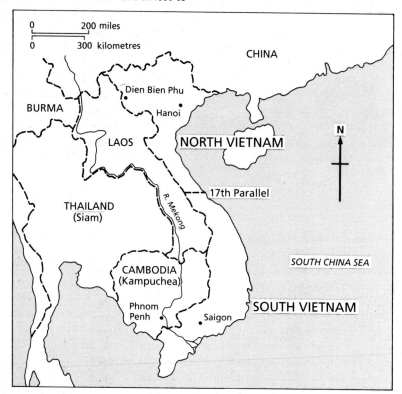

Explain in your own words what was meant by the 'Domino Theory'

(iv) *Assessment of the role of Kennedy in the Vietnam War:* Kennedy and most of his advisers accepted, without critical analysis, the assumption that a non-Communist Vietnam was vital to America's global interests, and their rhetoric in fact strengthened the hold of that assumption.

> George C. Herring, *America's Longest War, the United States and Vietnam, 1950–1975* (1979)

(v) *The role of President Johnson:* Johnson and his advisers...found compelling reasons to hold the line in Vietnam...Secretary of State Rusk hotly retorted that if the United States did not protect Vietnam 'our guarantees with regard to Berlin would lose their credibility.' It was all 'part of the same struggle.' A firm stand in Vietnam would discourage any Soviet tendencies toward adventurism and encourage the trend towards détente.

> George C. Herring, *America's Longest War, the United States and Vietnam, 1950–1975* (1979)

What do Rusk's comments tell you about America's perceptions of the Soviet Union?

What does the comment of the journalist reported in Source C (vi) suggest about perceptions of the Vietnam War in American circles?

(vi) *Escalation*: While visiting the aircraft carrier *Ranger* off the coast of Vietnam in 1965, Robert Shaplen overheard a fellow journalist remark: 'They just ought to show this ship to the Vietcong – that would make them give up.' From Lyndon Johnson in the White House to the G.I. in the field, the United States went to war in 1965 in much this frame of mind. The President had staked everything on the casual assumption that the enemy could be quickly brought to bay by the application of American military might...

Within two years, the optimism of 1965 had given way to deep and painful frustration. By 1967, the United States had nearly a half million combat troops in Vietnam. It had dropped more than $2 billion per month on the war.

George C. Herring, *America's Longest War, the United States and Vietnam, 1950–1975* (1979)

(vii) A FRIGHTENED VIETNAMESE FAMILY HUDDLED TOGETHER, WITH AMERICAN TROOPS IN THE BACKGROUND.

(viii) *Criticism of American policy:* Most liberals agreed that Vietnam was of no more than marginal significance to the United States and that the huge American investment there was diverting attention from more urgent problems at home and abroad, damaging America's relations with its allies, and inhibiting the development of a more constructive relationship with the Soviet Union. The liberal critique quickly broadened into an indictment of American 'globalism'. by attempting to impose its will on a chaotic world, Fulbright argued, the United States had fallen victim to the 'arrogance of power' and was flirting with disaster.

George C. Herring, *America's Longest War, the United States and Vietnam, 1950–1975* (1979)

(ix) SOUTH VIETNAMESE HELICOPTERS PICK UP MARINES DURING AN OPERATION (1971)

(x) *The role of President Nixon:* 'If, when the chips are down, the world's most powerful nation...acts like a pitiful, helpless giant, the forces of totalitarianism and anarchy will threaten the free nations and free institutions throughout the world.'

Extract from speech by President Nixon (30 April 1970)

Explain what Senator Fulbright meant by the term 'the arrogance of power'

(xi) 'The bastards have never been bombed like they're going to be bombed this time'.

Richard Nixon, transcript (29 June 1972) *New York Times* (30 June 1974)

(xii) *Collapse:* When North Vietnam mounted a major offensive in the spring of 1975, South Vietnam collapsed with stunning rapidity, dramatically ending the thirty-year war and leaving the United States, on the eve of its third century, frustrated and bewildered.

George C. Herring, *America's Longest War, the United States and Vietnam,*
1950–1975 (1979)

(xiii) THE VIETNAM WAR MEMORIAL, WASHINGTON DC

Which view of the Cold War would you now take having read both sections of evidence.

(a) Orthodox?
(b) Revisionist?
(c) Post-Revisionist

Give reasons for your answer and explain why you have rejected the other two viewpoints.

Nowhere has seemed to symbolise the conflict of the Cold War more than the divided city of Berlin. Read the following Focus 14.1 on the fate of Germany's capital.

1989: The Year of Revolution

We will now examine the context in which this great upheaval took place: the revolutions of 1989. What was the nature of the changes which took place in Eastern Europe in the greatest period of upheaval since the Second World War? Read Focus 14.2.

How was it possible for the reforms and revolutions in Eastern Europe in general, and Berlin in particular, to take place without the armed intervention of the Soviet Union? Many observers have attributed this to the role of the Soviet leader, Mikhail Gorbachev. Read Focus 14.3 for a study of Gorbachev.

FOCUS

14.1 The fate of Berlin - symbol of the Cold War

30 April 1945
Hitler commits suicide in Berlin.

1945
Berlin to be treated as a separate entity within the Reich, governed jointly by the four powers.

1948
East-West tension reaches a peak in a dispute over Berlin.

24 June 1948
The Soviets counter currency reform in Western zones by imposing a blockade. The blockade seeks to cut off all land and sea routes to West Berlin.

1948-49
The Allies mount an 11-month airlift during which the city's population of 2 million is sustained solely by plane.

12 May 1949
The Soviets lift the blockade on Berlin.

1953
Shortly after the death of Stalin a popular uprising against Soviet rule takes place in Berlin. The uprising is quickly crushed by use of force.

1955
The Federal Republic becomes a sovereign state but the Allies retain special rights in Berlin.

1949 to June 1961
2.6m refugees flee from East to West Germany.

July to August 1965
45,000 people cross from East to West.

ERECTING THE NEW WALL AT THE BRANDENBURG GATE IN BERLIN (NOVEMBER 1961)

Nikita Khrushchev (7 August 1961)
'The conclusion of a peace treaty with Germany would make it possible to normalize the situation in West Berlin...Should West Berlin be made a free city, that would not affect either the interests or the prestige of any State.

We proposed that it should be stipulated in the peace treaty that the free city of West Berlin be granted freedom of communications with the outside world. We agree to the establishment of effective guarantees for the independent development and security of the free city of West Berlin, but not on the basis of the maintenance of the military occupation.'

Building the Berlin Wall (August 1961)
13th The border between East and West Berlin and between West Berlin and the surrounding East Germany territory was closed leaving open only 13 crossing points.
14th The Brandenburg Gate was closed on a 'temporary' basis.
17th Communist workers put up a 6-foot high concrete barrier across the Potsdamer Platz and at other key points.
22nd Crossing points now down to six, and a 100-metre wide 'no man's land' declared. The Wall now surrounded all of West Berlin.

President Kennedy in Berlin (June 1963)
'Two thousand years ago the proudest boast in the world was Civis Romanus sum. Today, in the world of freedom, the proudest boast is Ich bin ein Berliner. There are many people in the world who do not understand what is the great issue between the free world and Communism. Let them come to Berlin. And there are some who say in Europe and elsewhere that we can work with the Communists. Let them come to Berlin.'

Year	Moved west at no personal risk	'Border obstacle breakers' who escaped at great risk
1978	3385	461
1979	1768	463
1980	2552	424
1981	2559	298
1982	2282	283
1983	2259	228
1984	3459	192
1985	3324	160
1986	4456	210
1987	5964	288
1988	9115	590

THE VISIT OF PRESIDENT KENNEDY TO BERLIN (JUNE 1963)

The Mayor of West Berlin

'This is the day that we have been waiting for for so long. The border will no longer keep us apart. It is a day of happiness for Berlin.'

Walter Momper (9 November 1989)

The Soviet reaction (10 November 1989)

'This is a symbolic event, a wise decision in my view, because it destroys all the stereotypes about the Iron Curtain...Politically it is not the time now to talk about reunification. The two Germanys belong to different military blocs.'

Gennady Gerasimov, Foreign Ministry Spokesman

Journalist's comment (10 November 1989)

'For most west Europeans now alive, the world has always ended at the East German border and the wall; beyond lay darkness...The opening of the frontiers declares that the world has no edge any more. Europe is becoming once more round and whole...When the Berlin Wall was built in 1961, the East Germans claimed that by sealing the Berlin border they had saved the peace. Then as now, the outrush of people to the West was threatening to bring about the collapse of the East German state, but in an utterly different world. It was the world of Nikita Khrushchev and that collapse would have brought the two super powers into violent collision.'

Neal Ascherson, The *Independent* newspaper

THE WALL COMES DOWN 1989

The US reaction

'Were we surprised by the speed of it? You bet your life...(The) most momentous event in East-West relations since the end of the war...a good development.'

Secretary of State James Baker (10 November 1989)

SLOGAN ON THE WALL (11 NOVEMBER 1989)
'DIE MAVERIST WEG!' - 'THE WALL IS DOWN!'

14.2 1989 - the year of revolution

East Germany

The crisis began with the mass movement of people out of East Germany via Hungary and Czechoslovakia. This was followed by enormous demonstrations in October which led to the total collapse of the hard-line regime. The Wall was breached at the end of 1989 and free elections promised for 1990.

Poland

In Poland, 1989 was the year in which the banned organisation Solidarity made its comeback. By the autumn, Solidarity had emerged from its period of repression and now provided the country's first non-Communist leader for 40 years.

BELOW: ABOUT 300,000 PEOPLE TAKING PART IN ANTI-GOVERNMENT DEMONSTRATIONS IN LEIPZIG, EAST GERMANY

Czechoslovakia

Another hard-line regime once again toppled in the wake of 'people power'. Initially the police had used violence against demonstrators but a further wave of huge demonstrations led to the downfall of the regime. Vaclav Havel emerged as the country's new president and free elections were promised for the future.

RIGHT: EAST BERLINERS MEET WEST BERLINERS THROUGH A NEW GAP IN THE BERLIN WALL (NOVEMBER 1989)

INSET: HUMAN RIGHTS RALLY IN PRAGUE (DECEMBER 1989)

Romania

After a long, bleak spell under the iron grip of Nicolae Ceausescu, the regime suddenly plunged into crisis when thousands were massacred in Timisoara. Retribution was taken by the people of Bucharest in December.

RIGHT: IN ROMANIA A TANK DRIVER PUTS ROSES IN THE BARREL OF A MACHINE GUN ON 26 DECEMBER 1989, CELEBRATING THE DEATH OF PRESIDENT CEAUSESCU

Hungary

In contrast to the other revolutions, the momentum of reform in Hungary came from the government itself, thanks chiefly to the efforts of Imre Pozsgay. Once again, free elections were promised for 1990.

Bulgaria

In Bulgaria the transition was relatively peaceful. Mass demonstrations in November prompted the resignation of Tudor Zhivkov, who had ruled Bulgaria since 1954. Once again, the people won the promise of free elections in 1990.

FOCUS

14.3 Biographical study: Mikhail Gorbachev

From peasantry to Politburo (1931-84)

1931-49 Born in 1931 in the village of Privolnoye in Stravropol province. His peasant grandfather supported Stalin's collectivisation drive and was a founder chairman of the first collective farm in the village. His father, Sergei, fought in the war and later became a Communist party official. Mikhail began work on the farm at the age of 13. His family had strong party connections and at an early age he joined too.

1950-56 Studied law at Moscow University and met his future wife Raisa. Returned to Stravropol after graduation.

1957-78 Worked as party official in Stravropol and came under the influence of Kulakov, the local party leader and Central Committee Secretary with responsibility for agriculture. After Kulakov's death in 1978 Gorbachev succeeded him and hence became a member of the Central Committee.

1980-84 Joined Politburo in 1980 at age of 49, serving under Brezhnev and Andropov and as number two under Chernenko. December 1984: made tremendous impression on the West when he visited London. Seemed to be a totally different Soviet politician: appeared confident, relaxed, dynamic and intelligent.

The first five years in power (1985-90)

1985 According to the long standing foreign minister, Gromyko, Gorbachev's ability was displayed during the last few weeks of Chernenko's illness when he led Politburo meetings 'brilliantly'. Gromyko said that Gorbachev's mind was 'sharp and deep ...anyone who has even met him only once, will confirm that'. On the day after Chernenko's death, at a hastily convened Politburo meeting Gorbachev was 'unanimously' elected as party leader. At the age of 54 he was by far the youngest of the four party leaders who had served in the past 30 months. After a succession of sick old men, Russia had been liberated by a man who was prepared to relinquish personal control of the people in exchange for freedom and prosperity. Key opponents were quickly removed. An anti-alcohol drive and a purge of corrupt officials followed. The first Soviet leader to talk to the people since 1917 soon discovered that economic collapse was imminent. It was with this, rather than political reform in mind, that *perestroika* (restructuring) was launched. The programme of *perestroika*, the policy of *glasnost* (publicity/openness), and his performance at the Geneva Summit in November 1985 confirmed that Gorbachev was a radically new leader.

1986 Dissident scientist Andrei Sakharov was released from exile, followed by many other political prisoners.

1987 For the first time Gorbachev openly referred to the 'victims of Stalin'.

1988 History examinations in school were suspended pending a review of textbooks. Bukharin was officially rehabilitated. A major speech in June condemned Russia's ossified system of government' and announced far-reaching proposals for 'self government for the people by the people'. However the 'new economic mechanism' led by Abalkin was clearly failing to provide a better standard of living.

1989 Problems mounted for Gorbachev. Nationalist uprisings, strikes, economic stagnation and outspoken criticism led to Gorbachev threatening to resign. Meanwhile, reform continued with a visit to the Vatican, sweeping trade agreements with the West and – crucially – free elections.

Keynote speech at the opening of the Soviet Communist Party Conference (28 June 1988)

Extracts from the speech

'Comrade delegates, the basic question facing us...is how to further the revolutionary restructuring launched in our country on the initiative and under the leadership of the Party and make it irreversible...that calls for radical solutions and vigorous and imaginative action...representation of working people in the top echelon of government should be extended considerably. ... All these deputies, elected for a five-year term, would comprise a new representative supreme government body – the Congress of the USSR People's Deputies... The Economy is gradually gaining pace...(but) for how long more are we to revolve within the vicious circle of outdated notions and formulas, such as production for the sake of production, and the plan for the sake of the right plan?...Perestroika has brought the question of people's political rights into sharp focus...We have no right to permit perestroika to founder...'

Press reaction

'What Mikhail Gorbachev set out in the enormous vastness of the Kremlin's Palace of Congresses yesterday was nothing less than a vision of a new socialism for a new millennium, in which not a shred of the evil authoritarianism of Stalin, nor of the slothful incompetence of Brezhnev remains.'

Robert Cornwell, The *Independent*
(29 June 1988)

Speech to the General Assembly of the United Nations (7 December 1988)

Extracts from the speech

'We have come here to show our respect for the United Nations, which increasingly has been manifesting its ability to act as a unique international centre in the service of peace and security...It is obvious...that the use or threat of force can no longer and must no longer be an instrument of foreign policy. This applies above all, to nuclear arms...All of us, and primarily the stronger of us, must exercise self-restraint and totally rule out any outward-oriented use of force...We are witness to the emergence of a new historic reality, a turning away from the principle of super-armament to the principle of reasonable defence sufficiency.'

SOVIET LEADER MIKHAIL GORBACHEV MEETS THE PEOPLE IN KIEV (FEBRUARY 1989)

Press reaction

'In a speech without precedent from a Soviet leader, Mikhail Gorbachev yesterday announced plans to cut his country's armed forces by 500,000 men or 10 per cent, and proposed a global mechanism for the conversion of military plants to peaceful civilian purposes...Gorbachev's historic speech to the General Assembly...is not only arguably the most comprehensive vision of international relations ever heard from the rostrum of the United Nations. It is also a statement of the Soviet Union's determination to rejoin a world from which it has largely severed itself for the past 70 years.'

The *Independent* (8 December 1988)

TALKING POINT

In the West, many people regard Gorbachev as a hero. In much of Eastern Europe and the Soviet Union he is deeply distrusted. Why should this be?

We shall conclude our examinations of the 'Year of Revolution' with an examination in detail of one revolution: the violent overthrow of the Romanian dictator, Nicolae Ceausescu. How does a modern-day revolution compare with those of the past?

Examining the Evidence

Anatomy of a revolution (December 1989)

Source A: The nature of President Ceausescu's regime

Nicolae Ceausescu's brutal tyranny, his megalomaniac architectural fantasies, his vast apparatus of naked power, ruthlessly exercised through a privileged secret police, remind us of Hitler and Stalin; but his open nepotism, his 'socialism in one family', as it has been called, and the insatiable greed of that disreputable clan, gave his rule a distinct character: personal, shameless and unique...

On 20 November we watched him on the television screen as he assured his docile Congress that 'scientific socialism' was in no danger. For six hours he deluged them with his oratory, and 67 times, in the course of it, they rose to their feet to applaud him. 'Romanian Communism!' 'Ceausescu heroism!' they chanted – a nauseating spectacle of servility – and they re-elected him, as so often before, as their absolute master. No wonder he assumed that he was safe.

Hugh Trevor Roper, *The Christmas Revolution* (1989)

Source B: The uprising begins – massacre in Timisoara (18 December)

Dozens, perhaps even hundreds, of people are reported to have been killed in the western Romanian town of Timisoara, after security forces intervened on Sunday with tanks and firearms against demonstrators who were attempting to protect an ethnic Hungarian Protestant pastor, Laszlo Tokes, from eviction by the authorities. Witnesses spoke of gunfire from helicopters, of smashed windows and cars overturned in the streets.

The *Independent* newspaper (Tuesday 19 December 1989)

RESIDENTS OF TIMISOARA VIEW BODIES TAKEN FROM A MASS GRAVE, VICTIMS OF THE UNREST THERE IN DECEMBER 1989

Source C ETHNIC GROUPS IN ROMANIA

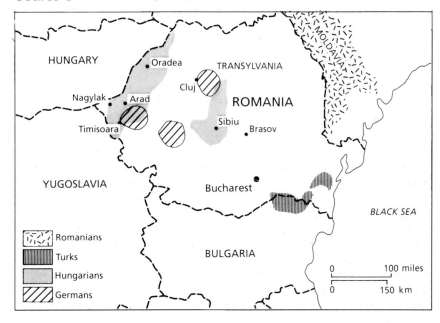

- Romanians
- Turks
- Hungarians
- Germans

(Map labels: HUNGARY, Oradea, TRANSYLVANIA, MOLDAVIA, Cluj, Nagylak, Arad, ROMANIA, Timisoara, Sibiu, Brasov, YUGOSLAVIA, Bucharest, BLACK SEA, BULGARIA)

0 100 miles
0 150 km

Source D: Uprising in Bucharest (21 December)

Bloody street fighting swamped the Romanian capital, Bucharest, yesterday, as thousands rose against the 24–year–long dictatorial reign of Nicolae Ceausescu. Tanks rolled over student rebels and troops opened fire on the growing mass of anti-government demonstrators...

The uprising in Bucharest followed a last desperate attempt by President Ceausescu to restore his image by addressing an open air rally of his 'supporters' – chiefly security service members and party bureaucrats acting under order. Shouting hoarsely through a microphone and rambling repeatedly about 'foreign imperialists acting in Timisoara' – where the uprising began at the weekend – the President was interrupted by boos and catcalls...Security forces tried to disperse the crowds with tear gas, but then the protest turned into a bloody riot. Witnesses said the protestors were mainly students and teenagers, who shouted 'down with the murderers' and 'yesterday Timisoara, today Bucharest'.

The *Independent* newspaper (Friday 22 December 1989)

Source E:

PRESIDENT CEAUSESCU ADDRESSES A RALLY IN BUCHAREST. AFTER ATTEMPTS TO SHOUT HIM DOWN, POLICE OPENED FIRE ON DEMONSTRATORS.

Source F:

The Bucharest rally – an eye-witness account When the President tried to talk, somebody from the first rows shouted: 'Down with Ceausescu!' Suddenly people dropped all the portraits and began to shout: 'Down with Ceausescu!'

You could see his face: he was amazed people could dare to do such a thing.

Viorica Butnaria, quoted in *The Observer* newspaper (31 December 1989)

Source G: A personal account of the Romanian revolution

Dear Kathy,

I write in this hour of despair and hope. Ceausescu ran away a few hours ago. You should have seen the joy, laughter and tears that came then...

I'm transfixed, staring out of the window as cannon go off on both sides of the house. I can see tracer-bullets whistling past...I must write to you now in case it's my last chance...

It's nearly midnight on Friday 22 December, a day we'll all remember...the army fights for us. Oh, God bless them. They refused to open fire against the people...

I was at the Presidential Palace with my brother when Ceausescu left by helicopter...the crowd was like a wild monster with a hundred mouths against Ceausescu. The crowd would have torn him to pieces and devoured him.

Saturday 23 December:

...Daylight brought some peace, but they wrote on the walls: 'We'll come back tonight' Now it is night and they've kept their word. They're back. The palace square is on fire. They're trying to destroy the palace and the Central Committee building, now that our people have taken it over.

There are not many terrorists left, but they're trained for this job, fanatics who destroy buildings and kill people for a dead cause.

Ceausescu and his family are caught and they know it. Still no sign of surrender. They break into the houses, kill the inhabitants and open fire from the windows...

Our killers are now dressed like us, and behave like us and are hardly noticed. The only difference between us is that they have a hidden gun.

Viorica Butnaria, quoted in *The Observer* newpaper (31 December 1989)

Source H: (Right)

A HELICOPTER WITH THE CEAUSESCU FAMILY INSIDE, TAKES OFF FROM THE COMMUNIST PARTY HEADQUARTERS IN BUCHAREST (22 DECEMBER 1989)

Source I: The capture of Ceausescu (23 December 1989)

The deposed Romanian President, Nicolae Ceausescu, and his family were yesterday reported to be under arrest as intense street fighting, which is believed to have cost thousands of lives, continued in the centre of Bucharest...

The disclosure followed conflicting reports about the Ceausescus' whereabouts in the past 24 hours, with Romanian television first saying that he had been arrested and finally that he had fled the country.

The Observer newspaper(24 December 1989)

Source J

Prosecutor: For 25 years you humiliated the population. For 25 years all you did was talk.

Ceausescu: I do not recognise any court. I recognise only the great National Assembly. This is a coup d'etat.

Prosecutor: We are judging you in accordance with the constitution of the country.

Ceausescu: I will not reply to any question...

Prosecutor: Who ordered genocide in Timisoara? Who gave orders to fire on the crowd in Bucharest? Even now innocent people are being fired on. Who are the fanatics who are shooting?

Ceausescu: I will not reply. No one fired on the Palace Square. No one has been killed...

Ceausescu: I recognise neither defeat nor anything...

Elena: No court. I sign nothing. I have struggled for the people since I was 14, and the people are our people.

Prosecutor: We consider that the accused are guilty, and the court announces the sentence sought: confiscation of all property and capital punishment. [The camera switches to show two bodies on a pavement and a bullet hole in Ceausescu's head.]

Extracts from the trial of Nicolae and Elena Ceausescu

Source K:

THE CORPSE OF FORMER ROMANIAN LEADER NICOLAE CEAUSESCU

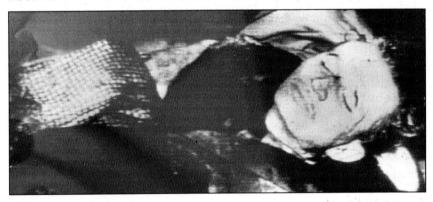

TALKING POINT

Was this a similar revolution to the one which brought down Nicholas II?

Source L: Analysis

Insulated from reality, blinded by power, by their own propaganda, and by its echoing flatter, the Ceausescu clan believed that they were insured against any change of fortune. Had they not fortresses, arms, secret police, control of the media, all the resources of the state? They forgot one thing: that even the most perfect machinery of repression must ultimately be operated by men.

Hugh Trevor Roper, *The Christmas Revolution* (1989)

Journalistic assignment

Provide a detailed news report giving as vivid an account as possible of the 'Christmas Revolution'

Conclusion

Events in Europe and the wider world in 1989-90 have moved on with breathtaking pace. Changes have taken place which, in the recent past, would have seemed unthinkable. Much evidence has still to be unearthed about these events and interpretations of these changes inevitably have to be provisional. Nevertheless, certain factors have remained constant. As was the case one hundred years ago, the fortunes of Russia and Germany remain of critical importance. To what extent, in 1990, is history repeating itself?

In the case of Russia, the issues faced by the leadership in 1990 are not totally different from those faced under the Tsar or under Lenin. In all three cases, for example, food shortages in the major towns and cities have been the source of anger amongst the people and concern for the government. Demands for political reform and the problem of managing the pace of change have been recurring problems in Russian history. The question of managing a massive empire and dealing with the nationalist aspirations in the Baltic States of Lithuania, Latvia and Estonia, which has troubled President Gorbachev, stems back to decisions made by Stalin in 1939. The issue of religious freedom has also been of recurring significance in Russian history. Management of the economy and the conduct of foreign policy, and the balance between these two aspects of the state, have also been of critical significance to Russian leaders past and present. The role of Russia in Eastern Europe and the wider world is a question which has still not been resolved.

In the case of Germany there are also striking parallels between the past and the present. Under the Kaiser and Hitler the issue of Germany's strength was of grave concern to her European neighbours. In 1990, as moves towards the economic and political reunification of Germany gathered pace, the extent of Germany's military and economic potential worried ordinary people as well as political leaders. What would be the role of a unified Germany in the new Europe? How would this new entity fit into the existing alliance system of East and West? Would Germany's new status change the essentially stable position which Europe has enjoyed since 1945? To what extent would the reunification of Germany be a welcome breakthrough of the barriers between East and West, or would this development mark a new and perhaps alarming surge in German nationalism? To what extent would anti-semitism recur?

In the wider sense, the changes which have taken place in Europe are also not entirely new. The nationalist aspirations which in part sparked off the First World War were a significant factor in the revolutions of 1989 and in the fortunes of countries such as Yugoslavia, which have experienced nationalist demonstrations without a revolution. The role of ordinary people, 'the masses', in the shift away from the Communist system and towards some form of market economy underlines the fact that not all changes are controlled by political leaders and that real power often resides in the street rather than in parliament. Perhaps a more novel aspect of the changes of 1989-90 is an increased sense among many people of being 'European' as well as being German, British or French. What changes do you anticipate in the next decade and into the Twenty-First century?

TALKING POINT

If you were asked to draw a map of Europe in 25 years time, what would be the major changes which you would predict? Now that you have 'challenged the past' what challenges do you anticipate in the future?

Index

Maurras, Charles, 44
Max, Prince of Baden, 175
Maximalists, 85
McCarthy, General, 335-6
McCarthyism, 335
Medved, 249-50
Mefo Bill, 289
Mein Kampf, 132, 180, 278, 286, 287
Mensheviks, 83, 85, 97, 205, 207, 217, 222, 247
Messimy, Adolphe, 64
Mexico, 247
Ministry of Popular Culture, 160
Miquel, Johannes von, 8
Molotov, V.M., 137, 316, 321
Moltke, Helmuth, Count von, chief of Prussian general staff (1858-91), 43
Moltke, Helmuth, Count von, chief of Prussian general staff (1906-14) and nephew of above, 24, 36, 37
Mommsen, Hans, 282
Momper, Walter, 349
Montenegro, 29
Moroccan Crisis – First, 1905, 21, 24, 52-3
Moroccan Crisis – Second, 1911, 22, 24, 52-3
Morocco, 26
Moscow, 79, 241, 331
Muller, George Alexander von, 22, 31
Muller, Hermann, 185
Munich, 175, 176, 274
Munich Conference, 137
Murzsteg Agreement, 29
Mussolini, Benito, 130-1, 135, 137-8, 142-70

Nagasaki, 327
Namier, Sir Lewis, 286
Napoleon III, Emperor, 4
Nasser, Col. Gamal Abdel, 338
Nationalism, 7
National Socialist German Workers Party (NSDAP), 176
NATO, 334
Nazi-Soviet Non-Aggression Pact, 135-41
Neuilly, Treaty of, 117
New Economic Policy, 226
New Mexico, 318
Nicholas II, 36, 46, 62, 64-5, 67-94
Nicholson, Harold, 111
Night of the Long Knives, 167, 264
Nikolaev, I., 248, 249
Nixon, Richard, 346
NKVD, 247-50
Noakes, Jeremy, 191
North Caucasus, 244
Nuremburg Laws, 274, 276-77
Nuremburg Trials, 283-5, 293

October Manifesto, 83
Octobrists, 83
Oder-Neisse line, 324
Odessa, 78
Oldenburg-Januschau, 198
Open door, 123
Orlando, Vittorio, 107
Otto Meisner, 193, 199
Ottoman Empire, 28-9

Overy, Richard, 128, 161, 191
Paléologue, Maurice, 64
Papen, von, 193-201
Pan German League, 22, 32
Pan-Slav Policy, 28
Panther Incident, 22, 53
Perestroika, 352-3
Paris, 277, 332
Persia, 26
Patacci, Clara, 142
Petrograd, 241
Piatakov, G., 247
Picquard, Major, 55
Plehve, Viacheslav, 75
Pobedonostov Constantin, 72, 94
Poincaré, Raymond, 35, 59, 61-5, 103, 106
Poland, 78, 106, 112, 119, 133, 136-7, 219, 274, 283, 316-8, 323, 324, 350
Populist Socialists, 84
Potemkin, 78
Potsdam War Council, 22, 24, 321-6, 330
Pozsgay, Imre, 350
Prague, 331
Princip, Gavrillo, 30, 31
Provisional Government (Russia) 204-7, 209, 211
Pugliese, General, 148, 151, 153
Pugo, General, 133
Punch Magazine, 6

Quantung Army, 128, 129

Radek, 247
Rapallo, Treaty of, 123
Rasputin, Gregory, 85
Rathenau, Walther, 32, 175, 178
Rayburn, Tom, 321
Read, Chris, 82
Red Army, 217, 219, 221, 309, 339
Reed, John, 210, 232
Reichstag, 7, 13, 16, 20, 22, 41, 102, 173, 180, 185
Reichstag Fire, 255-62
Reichswehr, 288
Reinsurance Treaty, 19-20, 24, 46
Reizler, Kurt, 32, 36
Revel, Admiral, 155
Revolutions: German (1918), 175; Russia (1905), 76-9; Russia (1917, Feb), 86-94; Russia (1917, Oct), 208-16; Eastern Europe (1989), 350-1; Romania (1989), 354-7
Rhineland, 112, 133, 310
Rhineland Pact, 125
Rhodes, Cecil, 20
Ribbentrop, Joachim von, 136, 138-9, 197, 288
Rich, Norman, 282
Roberts, J.M., 78
Rocco, Alfredo, 164
Rocco Law, 164
Rogger, Hans, 71, 75, 82
Röhl, John, 6, 11-12, 16
Röhm, Ernst, 200, 252, 264, 265
Romanov family, 67-8, 90
Roon, General, 43
Roosevelt, F.D., 130, 309-18, 320, 321
Rossi, Cesare, 158
Romania, 107, 119, 136, 324, 350, 354-7

ACKNOWLEDGEMENTS

The author and publishers wish to thank the following who have kindly given permission for the use of copyright material.

Edward Arnold for extracts from *France: The Third Republic 1870-1914* by Keith Randall, 1986; The Controller of Her Majesty's Stationery Office for an extract from *Documents on German Foreign Policy 1919-1945;* Newspaper Publishing plc for extracts from *The Independent;* Lofthouse Publications for extracts from *The United States and the Cold War 1941-1953* by Richard Crockatt, BAAS, 1989; Longman Group Ltd for a table from *Longman Handbook of Modern European History* by Cook and Stevenson, 1987; and a League of Nations chart from *Longman History of the USA* by Hugh Brogan, 1985; The Observer Ltd. for extracts from various issues of *The Observer;* Penguin Books Ltd for extracts from *Rise to Globalism: American Foreign Policy Since 1938* by Stephen E. Ambrose, Third Edition, 1983, copyright © Stephen E. Ambrose, 1971, 1976, 1980, 1983; Times Newspapers Ltd. for an extract from an article by Tony Osman, *The Sunday Times*, 17.11.85, copyright © Times Newspapers Ltd. 1985; George Weidenfeld & Nicolson Ltd. for extracts from *The Seizure of Power* by Adrian Lyttleton, 1987.

The following photographic sources have kindly given permission for photographs to be reproduced:

Popperfoto pp7 bottom, 10, 19, 22, 30 bottom, 68, 71, 72 top left, 72 bottom right, 74, 82, 90, 95 left, 108 bottom, 118 top, 118 bottom, 124, 128, 129, 131 top, 132 top, 132 bottom, 134 top, 134 bottom, 143, 144, 147 top, 147 bottom, 161, 162 top, 163, 165, 176, 178, 181 top, 181 bottom, 185, 192, 195, 198 top, 200 top, 200 bottom, 201, 202 top, 202 bottom, 204, 209, 211, 220, 229, 233, 234 top, 238, 243, 245, 254, 255 top, 255 bottom, 256, 259, 260, 264, 268 bottom, 276, 277, 278, 279, 280, 282, 289, 290, 298, 302 top, 306 top, 306 centre, 307, 308, 309, 310 top, 310 bottom, 311, 314, 319 top, 319 bottom, 320, 322 top, 322 bottom, 326, 327 top, 327 left, 327 right, 331, 333 top, 334, 335 top, 335 bottom, 337, 338, 339, 340, 342 left, 342 right, 343 top, 343 bottom, 345, 346, 347 top, 347 bottom, 348, 349 top, 349 centre, 349 bottom, 350, 351 (main), 351 (inset), 353, 354, 355, 356, 357; BBC Hulton Picture Library pp2, 3, 7 top, 9 top, 9 bottom, 15, 20, 25, 30 top, 34, 36, 70, 76 right, 76 left, 83, 86, 89, 96, 110, 171, 203 bottom, 205, 225, 231, 248, 253, 284, 285 bottom, 288, 301; Novosti pp40 top, 61, 67, 72 top right, 73 top, 73 bottom, 77, 80, 81, 87, 88 top, 88 bottom, 203 top, 212, 213, 218, 227, 232, 234 bottom, 236, 239, 242, 247; Radio Times Hulton-Deutsch Collection pp6, 40 bottom, 42 top, 42 bottom, 43, 47, 51, 53, 54, 57, 97, 101 top, 101 bottom, 105, 206-7, 224, 306 bottom; Moro pp142, 145, 148, 150, 151, 157 top, 158, 159, 166, 167; PUNCH pp52 top right, 108 top, 111, 131 bottom, 291, 333 bottom; Imperial War Museum pp37, 95 right, 103; Le Petit Journal Illustré pp2 bottom right, 44; Lords Gallery p162 bottom; Keystone Press Agency Ltd p328; Sadd Verlag p52; School of Slavonic Studies p285 top; H. Roger Viollet p85; Institute of Social History Amsterdam p241; V. Chochoia, Prague p302 top; Camera Press p349 centre; Associated Press P300; Library of Congress p114; Cover; Mary Evans Picture Library – St Petersburg Uprising at the Winter Palace; Paul Lowe/Network – Berlin unification celebration, October 1990 (inset).

Every effort has been made to trace all the copyright holders but if any have been inadvertently overlooked the publishers will be pleased to make the necessary arrangement at the first opportunity.